HERZL

Journey Through a Haunted Land

The Israelis, Founders and Sons

*Between Enemies: A Compassionate Dialogue
Between an Israeli and an Arab* (with Sana Hassan)

HERZL

by Amos Elon

HOLT, RINEHART and WINSTON

New York   Chicago   San Francisco

Published simultaneously in Canada by Holt, Rinehart
and Winston of Canada, Limited.

Library of Congress Cataloging in Publication Data

Elon, Amos.
Herzl.

Bibliography: p.
1. Herzl, Theodor, 1860–1904.
DS151.H4E57   956.94'001'0924 [B]   74–5128
ISBN 0–03–013126–X

All photographs courtesy of the Herzl Archive in Jerusalem.

First Edition

Designer: Mary M. Ahern

Printed in the United States of America

FOR *Beth*
who shares in everything

Contents

Conversion Table

1 pound sterling = 1 Turkish pound = 25 French francs

= 20 German marks = 8 Austrian guldens = 5 U.S. dollars

Author's Note

ALL INCIDENTS AND CONVERSATIONS in this book are based strictly on the written record. This is not a "fictionalized" biography, although in some parts the detail and the conversations may suggest a historical novel. The written record is found in Herzl's own massive notes, diaries, and letters, and in the related evidence of eyewitnesses and contemporaries. The material has been collected over the past forty years by the diligent researchers of the Herzl Archive in Jerusalem, or reposes in various European state archives which the author has consulted. No biographer could have wished for a richer resource of reliable material, or one as varied and representative of various points of view. Nothing has been construed or imagined— neither the words spoken nor the gestures. The source of each direct quotation is given on pages 419–32.

If I have seen one thing,
It is the passing preciousness of dreams;
That aspects are within us;
And who seems most kingly is the king.

Thomas Hardy, "A Young Man's Exhortation"

HERZL

1

The Turning Point

EARLY IN JUNE 1895, the solitary figure of a distinguished-looking
Austrian gentleman could be seen daily pacing the pebbled
walks of the Paris Tuileries gardens. Dark-bearded, in immaculate,
severe dress, he was clearly in a state of great agitation. His walk
was alternately slow and abrupt.

For most of the day he would remain closeted in his hotel room
on the nearby rue Cambon. At dusk he usually emerged, pale and
grave; his feverish eyes were surrounded by dark rings; the pallor of
his handsome face suggested an illness, or some serious mental
crisis. Clutching a little notebook in his hand, he would stop short
from time to time to jot down a few lines. Then he would resume
his nervous pace.

He was an uncommonly good-looking man, in his mid-thirties.
There was something distinctive about his grave countenance—
neither French nor Austrian—that was slightly mysterious, or perhaps theatrical. His clothes, his gloves, his hat, and his silver-plated
walking stick were elegant, almost dandified. His full beard, black
and perfectly trimmed, lent a forbidding appearance to his well-
proportioned head. His posture was proud, his body slim and supple.
The dignity of his solemn, somewhat pompous stance contrasted
oddly with the agitation apparent in his face. Its wan beauty
was enhanced by an aquiline nose and high forehead; the lips
were sensuous, finely chiseled, with perhaps just a touch of
weakness. The dark eyes were probably his most striking aspect,
large, velvety deep brown, searching and warmly expressive without being soft; through them flickered a strange, unquiet light.

Finally the frantic promenade would end. As though in great

physical pain the black-bearded man would collapse on a bench. His eyes might be flooded with tears.

This was Theodor Herzl, the founder of modern Zionism. In June 1895 he was in his fifth year as the Paris correspondent of Vienna's leading newspaper, the *Neue Freie Presse*. For the last ten years he had been a struggling, moderately successful playwright. To a casual passerby in the Tuileries he might have seemed to be suffering a psychotic shock. Herzl himself, as is evident in the notes he was then jotting down, and later copied into his diary, knew that he was "intoxicated." More than once he was "afraid of going insane." His own thoughts sometimes appeared to him "laughable, exaggerated, crazy." He recorded them dutifully, as they arose, avoiding the self-criticism that he would normally exercise in his literary work, for he was afraid to "cripple" his inspiration. "Artists will fully understand why I, who otherwise reason clearly, have allowed extravagances and dreams to vegetate wildly [in these notes]." He was in fact working on the first draft of a political pamphlet entitled *The Jewish State: An Attempt at a Modern Solution of the Jewish Question*. Published eight months later, the pamphlet was destined to become one of the most influential political tracts of modern times; it has affected the lives of millions down to our own day.

At that time Herzl did not yet know whether he would be able to carry out his program. But his mood was one of feverish exaltation, bordering on an ecstasy of which he was quite aware, and which at times he feared. In his diary he noted: "I believe that for me life has ended and world history has begun." He was living in a delirious trance. He compared himself to Bismarck, Savonarola, and Napoleon. For days and weeks, through the early summer of 1895, the idea "possessed me beyond the limits of consciousness." He wrote his book at every moment, everywhere, "walking, standing, lying down, in the street, during meals and at night when it tears me out of my dreams. . . . I am so filled with it that I relate everything to it like a lover to his beloved." He abandoned his normal work. For days he avoided his acquaintances by locking himself into his hotel room or walking for hours in the park. A man who saw him on June 16 remarked that he looked as if he had just risen from some terrible disease. The one acquaintance to whom he revealed details of his plan, a writer by profession but a physician by training, warned him that he was seriously ill and should immediately "see a doctor."

As he went on drafting his notes he was torn between bleak

despair and radiant self-confidence. He tested his sanity by seeing whether he could still add 2 and 2, or divide 348 by 12. He roused his flagging spirit by listening to Wagnerian music, especially *Tannhäuser*, whenever he could. It was his only relaxation. He confessed that only on those evenings when Wagner was not played at the Paris Opéra did he have "any doubts as to the truth of my ideas." A man possessed, he wrote to free himself of the ideas which "erupted within me like a volcano," conjuring up the detailed vision of an independent Jewish state in an as yet undetermined territory of the globe. His endless scribbles filled several hundred small sheets of paper. One passage read as follows:

> The promised land—nobody has thought of looking for it where it really is—within ourselves. . . . The promised land is where we shall take it. . . . The promised land, where we may at last have hooked noses, black and red beards, bow legs, without being despised for it. . . . Where we can at last live as free men on our soil. . . . Where the offensive cry of "Jew" may become an honorable appellation like German, Englishman, Frenchman; in short, like all civilized people.

2

Herzl had only nine years left to live. He died in July 1904, at the age of only forty-four. Within this extraordinarily brief space of time, he forged a national representation out of the most disorganized and fractional community on earth. Almost single-handedly, he built and sustained a movement which, within half a century, through a modern migration of outcasts and idealists, led to the establishment of the modern state of Israel. Herzl did not invent Zionism. Others had done that before him. He forged the instruments that would put Zionism into practice, for politics is the development of power. From nothing, he created first an illusion of that power, and then the power itself which would later make possible the return of the Jews to Palestine. His unusual life is a study in character, and a measure of the political impact that can be caused by one audacious individual.

At the beginning of most great enterprises stands an adventure, a defiance of time, or law, or some established notion. This is true of most new societies and states. There is always a trace of quixotism when devotion to a cause is extreme, logical, and saintlike. Herzl went beyond that. He walked a tightrope between charlatanism and genius. Throughout his career as a self-appointed leader of men he ran a very real danger of exposure as a fraud even as he was hailed as a savior. In his negotiations with kings, emperors, and ministers of state, even in his dealings with his closest disciples, he took great risks; he had to conjure up an entire world of make-believe in place of the real power he lacked.

Herzl was one of the great adventurers of the nineteenth century. His was not the common adventure of film, fiction, or of well-known political careers. The first part of his life unfolds as the inner drama of a man of letters who self-consciously recorded his every thought. The second part is more exposed; it takes place on the stage of international politics and intrigue, but in a setting so unusual as to seem at times unreal. One is not prepared for his life by the reading of such conventional histories as the saga of established kings and the clashes of mighty armies. Herzl was truly a hero of the nineteenth century, that era when the tale of lonely outsiders—reviewing life and society in the obscurity of a study and plotting new policies in the reading room of a public library—was often more fascinating and significant than the story of crowned heads, prime ministers, illustrious generals, and captains of industry.

Herzl had an uncanny premonition of the storm clouds gathering on Europe's horizon and the impending disaster of its Jews. His political techniques were sometimes shortsighted or naïve. Like many men in a hurry, he believed that the whole game of politics was played by strong men behind the scenes. He discovered his mistake before his early death. But for dispersed Jewry as it existed in his time, Herzl succeeded in transforming one mode of life into another, into a life which until then had been thought impossible. He imposed himself on his time with an idea that struck most observers, at first, as a wild, incongruous, ridiculous scheme. He handled this incongruity as though it were a sword, baring it when he wished, sheathing it at will. In his lifetime he was stigmatized by his detractors as a crank, a shallow litterateur dabbling in politics. There have been and always will be journalists with *idées fixes*, like Herzl, eccentrics with fanciful schemes. But how many of these fanciful, utopian schemes have been realized?

As a utopian Herzl was a child of his time, a period which was electric with hope of a New Age, a New Society, a New Woman, a New Justice. He was jeered in his lifetime as a "political Jules Verne." But the figment of his imagination was to materialize. The adventurer in history is sometimes regarded as a mere criminal if he

fails; if he succeeds he is often hailed as a genius. Herzl's posthumous success need not blind us to his shortcomings, nor should it
deafen our ears to the arguments of his critics, which were often
eminently reasonable. Success and failure are also functions of timing. Had Herzl lived in the Middle Ages he probably would have
been accused as a false messiah. Spared by the Jews, he might have
been burned at the stake by the Christians. But he was born into
the nineteenth century, the age of Mazzini and Kossuth, and grew
up in a veritable hotbed of messianic nationalisms. Herzl's maturity
coincided with the high point of liberalism and rationalism in his
native Austria-Hungary. Few men were as truly representative of
the age of liberalism, with its unbridled faith in a rational world
and in the orderly, sensible resolution of all problems. And yet by a
strange confluence of character and events, he seemed almost to
reincarnate in his own person the wilder spirit of a past age. He
followed a line of bizarre dreamers, gamblers, adventurers, and
audacious showmen which one assumed had ended with Cagliostro
or Sabbatai Zevi.

His personality, which so many found disarming, contained a
grain of self-hypnotism. He was a master at dropping veiled hints
and deft in the use of reticence. With the exception of D'Annunzio,
Herzl was the only modern European politician who was also a
playwright. For ten years, until 1895, his medium had been words.
Afterward it was human beings. As a professional playwright Herzl
was a great believer in the *mise-en-scène*. His statecraft was often
derived from his stagecraft. He had his own understanding of the
nature of politics—at one moment reality, and the next, a *grand
coup de théâtre*. He believed in manipulating men, mainly through
"imponderables"—by lights and sounds, the dazzling sights and the
suggestive music of the opera by which he himself was so moved.
The Vienna of Herzl's day regarded the opera as the highest form
of art and Wagner's so-called *Gesamtkunstwerk* as a culmination of
all wisdom.

As we consider his fate we are fascinated and sometimes
shocked by an odd combination of accident and design, and by that
utter naïveté which is perhaps the very essence—and the tragedy—
of a life of adventure. It is difficult to resist the thrill of Herzl's
story. It exudes a strange charm and touches us in a most elemental
way. Perhaps this is so because what we take for genius is often
little more than a prodigious innocence. It flatters us by its simplicity and allows us to feel cheaply wise after the event.

The extravagant timing of history linked Herzl with three

events of tremendous importance. The old European order was in decline, exemplified especially by the decay and chaotic disintegration of Herzl's native country, the multinational Austro-Hungarian Empire. Second, there was the crisis of liberalism and rationalism, which was brought about by the third, most shattering event, the rise of nationalism and racism. Because of his involvement in these three developments—as a man, as a writer, and as a Jew— Herzl would have been an interesting figure had he not altered the course of modern Jewish and Near Eastern history.

The dramatic quality of his life also derived from the unusual convergence in his character and career of the literary and the political, the state and the stage, a dream world and a true world, the false and the real. He was aware of this confluence himself and articulated it freely in his extensive diaries. Herzl was a vain man, but his vanity was in a grand style. It permitted him the remarkable candor of his diaries. He readily confessed his pettiest and his grandest fantasies. The compelling frankness of his diaries is rare in modern political literature. Herzl dissected himself with considerable detachment and irony. A study of his life may thus throw light not merely on today's Israeli and Jewish affairs, or on the peculiar world of *fin de siècle* Europe, but on the process of history-making and on the creation of ideologies. His literary work affords some insights into darker, less accessible recesses of the political mind. The combination in Herzl of charismatic leader and playwright is probably unique. D'Annunzio was not charismatic. Disraeli wrote novels. Churchill and de Gaulle were historians. Karl Marx was an economist. Herzl not merely endeavored to contemplate the last act of the Jewish drama, but wanted to stage it. It is difficult to think of another major political figure who came to politics from the theater, let alone from the light drama that was Herzl's specialty.

There are both profound and ridiculous aspects to this circumstance. Herzl was not a great playwright. On the contrary, his writing, apart from his journalism, was mostly mediocre. He began as a *poseur*, a superficial wordsmith, an elegant fop, a tedious chatterer, an absurd sentimentalist. But he broke away from the aridity of his milieu and threw off the empty pose, the petulance and shallow emotionalism of his early days, to become a real force in human affairs. Having failed in the theater, he made the whole world his stage. He had the audacity to become a statesman without a country and without a people. Other founders of national movements might have hesitated before such a heavy, improbable task. None has been the progenitor of a country to the degree Herzl was the founding father of modern Israel. There is almost a poetic quality in this singular achievement.

Herzl often poeticized his role, forever aware of the intermingling of life and letters. His plays give an indication of his psychological makeup. They are a minor but not insignificant element in the story of his life. His short stories and plays neither enhance nor diminish his reputation as a man of action, but they might well help us to a better understanding of Herzl the human being. Few prominent men of action have left behind such a wealth of unconscious indices to their neuroses.

Herzl epitomized nearly all the ideal and dubious qualities often attributed to the modern Jew: imagination, showmanship, vanity, irritability, relentless drive, utopian yearnings for the just society, alienation, snobbery, pride in Judaism, and Jewish self-hatred. A masterful intellect came coupled with absurd sentimentalism. He had a good head for business and that biting, self-critical irony that since Heine has been a hallmark of the Jewish sense of humor.

3

Yet Herzl was also, perhaps first and foremost, a Viennese. In the context of *fin de siècle* Vienna, Herzl's figure assumes a special plasticity and gains a measure of conviction that is lacking if he is viewed solely against his Jewish background. He was not born in Vienna but in Budapest. Like many national leaders he came not from the center of culture but from the uneasy border area. His birthplace stood between Western and Eastern Europe, in that intermediate area where the very precariousness and relativity of all things greatly sharpened the sensitivities. Vienna, where he spent his formative years, was his adopted home. It was an imperial, not a national, capital. In its endless variety Vienna was a microcosm of the larger, already decaying and disintegrating empire. It was a great school for ambivalence, though at the time its lessons were not apparent to many. Herzl—Hungarian by birth, Jewish by religion, Austrian by naturalization, German by culture—was ambivalent about his roots. A nationalist Jew by choice, he was too civilized to be so without great reservation. His nationalism was humane, tolerant, and marked by strong moral and cultural reservations. His life must be viewed against the decor of macabre gaiety which marked the decline and fall of the multinational Austro-Hungarian Empire. As with many men of destiny, his time summed itself up in him just as it was becoming out of date: he lived through the dusk of liberalism, the decline of humane nationalism, and the end of European colonization in territories overseas.

Herzl combined in his personality the two most prominent, most heralded features of the Viennese mind in the autumn of empire: the playful and the apocalyptic. Tired resignation alternated with revolutionary fervor, and sometimes one flowed into the other—decay and rebirth, death in life, life in death.

On the one hand we see the worldly, cynical, sophisticated playfulness of a disintegrating society. The idea of death, so "fashionable" in *fin de siècle* art, was always alive in Herzl's mind. He constantly toyed with it. As we look over his life, it sometimes seems as though he stepped out of a novel by Arthur Schnitzler. He himself might have acted out Schnitzler's lines in *Paracelsus*:

> We are all actors;
> He who is aware of it is wise.

Or he might have exclaimed with Hugo von Hoffmannsthal:

> We are all playacting,
> Acting out our own piece,
> The comedy of our soul.

The Vienna of that time was said to be a *Versuchsstation des Weltunterganges* (proving ground of world destruction). There already arose from the gutters a flood of sheer hatred, venomous prejudice, and chaotic violence. The stifling hothouse atmosphere of *fin de siècle* Vienna sprouted all kinds of flowers, some sweet, others poisonous, but all of a strange luxuriousness, all related and somehow nurtured through the half-hidden convergence of ideas, of cause and effect. It is perhaps no mere coincidence that the same city, the same decaying crucible of passion and hope, love and hatred, anticipation and invention, produced a Herzl as well as a Hitler; the antidote before the poison. It is difficult to imagine another city that could have nurtured these two men. Both were born in the provinces but came to Vienna in their formative years; both had to leave it behind to find their own peoples. The same Vienna also produced Sigmund Freud, who, as Herzl was converting to Zionism, was developing his theory of psychoanalysis. In its urgent quest to cure, psychoanalysis was probably by itself an index of the general disease.

In this wide political and cultural context Herzl stands out as a man of considerable foresight and great humaneness. He was of much greater complexity than was apparent in the iconography that sprang up around him in his lifetime, and even more so after his death. No one ever knew him intimately, not even members of his own family. Already in his lifetime, legend obscured the complicated kernel of his personality and simplified his motives. His private life was marked by tremendous emotional complexes, sickness, and the effects of a ruined marriage. But so dignified were his personality and bearing, that together they often induced an almost religious awe. Many spoke to him with reverence even while they disagreed with him. His physical appearance seemed to take on unusual attributes in the minds of his beholders. Thus he was invariably described by his admirers as "majestically tall," towering over everyone. In his army medical examination papers, however, he is described as being of medium height; the French *Préfecture de Police* listed his height at five feet eight inches. And yet there cannot be any doubt that in the eyes of those who met him he appeared much taller.

He figured strangely in the consciousness of many of his contemporaries. Sigmund Freud claimed to have seen him in a dream even before he saw him in the flesh. Sidney Whitman of the New York *Herald* wrote that he had never seen a man whose role was so clearly written on his body. To the Sultan of Turkey he looked like an ancient Hebrew prophet; to Ibrahim Bey, the Sultan's master of ceremonies, like "Jesus Christ." Franz Rosenzweig, the theologian, said that Herzl proved, finally and beyond all critical doubt, that the biblical Moses had indeed been a historic person. Max Nordau, the atheist, was prompted by Herzl to say, "Were I a believer I would state that your appearance at this critical point in history is the hand of Providence." To Martin Buber he was "a statue without error or mistake, a countenance lit with the glance of the Messiah."

The very brevity of his life added to its popular splendor. His sudden death at forty-four contributed a touch of Byronesque romance to his legend. Patriotic art has joined its own peculiar lore. E.M. Lilien, the gifted disciple of Aubrey Beardsley and Walter Crane, painted Herzl as half-Wotan, half-Moses, bearing the Tablets of the Law in a pair of gigantic, muscular arms. In another picture by Lilien, Herzl appears as a nude, bearded angel presiding in heaven over the birth of man.

In the case of all national heroes it is never easy to disentangle the image from the blinding halo. Herzl himself would most probably have welcomed the effort. Speaking of his desire for a frank treatment of his life, he said that "the Bible spared Moses nothing." In his own writing he found it essential to "study the small side of great men." On one occasion, observing the German Kaiser, he deliberately "concentrated on his physical deformity." This was "an abnormality essential for his image. It brings him closer to me as a human being."

In Israel today, Herzl is a national hero. His popular image has become as two-dimensionally dull as the stylized Herzl portrait that adorns Israel's hundred-lira bank notes. Behind the stately beard the human face has disappeared. We must shave that beard that has become a national symbol on postage stamps and on the walls of dreary schoolrooms, to seek his real features. We must delve inward, as it were, to reach the complex core of a most fascinating personality. And at the same time we must reach out beyond the man himself, to the culture that produced him at a particular moment of crisis in European civilization.

2

German Boy in Budapest

E WAS BORN on May 2, 1860, in Budapest, the "other" capital city of the multinational Hapsburg Empire. There was little reason to foresee his destiny. Theodor was the second child of Jeannette and Jakob Herzl. His father was a wealthy businessman and the director of a small bank. His mother was enamored of German *Kultur*.

Like so many Jews of their time, the Herzls were "assimilated," but too proud, or perhaps too inert, to cross the line into Christianity. Their Judaism was vague and superficial, a mechanical routine of little meaning, sporadically observed. Throughout Europe hundreds of thousands of Jews were slowly fusing with the political, even religious, culture of the Gentile majority. The Herzls were among them. Trusting in the inevitable triumph of social progress and democracy, committed to the quasi-liberal Hapsburg regime, piously devoted to the German culture of the master nation, Jakob and Jeannette Herzl had no special interest in Jewish questions. There was nothing about them to suggest that their only son would influence history as the spiritual father of a modern Jewish state.

Their home, on the Tabakgasse, was a large, elegant structure of yellow brick and stone. A stately line of tall Doric columns was topped by gracious architraves. Next door on the right stood the vast, if tasteless, edifice of the new main synagogue of Budapest. The synagogue had been completed only a year before Herzl's birth, in 1859. A reformed house of worship, it symbolized the rising tide of adaptation, both social and religious, which was expected to bring Judaism into harmony with modern life. The architecture reflected the awkward constraint by which this harmony was attempted. A broad Gothic facade, flanked by two high pseudo-Moorish towers, gave the building an oddly eclectic look, rather like a Norman mosque. (Here, thirty-seven years later, Herzl would be denounced from the pulpit as a dangerous rabble-rouser, for to most Jews, both Orthodox and Reformed, Zionism was the great heresy of the nineteenth century.)

Beyond the synagogue, on a wide street, to the right, stood the Hungarian National Theater. Farther down, in the distance, flowed the Danube, an opaque, gleaming surface of water that divided Pest on this bank from Buda on the other. A light haze hung over the meadows and craggy hills of Buda; above its medieval rooftops the grim castle of the kings of Hungary hovered like a distant iron crown.

Here Herzl grew up. Budapest, in the throes of expansion, was still a small provincial capital. Nestled between the hills of Buda and the flat plain of Pest, its avenues, river islands, and embankments were lined with blooming chestnut and acacia trees. The beauty of Budapest was enhanced by the natural gaiety, music, and good food of the colorful Magyar population. Its glamour was further heightened by a strong Gypsy strain and the carefree flamboyance of the native aristocracy. There were tremendous social differences, but the world of Herzl's early youth was firm in its self-confidence. Today it is difficult to convey the sense of utter stability that marked the rising Jewish middle class in particular. Most writers of the time have borne it eloquent witness.

Steam power and democracy were finally ushering in a golden "age of security," which the state would guarantee. The thousand-year-old monarchy was headed by the universally beloved Franz Josef. As Emperor of Austria and King of Hungary, Franz Josef was committed to the well-being and happiness of all. He addressed his subjects as "My dear peoples." The Jewish bourgeoisie was supranational like the Emperor himself; it was particularly loyal and attached to him personally.

Elsewhere too the 1860s were marked by liberal breakthroughs and reforms. Lincoln was President of the United States. Marx presided over the first International. Lassalle created the German labor movement. In England Disraeli was in power; in Prussia the progressives achieved a majority for the first time. Even in Russia, Alexander II, the "liberal Czar," created the brief illusion of a new dawn, which prompted the Hebrew poet J.L. Gordon to announce ecstatically:

Now hath the dawn come forth,
The sun has risen, .
Bright light shineth all over man,
It has touched *us* also.

It was a time of hope, in Budapest perhaps even more than elsewhere on the continent. The city's German-speaking Jews— ignorant of Gordon—were more likely to exclaim with Ludwig Uhland: "The world is more beautiful every day;/now everything, everything must change."

Twenty or twenty-five years later things would look menacing again. But no one could foresee this during the first ten years of Herzl's life. The population of Budapest grew by almost 50 percent, to 280,000; it had nearly doubled since 1850. Some 45,000, or 15 percent of the total, were Jews. The tremendous upsurge in economic growth and population was greatly encouraged by the Austro-Hungarian Compromise of 1867, which established the principle of dualism. At least for the time being, the prevailing national rivalries were set aside; the Compromise of 1867 created two interlocked political systems under one benign monarch.

The number of Jews in Budapest grew even more rapidly than the general population. Culturally they leaned toward things German, as did the Hungarian aristocracy. Esterhazys, Karolys, Andrassys, and other nobles often spoke better German than Hungarian. Count Stefan Szecheny, "the greatest Hungarian," wrote his private journal in German. There was as yet no contradiction between political allegiance to Hungary and aesthetic preference for German culture. Even as they spoke German and looked to Vienna for their books, their theater, their music, and their daily newspapers, secularized Hungarian Jews felt thoroughly at home in Hungary.

They were by no means newcomers to the region. Jewish settlements had existed in Hungary under the Romans, long before the arrival of the Magyars. Many Jews boasted of their "Magyar blood." Samuel Kohn, the Chief Rabbi of Budapest, claimed a racial kinship between Jews and Magyars through the Khasars, a central Asian people who had converted to Judaism in the sixth century and joined the Magyars on the trek to the west.

Jews had participated in the Hungarian revolution of 1848. Herzl's uncle on his mother's side was a lieutenant in the revolutionary army. For their participation in the revolution the Jews were rewarded by the short-lived emancipation of 1849. But the revolution was crushed by the combined forces of the Austrian Emperor and the Russian Czar, and the constitution was suspended. Yet the liberal trend continued, and with the new constitution of 1867 the last vestiges of discrimination were at least theoretically abolished. Any surviving bigotry and prejudice in daily life, most educated Jews believed, was doomed by the Age of Science and would wither away along with other vestiges of medieval superstition. There was, in fact, much less overt anti-Semitism in Hungary than in Austria, Germany, the Czech lands, or Poland. The reasons were partly political. Without Jewish votes, the ruling Magyars might have lost their narrow majority to the resurgent Romanian, Slovak, Serb, and Croatian minorities. For the Jews of Hungary it was a time of good faith and unbridled optimism. This atmosphere is important as a backdrop to Herzl's subsequent development. If liberalism and tolerance had triumphed, as they were generally expected to do during his youth, his life would have taken a totally different course. His driving ambition might have elevated him to a position of prominence, but it would have been most likely in the arts, not in politics.

2

Herzl's story was unusual enough; there is no reason to make it even more unusual. Myths about him circulated early in his public career. Some were spread by disciples, others by members of his family. There was often a touching naïveté about such exaggerations, but they were falsehoods nonetheless. Well after his rise in Jewish and European politics, his aging mother claimed that the family was descended from royal Hebrew blood. This was a doting old mother's fantasy, related perhaps in half-jest. The Herzl family, in fact, could barely trace its origins to the early eighteenth century. At least twenty-three unaccounted centuries lay between the legendary House of David and Solomon and 1751, the birth year of the earliest known Herzl, one Moises Herzl, who became a glazier in Semlin, a little town on the outskirts of Belgrade.

Herzl shared in his family's tendency to romanticize its origins. He often spoke of "the novel of my life." He told at least one biographer that he was descended from noble Spanish Marraños. He informed Reuben Brainin, his first biographer, a few months before his death, that there had been two brothers in Spain who were forced by the Inquisition to adopt Christianity and to enter monastic orders. Following their conversion, the two brothers had risen high in the hierarchy of their order, but they secretly remained loyal to the ancient faith of their fathers. Sent abroad on a confidential mission of the order, they reached Innsbruck, Austria, and the long-awaited opportunity to escape. After many difficulties and adventures they arrived in Turkey, where they returned to Judaism. His family, Herzl told Brainin, was descended from one of the brothers.

This charming story is interesting for the light it sheds on the self-delusion that grips famous men, and on the prevailing snobberies of the age. In the nineteenth century many assimilated Western Jews professed a Sephardic origin. The romantic poets, in particular Byron and Heine, had attached an aura of marvelous nobility to the proud Jews of medieval Spain. Moreover, at a time when the rich, liberated Jews of the West sought to dissociate themselves from their poor and outcast coreligionists in Poland and Russia, only a Sephardic origin was conclusive proof that one did not come from the primitive *Ostjuden* (Eastern Jews).

Herzl was a political romantic; he admired the aristocracy of his time. He once admitted that had the choice been his, he would have been born a Prussian nobleman. The desire to compensate for reality by the invention of nobler antecedents was a characteristic of many historical personalities, from Cola di Rienzi to Benjamin Disraeli. The romantic mind requires that power or success or fame be somehow legitimized by heritage. Herzl's father's family was in fact Ashkanazi, not Shephardi. It came not from Spain but from Silesia, Bohemia, and Moravia. The name Herzl is a German translation of the Hebrew *lev* (heart). Early in the eighteenth century the family migrated south and settled in Belgrade, which had come under Austrian rule in 1719. Twenty years later, when Belgrade reverted to the Turks, the Herzls moved across the Sava River into Semlin, which had remained within Austrian territory. The move was an act of loyalty to the imperial crown for which the family was awarded special privileges. Semlin today is a suburb of Belgrade; at that time it was a small fortified town and already memorable in Jewish history. There, in 1096, the knights of the First Crusade had crossed into Byzantine territory, littering their way to the Holy Land with the corpses of slain Jews. Theodor's great-grandfather, Loebl Herzl, born in 1761, worked most of his life as a day laborer in Semlin; he later turned to commerce and achieved a modest prosperity.

Of Loebl's three sons, two converted to Christianity. The third, Simon Loeb Herzl, remained within the fold, and perhaps compensated for his brothers' apostasy by an increased adherence to sacred law. His son, Jakob, Herzl's father, however, shared the sentiments of his more liberal uncles and became an assimilated Jew.

3

Such were Herzl's antecedents. He had a tendency to poeticize them. In keeping, perhaps, with the literary tradition of *fin de siècle* Vienna, he saw a dreamlike quality in his own life, and he reacted to it with a mixture of melancholy and wonder. He claimed that he had experienced some of the major events of his own life before, as a fantasy or in a dream. Shortly before his death he told Reuben Brainin that, at the age of twelve, the "King-Messiah" had himself appeared to him in a dream:

> He took me in his arms and carried me off on wings of heaven. On one of the iridescent clouds we met . . . Moses. (His features resembled those of Michelangelo's statue. As a child I loved . . . this marble portrait.) The Messiah called out to Moses, *"For this child I have prayed!"* To me he said, "Go and announce to the Jews that I shall soon come and perform great and wondrous deeds for my people and for all mankind!" I kept this dream to myself and did not dare tell anyone.

Brainin himself wrote that he could not be sure whether Herzl was remembering a real dream, or "merely a childish tale born in his mind even as he was talking to me." Was it a true dream, which Herzl had kept secret until a few months before his death or the belated construction of a fertile literary and political mind? In either case there is a quaint peculiarity about his dream. It throws light on Herzl's effusive character and betrays Herzl's relationship to the unconscious, which, according to Jung, is the essence of all creativity. Perhaps it was what Freud has called a "screen memory," an unimportant memory recalled in place of an important one and associated with it. Freud remembered a similar urge in his youth to identify with Moses. A man's recollections of his early childhood are at best puppet shows of memory, remembrances not of events themselves, but of having remembered them once, confused feelings mixed up with associations whose origin is lost in obscurity. In his conversation with Brainin, Herzl rationalized his dream. He noted that even as a boy, soon after the dream, he had become convinced that modern technology—"the electron!"—was the real Messiah. Electricity would redeem men from their lowly bondage. "Then and there I decided to become a great engineer."

One explanation for Herzl's fantasy might possibly be sought, with Freudian hindsight, in the overpowering personality of his mother. From his earliest years Jeannette Herzl consciously and deliberately prepared her son for great things. As Freud wrote, "A man who has been the indisputable favorite of his mother keeps his entire life the feeling of a conqueror, that confidence of success which often induces real success."

Jeannette Herzl was the daughter of well-to-do Budapest Jewish parents. Her family had migrated to Hungary in the eighteenth century from Moravia and Slovakia. Her father was in the clothing business. In her maiden days Jeannette Diamant had been a celebrated beauty. She married Jakob Herzl in 1857 at the age of nineteen. The marriage seems to have been extremely happy, clearly dominated by her stronger personality. Her husband deferred to her throughout their life together.

Jeannette Herzl's vast ambitions for her son were matched only by her boundless love. In this she was also a child of her class and time. The first generation of Jews emancipated from the ghetto produced an abundance of overprotective, overindulgent Jewish mothers. Many of them were convinced that their sons were born to greatness. Hard work and self-sacrifice, along with the new freedom, were enabling the sons to acquire a thorough secular education. Innumerable Jewish parents saw their little boys destined for a ministerial portfolio or at least the equivalent of a Nobel Prize.

In this sense Herzl had much in common with Freud. Both grew up at the same time in the same Austro-Hungarian, urban, Jewish, middle-class milieu. Freud's mother, told that her baby was "born in a caul . . . [and thereby] ensured of fame," firmly "believed in the prediction." There were no such augurs at Herzl's birth, but his mother was nevertheless fully convinced of his great destiny.

No effort was spared to assure his advancement. A succession of private tutors was hired to supplement his formal schooling. Lessons started some fifteen months before he entered, at the age of six, the first form of the Israelite Community Elementary School of Pest. He began to study the piano and learned French, English, Italian, and Hebrew. But in Hebrew "he was an unwilling pupil," and the subject was soon discontinued. His tutoring was limited to one hour a day; Jeannette was afraid of exhausting the child's energies. The rest of the day was rigidly allocated to set periods of walking, playing, and resting at home. Nevertheless, the five-year-old child is said to have mastered reading and writing within only two weeks, and to have gained a smattering of French within barely three more.

It is not necessary to accept all reports of the child's marvelous progress except as an indication of Jeannette's admitted faith in his genius. Herzl's remarkable mother was a beautiful woman, stately and statuesque. Her dark eyes flashed imperiously; the small, firm mouth was slightly hard. Her long black hair was piled over a high forehead, and she had a strong, straight, well-formed nose. Powerful, domineering, possessed of an iron will, worshiped by a pliant husband, Jeannette Herzl presided jealously over the affairs of her small family. She imparted her great love for German poetry to her son. At the age of eight or nine Theodor reportedly knew entire sections of German poetry by heart. Jeannette's particular favorites, from her maiden days, were Goethe, Schiller, Heine, and Lenau.

But her most distinctive stricture was a rigid Victorian sense of moral rectitude. The child was brought up by his mother to believe that there was nothing worse than "moral weakness"; truthfulness was the highest virtue.

Jeannette was not liked outside of her immediate family circle. Arthur Schnitzler's wife, Olga, remembered her as another Cornelia —ambitious and arrogant, hard, scheming, and aloof: " 'Mother of the Gracchi'—so the stately, proud, and virtuous woman was called in that part of the family where one lived slightly less grandly but a little more gaily." Olga Schnitzler complained of Jeannette's utter lack of humor. Jeannette's speech was marked by a "solemn pathos." She was sometimes asked not to be "so antique."

Herzl's father, Jakob, was less imaginative than his wife, with none of her intellectual ambitions and artistic tastes. He complemented her rigid sense of propriety with a stiff uprightness, an apprehensive, fussy pedantry, and a penchant for ceremonious solemnity. This last he bequeathed to his son. His contemporaries remembered him as a practical, hardworking, enterprising businessman. Though taciturn, he sometimes gave in to excessive rhetoric. "Many ships sank under me," he once wrote of his various business failures, "but time and again I threw myself into battle with the billows of the sea."

Jakob's wealth, which at one time was considerable, was self-made. His formal education was incomplete. At fifteen he had left his native Semlin to be apprenticed in the commissary and transportation business of a relative, Philipp Fleischel, at Debrecen. His native language had been German; in Debrecen he first learned Hungarian, but his command of that language would always be incomplete.

In 1856 the twenty-one-year-old Jakob moved to Budapest to open his own firm. His marriage the next year to Jeannette was a love match, a rare thing in his class, at a time when most engagements were carefully negotiated and arranged by ambitious relatives. As a contemporary characteristically remarked, "Although it was a love match, it was highly successful. There has never been a happier pair." Throughout their lives Jeannette and Jakob remained deeply attached to one another. Their mutual love was matched only by a passionate, possessive attachment to their only son.

Following his marriage to Jeannette, Jakob's business affairs in Budapest quickly prospered. He branched out into banking. By the early 1870s he was rumored to be a millionaire. His wife's social tastes favored an "aristocratic" early retirement, but Jakob was too active a man to retire young, even on his considerable income. It was probably the only time in his life that he ignored his wife's firm advice. In 1873 he speculated rashly and promptly lost a fortune estimated at half a million gold crowns. He never fully recovered from the blow. Jakob's misfortune was due partly to his own imprudence, partly to the economic crash of 1873. His father's experience had a strong effect on Theodor. It gave him a profound aversion to business. Herzl thereafter considered the stock exchange unclean, unsavory, and manipulated by unscrupulous scoundrels. And since, in the West, it was also a sinecure for Jews—the so-called *Börsejuden*—it epitomized everything shameful about Judaism.

4

This then was young Herzl's immediate family background. His father was often away from home on business. Herzl was raised almost solely by his mother. Since the company of other children was discouraged by the possessive Jeannette, his sister Pauline was his closest, most permanent, perhaps his only playmate. Pauline, one year older than Theodor, bore a remarkable resemblance to her mother. Herzl grew up in a feminine atmosphere. Its gentle monotony was rarely broken by rudeness or impetuosity. He was surrounded with loving care. Many of his early scribblings and copybooks were preserved by his mother. The collection comprises his first literary experiments and his correspondence, including this early letter to his father, written when he was six:

Heissgeliebter Papa!
I am also in good health and am very much longing to be able to see you soon again. Greetings from your good son,
Dori

The remaining papers convey a general, if incomplete, impression of his youth. He was a precocious child. Contemporaries remembered his being elegantly dressed at all times, in black and expensive finery. In one remarkable photograph taken when he was five, Herzl stands tensely erect, dressed in black velvet with white lace cuffs and collar and high-buttoned black patent leather boots. He looks very self-assured, full of himself. The childish eyes are sad and wizened. His chin is thrust forward petulantly, and his left hand rests nonchalantly on a book placed on an elaborately carved chair. The corners of his pressed lips droop in an expression almost of disdain, surprising in so young a boy. The princely pose is reminiscent of the famous Velázquez portrait of the children of Philip II; it is easy to imagine the proud, high-spirited, ambitious mother arranging her son's first formal portrait.

But one senses a moody, high-strung child as well. He was a daydreamer. His imagination, nurtured by his mother's rich store of German fairy tales, was heightened by solitude and reading. He sometimes pictured strange and brilliant scenes to himself. He saw himself perform majestic feats. Fabled romance alternated with science fiction. He would meet creatures of great beauty and nobility: a shining knight; a blond, blue-eyed princess, she would pledge herself to him, and he to her. Or he might be a great inventor crossing the sky in a flying ship, or an engineer who would construct powerful machines to move mountains.

His boyhood was nonetheless quite straightforward. The elementary school he attended was bilingual; German and Hungarian were taught on an equal basis. Although it was a parochial school, Jewish or religious studies were marginal. Nevertheless, the future Zionist leader disliked it for the little Jewishness it possessed. One harrowing memory of the parochial school lasted into adulthood. This was "the thrashing I received because I did not remember the details of the Exodus of the Jews from Egypt," Herzl wrote in 1898, when his Zionist project had already aroused great controversy. And he added with characteristic sarcasm: "Nowadays, many schoolmasters would like to thrash me because I remember that Exodus only too well."

At ten, Herzl transferred to the municipal *Realschule* of Pest. The child probably chose this science-oriented school over the more conventional classical *Gymnasium*. His parents were sensitive and sympathetic to his every wish. He soon regretted the choice, but for some time at least it seemed that technology was Herzl's natural bent.

He entered the *Realschule* in 1869, shortly after the opening of the Suez Canal. The boy's imagination was fired by the great technical feat. He followed newspaper accounts of the colorful opening ceremonies in Port Said and Cairo, in the presence of kings and queens, and to the music of Verdi's newly composed *Aïda*. The combination of medieval pomp and modern technology appealed to the boy's taste. Ferdinand de Lesseps, builder of the canal, was the hero of the day and Herzl's great idol. The boy confided to his father that he would follow in Lesseps' footsteps; when he grew up he would cut through the Isthmus of Panama to unite the Pacific and Atlantic oceans. He asked his father to guard his secret well, so that no one else would beat him to the task.

At the *Realschule*, however, the would-be engineer was not a success. Although he remained more than four years, he was plagued by growing discomfort, failure, and frustration. His marks in German and in history were good or excellent, but he was mediocre in mathematics, geometry, and science. The marks grew worse as the years went by. His early "love of logarithms and trigonometry" was fading. In retrospect, more than thirty years later, he analyzed his disenchantment with trigonometry as stemming from "the anti-Semitic spirit" at that school. One teacher had explained the term "pagan," adding that it included "idol worshipers, Mohammedans, and Jews." After this explanation, "I became fed up with the *Realschule* and wanted to transfer to a classical *Gymnasium*."

Herzl's complaint of anti-Semitism at the *Realschule* is plausible. The stock exchange crash of 1873, during which Herzl's father had lost almost his entire fortune, briefly rekindled anti-Semitic agitation in the city. But the real reason for the boy's disenchantment with the *Realschule* was his growing passion for poetry and humanistic studies, an interest that was not sufficiently requited at the science-oriented school. He had lost interest in science; perhaps he had never had any real interest beyond its glamour as a subject for romantic literary treatment. An unsympathetic or anti-Semitic teacher further spoiled his taste. But his marks in Jewish religion were equally bad, and that teacher was certainly no anti-Semite. The same growing passion for German poetry and German history for which young Herzl neglected his mathematics caused him to neglect his Jewish studies as well.

He had little, if any, interest in Judaism. He regarded Jewry with some arrogance and even a little disdain. As a small boy he had occasionally been taken to Friday evening services in the synagogue. But this never became a habit, and as he grew older he stopped attending altogether. When he was eight his father inscribed him as a member of the local *Chevra Kadisha*, a charitable synagogue society. He was registered in the records as "Habachur [the lad] Benjamin Zev, son of Jacob." Benjamin Zev was his Hebrew name, which like most Jews at the time he carried informally next to his official name, Theodor. But except for such occasions, he never used it. The ceremony took place in a candlelit prayer room. An elder shook the boy's hand and pronounced, "*Achinu Ata*" (Thou art our brother). The ceremony made little impression on Herzl; he never mentioned it anywhere. Thirty-six years later, in 1904, when Herzl was at the peak of his fame as a modern Jewish leader, his name was struck from the society's rolls for inactivity and apparent nonpayment of dues.

His mother derived her strict notions of charity and moral rectitude not from any conscious sense of Jewish ethics—she was ignorant of those—but from her interpretation of German humanist *Kultur*. On Herzl's thirteenth birthday, invitations went out, not to his *Bar Mitzvah*, but to his "confirmation." It took place at eleven o'clock in the morning at the Herzl home. There is no evidence of a synagogue service. After Herzl's death an uncle remembered a proper synagogue *Bar Mitzvah* during which the boy supposedly read the Torah and vowed eternal loyalty to Judaism. But this was an apocryphal account, related long after Herzl's apotheosis as a latter-day Jewish saint. The "confirmation" made no impression on Herzl's memory. The future Zionist leader grew up as a thoroughly emancipated, antitraditional, secular, would-be German boy.

He dismissed *all* religion. In a little essay he wrote in high school he developed a fully rationalistic outlook on life. It began with a characteristic sentence: "I have pondered a great deal (in my own way of course) on the purpose of human existence." And it concluded with the observation that the false miracles of all "clever frauds from Moses and Jesus to the Count of Saint Germain have already been exposed by the human spirit. It will undoubtedly soon unravel the last and final secrets of the human order."

His juvenile arrogance was nourished by his mother's imperious pride. Unlike her husband, who had come from provincial Semlin, Jeannette Herzl had been born in metropolitan Budapest. Her family was at once more sophisticated, more assimilated, and more secular. Jeannette was a social and cultural snob. Like many other emancipated Jewish mothers, she imparted to her son her own genteel resentment of the alleged crudity and materialism of the *nouveau riche* Jewish milieu. Her son, as a high school student, deplored the Jews' alleged warped morality. He professed shock at what he felt was their lack of "ethical seriousness." It is difficult now to understand precisely what he meant, but clearly young Herzl was inadvertently adopting some of the stereotyped anti-Semitic attitudes of his day. They would remain with him for many years.

5

A Hungarian fellow student remembered him from his high school days as a "dark, slim boy, always elegantly dressed. He was always in a good mood . . . but mostly acting superior, ironic, even sarcastic." There was a "smooth nihilism" about him. He was not unpopular, but he had no close friends, and from this description it is not difficult to see why. Nor did he want any. Today he would be called a loner. Surviving photographs of Herzl in his teens show the dark eyes, which had had a touch of sadness in them at the age of five, clouded by a new melancholy. The chin had grown even stronger. He looked older than his age.

To the Hungarian schoolmate, Herzl's later prominence as "an apostle of Zionism" came as a great surprise. In high school he had spoken of Judaism with "mocking cynicism." His primary interests were German literature, German history, and politics. The family spoke German at home. He was as fluent in Hungarian as in German, but German was his first love. And not surprisingly. In the early 1870s "culture" in Budapest was still synonymous with German *Kultur*. Hungarian nationalism had received a tremendous uplift by the Compromise of 1867 which had established the dual

monarchy, but German culture still reigned supreme. The best theater was German; the most prestigious and best-written daily newspaper was the German-language *Pester Journal*. It was edited,
again not surprisingly, by the brilliant Jewish publicist Adolf Silberstein, a friend of the Herzls. In Hungary, as almost everywhere
in the eastern parts of the far-flung Hapsburg Empire, Jews were
the vanguard of the German language and *Kultur*.*

While still at the science-oriented *Realschule*, Herzl spent much
of his free time writing short stories and poems. His style and
subject matter revealed the strong influence of Heine on the boy's
unformed mind. In February 1874 he founded and became president of a literary society of four or five young boys, self-confidently
called *Wir* (We). The "Ground Rules . . . formulated by Theodor
Herzl, adopted at Meeting I, 22 Febr. 1874," have survived. The
purpose of Wir was to enrich its members' knowledge and to improve their German style. Works by members of Wir were read and
criticized in public session. The procedure followed a solemn ritual
laid down by young Herzl in the Ground Rules.

The rules give an early insight into Herzl's keen sense of ceremony. The boys were required to address each other not in the
familiar *du* but in the formal *Sie*. They were enjoined to observe
strict rules of presentation and demeanor.

According to the minutes, the sessions were monopolized by
the president. His works were cited in the minutes as "good" or
"accepted with praise." Other members fared less well. The minutes
of each meeting were signed "certified correct and accepted by
Theodor Herzl, President." Much of the time was taken up by discussions of Herzl's works and by his "informal addresses" on such
subjects as "Mythology," "Heroism," or "Order and Obedience." The
society collapsed after two months, perhaps from the exercise of too
much presidential leadership. The five members clearly found him
too overbearing.

One of his own works that Herzl read to the group, the fairy
tale "Charmed Harp," has survived in manuscript. It reveals a facility for language remarkable in a thirteen-and-a-half-year-old boy.

* A decade later this attitude would change; in the 1880s and 1890s Hungarian Jews would begin to dedicate themselves to Hungarian letters as
passionately as young Herzl in the early 1870s devoted himself to German.
Herzl's cousin, Joseph Heltai, eleven years his junior, rejected German and
became the "father of Hungarian journalism." In 1897, when Herzl was already
prominent in German letters, he urged his cousin to move to Vienna and
offered him a promising career. Heltai refused; he wanted to be a Hungarian
writer, and he wrote back saying he desired to remain "at home."

The breakup of Wir did not interrupt his literary experiments. On the contrary, he wrote more than before. In the process he neglected his schoolwork. At fifteen he became interested in politics. Bismarck, the Iron Chancellor of the new German Reich, replaced Ferdinand de Lesseps as the boy's idol. The cult of Bismarck was shared by innumerable liberal Jews of the time. Freud's father was such an admirer of Bismarck that when he had to translate the date of his own birth from the Hebrew calendar to the Christian, he juggled the dates somewhat to choose Bismarck's birthdate.

There was something natural and obvious in young Herzl's support of German nationalism and grandeur. He expressed his sentiments in a historical poem written under the impact of Bismarck's aggressive diplomacy in the wake of the Prussian victory over France in 1870. Its title, "To Canossa We Won't Go," echoes the resurgence of German nationalism and German Protestantism after the establishment of the united Reich in 1870. Herzl extols the Holy Roman Emperor Henry IV and his humiliation at Canossa in 1077 at the "dark and treacherous hand of Rome." In the centuries that have passed since Henry's terrible penance, the "noble tribe" of Germany has cast off its old faults and recovered its might:

> Out of the long, long night
> Through Luther's power and might
> The German spirit came to light.

> And Liberty's glorious sight
> Shines upon all awake; for lo,
> To Canossa we won't go!

> (Es ist aus langer Nacht
> Durch Luther's gewaltige Kraft
> Der deutsche Geist erwacht.

> Und der Freiheit goldnes Licht
> Bestrahlt der Erwachenden Angesicht
> Nach Canossa gehn wir nicht.)

There were moments, however, when this young admirer of German *Kultur*, of Luther's might and Bismarck's glory, encountered an older, radically different view of life in the person of his paternal grandfather, Simon. The old man was in his early seventies. He still lived in Semlin, some two hundred miles south of Budapest. It was a six-hour train ride; in some ways it bridged entire centuries. Young Herzl's grandfather represented a different

type of Jewish piety, old-fashioned, simple-minded, deeply rooted
in ancient lore. Simon's stark, unreflective faith contrasted sharply
with Herzl's Budapest milieu of flippant sophistication and secularism. Simon Herzl resented his son's secularism. He must have
been even more critical of his grandson's upbringing. Theodor's
feelings about his grandfather are not known. In later years he
wrote of him only once, in a brief and perhaps wistful note hur-
riedly jotted down in 1896 after a moving, tearful, and, for Herzl,
"completely dumbfounding" reception given to the visiting Zionist
leader by masses of pious Sofia Jews. He wrote: "I . . . surveyed the
crowd. The most varied types. An old man with a fur cap looked like
my grandfather, Simon Herzl." Herzl had a strong sense of family,
yet in the vast collection of Herzl's private and public papers, diaries, and letters, there is no further reference to his grandfather.
Perhaps he was embarrassed by him. More likely he treated him
with the same air of reserve he showed toward his younger contemporaries.

Simon was a great storyteller. He may have told his grandson
the strange saga of Yehuda Alkalai. Alkalai was a Sephardic rabbi
in Simon Herzl's hometown, Semlin. In 1834 he created a stir
among the townspeople by publishing a little Hebrew booklet that
called for the establishment of Jewish colonies in the Holy Land.
This, he argued, was a necessary step toward messianic redemption.
Yehuda Alkalai was influenced by religion as well as by the Greek
War of Independence and the national strivings of the Serbs among
whom he lived. To sponsor his project, he traveled to various European cities and organized a few short-lived circles, including one in
London. In 1874, shortly after Herzl's "confirmation," Alkalai created another little stir in Semlin by moving himself and his family
to Jerusalem, where he died four years later. He was one of Herzl's
precursors as a Zionist agitator, a romantic, bizarre figure of considerable charm.

When Herzl later, in his articles and diaries, traced his development as a Zionist, he mentioned neither his grandfather nor Alkalai. Either he was ignorant of Alkalai's history, or, having heard it
once in his youth, had dismissed it or laughed it off. Perhaps he had
banished it to a corner of his mind, like sweat or sex in a Victorian
novel, where it lay dormant only to reemerge after many years,
unrecognizable, in a new form.

6

In February 1875, in the middle of the school year, Herzl's parents finally removed him from the *Realschule*. It was high time. The boy was thoroughly miserable. His marks had reached the lowest point of his entire high school career. Gone were all the "excellents" and "very goods" of former years. In his last term report he was rated "insufficient" in geometry, draftsmanship, and religion. Hungarian language, chemistry, mathematics, and caligraphy were "sufficient"; so was his "industry." Even his German was merely "good." Private teachers were now hired to prepare him for a classical *Gymnasium*. He knew neither Greek nor Latin. But he had a natural facility for languages, an "easy grasp," and an unusually strong memory.

Such qualities now combined within the stubborn, moody, independent-minded boy to produce quick results. He gave up his piano lessons, which he regarded as "medieval torture." But with great exuberance he threw himself into his Latin and Greek. Approvingly, he inscribed one of his copybooks with two lines from Hölderlin:

> We are nothing,
> What we *will* is everything.
>
> (Wir sind nichts,
> Was wir *wollen* its alles.)

Later in the year he entered the Evangelical *Gymnasium* of Pest. Despite its name, the majority of the pupils were Jewish. The school was a high temple of German language and *Kultur* set in the heart of a great Hungarian city. It emphasized ancient languages and the modern German classics. Here Herzl soon felt at home, and it quickly showed in his marks. Within only a few months his performance was again "excellent" and "praiseworthy." Even in *doctrina religionis*, he now rated *eximius* as he did in *lingua germanica*. He became active in the *Deutscher Selbstbildungsverein*, a pupils' society devoted to the study and practice of German letters. Like the late Wir, it engaged its members in elaborate discussions of their poems and short stories.

Herzl was happy at the *Gymnasium*. He took long walks in the environs of Budapest. He even made friends with a boy of his own age. This friendship was short-lived; Herzl soon sneeringly referred to this companion as a "simple-minded" fellow. But while the friendship lasted the two boys toured the pretty wooded riverbanks or watched "the sun as it set majestically beyond the hills of Buda." He also fell in love. In later years, he confessed that it had been the "first and only" real love of his life. In view of his subsequent bitterly unhappy marriage, there is good reason to take this confession seriously. The girl's name was Madeleine. Very little is known of her. She was fourteen years old, and she apparently died while still in her teens. Her blond hair and blue eyes, a Germanic ideal of beauty, left an indelible impression on Herzl. His novels, short stories, and plays would be crowded with blue-eyed, golden-haired heroines. The one exception, Miriam, the heroine of *Altneuland* (1902), was "black haired . . . *nevertheless* she did not cut a bad figure next to the tall, blond Englishwoman [italics mine]."

It is doubtful that Herzl and Madeleine ever exchanged more than a few words. He was overcome with shyness and worshiped Madeleine from a distance. "I hid my love from its object with greater fear than that of a poacher who hides a slain deer from the hunter's watchful eyes." Instead he poured his feelings into rhyme. And he walked even longer hours on the banks of the Danube "in the good company of sweet, sentimental Lady Melancholy."

We must picture him at this time, a seventeen-year-old youth, enjoying an easy success at the *Gymnasium*, pampered by a loving mother, and adored by a sweet and pretty sister. Sulky and sensitive, he affected the fashionable *Weltschmerz* of his age group and time, and was much given to solitude. He was an avid reader. His favorites were Heinrich Heine and Nikolaus Lenau, both anticlerical romanticists. Heine was a Jew, perhaps the finest lyric poet in modern German letters. His prose excelled in a kind of subtle irony that Herzl tried all his life to emulate. Lenau was born, like Herzl, in Hungary and had become a well-known German poet. Lenau's *Polenlieder* (1830) extolled the Polish wars of independence. In *Johannes Ziska* (1837) Lenau celebrated a famous Czech national hero. Herzl knew long excerpts from Heine and Lenau by heart.

At sixteen, Herzl still jestingly referred to himself, in a letter to his father, as a *"Deutscher Schriftsteller"* (a German writer). By the age of seventeen he had definitely decided to become a writer. Several poems, sketches, and the outlines for some fifteen plays have survived from this period. They reveal no special talent. The poems are strongly imitative of Heine. ("Ach, die Lippen die ich küsste!" "Lieder singt meine Leiden.") Three years later, at twenty, he himself disparagingly referred to them as plagiaristic. His prose —later his forte—rarely rose above the level of conventional society novels. ("In the early fifties I was living in the chateau of a relative in northern Hungary. It was the hunting season. Guests at the castle were ladies and gentlemen of the highest class. In the brilliant wreath of charming ladies, one in particular stood out, Fräulein von . . .")

He worked hard on his French, which was near perfect, and on his Italian and English. He devised his own little English-German dictionary. The first thirteen English words he listed are noteworthy:

> mellow
> boyish
> ambition
> voluptuous
> indolence
> lofty-minded
> resolve
> eloquence
> cheek
> exhortation
> lingering gaze
> clever

He sent some of his work to a newspaper for possible publication. In an exuberant accompanying note he claimed to be just as capable as the editor at any task. "Furthermore I beg of you, very esteemed sir, not to take this as proof of a fool's ridiculous arrogance—or unjustified pride—but as the calm certitude of one who knows his capability but scorns to display a show of absurd modesty."

His parents strongly encouraged him in his literary ambitions. They were sure of his eventual success as a playwright or novelist. With his resolve to become a German writer, his interest in Hungary diminished even more. He adopted a sardonic, superior tone toward Hungarian affairs and a disparaging attitude toward politics. At seventeen and a half he sent a patronizing, albeit witty, account of Hungarian parliamentary life to the Viennese weekly *Leben*. He was pleased to see it printed, anonymously of course. As a *Gymnasium* student he would have suffered a severe reprimand for publishing even a short piece in a newspaper.

He also wrote book reviews, which were anonymously published in Adolf Silberstein's *Pester Journal*. His progress in the

Gymnasium continued satisfactorily. In his eighth and final year he was nearly a model pupil. In the winter of 1877–1878 his report card showed five marks of "excellent." His "behavior" was less admirable and rated a mere "vorschriftsmässig" (according to regulation).

As he approached his final examination, the family began to consider his immediate future. Jakob and Jeannette contemplated moving the household to Vienna. It would give young Theodor an opportunity to attend the best, most prestigious university in the Austro-Hungarian Empire. He would breathe the exhilarating air of a great European literary and theatrical metropolis. Herzl's own heart strongly "went out to Vienna." It was unthinkable that Theodor should go alone; the Herzls were too closely knit a family.

Then a terrible blow suddenly fell on the happy little circle. On February 7, 1878, Pauline, Herzl's nineteen-year-old sister, fell ill with typhoid fever. That evening, the visiting doctor was still confident that she would recover but within a few hours she was dead.

Her flower-covered coffin was placed in the living room. Herzl knelt by it, crying silently. His father's inchoate cries echoed through the house. Jeannette, completely shattered, "did not cry. She cried afterward, without interruption, for many years." Herzl bitterly reproached himself later for not having properly mourned his beloved sister. He confessed to having displayed a fake show of pain. In a brief note ("In Memoriam") written in an almost suicidal tone in 1882, he accused himself of cold callousness. At Pauline's funeral "I shouted something, as is customary, and I cried a great deal, but I [also] edited the death announcement with circumspection and a fine ear to its oratorical impact. My pain was somewhat theatrical. I felt very sorry for myself, but mostly because I knew that others were sorry for me."

Pauline had been a popular girl, an actress in amateur theatricals. Herzl later confessed that he had derived

> no little satisfaction from the fact that the newspapers were writing about our misfortunes. . . . I thought of my black tie and black gloves. I did not lose my control. Nor did I overlook the consequence of my absence from school. . . . I was a very wretched fellow. Yes, even while my good, beloved sister was dying, I still visited the coffeehouse to play dominoes, though with a solemn air of seriousness as befitted the situation, and with a certain kind of artistic sadness—for my sister's sickness was known. . . .

There was an element of theatricality even in this remarkable confession, but also something of that desperate search for disillusioned truth which later marked the Zionist leader. Whatever had been the youth's immediate reaction to his only sister's death, he nevertheless remained inconsolable over her loss for many years. He had loved her dearly, and realizing later how hard it was to find lasting love, he missed her even more. On the anniversary of her death Herzl often traveled to Budapest and brought home to Vienna a flower from her grave. He named his first-born daughter after her. In his novel *Altneuland* he drew a loving portrait of Pauline in the person of Miriam. The loss of Pauline had been Herzl's first encounter with death; henceforth its sad shadow would always be with him.

After Pauline's death, Herzl and his parents became even closer and more withdrawn. Jeannette Herzl was in a state of shock. She could not bear to remain in the house, or the city, where she had raised Pauline. The family decided to move to Vienna immediately. Herzl was taken out of school. Barely a week after the funeral they were on their way. Jakob Herzl returned several times to Hungary to wind up his affairs and to arrange for the transfer of the furniture. Theodor remained in Vienna with his grief-stricken mother. He answered the letters of condolence. "Dear good Aunt," he wrote his mother's sister Rosalie from Vienna on February 23, 1878:

> . . . my poor dear parents instruct me to write you and all our relatives to thank you for the warm, but unfortunately vain, words of consolation, that you have expressed to us. Since a few days ago I have been in Vienna with my sweet Mama; here in Vienna she will try, as much as possible, to forget the painful loss that shattered our whole life, which until now has been so pleasant and nice. One can only hope that it will work, that she might forget even slightly and console herself for her loss with what has remained to her. And yet one cannot be sure, for even now, with the days of the heaviest pain over, she still occupies her whole time with fruitless, unnerving anguish.

At the same time, Herzl prepared himself at home for his final high school examinations, which were now only four months off. He traveled back to Budapest in June to sit for his exams and barely passed with minimal marks, except in German and religion. Herzl quickly returned to Vienna and his parents, relieved to leave Budapest behind him. He would return only briefly thereafter, and always with some displeasure and misgiving.

3

Viennese Masquerade

THE BIG, ELONGATED HOUSE at Praterstrasse 25 looked out over a vast expanse of cobblestones. It was built of yellow brick, in the graceful style of the late Biedermeier period. Here the Herzls took up residence early in 1878. The spacious apartment occupied half of the third floor. Its tall and narrow windows, topped by delicately cut ledgestones, overlooked the broad and stately avenue. Below, the road was bordered by massively carved granite pillars erected on both sides for effect and the protection of pedestrians. Beyond, over the rooftops, stretched the wide, treelined quay of the walled-in Danube basin.

The Praterstrasse, located in the second district of Vienna, was a prosperous residential section. Here, within an area of three or four blocks, a surprisingly large number of distinguished men had taken their first steps. Arthur Schnitzler was born in 1862 a few houses down the road from Herzl's home. His father, a successful physician, had come to Vienna, like Herzl's parents, from Hungary. Around the corner from Praterstrasse 25, young Sigmund Freud had lived in 1866 with his parents, just after their arrival from Bohemia. Now, in 1878, the young Gustav Mahler, born like Herzl in 1860, huddled in a little room a few steps away from the Herzl residence, practicing his music. In the nearby Tempelgasse, a new synagogue was rising next to a canteen for poor Jewish immigrants from the East.

If the Leopoldstadt, as the area was called, was popular with Jews, it was not yet an exclusively Jewish ghetto. Everywhere in the Leopoldstadt Jews and Catholics lived side by side in the same streets and apartment houses. On the Praterstrasse, which was the former Jaegerzeile (hunter's row, so called because early in the

VIENNESE MASQUERADE   33

century a Hapsburg archduke had donated the land for town
houses for retainers of the imperial household), only a handful of
wealthy Jews made their homes among staunchly Catholic bur-
ghers, pensioned widows, and retired bureaucrats. The Praterstrasse
was touched by Bohemian flair and aristocratic bonhomie. At number 29, a few yards to the left of the Herzls' house, a neoclassic
portico of heavy columns led to the famous Carl-Theater. The Carl-
Theater was Vienna's second most important stage after the imperial Burgtheater. It was as distinguished in drama as in music.
When it was not launching Offenbach or Strauss operettas on triumphal marches across Europe, or engaging Gustav Mahler or the
young Arnold Schönberg to conduct visiting Italian opera groups, it
mounted brilliant productions of classic Austrian plays by Grillparzer, Raimund, or Nestroy.

The stately road led to the magnificent gardens of the Prater.
Its races and flower shows attracted carefree pleasure-seekers with
their equipages and fiacres and liveried footmen and handmaids.
On fine days gentlemen riders passed under young Theodor's windows on their way to the park, the image of resplendent elegance
and aristocratic ease. And on Sundays, long processions of open
carriages, filled with elegant ladies in huge hats, made their way to
the fashionable promenade, the Corso, in the wooded park.

Herzl was happy to be in Vienna. He felt he belonged here.
Many years later, dejected by his failure as a writer, except as a
"journalistic handyman," and seized like most Viennese intellectuals
by the city's perennial air of despondency, he called Vienna the city
of his "pains and travails." But in 1878 he clearly preferred the pains
of Vienna to those of his former life in Hungary. His parents, inconsolable over the loss of Pauline, lived in a state of self-imposed
seclusion. After their move to Vienna, Jakob and Jeannette remained quietly at home. They made no such demand on Theodor,
who threw himself wholeheartedly into the hectic Viennese life of
literary cafés and first nights at the opera. For a young man of
strong literary ambitions from the provinces, it was a pleasantly
stimulating life with all its concomitant loves, feuds, and heated
arguments. The theater was the great Viennese passion, far exceed-
ing politics in importance.

Eight months after his arrival, in the fall of 1878, Herzl en-
rolled as a student in the University of Vienna Faculty of Law. His
choice of so mundane a subject may seem surprising. He was led by
tradition and circumstance. Many German men of letters had pursued an identical course, including the great Goethe and Heinrich

Heine whom the poet Herzl considered closest to himself in background and temperament. Circumstance was another factor. Although Jews now legally enjoyed full civil rights, in practice they
were still excluded from the middle or higher echelons of public administration; a full professorship at a university was attainable only
after conversion to Christianity. To overcome such handicaps and yet
gain a measure of economic security, Jewish students naturally
tended to one of the two truly free professions, law and medicine.
Both held out a promise of achievement, comfort, and independence.
Shortly before the Herzls' departure from Budapest, the Chief
Rabbi, during a condolence call, had asked young Theodor what
career he was planning.

Herzl answered, "A writer."

The Chief Rabbi responded, "But you can't call that a real
career."

His parents, despite their faith in his talent, were also concerned for his future. He was not interested in medicine. But to a
lawyer, as a current saying went, "the whole world stood open."

His legal studies barely distracted him. Soon after his arrival in
Vienna he began writing again. He bombarded newspaper editors
and book publishers with poems, short pieces, novellas, and offers to
translate French plays into German. He subscribed to half a dozen
literary magazines, including the *Deutsches Dichterheim*. The move
from Budapest to Vienna was easy and called for no cultural or
linguistic change. Herzl had always felt like a German-Austrian boy
growing up in a Hungarian town; now that he was becoming an
adult, it was only fitting that he lived in Vienna, perhaps the greatest German cultural center of the time. He was a young man suddenly matured by a terrible personal loss. Like many young adults he
sought an identity. For a time he thought he had found one. One of
the first pseudonyms he picked was "Theodor Viennensis."

Budapest quickly receded into the past. In March 1882 he was
ordered by the army to report to Budapest for his medical examination. The three days he spent there were highly disagreeable. He
was now a sophisticate from the big city who found his hometown
unbearably confining. Its provinciality startled him and he was repelled even by its appearance. "How it has shrunk . . . the streets
have narrowed and shortened," and even the houses "look like se-
nile old men." In Budapest this was a time of growing self-assertion
among the Magyars. Herzl was especially derisive of the nationalist
movement and wrote a friend in a mocking tone:

Since I left, Hungary has unfortunately become even more Hungarian. Alas! How some of my friends and colleagues . . . have in the meantime developed into extremely Hungarian idiots! Their Hungarian is bad, but they speak it with great tenacity; and those who were named Sonnenberg and Faigl-stock are now calling themselves Murányi and Figályi. Isn't that pretty!

Your faithful Theodor

P.S. With great consequence I have not uttered a single Hungarian syllable here.

2

Vienna, at the time of Herzl's arrival, was a city of unique character. The vast empire it ruled was the oldest in all Europe. It was bound together neither by geography, nationality, nor a common culture or language, but by the dynastic principle inherited from a previous age. Like the empire, the city's character was "out of time and out of place." Vienna lagged a hundred years behind Paris or Berlin. Some Viennese deliberately lived in the age of the baroque or the rococo.

Raoul Auernheimer, Herzl's cousin, a writer of considerable local renown, aptly summed up the mood and basic sensibility of refined Viennese culture shortly before it was drowned by the tide of nationalism and finally destroyed by war. Although "born in Vienna in the last quarter of the nineteenth century," he wrote, "I actually lived in the eighteenth." Young Herzl might have made the same statement.

Vienna was not a national but an imperial capital, and not merely a capital, but the soul of the Hapsburg Empire. It reflected and controlled, as best it could, a supranational alignment of feudal and clericalist forces, stretching across half of Europe, that had survived from the Middle Ages into the nineteenth century. There were more Czechs in Vienna than in Prague, more Croatians than in Zagreb, and five times as many Jews as in Jerusalem. Vienna's cultural atmosphere was more cosmopolitan than that of any other European city since the fall of Rome.

"Nowhere was it easier to be a European," Stefan Zweig wrote nostalgically many years later, in exile, of his beloved "world of yesterday," desperately invoking its lost grandeur. "Whoever lived there and worked there felt himself free of all confinement and prejudice."

Not everyone. It was not all sun and light, as it seemed to the aging Zweig. Already the unmistakable subterranean rumblings of a nationalist volcano, slowly warming up, were heard and sometimes feared, but they were not taken much to heart. The poet Franz Grillparzer warned that Austria might be heading "from humanism, through nationalism, into barbarism," yet the typical Viennese reply was, "The situation is desperate, but not serious." To each of the empire's warring nationalities (especially the dominant Germans) only his own nationalism was civilized and patriotic. The national aspirations of the remaining eight or nine segments of the empire were dismissed as chauvinistic and disruptive barbarism. Meanwhile, few people worried. Such cracks as there were in the glittering edifice of Europe's oldest empire were covered up, at least in Vienna, by a fabulous late flowering of rococo frivolity, the well-organized gaiety of masked balls in endless succession, in which all but the very poor regularly took part. Here "every middle-class lady was made to feel like Marie Antoinette, and every stockbroker like the Duc de Lauzun."

The masquerade went beyond the narrow confines of gilded ballrooms. The prevailing fashions in interior design and in clothes were a good case in point. A gentleman's study was decorated like a knightly Gothic hall, with banners and swords draping the walls. Drawing rooms were oriental tents encased in worm-eaten Gobelins. For the well-to-do—it was the great age of *modistes*. Women's heads were bizarrely coiffed, emulating the style of Livia or Plotina, or of medieval pages and knights. The outlines of the female figure were lost under corsets. Children were costumed just as absurdly: little girls in grandmother bonnets, boys in admiral's uniform, twins in Spanish page outfits.

The spectacular pageantry of the imperial court often spilled out into the streets. Its rigid rules of etiquette were derived from Spain; under the iron skies of Central Europe, the Hapsburgs successfully reenacted a frozen version of the sheen and dazzle and color of El Escorial. The Emperor rode through his city in a gilded carriage drawn by eight white horses, mounted by lackeys in raven black, gold-trimmed uniforms and white perukes. On each side of the imperial carriage strode two Hungarian guards, yellow-black panther furs thrown over their wide shoulders. "They looked like gods, but were merely the servants of demigods"

Nor were such spectacles confined to affairs of the imperial court. Periodically the entire city became a gigantic stage for vast festivals, processions, and parades. One of the first Herzl saw after his arrival in Vienna was the elaborate *Makartfestzug*, held on April 28, 1879, in honor of the Emperor's silver wedding anniversary. The procession passed under Herzl's windows on the Praterstrasse. Its sheer resplendence, its elaborately staged tableaux, its fusion of theatrical and political motifs dazzled the young man, along with nearly everyone else in Vienna. Undoubtedly, it influenced Herzl's later faith in the political role of liturgy and the *mise-en-scène*.

Many chroniclers of nineteenth-century Austria have seen this procession as an index to the taste and temper of the time. It was "produced" by Hans Makart, the most popular and successful painter of his day, who had briefly diverted popular attention from the musicians, contrary to all Viennese tradition. Makart himself rode on a gilded horse at the head of the procession, dressed as a latter-day Tiepolo in a costume of black velvet. Makart believed not only in the costuming of his world but of himself as well. No more fitting man could have staged this particular pageant to suit the taste of this particular time. Makart had a natural, typically Viennese instinct for decor, and for everything that glittered, adorned, richly unfolded, and hid what was ugly. He was a virtuoso of grandiose stage effects, vast spaces, lights, blinding golds and silvers. It was all very intoxicating, but had little in common with real life.

In the masquerade that was Vienna in the 1870s and 1880s—crucial, formative years in Herzl's life—Makart created the biggest, most dazzling mask to hide the real face of the decaying city. The Viennese way of life was still "easygoing" and "lighthearted," full of a conviviality that kept everything on the surface. The contrast with Berlin, the other German capital, was considerable. The Viennese spoke a softer, more gracious, musical southern German. They had a reputation for gluttony and affectation. Schiller, echoing a more Spartan northern Germany, derided the easy-living Austrians as a bunch of "Phaecians"; in Austria "it is always Sunday, the spit is constantly turning on the stove." The Viennese were equally suspicious and resentful of the militaristic, crude Prussians. The feeling prevailing in the liberal 1870s, before the rise in Austria of pan-German nationalism and anti-Semitism, was well expressed in a popular song:

> There is only one royal city,
> Vienna is its name.

There's only one robber's nest,
Berlin is its name.

(Es gibt nur eine Kaiserstadt,
Es gibt nur ein Wien.
Es gibt nur ein Räubernest,
Das heisst Berlin.)

Few suspected that the famous Viennese *Gemütlichkeit*, still largely liberal, tolerant, and cosmopolitan, was only a thin veneer covering a chaotic mass of dark, barbaric forces. "It was sweet to live here," Stefan Zweig wrote of the old Vienna. It is not difficult to see why. The Viennese world of yesterday, which had so great an influence on Herzl's mind and temperament, was essentially liberal and rationalist, though perhaps also impractical and unduly naïve. From the vantage point of our own era of fierce tribal loyalties, this Vienna retains a marvelous appeal.

Vienna in the last part of the nineteenth century was what New York would be a century later. Because of its diversity, the intellectual span of Viennese life was wider than in any other European capital. Culturally and ethnically it was the melting pot of Europe —at least until the new century, when the pot exploded into pieces that tore all of Europe apart. There was hardly another city in Europe where a passionate concern for music and theater was such an integral part of public life. Vienna was a showpiece of intensive creativity brought about by cultural diversity. Though not really open-minded, with its curious sense of receptiveness it attracted and absorbed the most disparate intellectual forces from the vast Hapsburg Empire. The principle of ethnic and cultural diversity was followed, in varying degrees, on all levels of society. At the top of the social pyramid, the Hapsburgs were intermarried with most of Europe—England, Burgundy, Italy, Byzantium, Spain, and Poland. The resultant aristocracy was a mixed breed of Germans, Italians, Frenchmen, Spaniards, Poles, Irish, and Walloons.

Early in the century, Metternich's secretary, Gentz, reflecting on the diversity of Vienna's upper classes, remarked, "Thou art no more a city, Vienna, but Europe!" In the 1870s the vast population influx from Eastern, Central, and Southern Europe was making Gentz's remark applicable to the middle and working classes as well. It cannot be said that they got on well with each other, but the constant challenge and potential of diversity was ever present. Few, if any, townspeople were "thoroughbred" Viennese, or even *Aus-*

trian—whatever that meant. The majority were Czechs, Magyars, Serbs, Italians, Jews, Croatians, Poles, Swabians, and Bavarians. Vienna was a German-speaking city, but in the nineteenth century it was not really German, as were Munich and Berlin. Its culture was cosmopolitan. Henri de Blowitz, the Austrian-born, world-famous Paris correspondent of the London *Times*, exemplified the supranational affinities of many civilized Viennese of his day. The Queen of Romania once asked him his nationality. "Heavens, Majesty!" he answered in French, "I don't know anything of that. I was born in Bohemia. I live in France, where I write in English."

It is possible that the musical genius of Vienna helped to harmonize for a time many of the prevailing contrasts. As long as it worked it was beautiful. In 1881 the Emperor, speaking as a "German prince," decried nationalism as the "plague of the century." Try as he might, he could not stem the tide. Our own time, which has witnessed nationalism as the gravedigger of Europe, cannot help sympathizing with his sentiments. At least until the early 1890s, when anti-Semitism of a particularly rabid form made its way through the streets and universities of Vienna, the position of Jews was also continually improving. The last vestiges of formal legal discrimination had come to an end in the early 1860s. The result was a vast influx of Jews from Galicia, Bohemia, and Romania. The rate of conversion to Christianity was higher in Vienna than in any other urban Jewish community in Europe. In 1880 every tenth Viennese was Jewish. The Jews were attached to Viennese civilization with a stronger—and more fruitful—passion than they had ever felt for a host country, except perhaps in medieval Spain before their expulsion in 1492.

Stefan Zweig undoubtedly exaggerated when he wrote later that "subconsciously every citizen [of Vienna] became supranational, cosmopolitan and a citizen of the world." The situation before the deluge was better defined by Daniel Spitzer, the most popular Viennese journalist of the 1870s, who wrote, "Even if we Austrians are Germans at heart, we are cosmopolitans in our buttonholes."

3

This was the world Herzl entered readily in the spring of 1878, a young man fresh from the provinces, proud and ambitious, pampered by his parents, realizing a long-cherished dream. Vienna was

in a time of change, but few people noticed its profundity. Herzl
and his family certainly did not see beyond the superficiality of the
general bonhomie. Like most Viennese Jews, they had an implicit
faith in the future of the city and of the country.

Their sense of security as Jews was supported by the best
authority. Only eight years earlier, in 1871, Heinrich Graetz, the
great Jewish historian, had concluded the eleventh and final volume
of his monumental *History of the Jewish People* on a note of supreme confidence:

> Happier than any of my predecessors, I may conclude my his-
> tory with the joyous feeling that in the civilized world the Jew-
> ish tribe has found at last not only justice and freedom but also
> a certain recognition. It now finally has unlimited freedom to
> develop its talents, not due to [Gentile] mercy but as a right
> acquired through thousandfold suffering.

Such was the unbridled optimism of assimilated or assimilating
Jewry. The Herzls shared it completely. Wasn't Austria ruled by a
kind monarch? Wasn't Vienna the very heart of that civilized world
Graetz had written about so confidently? Didn't Viennese society
now include a number of Jewish barons, and even (after baptism)
some counts? There was still some prejudice, yes; but it was fated to
die with the advent of mass education. "We can wait. Knowledge is
liberty" had been the famous words of Anton von Schmerling, the
Liberal leader. Most Jews were content to wait.

The city's mood was gay. Sentimentalism was a Viennese trait,
a mixture of reason and mood, perhaps an affliction like a kind of
flu. It reigned supreme in the press, which was otherwise on a
superbly high level, and on the popular stage. Both in the press and
on the stage, sentimentalism's main progenitors were Jews.

There was so much sickly sweetness in the atmosphere that one
cool observer, fresh from abroad, expressed the fear that an entire
civilization might succumb to a "severe attack of diabetes." And yet
the sentimentalism of Vienna was of a special sort. Even at this
early stage it was really bittersweet. A kind of melodious sensuality
was combined with a touch of playful morbidity. Both were characteristically Viennese. The morbidity was partly an inheritance from
the death-conscious age of the baroque, and partly inspired by the
misfortunes of the old empire. Long before the advent, in the 1890s,
of the Viennese school of expressionism, with all its heavy overtones
of morbid decay, years before Gustav Klimt and Gustav Mahler, the

weary worldliness of Vienna echoed in its famous waltz, the musical epitome of Victorian *joie de vivre*. The Strauss fashion was at its height when Herzl settled in Vienna. The "Emperor Waltz," composed to celebrate the fortieth anniversary of the Kaiser's ascent to the throne, was typical of this period. A deep melancholy rang through the tones of unbridled gaiety.

Such ambivalence could hardly have found itself a better setting. The physiognomy of Vienna was ideally suited to it. Viennese baroque emphasized the unreal and transitory in earthly life, a synthesis of faith and sensuality, of splendid, lighthearted gaiety and a feeling of despair and tragic uncertainty. Herzl's temperament absorbed the theatricality as well as the pessimism, tedium, and futility of his adopted city. In a setting of display and make-believe, the only reality is that of the imagination. Viennese baroque was all theater, or perhaps operetta. In the central city a spectacular array of baroque and rococo ringed the Gothic dome of St. Stephen's. The gaudy town houses of the Czech, Hungarian, German, Polish, and Italian nobility clustered around the huge, rambling imperial palace. The city's decor, with all its grand facades of desperate frivolity, sometimes taken for "Viennese charm," was a hollow sham.

The insides of the palaces were unsanitary, cramped, damp in winter, and airless in the stifling summer heat. Beyond the gilded set pieces of official Vienna, the new suburbs were crammed with the vast population influx of the recent decades. The poor slaved for the rich; their work hours were longer than those of animals. Streetcar employees were forced to work fourteen hours a day, their horses only four. The lower classes lived in miserable slums that were among the most wretched in nineteenth-century Europe. Here, among the poor of different ethnic origins, "mutual dislike intensified into a strong sense of community." The words are Robert Musil's, author of *The Man Without Qualities*, the celebrated, haunting portrait of prewar Austria: "Even mistrust of oneself and of one's own destiny here assumed the character of profound self-certainty."

Yet in sheer beauty and surface texture there were few places in Herzl's time, or in ours, so pleasing to the eye as the old inner city of Vienna. Herzl loved the noble palaces for their delicate message of beauty and well-ordered shapliness. He liked the majestically laid-out parks, planted in the style of the eighteenth century. Here he would linger many hours, reading books, daydreaming. The splendid munificence of old Vienna began only a few steps from his parents' house. The young man, with his inborn worship of beauty, jealously admired the old aristocracy. He often walked the narrow streets of the inner city with its magnificent portals, noble staircases, and steep majestic ramps. "Only good horses manage to get up there," he wrote. (Did he hate himself for not being a noble horse himself, but the son of middle-class Jews?) He suffered deep fits of melancholy. More than anything, he would have liked to be a nobleman. Later, when he conceived the idea of a Jewish state, one of his first plans was to re-create in the new state the sophisticated urban and landed aristocracy he had so envied in his youth. He gushed about the aristocracy, or rather its ideal form: worldliness, a lordly style, combined with chivalry and masculinity.

All the heroes of his novels and short stories between 1878 and 1881 were noble barons, lords, and steadfast knights. "From this single enthusiasm (*Schwärmerei*) of mine," he wrote in 1880, "all my other enthusiasms, however contradictory, can be derived." His artistic sense, his perennial melancholy, his feeling for music and disciplined beauty, his marvelous command of the German language, the sad, slightly aloof but always strangely melodious quality of his literary style, were all inspired and provoked during his formative years in Vienna before the deluge. It is difficult to imagine Herzl and *fin de siècle* Vienna separate from one another. Although he was born elsewhere, in his mental makeup, style, and basic sensibilities he came to epitomize—like Freud, Mahler, and Schnitzler —the very essence of the Viennese soul.

4

As he walked the streets to the university, to the theater, or to his favorite Bohemian café, he noted the huge physical changes apparent everywhere. Beyond the ancient inner core, Vienna was one vast construction site. The massive ramparts that had ringed the city since the Middle Ages had been torn down to make way for a series of monumental new buildings and a broad promenade-thoroughfare, the Ring, Vienna's Via Triumphalis, her answer to the Paris Champs Élysées.

Here on the new Ring, the old system of magnificent make-believe reappeared in a new, contemporary interpretation. If the old baroque had been a fusion of faith and sensuality, the new eclecticism of the Ring represented "a fleeting carnality and no faith at all save in the blessings of the stock exchange," whose massive edifice in mock Renaissance style rose proudly on the Ring's inner circumference. If architecture is a mirror of civilization, truer than others because of its unconsciousness, the architecture of the Ring reflected a deplorable nadir; decor was no longer naïve, but contrived and therefore cynical.

The decor covered the inner void. The Ring was mostly facade, a gaudy backdrop to the newly risen bourgeoisie. It was the playground of a new café society of impoverished noblemen, new rich, *bon vivants*, actors along with their vast entourage of waiters, prostitutes, tailors, sycophants, and aspiring starlets.

In an age that prided itself on its hardheaded realism, the buildings on the Ring endeavored above all to escape from their own time. Each edifice reached into the past and recast it in cheap plaster: a parliament building in the style of a Greek temple; bankers' palaces in pseudo-Renaissance; an army barracks in the style of a medieval fortress (but with no lavatories for the men); two museums to function mainly as backdrops to a grand square rather than to house the Hapsburgs' enormous art collections; a Gothic town hall, behind whose windowless facade scribes worked by candlelight even in daytime. The Ring might have indeed sprung from one of Makart's gigantic canvases. Its style was imitated all over the empire. Replicas appeared everywhere, from Trieste to Cracow. On the Ring the age of bombastic decor had finally taken over, suggesting a confusion, a crudity, a veneer of civilization as fake, thin, and fragile as the stucco ornaments of its gaudy facades.

This was Herzl's Vienna. Within months of his arrival in the city, he felt a part of it, as though he had lived here his entire life. This was strongly implicit in his mood, which quickly responded to the prevailing fashion. Even in his writing he sometimes pretended that he had never lived anywhere else.

He was now approaching twenty—moody, full of adolescent restlessness, sensitive to every movement in the air. In the photographs that have survived from this period he appears gaunt, bony, and nervously tense. His chin, now fully developed, is wide and willful, his neck high and muscular, his dress elegant, a dandy flashing an ebony-handled stick. The impression of tension is heightened by the unrest apparent in his large, dark, velvety eyes.

The tired worldliness and gay morbidity of the Viennese atmosphere were admirably suited to his precocious temperament. "I have much cause to complain about the changes in my moods," he wrote a friend on September 4, 1879, "to exalt to high heaven, to be deadly depressed, soon to delude myself with hope . . . then again to die but soon to be rejected by death. . . . Pain is the basic feeling of life. There is joy only when, by sheer accident, there is a temporary absence of pain." Herzl's letters and notes of the period are filled with similar remarks. At twenty he was young enough to enjoy his melancholy, to find it sweet and voluptuous: "I can only be happy when I am absolutely miserable." Of the Viennese he wrote, with dramatic admiration, "For and of what do these people die? Of *Morbis Viennensis.*"

He attended his law courses in a lovely rococo palace on the Jesuitenplatz, in the heart of the old city; the University of Vienna had not yet moved to its present location on the Ring, which was then under construction. His pursuit of the law was casual. Quick to learn, he was not made for listening to long lectures, especially in "Austrian Material Law and Procedure of Inheritance," or "Bills of Exchange and Laws of Commerce." He was soon bored. He read philosophy of law under the renowned Lorenz von Stein, who preached the Hegelian idea that the *Volksgeist*, or "spirit of a people," reaches its apex in the state. Of his legal studies only Roman law seems to have had a direct impact on his mind. Fifteen years later, when he was writing *The Jewish State*, under the crushing impact of resurgent anti-Semitism, he used the Roman concept of *negostorium gestio* to advocate the right of a small minority of high-minded Jews to assume responsibility for and act on behalf of an entire people in distress.

Herzl's heart was not in law, but in literature and in the arts. He avidly read everything he could acquire in German, French, Italian, and English. He had that facility for foreign languages that came almost naturally to middle-class Austro-Hungarian Jews. The Prague-born philosopher and German philologist Fritz Mauthner noted in his memoirs: "I find it incomprehensible whenever I see a Jew who isn't simply driven into becoming a theoretical linguist." Herzl, in addition, also had a fair command of Hungarian, Latin, and Greek.

In his passion for theater and Wagnerian music, Herzl readily shared in the standard Viennese idol worship. Every Viennese "student was a Wagnerian, even before he had even heard a single bar of his music." Herzl's contemporary, Max Burckhardt, later his colleague in the theater world, reportedly spent three days and nights at the railroad station only because it was rumored that Wagner was arriving. He wanted nothing—autographs were not yet fashionable—except to be able to say, "I saw him."

The general passion for theater was strong among the wealthy and schooled as well as the poor and illiterate, for whom theater was a kind of substitute for politics, a pleasant escape like the Hollywood movies of a later age. The prime minister could walk the streets unrecognized, but the leading actor in the Burgtheater was cheered everywhere. The public attended the theater less for the plays than for the actors. The new bourgeoisie were especially fanatical theatergoers; it was said that the theater taught them how to behave, what to wear, and how to speak. Felix Salten wrote of Girardi, the famous actor, that he taught people how to be Viennese. "Eventually, every second young gentleman one met in the street, every postman, every philistine was acting out some Girardi role."

Young Herzl emulated the musical, slightly nasal German of the upper echelons of the imperial bureaucracy, the gentry, and the literary intelligentsia of the cafés. He began a long novel. He frequented the Café Griensteidl, where every other table was filled with celebrities and where the latest literary gossip and verdict was handed down. The café was a citadel of Viennese cynicism, an institution almost as hallowed as the crown. For the price of a mocha, one could read newspapers and literary magazines in six languages from all over Europe and listen in on the flowing conversation of great writers and brilliant charlatans, playwrights, journalists, poets, painters, and dentists with a passion for the arts. The air was thick with the smoke of cigars; a soft lassitude prevailed, as one practiced a marvelous superiority toward everyone and everything, an all-understanding, all-condemning, all-excusing, always mocking superficial cleverness that was a specialty of Viennese literati of the period, and that often came hand in hand, unabashedly, with the most saccharine sentimentalism.

Life at the cafés was real. Herzl preferred it to the university. In the back rooms he played billiards and gambled at cards. At home, late at night, he sat up in his little room high above the Praterstrasse and labored over his literary projects. He wrote and rewrote plans and dialogues for the light comedies with which he was hoping to quickly break onto the Viennese stage. His *Ritter vom Gemeinplatz* (*The Knights of Phraseology*) was a satire of political hypocrisy. As in many decaying empires, satire was a high art form in Austria-Hungary. Herzl had started the play at the age of eighteen, in the summer before his admission to the university. His prescribed remedy to the venom of hypocrisy expresses Herzl's romantic hero-ideal; it already bears the marks of his future stance as a Zionist Don Quixote.

The play celebrates an act of courage by a man of noble heart who hides his passionate concern under an immovable exterior of "icy calm." His seeming naïveté is deliberate; he is a Swiftian "fool among knaves." Shortly afterward Herzl wrote another play, entitled *Kompagniearbeit* (*Joint Effort*). This comedy dealt with two young dandies, aspiring like Herzl to write for the theater. They decide, with disastrous consequences, to act out their proposed play in real life, prior to committing it to paper. Here again there was a premonition of the future, the temptation to move from real life into theater and back into real life.

Both plays, and a half-dozen other projects, were curtly rejected by everyone Herzl approached. Herzl also tried his hand at the popular *feuilletons*, sketches from life written in a light, whimsical tone, which at that time formed an important part of daily newspaper fare. The *feuilleton* was a French import. In its imaginative subjectiveness and loose style it was expressive of the fashionable emotions of the bourgeoisie, their cult of art and their sentimentalism. It was called by one detractor "the French disease carried into German by Heine, who had so loosened the language's corset that today every clerk may finger her breast." The *feuilleton* was a pastiche of vignettes—much like the *New Yorker's* "Talk of the Town" a century later—reflecting a reporter's wit, his philosophic insights, and his subjective response to a particular event. Generally considered an art form, it was practiced by the best novelists, poets, and playwrights of the time. Herzl was destined in later years to be one of its leading masters in the German-speaking world. But at this early stage he failed in his numerous attempts to place a *feuilleton* in one of Vienna's leading dailies. He was frustrated and driven to self-hatred by his failure.*

One evening, during a concert, he extracted a visiting card from his pocket and wrote on it: "At the sound of the music, sweet intoxicating dreams of future fame and glory envelop my drunken heart . . . raptures of hope."

* The student of Herzl's early life is fortunate in the uncommon wealth of written evidence left by Herzl himself. Herzl saved and carefully sealed in envelopes every scrap of paper, even bills or railroad tickets, on which he had scribbled some remark. Every few years he reviewed these jottings and added comments in the margins. ("On February 1, 1882, leafed through this heap of reminiscences, consisting of childishly scribbled scraps of paper, for the sake of smilingly melancholic self-edification. . . .") Not everything was later saved by his heirs, and a part seems to have been destroyed, but enough is left to throw a light on the inner workings of his mind. A fragmentary diary from the years 1881–1884 is also extant.

But soon after, shattered by failure to win even honorable mention in a popular literary competition, he confided to his diary: "Impotence! Impotence! To be defeated is infamous because victory is an honor . . . the only thing to do is crawl away, and hide a tear of pain like a man. But the tear is not shed for a lost victory, but for one's own feeling of impotence; for not being able. *Castratis* off!" He was consumed by self-hatred for groping one moment for a success that in another moment he himself despised. "It is in writing that I feel how false I am. Not to be able to! Another *impedimentum matrimonii* with the muse. Unfortunately this is one impotence which is thought curable, even when it is not." He felt suicidal, as he would often feel again thereafter. "Is everything over?" "Miserable, miserable life." "What for?" "I do not carry a great work in me. Break your pen, poor devil."

In the fall of 1883, he wrote, "No success will come. And I so need success. I thrive only in success." On October 11, 1885: "Come Book of Disillusion . . . Book of Fatigue . . . of Pains . . . of my life's misery and disconsolation."

5

There was, undoubtedly, an element of romantic pose in all this. Herzl's fits of depression were linked to the extreme poverty of his emotional life, his incapacity to love any woman other than his mother, and a lack of real friends. Nor could he commit himself to any public cause, except playfully, ironically, superficially. In his notes and diaries he freely mixed images of literary and sexual impotence, extracting a characteristic sense of pained dignity from both. Herzl had more than his share of the complexes and obfuscations of middle-class sexual morality, so rampant in the age of Victorian hypocrisy. In Stefan Zweig's words, it was an age that no longer believed in the Devil and scarcely believed in God, but looked upon sexuality as an anarchical, disturbing threat to middle-class morality.

To make up for it there was massive prostitution. The resultant syphilis marched behind Victorian Vienna like Sancho Panza behind Don Quixote. In 1874 there were rumored to be fifteen thousand streetwalkers in Vienna alone; propositioning was normal along the main streets, on the Kärntnerstrasse, and in most cafés. Venereal disease, still incurable in some forms, was widespread, particularly among the dashing and fashionable. Arthur Schnitzler's father (a doctor) took him to his study and told him to leaf through three huge medical encyclopedias on syphilis and skin disease, in order "that I might learn the consequences of a sinful life." Schnitzler, in despair, asked his father point-blank how a young man could evade the dilemma of having to violate either "morality" or "hygiene." He demanded a clear answer. Schnitzler senior answered darkly, "One dismisses it."

Herzl's own inhibitions and those of Victorian society surfaced throughout his letters, short stories, plays, and novels. The women in his short stories—and in his private life—were of two kinds, either coarse, sensual, and therefore emotionally dangerous, or untouchable—desensualized virgins, "blond, sunny, and blue-eyed," fairy-tale creatures, divine, dreamy, and remote. As a young man he often dreamed of marital life. He expressed his desensualized view of marriageable women in a daydream he recorded in 1883 while on a trip to Switzerland. As he glanced through his railroad compartment window, he saw the enticing figure of his ideal desire fleeting in the fogs across distant mountain horizons. "It is strange how dreams of intimate marital bliss creep in on you on a trip," he recorded in his notebook. As he watched this mirage take shape in the mists, he noted his "enchantment at the sweet softness of her body's lines . . . I foretaste the scent of her golden hair. Will I ever find you, seize you, ravishing daughter of fanciful desire?"

As if to underline his inability to combine love with sexuality, Herzl quite frequently fell for young nymphets. He talked himself into loving little girls of ten and twelve. He always eyed them, trembling, from a distance. While on a short trip to Budapest he fell madly in love with his little cousin, "a girl as sweet as one normally sees only in dreams . . . I yearn for this child." She was like "a lyrical poem. I cannot think of a nicer purpose in life than to read this poem eternally." He does not seem to have exchanged more than a dozen words with her. After securing her photograph "with wearisome difficulty," he sat in his hotel room gazing at it for hours.

A year later he swooned for days over a little girl he had first seen at a resort and later encountered aboard a steamship on the Rhine. "Blond, clever-eyed little girl . . . today I realized for the first time that it is possible to fall in love with a little girl . . . as I boarded the ship at Mainz I immediately saw the *allerliebste Kleine* . . . so as not to lose a thing, I posted my deck chair not too closely." He was twenty-three at the time and the girl was eight.

The theme of "pure, untouchable love" recurs time and again in his writing. The objects of his love, such as it was, were distant, ephemeral, unattainable. Or else they would be those who rejected his approaches. "Have I already told you," he wrote an acquaintance on November 22, 1882, "that I love only those women who step on me . . . ?"

There was a second type of woman—young actresses and chorus girls, easily attainable through charm, dash, or money. A good-looking young man of means like Herzl had no trouble winning them. Throughout his life Herzl was pursued by women, sometimes worshiped by them. Yet attainable love, sensual and concrete, frightened him. Nudity appalled him; it was suggestive of death. At Dieppe, on the beach, he observed young Frenchwomen in bathing suits and complained, "The bathing costume *distorts* even the most beautiful of women." Sensual women he compared to vipers:

> Snake-girls, girl-snakes
> Are a dangerous lot.
> Don't become involved with them.
> Or else it will be bad for you.

> (Schlangenmädchen, Mädchenschlangen
> Sind ein gefährliches Geschlecht.
> Hut' dich mit ihnen anzufangen,
> Sonst geht es bald dir schlecht.)

Prostitutes disgusted him. But his flesh succumbed to the sordid and forbidden. Like most young men, he went to brothels and spent nights pretending, with a heavy heart, the gay abandon of the *bon vivant*. Afterward he hated and despised himself for having lost his self-control and for having soiled himself. In June 1880 he contracted a venereal infection, probably gonorrhea.

The affliction may well have passed without trace. But the general state of his health seems to have declined seriously over the next six months. Earlier in the year (January 1880), Herzl had undergone his first medical examination by the army draft board and had been found fit and able. After a second examination (December 1880) this decision was reversed, and Herzl was declared "*derzeit felddienstuntauglich*" (unfit for military field service at this time). No reason for the rejection was given by the army doctors. It is possible—but not probable—that they suspected the heart failure which would kill him at forty-four. (The first official diagnosis of heart trouble came only sixteen years later.) He was otherwise strong and sturdy. He may have been suffering the aftereffects of the infection of 1880. These aftereffects may possibly have caused the infections and abscesses from which he later suffered in his loins, his fits of fainting, recurrent attacks of brain anemia, and finally his heart failure. Any mental effects would be impossible to gauge.

He revealed his infection to one man only—Heinrich Kana, who was just then nursing a similar complaint and obligingly sent Herzl his syringe and medicating powders. Kana was his trusted confidant at that time and the only close friend Herzl made during his entire lifetime. The two young men had met shortly after Herzl's arrival in Vienna. Kana was three years older, the son of impecunious Romanian Jews. The two young men had much in common. Both were students of law but were planning to become famous German writers. Both cultivated the vain pose of supercilious arrogance and worldly disdain that was a good index of their insecurity. Both were paragons of turn-of-the-century *Weltschmerz*. They fed one another's spleen with a moodiness calculated to assuage their self-inflicted wounds. Their exchanges would be amusing if they were not foreboding of coming tragedy:

[*Kana to Herzl:*] Days, hours, minutes . . . tasteless, desolate, monotonous. . . . Such a dark sense of time weighs heavily upon the soul; one feels chained by invisible fetters.

[*Herzl to Kana:*] . . . we two are in need of a mighty passion, an unhappy love.

[*Kana to Herzl:*] But where find her, the tall or petite, blond or brunette, unknown? It would be vain or too ridiculous to search for a Dulcinea as a modern Don Quixote. . . .

On another occasion Kana told Herzl that life could be bearable if only "we would reconcile ourselves with the thought that while we are not zeros we merely exist in the banal humdrum of eternity."

Soon after they met, Herzl called Kana "my only friend." To everybody else, including his adoring parents, Herzl presented his usual facade of playful wit and dandy without a worry in the world. Only Kana was allowed, in Herzl's words, to look "under my vest." Kana was sharply critical of what he saw there. He believed in Herzl's future. But he counseled his friend to abandon his sentimental pose, to be more serious and less deliberately clever in his writing. He nicknamed Herzl "Tartarin de Tarascon" after Alphonse Daudet's Gascogne phrasemonger. Kana castigated Herzl for his style. It was unbalanced, too sweet, forced, and artificial; in his relations with others he was haughty, inhuman, and intolerant. Kana, though bitter because of his own failure, was honest and mostly right in his censure of his rich, dashing, infinitely more successful friend.

Herzl at first took his reproofs with good humor. "Please inform me by return mail of my latest sin, in order that you might be my own little Canossa." He even encouraged the censure: "A diffuse fellow like me needs firm disciplining." But in time his impatience grew and he suspected that Kana might be envious of him. Soon Kana moved to Berlin. Their correspondence continued sporadically, but the friendship cooled. Herzl continued to think fondly of Kana until the latter's suicide in 1891. Never again in Herzl's life would there be another man who combined the roles of frank critic and close friend. Intolerant of criticism, shy of tender friendship, Herzl would henceforth evade both.

4

Faces Unmasked

ON OCTOBER 15, 1881, Herzl and a hundred other students
spent a raucous night in the smoke-filled back room of a
Vienna pub. The place was gaudily decorated. The wine-stained
walls were hung with ornate flags and medieval emblems. The company drank heavily and sang:

> We love Germanic gaiety
> and old Germanic customs.
>
> (Wir lieben deutsches Fröhlichsein
> und alte deutsche Sitten.)

and

> Only in Germany, in Germany only
> Would I forever live.
>
> (In Deutschland, in Deutschland
> da will ich ewig sein.)

The students wore colorful sashes; many of those present
donned elaborate swords that hung at their sides under the heavy
table like so many tin legs rattling on the wooden floor. The occasion was the *Eroffnungskneipe*—drinking bout—that marked the
opening of the new *Deutsche Lesehalle*. The *Lesehalle* was a student fraternity. A large part of the membership insisted on Austria's
subservience to Germany, arrogantly dismissed the rights of other
nationalities, and supported Austria's eventual union with Bismarck's militant empire.

Herzl liked the complex, romantic ritual of the German student fraternities. It appealed to his inherent conservatism and sense of "noble manliness." He was not a "political" person. But in joining a Teutonic student fraternity, he was continuing the old flirtation with conservative German nationalism that began when he fell under the spell of German culture in Budapest.

Herzl's early German nationalism has been a cause of some embarrassment to many of his later admirers. The excesses of German nationalism in the twentieth century have made it a difficult thing to stomach. In his biography of Herzl written in 1933, Alex Bein tended to underplay Herzl's commitment to the Teutonic cause. Yet the evidence suggests that Herzl's enthusiasm for Germany and German culture was strong. It did not falter, at least until the time his own fraternity officially endorsed anti-Semitic policies.

He was not a fanatic, and was naturally repelled by crudity and rabble rousing. His conservative nature shied away from all extremes, in attitudes and in manners. The breeding ground of German nationalism in the nineteenth century was usually a foul-smelling beer cellar where the haze of alcohol easily blended with half-baked ideas. Beer was consumed in huge, oversized steins. It was said at the time that the *Jewish* contribution to German nationalist student politics was a "*small* glass" of beer. The statement aptly sums up Herzl's approach. Yet there is little doubt now where his heart lay.

At the time there was nothing unusual about this. Many, if not most, Jewish students in Austria were ardent German patriots. If ever a people spontaneously and wholeheartedly entered the service of another, the Jews of Austria did so for the ruling Germans of Austria. Never was an attachment by a minority to a majority so strong; never was it expressed in such magnificent cultural contributions. Austrian middle-class Jews generally supported the so-called Constitutionalist party. The Constitutionalists endorsed the liberal creed of their kin in England and France—laissez-faire, rule of law, freedom of speech, separation of church and state—but they upheld the right of the German-speaking population to rule the vast majority of poor, uncivilized Slavs. The German speakers monopolized power, destined to rule by virtue of their higher culture and superior language; the Slavs were commonly called *Bedientenvölker* (servant peoples).

Many Jewish intellectuals were dazzled by the rise of German power under Bismarck. Like Herzl, many other Austrian Jews—

Freud, Mahler, Schnitzler, and the socialist Victor Adler (one of the founders of the first Austrian republic in 1919)—went through an early phase of German nationalist enthusiasm. One remarkable scene in the late 1870s was recorded by Richard von Kralik, the Austrian historian. He recalled a certain student celebration in Vienna. Two young Jews, Victor Adler and Heinrich Friedjung (one future socialist leader and one ardent German nationalist), joined in an enthusiastic rendering of "Deutschland über Alles" while a third young Jew, Gustav Mahler, "assisted at the piano with a passionate rendition of 'O du Deutschland, ich muss marschieren.'"

At Linz, in 1880, Adler, Friedjung, and Georg von Schönerer (two Jews and one future anti-Semitic rabble-rouser) jointly formulated the program of the National German party. Adler quickly dropped out, Friedjung was pushed aside, and Schönerer's party soon threatened to break up the multinational Hapsburg Empire in the name of German glory and *Kultur*.

"Nowadays one must be blond," Herzl wrote in a revealing little note found among his papers from that time. Was this irony? The evidence suggests that he may have meant it in all earnestness, manifesting in one short, casual line all the tortured convulsions of a sensitive secularized Jew's search for identity. One good way for a dark-haired Jew to appear blond, figuratively speaking, was to be active in one of the prestigious dueling fraternities.

The best Viennese fraternities still accepted a carefully prescribed number of Jews with pronounced "Aryan" sentiments. In 1881 Herzl joined the fraternity of *Albia*. The fraternity had not yet adopted an official political stand, but the spirit of the National German party was already dominant in its ranks. Herzl enjoyed the glamorous swords, the colored caps and ribbons worn by members at official functions. Arthur Schnitzler, who opposed dueling on principle, remembered Herzl snobbishly stalking the promenades of Vienna "in the blue *Albia* cap, with a black ebony-handled stick inscribed with the letters F.V.C. (*Floriat Vivat Crescat*—To Flourish, To Live, To Grow)." Schnitzler resented the fraternities' *Biederkeit* (stiff uprightness), which he defined as a mixture of guile and stupidity. A snapshot of Herzl as a haughty fraternity member has been preserved. He is seen standing in full regalia, with two fellow members of *Albia* and a black dog—four figures, solemn, proud, and frozen like porcelain soldiers. He relished the test and adventure of the duel, the so-called *Mensur*, which was considered manly and edifying. ("I took part in all student follies," Herzl wrote eighteen years later.)

The *Mensur* was a ritual that German students shared with primitive African and Australian tribes. The resulting facial scars, which in Guinea are known as *Khanti*, were called *Schmisse* in Germany and Austria. The *Mensur*, unlike fencing, was neither elegant nor sporting; its result was mutilation. Yet in its aura of manliness and aristocratic chivalry the *Mensur* exerted a fatal charm, especially on ambitious sons of the urban bourgeoisie. Herzl was not immune to it.

During the winter of 1880–1881 he was very active in the life of the fraternity. As a fraternity name he picked, or was given, that of a famous Christian prince, Tancred, the rakish Crusader conqueror of Palestine and "Prince of Galilee." Was this a tribute to his proud bearing, his outlandish dark hair and olive skin? The echo of a dominant romantic fashion? A portent? He prepared assiduously for the *Mensur*. Twice daily, afternoon and evening, he took part in the fraternity's official training program. Eager to achieve his mark, he took private fencing lessons as well. Herzl fought his first *Mensur* on May 11, 1881. He was in a mood of high elation. His opponent was a member of another student fraternity, *Allemania*. After a few rounds, the prescribed mutilations were successfully inflicted. The umpire called out, "*Silentium* on the battleground! *Mensur Ex*." The combatants retired to present their gashed faces to the attending surgeon, who promptly stitched them. The same night Herzl's manliness was celebrated with beer and young wine by his companions in *Albia*, for whom he had written the following song:

> Drink, lads,
> Drink up, men,
> In your hand the noble sword,
> Mirth and merry in your breasts.

> (Trinket, Knaben,
> Trinket Männer,
> In der Hand den blanken Schläger,
> Lebensfreude in der Brust.)

For Herzl, however, the drinking bouts and fencing rites of *Albia* were not enough. Shortly after his first *Mensur* he relapsed into one of his periodic fits of depression. He participated less in the hectic drinking-fencing-and-debating life of the fraternity. Actually, he was bored. For all we know, the *Mensur* of May 11 was his last. His fellow members grew to dislike him. Haughty and self-centered, he was incapable of friendship among equals, a quality his contemporaries would comment on throughout his life. Fraternity members took exception to Herzl's habit of addressing them with "patronizing mockery." He still showed up occasionally at the fraternity clubrooms in Protowiner's *Bierhalle* on the Heugasse. Members resented his interruptions during debates—for what he said, and even more for his tone. The bulletin of *Albia* complained that with "less than average" achievements as a member, he claimed for himself a position of special privilege even as "he overtly jeered and covertly scorned what was dear to fraternity members' hearts."

He withdrew into himself. He read a great deal and filled a thick notebook with lengthy book reviews and comments. He also wrote many passionate exclamations and disclaimers. In the winter of 1881–1882 Herzl lived as a recluse. He spent most of his evenings at home, reading more than a hundred books within a few weeks. He worked his way through Shakespeare, Byron, Spinoza, Macaulay's *History of England*, Mark Twain, Dostoevski, Voltaire, Rousseau, Balzac, Flaubert, Zola, and a large number of contemporary French playwrights. He was sharply critical of what he read. He expressed his censure from the point of view of "we Germans." Interspersed with his literary criticism are the somber reflections of his loneliness, his vain search for love, the dejection over his continued failure to get his work published or produced. On his twenty-second birthday, May 2, 1882, he wrote, "Twenty-two years! And damn little achieved . . . I haven't even the tiniest success to show, nothing to be proud of . . . I sense my insincerity in my own writing."

2

Herzl's literary taste remained extremely conventional. He was repelled by the inchoate formlessness of Dostoevski. *Crime and Punishment* "disgusted" him. He was deeply troubled by Émile Zola's naturalism; Zola stung his sense of propriety with his "evil-smelling whores" and "original stench of filth." *Nana* was Zola's "impure abortion of smut and Spanish fire."

On February 9, 1882, Herzl wrote his reaction to a different kind of book, one which drove him into a fury for a short time. It was Eugen Dühring's anti-Semitic diatribe, *The Jewish Question as a Racial, Ethical, and Cultural Question.* Dühring was a renowned German scholar. His contribution to philosophy and economics was significant at the time, though not earthshaking. But his "science" of racialism made him one of the most influential thinkers of the nineteenth century. His vitriolic attack on the Jewish "race" first appeared in 1881, shortly after his resignation from the University of Berlin, where he had quarreled so much with everybody that the Senate finally forced him to leave. His book came amid a wave of anti-Semitism which suddenly inundated large parts of Europe. In France the new anti-Semitism was expressed in books and political speeches. In Russia the first great wave of pogroms swept the Ukraine, partly instigated by the czarist police to divert popular energies from the revolutionary cause. In Germany there were riots in Brandenburg and Pomerania (1881). Here the new racialism was given respectability by the official chaplain to the imperial court at Berlin, Adolf Stöcker, a leading anti-Semitic agitator. In Austria too there were beginnings of an anti-Semitic mass movement. In Prague Dr. A. Rohling had just published his phenomenally successful diatribe, *Der Talmudjude.* Rohling was an ordained Catholic priest and professor of theology at the German University of Prague. He claimed that Jews were authorized by their religion to destroy the lives, honor, and property of all Gentiles. And in Hungary the Dark Ages returned in the trial at Tiszaeszle, where a Jew was accused of the ritual murder of a Christian child to celebrate the Passover, the first of a rash of similar cases that swept the rural areas of the Hapsburg Empire.

Among Herzl's otherwise extensive papers, there is no record that he was in any way distressed or even vaguely impressed by these harbingers, which had been building up for two or three years. Dühring's book shocked him out of the complacency of his own untroubled personal milieu. Filled with malicious travesties and vile calumnies, Dühring's book called for the abolition of all civil rights for Jews. They were to be locked up in ghettos.

"An infamous book," Herzl noted in his diary. As the immediate afterthought of a German stylist, he added, painfully: "Unfortunately it is so well written . . . in such a deliciously pure, excellent German. . . . When such vile stuff is expressed so sincerely, when Dühring with a mind so well trained and penetrating, and with deep universal learning, is capable of writing such stuff—what then are we to expect of the ignorant rabble?" If Jews were really as mean, as beastly, and as untalented a race as Dühring claimed, how could they have "survived fifteen hundred years of inhuman repression? How was this possible unless they possessed some good qualities?"

The first chapters in Dühring's book, Herzl thought, were "informative enough, despite its obvious hatefulness and exaggerations. *Every Jew should read it.*" Dühring confirmed and apparently sharpened some of Herzl's own youthful prejudices against his own race. Herzl partially endorsed Dühring's criticism of the "crookedness of Jew morality" (sic!). The lack of "ethical seriousness in many Jews (Dühring says 'in all') is mercilessly exposed and characterized," Herzl noted. Was he saying, then, that anti-Semitism made sense? Yes and no. "There is much to learn from this! But as one reads on, it becomes obvious that some true observations have been mixed with many false ones and with deliberately infamous falsifications. Dühring is at first dangerous, then downright ridiculous." Herzl next discussed and refuted various charges made by Dühring. His book, said Herzl, in effect presented medieval superstitions in modern, pseudoscientific dress.

It is unclear what Herzl meant by "crookedness of Jew morality" and lack of "ethical seriousness." One safe guess is that he meant the morality of Jewish brokers at the stock exchange. A modern reader is prompted immediately to ask what was so "Jewish" about trading in stocks and bonds—was there something that non-Jewish brokers, engaged in the same trade, lacked? Herzl's own father at that time was a broker at the Viennese *bourse.*

Whatever the reasons, Herzl's lengthy notes on Dühring's book marked his first break with the liberal clichés of his youth. Dühring proved to Herzl that education did not necessarily "liberate" mankind; on the contrary, it might herald the advent of a new tyranny. For Herzl the break was still very tentative. Many years later he said that his first concern with the Jewish problem came after reading Dühring's book. The concern cannot have been very serious or worrisome for him. Dühring's book was a passing phenomenon, a *literary* event that was soon superseded by other literary events. Herzl played with the idea of conversion to Christianity, but since baptism implied an act of renunciation that offended his personal sense of pride, he could not consider it seriously. In any case, he did not care much for either religion. He believed that intermarriage between Jews and Gentiles on the "basis of a common state religion" would benefit all; it might also improve the Jews' "so alien-looking, despised physiognomy."

Herzl did not pursue his furious reaction to Dühring's book. He remained ignorant of the Jewish national revival in Russia, which sprouted everywhere in the Pale of Settlement as a direct result of the 1882 pogroms. He never read the best-known pragmatic statement of that revival, Leo Pinsker's pamphlet *Auto-Emancipation—An Appeal to His People by a Russian Jew*, which was brought out in German by a Berlin publisher. Dr. Pinsker, a physician in Odessa, was so shocked by the pogroms of 1882 that he completely despaired of emancipation. "To the living, the modern Jew is a dead man," Pinsker wrote. "To the native born he is a stranger, to the long settled a vagabond, to the wealthy a beggar, to the poor a millionaire and exploiter, to the citizen a man without country, to all classes a hated competitor." Jews therefore had no alternative, Pinsker wrote, but to become a nation once more and possess their own territory. Pinsker did not much care where that territory was. Palestine was one possibility, but not the only one.

Pinsker traveled to Vienna but was dismissed there as a lunatic. The Chief Rabbi of Vienna, Dr. Adolf Jellinek, told him to see a doctor immediately.

Herzl remained ignorant of all this. He also ignored the first Jewish nationalist clubs which poor Jewish students from Poland and Romania were just forming at his own university. Vienna was after all a center of exiled nationalist agitators of all shades; the first Ukrainian, Serbian, and Greek nationalist newspapers were published there, and the first Hebrew-Zionist magazines would also appear there, in 1883. Herzl undoubtedly dismissed such stirrings as childish and irrelevant. A day after reading Dühring's book, he withdrew again into his shell.

3

The shell was not very thick. Within a year he broke out of it again. During the year 1882 the Viennese student body was considerably radicalized. The pro-German Prime Minister Auersperg had been replaced by an aristocrat of Irish origin, the Kaiser's boyhood friend Eduard Taafe, who believed that the empire could be held together by maintaining its warring nationalities "in a state of well-tempered mutual dissatisfaction." His first step was to placate the Czechs. His measures infuriated the Germans. An increasing number of agitators told the aroused student body of Vienna that an onslaught of wild Slavs from the East was endangering German *Kultur*, the very ethic of Western civilization, and that Taafe was responsible for it. Most Jews were pro-German and anti-Czech, yet both sides quickly fell upon the Jews. They were denounced in Prague by the Czech nationalists and in Vienna by the German anti-Semites.

Things came to a head in February 1883. On the thirteenth Wagner died in Venice. His memorial rites occasioned rabid anti-Semitic outbursts. In his lifetime Wagner had been a cult figure; music lovers, many of them Jews, as well as German nationalists and rabid anti-Semites, worshiped at his feet. Wagner was as famous for his music as for his call to "emancipate German *Kultur* from the yoke of Judaism." One Wagner memorial meeting was of particular significance to Herzl. On March 5, 1883, a number of German nationalist student societies, including Herzl's fraternity, *Albia*, arranged a memorial at Vienna's Sophiensaal. The main speaker at the mass meeting was Herzl's fraternity brother, Hermann Bahr. Bahr voiced a violent attack on the Austrian regime and brought the house down by endorsing "Aryan" pan-Germanism. "A penitent Kundry [Austria]," he announced, "expects its salvation by Deutschland," a spiritual renewal through the endorsement of "Wagnerian anti-Semitism." The rowdy meeting was broken up by the police. Bahr was suspended from the university. The men of *Albia*, in a tremendous drinking bout, celebrated him as a martyr and hero.

Herzl did not attend the meeting; he may well have spent the evening of March 5 at the premiere of a new opera by Suppé, where the latest innovation—electrical stage lights—was being tried out. Herzl read about the meeting in the newspapers. He waited another day in the vain hope that the governing body of *Albia* would dissociate the fraternity from its official speaker. On March 7 he penned a letter to the "commendable fraternity of *Albia*." Seething with anger and offended pride, he wrote:

> From the daily papers I gather with great regret that the Richard Wagner meeting developed . . . into an anti-Semitic demonstration. The meeting was called by, among others, the fraternity of which I have the honor of being an inactive member.
>
> It does not even occur to me to polemicize here against this regressive fashion of the day. I would mention incidentally that as a lover of liberty, even as a non-Jew, I would have to condemn this very movement which my fraternity seems to have joined. I say "seems to," for when one does not protest audibly against such events, one shares responsibility for them. *Qui*

tacet, consentire videtur! [He who keeps silent, seems to be consenting.]

. . . It is pretty clear that handicapped as I am by the impediment of *Semitism* (the word was not yet known at the time of my entry), I would today refrain from seeking membership in the fraternity. It would probably refuse me anyway, for the above-mentioned reason. It must therefore be obvious to every decent person that I do not wish to retain my membership. . . . Since, as far as I know, there is nothing dishonorable in the records about my person, I count on honorable discharge.

Respectfully faithf. to a d(ear) f(raternity)
cand. jur. Theodor Herzl
Al. B. Tancred

7 III 83

The men of *Albia* were outraged at the tone and content of this letter. Herzl's request was discussed at a plenary meeting. His resignation and "honorable discharge" were refused. The fraternity decided to cashier him. A curt letter of one sentence, without polite salutation, informed Herzl on April 3, 1883, that by plenary decision his name had been struck from the fraternity's roster. He was requested to return the fraternity's insignia, cap, ribbons, and drinking mug.

Herzl did not give in. He wrote again to an officer of *Albia*, one E. Hoerne, a close acquaintance and fellow law student. He complained that the curt letter of dismissal had failed to acknowledge the fact of "honorable discharge" and that he had himself resigned. He appealed to their past friendship and asked Hoerne to send him a written confirmation "as a proof of loyalty." The letter was couched in the intimate second person, *du*, and assured Hoerne of Herzl's "lasting, friendly sentiments."

Hoerne chose to ignore these. One month later he sent Herzl an icy note informing him that he had been dismissed regardless of his application, because of his "tone of disrespect" for the fraternity. "With fitting regards, E. Hoerne, *stud. jur.*"

The pressures on young Jews who joined fraternities like *Albia* were exemplified by the case of Paul von Portheim, one of three other Jews in *Albia*. What a mixed-up group they were, confused victims of a world they wished were real! After Herzl's dismissal, Portheim himself proposed that no more Jews be admitted to membership. The motion was approved in plenary session. Shortly afterward, the few remaining Jews were also forced out. Portheim shot himself on July 13, 1883.

Portheim's paranoiac proposal and his subsequent suicide were expressions of a crisis which ranged far beyond himself. The ground was beginning to shake under the feet of many educated, secularized young Jews in Austria, in Germany, and in France. As yet, only a handful were sensitive enough to notice it.

4

Herzl was not among them. His personal sense of pride had been affronted once by Dühring's book; pride brought forth another burst of pain and indignation, even wrath, during his unpleasant exchange with the men of *Albia*. The wrath did not last, nor did it yet prompt him to conclusions of a more general nature. These would come only much later.

Meanwhile he continued his studies and renewed his attempts to have a play produced on the German stage. He concluded a one-act comedy of "legal ennui," *The Causa Hirschkorn*, a satire on dull lawyers caught up in the comic maze of an inheritance suit. The play was well received at an amateur performance in the home of Rosa Eidlitz, a Viennese society lady whose salon Herzl frequented. But the Burgtheater refused it. Shortly after the *Albia* incident, in May 1883, Herzl begged Ernst Hartmann, a leading actor at the Burgtheater, at least to include the play in the summer stock. He wrote Hartmann an unhappy letter and was refused. To his diary he confided again, after almost a year's silence, the pain he felt at not getting on in the world. But he did not lose heart. One autumn evening, in the company of Arthur Schnitzler, he walked by the scaffolding of the new Burgtheater building which was just going up on the Ring. Herzl waved at the edifice and grandly pronounced: "You'll see! I will get in here one day!"

As a "German writer" he also offered a piece to Heinrich Friedjung's German nationalist weekly, *Deutsche Wochenschrift*. Friedjung advised him to adopt a pen name less Jewish than his own. Herzl flatly refused. "I want to continue to carry the name of my father," he said and offered to withdraw the manuscript. Friedjung accepted it anyway. Herzl did not give this incident any more thought than he had given *Albia* after his dismissal. In a letter to

Kana (May 25, 1883) he joked about anti-Semitism as though it did not touch him personally; it was for "the birds."

Anti-Semitism was deplorable, of course, from the *general* viewpoint of progress and justice and love of liberty. But it was not something that affected Herzl's own life, which remained sheltered, or his career as a German artist. He did not identify with the Jews, as a people or as a faith. The very same Hermann Bahr whose anti-Semitic speech at the Wagner memorial meeting had caused Herzl's unpleasant clash with *Albia*, remained a close acquaintance. They met frequently, at times almost daily.

5

Fool Among Knaves

NEVERTHELESS, these were seminal years in Herzl's life. He deliberately evaded his problem as a Jew. But it lurked all around him; in later years he reproached himself bitterly for this evasion. "I was just a writer of sorts, with petty ambitions and mean vanities." The reproach was unduly harsh. In the context of his time and place, Herzl was neither petty nor mean.

Had he lived in Russia, he might well have been driven to radicalism. In the pseudoliberal Austro-Hungarian Empire, Herzl could still have a sense of great personal freedom and security. As a law-abiding man of means, he could go about his business and hardly recognize the increasing pressures. In one important sense, Herzl's generation was freer than the next two. Herzl could travel almost anywhere without a passport or permit, and he made full use of the privilege. He was sufficiently well-off to devote himself almost exclusively to art, literature, travel, and intellectual refinement, without having to pay much attention to world or domestic politics. He could live wherever he liked. His wide command of languages enabled him to feel at home in half a dozen Western European countries.

Undoubtedly, however, something was slowly building up in him. It is not easy today to convey a correct impression of what it really meant in the nineteenth century to be a Jew. In the lands of overt oppression, czarist Russia or Romania, the meaning was clear. In the emancipated West, it remained ambiguous. In our own days, the Nazi holocaust has driven most Jews to a kind of militant self-assertion. In the 1880s the opposite was true. In Germany and Austria barely two decades had passed since the Jewish emancipation. Having just emerged from the seclusion of the ghetto, many emancipated Jews were extremely self-conscious and uneasy, like prisoners who had suddenly emerged into broad daylight after years in a dungeon.

There was still rudeness and no little bigotry. Its victims were mostly the poor. Freud's father was humiliated on a Vienna street one day in 1868 by a ruffian who knocked off his hat and screamed, "Get off the pavement, Jew!" Freud's father simply stepped into the roadway and silently picked up his hat. His father's "unheroic conduct" haunted young Sigmund for years, a trauma that he later analyzed.

No such incident ever clouded Herzl's youth. But the psychological stresses on newly emancipated Jews like the Herzls were compounded by a number of factors. Gentiles displayed an almost pornographic curiosity about the most intimate details of Jewish life. Everywhere in the West in the 1880s there was suddenly talk of a Jewish "problem." It was invented by those who opposed the emancipation of Jews on grounds of "moral" and "racial" principles. It is difficult today to imagine the importance attached to this "problem" at the time. It weighed heavily on the minds of men "spiritually almost more than politically and socially." Herzl's own notes on the subject are amply corroborated by the rich literary evidence of the time. His contemporary Arthur Schnitzler complained that as a Jew "you had the choice of being considered insensitive, obtuse, and fresh, or of being oversensitive, shy, and suffering from feelings of persecution."

The assimilated Jew was psychologically troubled because, having lost his Jewish links, he was still denied the equality he so desired. Barely twenty years after emancipation, Jews were accused of "polluting" the very *Kultur* they so admired. The resulting schizophrenia colored their every move. The new "scientific" racialism was at first somewhat *gemütlich*, at least in Austria. Karl Lueger, a populist anti-Semite with an enormous following in Vienna—Hitler would recognize him as a spiritual father—had Jewish friends. Challenged to explain this inconsistency, Lueger announced, "I decide who is a Jew."

In this confused milieu, an anti-Semitic rabble-rouser like Rohling* could be professor of Hebrew studies at Prague University and a Dr. Theodor Cohen could serve as Prince-Archbishop of Olmütz, the most distinguished Catholic diocese in Austria. The Emperor once jestingly inquired whether the Archbishop had in

* See Chapter 4, p. 57.

fact converted. Prime Minister Taafe put the same question to Joseph Bloch, a Jewish deputy from Galicia. Bloch responded, "Never fear, your Excellency, if he were still a Jew he would no longer be called Cohen." Just as there was an Archbishop Cohen, so a leader of the German nationalists was a Czech named Bielehlawek.

It was easy at first to laugh it all off as a short-lived fad. Many people succumbed to the temptation. When a number of frightened Jewish scholars publicly endorsed the new "scientific" anti-Semitism and admitted the "biological" inferiority of their race, other Jewish wits replied that "anti-Semitism did not really succeed until the Jews began to sponsor it." On a more serious level, there were diligent attempts by reasonable men to rationalize something that they might still have found inexplicable a decade earlier. One common rationalization was based on economic factors. Earlier in the century, enemies of capitalism had fixed their hatred on Protestantism; now the Jews were held responsible for ushering in the materialism of the industrial age. In the past, Swiss bankers had been slandered, though never persecuted, and accused of bloodsucking and stealing the wealth of the people. Mark Twain, on a short visit to Vienna, surmised that the whole Jewish "problem" was a "trade union conflict in religious disguise."

With the growth of national banking, the house of Rothschild was already in decline, but its conspicuousness on the European scene facilitated the sudden growth of a myth of Jewish power. A committee of rabbis and Jewish financiers was said to be meeting in secret and controlling the fate of the world. Word that the new Paris métro was partly owned by Jewish stockholders led to rumors of a Jewish plot to blow up Paris and other European capitals from underground. Jewish businessmen of the time shared in the moral evasions and false pathos of Victorian humanism. But they were neither better nor worse than other businessmen. There were only fewer of them. The vast majority of Jews were desperately poor or struggled along in the lowest ranks of the new middle class.

Another common explanation for the new racism was based on population statistics. In twenty-three years the Jewish population of Vienna had grown more than tenfold, from 6,217 in 1857 (2.16 percent of the total population) to 72,588 in 1880 (10.06 percent). But other ethnic groups grew as rapidly, and no similar phobia was released against Czech, Magyar, or Croatian immigrants to the city. The main spiritual center of modern racism was not, as is often thought, Germany or Russia, but France, where the Jewish population had grown only marginally.

The lower middle class in Austria and Germany turned anti-Semitic in the 1880s; France's lower middle class had been anti-Semitic at least thirty years earlier. French *savants* spearheaded the new racism long before it was taken up seriously by German *Wissenschaftler*. Alphonse Toussenel's diatribe *Les Juifs, Rois de l'Époque* was favorably received by the French left in 1845. Paul De Lagarde declared that Jews were "vermin"; no compromise with Jews was possible, for "with trichinae and bacilli one does not negotiate, nor are trichinae and bacilli subjected to education. They are exterminated as quickly and as thoroughly as possible." The French Count Arthur de Gobineau published his famous *Essai sur l'Inégalité des Races Humaines* in 1853, long before the German Wilhelm Marr came out with his *Der Sieg des Judentums über das Germanentum* (*The Victory of Judaism over Germanism*) in 1879. Marr argued from a secular point of view and first introduced the term "anti-Semitism." The Germans have generally been credited also with having invented the apposition of "Aryan" and "Semite," but actually the first to do so was a Frenchman, Ernest Renan. The early racism in France was helped along by a series of financial scandals in which Jews had been implicated. But the involvement of Jews in these scandals was marginal compared to the widespread venality and corruption of French politicians and civil servants.

There was one area of life in Vienna in which the predominance of Jews was unquestionable. This was in culture. Stefan Zweig claimed that nine-tenths of what the world celebrated as Viennese culture in the nineteenth century was nourished, promoted, and often created by Viennese Jews. It was by no means Jewish art. Jews gave Austria and Vienna their highest expression, in folk songs and symphonic music, in theater, in literature. Jews were especially prominent in the metropolitan press; some thought that Viennese anti-Semitism was really a form of anti-journalism. Worldly, ironical, and with a tendency to psychologize about everything, Jewish litterateurs elicited as much uneasiness as admiration. "They really make you nervous sometimes," said Georg von Wergenthin (the Christian protagonist of Schnitzler's novel *Der Weg ins Freie* [*The Road to Freedom*], a portrait of *fin de siècle* Viennese bourgeois life), "these Jewish-super-clever, unsparingly incisive judges of men."

The tacit exclusion in Austria of nonbaptized Jews from the

upper ranks of the universities and the civil service naturally drove Jewish students, as it had driven Herzl, into the "free" professions of journalism, the arts, medicine, law, and engineering. This in turn nourished resentment among non-Jewish professionals, who complained that the number of Jewish doctors and lawyers was four or five times greater than the ratio of Jews to the population as a whole.

The growth of anti-Semitism at the University of Vienna, which affected Herzl as a student, was paralleled among the non-educated masses by the rise in the 1880s of a populist know-nothing movement of workers and lower-middle-class Catholics. It was led by the rabble-rousing Karl Lueger, a municipal politician of rare talent and great charismatic charm. Known as the *Herrgott* of Vienna, Lueger combined a genuine concern for social welfare with loose anti-Semitic talk. He began as a municipal reformer and enemy of "corruption," then extended his criticism to the new industrial civilization in general. Soon he was winning the crowds with claims that their true enemy was the Jew. Lueger's anti-Semitism came from the left; it was "fools' socialism." Science, he said, was what one Jew copies from another. He was taken very seriously as a political force by the conservative right as well as the socialist left. Karl Kautsky wrote in 1884 that in Austria, anti-Semitism was more dangerous than in Germany because its appearance was oppositional, pseudodemocratic, and therefore appealed to the instincts of the worker.

The Emperor despised Lueger, but try as he might, could not prevent his rise. Lueger ended his career as one of the most popular lord mayors Vienna had seen. One of Lueger's young admirers was Adolf Hitler. Hatred of the Jew was perhaps Hitler's most sincere emotion. It was first born in his heart during his stay in Lueger's Vienna, where he observed the Jew's "alien face" from the vantage point of the gutter. Vienna, Hitler said later, was "the hardest, but also the most thorough, school of my life." In Vienna he "laid the foundations for a world conception in general and a way of political thinking in particular that I had later only to complete in detail."

2

What then did it mean to be a Jew in these critical years, when the seeds of the future disaster were planted, sometimes unconsciously, in the hearts of men? During the last two or three decades of the nineteenth century, the so-called Jewish "problem" became one of the most debated subjects in Europe. Jews were baffled and shocked by this obsession. Should they react to the attacks or ignore them? Was it something they had done? Many sensitive young Jews were tormented by these questions. Rich Jews tended to blame poor Jews, and vice versa. Intellectual Jews, like Herzl, were embarrassed by both. There was much loose talk of Jewish "bad manners." Coarse manners were of course not a monopoly of Jews alone. But Jewish manners were more conspicuous because of the obsessive interest in their lives and the general belief in the existence of a "problem," which even Jews paranoiacally began to share themselves. With characteristic disdain, Herzl, in 1885, described an elegant party he had attended in Berlin at the house of a wealthy businessman, a friend of his father: "Yesterday grande soirée at the Treitels'. Some thirty or forty ugly little Jews and Jewesses. No consoling sight." From the beach at Ostende, he wrote his parents: ". . . Although there are many Viennese and Budapest Jews here [on the beach], the rest of the vacationing population is very pleasant. . . ."

Could the new anti-Semitism be the Jews' own fault? A number of sensitive young Jews talked themselves into believing it was. Some destroyed themselves in the process. The brilliant young Viennese prodigy Otto Weininger was perhaps the best-known of those who have since entered the annals of psychology as tragic victims of Jewish self-hatred. At the age of nineteen he wrote his obtuse but vastly successful book *Geschlecht und Charakter* (*Sex and Character*), a double attack on the female sex and the Jewish "race." It became one of the most influential books of the period. As a Jew, Weininger was fully aware of the consequences of his deed. "What I have found here pains no man more than it pains me," he wrote. "This book constitutes a death verdict; it will strike either the book or its author." The book was an instant success and Weininger promptly killed himself.

Schnitzler remembered a Jewish friend, Louis Friedmann, a strikingly handsome man, a successful industrialist, champion skier, and renowned alpinist. He determined, said Schnitzler, to remain single, or at least childless, so that the hated blood flowing in his veins might not again be propagated. Paul Ree, Nietzsche's Jewish friend, bemoaned his origin like a disease, a miscarriage at birth.

Weininger, Friedmann, and Ree were extreme cases, of course.

Their imbalance undoubtedly stemmed from more than one source. Yet they all embodied an agony—which in our days has become almost incomprehensible—a confusion, a lament, a nausea generated within sensitive souls by the emergence of the new barbarism from the gutters of Victorian society. In varying degrees the torment was felt by many Jews. It struck less often among the poor, whose daily struggle left little time for agonizing soul-searching. It was more common with the rich, the baptized, and those who believed they had successfully crossed the line into Gentile society. The Viennese Rothschild, Baron Nathaniel, rarely asked Jews to the splendid parties in his city palace. Prince Schwarzenberg, invited to attend Nathaniel's grand ball, was assured that he would not meet any Jews there. The Prince declined rather maliciously: "Rothschild does not associate with Jews. Nor do I."

The plight of the wealthy bourgeoisie was vividly described by Schnitzler's hero, Georg von Wergenthin: "Wherever he went he met only Jews who were ashamed of being Jews, or such that were proud of it but frightened that someone might think they were ashamed." Joseph Roth, in *Radetzkimarsch* (*The Radetzky March*), a magnificent panorama of Old Austria in decline, portrayed the Jewish Baron Nagyjenö as one who "successfully forgot the Semitic race from which he was extracted, by adopting all the faults of the Hungarian gentry."

In the 1820s the young Heinrich Heine had called a baptismal certificate the entrance ticket to European civilization. The old Heine, in 1855, doubted that even conversion would solve the problem. In a poem dedicated to the "new Israelite hospital in Hamburg," he lamented the poor outcasts who "groan beneath the heavy threefold evil—of pain, of poverty, and of Judaism," of which the most malignant was the last. Judaism was a plague, a family disease, an

> Incurable deep ill! defying treatment
> Of shower and vapor bath, and apparatus
> Of surgery, and all the healing medicine
> This house can offer to its sickly inmates.

Gustav Mahler, the composer, had converted to Christianity out of deep involvement with Catholic mysticism—and also to win the coveted post of conductor of the Vienna Court Opera. Yet even a man of Mahler's stature, fame, and success failed to achieve his end. The atmosphere was dominated by the popular slogan,

What the Jew believes is all the same;
It's the race that's all the filth and shame.

Shortly before his death Mahler complained bitterly: "I am thrice homeless. As a native of Bohemia in Austria; as an Austrian among Germans; as a Jew throughout the world. Everywhere an intruder, nowhere welcome."

The vast majority of Western Jews, however, remained firm in the faith that their future was secure. Rejected by their homelands, they continued to offer tokens of boundless patriotic loyalty. As Adolf Dessauer, a close acquaintance of Herzl's, put it in his vastly popular novel *Grossstadtjuden* (*Jews of the Metropolis*), the toll paid for each one-sided loyalty was "a violent denial of self," a lack of "relaxed self-assurance" among Jews, which in turn fed anti-Semitism even more. Dessauer believed that Viennese anti-Semitism was just "a passing fashion, a mood, a joke. Fashions change."

Such an optimistic statement seems strange only in retrospect; at the time it was perfectly natural. Only a handful of Jewish men and women began to feel that new, more insidious shackles were slowly replacing the old medieval walls. They sensed it in their bones, but as yet no one saw a remedy.

3

In Herzl all these moods and notions overlapped and encroached on one another. They were conditioned by his own sudden shifts of temperament. He still affected a blasé languor and the tired maturity of the young dandy which made him write in his notebook: "Nothing on earth, or very little, deserves our wrath. With disdain and pity it is possible after the age of thirty to get on very well in the world."

In May 1883 his parents gave up their flat on the Praterstrasse. By now the area had become predominantly Jewish. The Herzls moved to Zelinkagasse 11, in the aristocratic inner city, around the corner from the Ring. The new milieu suited Herzl's taste for refined living. He played with the idea of conversion. Yet, though indifferent to Judaism as a faith, he was too proud to take that step. Scornful of the new Jewish bourgeoisie, he was also repelled by the crudity of the rabble-rousers. The German Nationalists of Vienna were now fusing anti-Semitism with pan-Germanism. In the streets of the inner city Herzl watched his former *Albia* fraternity brothers

stride up and down the promenades chanting the battle song of a
new movement to lead Austria home to the Reich:

> Without Judas, Hapsburg, Rome,
> Let us build the German dome!

He met the new trends in a mood of pained resignation, aloof-
ness, and mocking irony. With some relish he cut an advertisement
out of a daily paper and pasted it in his notebook:

> A new financial boom is in sight. Shares are rising daily and
> after an intermission of years it is again possible to become rich
> overnight.
>   The representative of a local bank, recommended by the
> highest aristocratic circles, CHRISTIAN, undertakes execution of
> well-inspired speculations. . . .

He was provoked as much by his ire against Jewish stockbrokers,
whose materialism he detested, as by his resentment of other prac-
titioners of the craft, like the advertiser, who protested his Christianity. He consoled himself with the thought that the new racists
were too ridiculous for words. The right thing to do was to hold
one's nose and walk by, calm and composed. He emulated Raoul
von Wengenheim, the Kiplingesque hero of his early play *The
Knights of Phraseology*, who hid his passions under an impenetrable
cover of "icy calm."

Early in July 1883, he sat for his state examination in law, but
his heart was not in it. The unhappy results of his examination
provoked another outburst of that imperious, proud, almost
compulsive sense of straitlaced sincerity, which by now was a distinctive trait of his solemn character. His friend Heinrich Kana
attempted to save face for Herzl by circulating a rumor that he had
passed his examinations with distinction. Herzl lashed out at Kana
angrily: "It seems that you have still not found the key to my
character. I do not always speak the truth, not even often. Yet I am
a sincere animal." He would readily lie for a grand purpose, he
announced, but not for anything so petty as his own personal reputation or profit.

His adoring parents swallowed their disappointment. This was
merely a temporary setback. Jakob Herzl gladly treated his son to a
tour of Switzerland and Germany in order that he might relax and
recover from the strains of his legal studies. Jeannette Herzl be-

lieved the trip would inspire his literary efforts. She took leave of her twenty-three-year-old son with the following words: "My precious child, write to us every day, for in spirit we are always with you and live by you alone. But a postcard will suffice. Whatever you find en route in impressions, and ideas, work these out as a writer, for they do not belong to us but to the world."

With 200 guldens, 200 marks, and 150 Swiss francs, Herzl set out by train on July 9, 1883, from Baden, his parents' summer home. He traveled alone, at a leisurely pace, shunning all company, silently relishing every moment, carefully noting everything he saw. His first stop was Linz, barely two hours away. He liked the main square at Linz, the narrow alleys and arcaded courts of this picturesque old town nestled pleasantly on the banks of the Danube. Its massive fortifications bore the proudest of all Hapsburgian heraldic inscriptions, Frederick III's acronym on the city gates: *A.E.I.O.U. 1481—Alles Erdreich Ist Österreich Untertan* (The entire universe is to Austria subservient). The inscription appealed to the young man's sense of irony. That same evening, on the hotel terrace, tired and content, Herzl disregarded his mother's admonition and recorded his pleasure in a long letter home, the first of many—sometimes two a day—that he dispatched during his three weeks of travels. He penned slightly verbose, but often incisive, little sketches of people, scenery, and mood.

He continued from Linz through Germany to Ischl. He inspected the resort town where the Emperor had his summer residence, and which the court shared with wealthy Viennese merchants and operetta kings like Franz Lehár. He continued by train and boat through the magnificent lake district of Upper Austria. From Wolfgangsee he went to Munich, through southern Germany, and then to Switzerland. He stayed in the best hotels. When his money ran out, Jakob Herzl obligingly cabled him more. Herzl filled a notebook with penciled impromptu impressions and observations on life. Despite all the pleasure, he was churlish and morose. Characteristically, it was not any human encounter but the contemplation of distant landscapes in the Swiss Alps that conjured up erotic fantasies in his mind. "If I ever get married, I am sure I'll cheat myself horribly," he noted on July 25, 1883.

Nothing of this moroseness was even remotely hinted at in his letters to his parents. In these he was worldly and let his wit play freely, often about food and drink, to convey a picture of careless gaiety and youthful abandon. "Shall I describe to you the elegant waiter's noble consternation over my vulgar hunger? . . . [My stomach] is capable of unbelievable feats . . . three servings of fish, three of roast beef, four of roast, vegetables, compote, poultry, cake, cheese, fruit, and at the end . . . a buttered slice of bread."

On July 17 the sophisticated traveler, scoffing at the provinces, wrote from Switzerland:

> Since I left the frontiers of the fatherland I haven't had a single cup of potable coffee. In Bavaria it was still possible to bear this misfortune; there the beer was a consolation. But here even the beer is undrinkable. . . . At breakfast today my neighbor unfathomably ordered a third cup of coffee. I looked up from my teacup, and eyed him offensively.
>
> "Der koffee here ist zo goot," he said apologetically.
>
> "Undoubtedly you are a Saxonian?" I asked ironically.
>
> "Ja, ja, zot's ver I come from. It's amasing how beople can tell zat right away."

4

He returned to Vienna in the autumn to prepare for his final doctorate examinations, outwardly confident, but inwardly as insecure and lonely as ever. In September he again entered a short story competition. Once more he failed. His entry did not receive even an honorable mention.

For the first time, apparently, he considered abandoning his literary ambitions to become a lawyer after all. He shunned people. He was attractive to women but felt timid in their company, afraid always that they might betray him. Herzl had the prissy prudishness of a youth who keeps himself pure for marriage. As before, he found it difficult to combine tender love and sensual pleasure. "Sexual love is no love at all," he wrote; any other was a hoax, a fairy tale for children.

Nevertheless, he followed the example of many dashing young Viennese and took a mistress, with apparently disastrous consequences. She was probably an actress, or perhaps a lively suburban girl of the lower classes, carefree and gay, the *grisette* so common in Vienna at the time, the type Schnitzler immortalized in *La Ronde* and *Anatol* as the "sweet Viennese girl."

"I have a mistress, an appetizing female, created for love, a *bonne fortune*," Herzl recorded in his diary on December 31, 1883. But, alas, "I am no longer fit for love! Not anymore." There are a few pages missing in the manuscript; then this entry: "Torn out at a later reading because they include memories of an ignominious low woman."

A few months later Herzl sat for his final examinations. In May 1884, he was awarded the degree of *Doctor Juris* (Doctor of Law). He was immensely relieved. His parents were delighted. Jakob Herzl offered him another journey, longer and more extensive than the first. Herzl welcomed the opportunity. He traveled through Germany at his usual leisurely pace, alone, slowly savoring Karlsruhe and its charming ducal palace, where twelve years later he would begin his relentless diplomatic quest. On June 2 he stopped briefly at Strasbourg—in 1884 under German rule—to inform his parents of a marvelous meal on the Kurhausterasse: "Warm fish with sauce (I was sorely tempted to cable you a piece, Mama)." A day touring Nancy followed, and the same evening he was in Paris at a performance given by Sarah Bernhardt. Herzl stayed in Paris for nearly a month. He was taken by the city immediately. In Paris, as much as in Herzl's Vienna, the frivolity of the 1880s was in the air. It was here that the new mood of despondency and decadence in art, as in life, was first consciously realized and given its name: *fin de siècle*.

Paris was the enchanting capital of pleasure and elegant living. The literary skies of Paris were aflame in the weird glow of Mallarmé, as Vienna's would soon be in the tired glint of Hofmannsthal. Artistically, Paris was a decade ahead of Vienna. Herzl plunged into Paris as eagerly as he had into Vienna as a teen-ager. His French was fluent. He was enthralled by the city and by French culture, the traditional aspects of which appealed to him more than the new or the experimental, which he dismissed as a bizarre passing fancy. His perennial gloom gave way for a few weeks to a pleasant exuberance. One night he had a nightmare that he had not yet passed his doctoral examinations, and he was pleased to wake up to his sunlit hotel room on the rue Castiglione.

He went to the theater almost every evening. It was the great time of the Comédie Française, of Sarah Bernhardt, Coquelin, Meunet-Sully, Sardou, and Alexandre Dumas. He visited the grave of his idol, Heinrich Heine, whose style he had imitated in his youth; even now he admired Heine's unique symbiosis of German and Jewish sensibilities. From the heights of Père Lachaise cemetery, he looked down on the Latin Quarter, barely visible in the rising mist of the evening. He also attended a sensational trial, a public execution, a lecture by Ernest Renan on the Bible. He sat through a mass meeting with William Booth, founder of the Salvation Army, and sent his parents a graphic description of "this weirdly howling sect."

He was happy in Paris, preoccupied exclusively by beauty and the arts. One sunny afternoon he walked through the Jardin des Tuileries, where eleven years later he would experience the ecstatic inspiration that would change his own life and the lives of millions in the future. He looked through the trees across the river to the imposing edifice of the Palais Bourbon, the seat of the French parliament. He smiled derisively. Politics still bored him; it was too banal and corrupt for his aesthetic nature. Politics was something to be passed by, and ignored, in icy composure.

He returned to Vienna in July, only to face another setback in his literary aspirations. *Die Enttäuschten* (*The Disillusioned*), a play he had worked on for most of 1883, was rejected. It was rich in autobiographical suggestion. One short line sounded a note of strange premonition: "But you, my mourning friend, I shall cure of disillusionment, through politics." He read the play to Friedrich Mitterwurtzer, a leading actor of the Burgtheater, who interrupted Herzl in the middle to exclaim that he simply could not bear such tedium.

5

Herzl was now in his twenty-fifth year; despite his father's generosity he had to think of earning at least part of his keep. Reluctantly, and in very ill humor, he became a law clerk at the Vienna District Court. The endless boredom of his mornings in court, as he filled out one legal form after another, weighed heavily on him. His afternoons were more pleasant. "I read, dream, smoke, write."

He grew a beard, perhaps as a concession to an age when youth was a hindrance to all careers. Many twenty-four-year-old Viennese hid behind full beards to convey an impression of experience. The beard suited Herzl's delicate, slightly hooked nose and high forehead, and seemed to soften his deep voice. He still led a solitary life. With all his obvious charm, quick wit, and easy irony, he lacked the most precious gift, the art of making friends. And when Kana left Vienna to accept a tutor's job in the provinces, and then moved to Berlin, Herzl became a very lonely man. A brief friendship with Julius von Ludassy (later editor of the *Wiener*

Allgemeine Zeitung) faltered because Ludassy considered Herzl too "haughty, cool, condescending, and superior."

Dejection and loneliness heightened his irritability. During the winter of 1884–1885, he was entangled in at least three "affairs of honor," an average of one every six weeks. He brawled once with a Herr von Scheidlein, a lawyer who had accused him of "silly arrogance." Herzl promptly dispatched his seconds to challenge the man to a duel. Scheidlein, refusing even to hear Herzl's seconds out, dismissed them bluntly with the words: "I do not have anything to do with Dr. Herzl!" Herzl's seconds deplored this violation of the Code of Honor and declared Scheidlein "unworthy of satisfaction," and the incident was closed. Soon afterward, Herzl was infuriated by Ludwig Widecky, Secretary of the Exchange Commission, and challenged him to a duel with pistols. This time the case was peacefully resolved through mutual apologies. On another occasion he felt slighted by a man who had taken his chair in a club. Herzl handed the man his card, and a duel was arranged. At the very last minute Herzl could not show up because his father had suddenly fallen ill and summoned him to his bedside. No record remains to explain why the duel was not held at a later date. Years later Herzl was still haunted by the thought that because of this "cancellation" he may have been judged a coward.

Fortunately all of these outbursts ended without bloodshed. Their frequency, nevertheless, reflected Herzl's tense temper, as well as his subservience to an obtuse institution of a bourgeois society still subject to feudal ideas. Many young intellectual liberals were eager to emulate the behavioral code of shallow, prejudiced army officers. They were spellbound by the style of a military caste hiding its crudity behind a romantic mask of "manliness." Like most educated young Jews, Herzl was anxious to "prove" himself by cultivating a grotesque chivalrous style.

It pervaded everyday language. Even a press reporter was said to have "won his spurs" by his coverage of this or that event. In an age that prided itself on its individualism, the duel proved that the herd instinct was still more powerful than the instinct for self-preservation. Men endangered themselves for banal reasons, simply for fear of what their peers might say.

Herzl's devoted parents were his only emotional support in his loneliness and melancholy. He lived with them until his marriage in 1889, at the age of twenty-nine. He loved his parents deeply, with an attachment so strong, so complete, and so moving as to be rare and enviable. The Herzls had always been close. After Pauline's death they drew even more tightly together. In his earlier days, Herzl's father had been an active, enterprising businessman, banker, and financier. Now semi-retired, he and his wife lived for their only son, whose literary career he was sorely tempted to manage. The warmth of Herzl's filial devotion was all the more remarkable when one considers his difficulty in forming a lasting attachment to anyone else. If he hid his frequent dejection and moroseness behind a facade of playful wit, it was not because of any lack of trust in his parents, but to spare their feelings. He constantly worried about their health. His beautiful letters to his parents, of which hundreds have been preserved, are unusual examples of care and devotion. During his trips abroad he wrote his parents daily, sometimes two or three times a day: "Good Mama!" "Good Papa!" "My Precious!" "My Golden Ones!" "How is my dearest?" "How fares my golden?" "My precious golden heart!" When a day passed without a letter from his parents, he would hasten to the telegraph office to cable his concern. "I beg of you again, most urgently, to deliver your letters to the post office daily at the same time if you do not want to cause me hours of unbearable torment." He never traveled without a picture of his parents on the table next to his bed. His parents' overpossessiveness was sometimes a strain; he bore it gladly, lovingly, with a touch of good-natured humor. In a little essay written in 1886, he delivered a mock lecture on "Parentagogy," a disease afflicting parents, who burn with a "noble thirst for learning. Everything they have not learned themselves—and that's a lot—the child must be taught." Parents "*sometimes* bring up their children, but parents are *always* brought up by their children." When a young man picks a profession his father "follows him blindly . . . the father of a lawyer always becomes a great jurist, and the progenitor of an artist becomes a dangerous critic."

Herzl's parents were both ailing. Jakob Herzl suffered from a chronic ear disorder. In June 1885 his doctors sent Jakob on a cure to Hall, in Upper Austria. In order to be near his father and mother, Herzl, after nine months of training at the Vienna District Court, arranged for a transfer to Salzburg. He was able to visit his parents at Hall every weekend. The daily correspondence with his parents continued during the week. His mother was worried that he did not eat enough. He had to constantly reassure her that he was getting fat. "I eat very well. Two meat courses for lunch, dessert, and a glass of Bavarian beer." On hearing that he had taken rooms on the ground floor, she fretted over his safety, and he had to reassure her that his windows had iron shutters and bars. He was no less concerned for their well-being than they were for his.

> I would like to receive a detailed report on the condition of my beloved Pa. Is there still mucus in the ear? Have your headaches completely relaxed . . . how is the throat? Are you still coughing up pus? What does the doctor say? And how do you feel, my beloved Mama? Do you think that the baths do you good? How are your looks, my good ones? Have you appetite? Good and healthy sleep?

Herzl enjoyed Salzburg. Many years later he said that he had spent "some of the happiest hours" of his life there. His office was in an old fortified palace. The windows opened on a marvelous panorama of stately gardens and baroque churches and palaces. The chimes, three times a day, "rang prettily in my ears." He started a new play, *Muttersöhnchen* (*Mother's Boy*), another dramatization of his perennial hero-ideal—the aristocratic happy-go-lucky gourmet and seducer of women—the opposite of his own shy nature.

Fifteen years afterward, as a Zionist leader, Herzl said that he might well have remained in Salzburg forever, if only there had been the chance of steady promotion. But, for a Jew who refused to convert to Christianity, a career in the state judiciary held no promise.

Herzl had now made the final decision not to become a lawyer. Seven weeks after his arrival in Salzburg, at the conclusion of his father's cure, he resigned his post. Brimming with an urge to write, to travel, and to succeed—quickly!—he resolved once more to make his fortune by his pen.

6

For a start, his parents gave him another extensive journey. Herzl spent much of the remaining autumn and early winter traveling. He went to Germany, Belgium, and Holland. His mood continued to shift abruptly between utter euphoria and suicidal depression. Thoughts of death crossed his mind in Brussels; Bruges and Ghent restored his flagging spirits. He sighed at the soft contours of the Lowlands in the gentle, grayish northern light. In Amsterdam he was enthralled by Franz Hals's "Flute Player" and

Rembrandt's "Night Watch." Heidelberg provoked nostalgic memories of his days as a gallant fraternity man in *Albia*. His feelings as a German-oriented Austrian deepened, and on his return to Vienna he gave up his Hungarian citizenship and became an Austrian national. In a review he wrote of the Viennese production of *König Kobman* by the Hungarian playwright Mauruz Jokai, he noted that "Jokai, like Turgenev, is well known in Germany." He crossed out the last phrase and wrote instead "is well known to *us Germans*."

In September at long last he received a first token of recognition as a writer. As in previous years he entered a literary competition. He failed again to win the coveted prize, but this time at least his short story won honorable mention and received special commendation for form and content. Encouraged by this small success, Herzl set out to achieve more. By November he finished *Muttersöhnchen*, the new play which he had started in Salzburg during the summer. In a spur-of-the-moment decision he packed up the manuscript, along with two or three older plays, and traveled to Germany to seek his success on the Berlin stage. His greatest ambition remained the Vienna Burgtheater, the one and only proof of success in the theater for any Viennese, but he hoped to reach it indirectly, through a prior triumph in Berlin. To his parents he wrote from Berlin, "Will get to the Burgtheater at age twenty-six, latest twenty-seven. But get there I will. It would be the pinnacle of my career."

Because of his father's connections, Herzl was well received in Berlin. He was introduced to leading actors and theater directors. He was wined and dined and met a wide range of playwrights and editors. But as far as his theatrical ambitions were concerned, the trip was a failure. Although he was a social success, his plays were rejected.

Back in Vienna, he presented the usual stiff upper lip to his parents. He told them that in Berlin he had, after all, established important connections that might prove useful in the future. His true mood, confided to his diary, was one of utmost despair. "Miserable, miserable life. No success. When is it time? I grow colder." The minor success of his short story in the September competition had given him entrée to a few Viennese weeklies and second-class daily newspapers. Herzl's *feuilletons* and humorous sketches were now published regularly. But his true ambition was the theater.

In his emotions he remained unsteady. He longed to fall in love, but did not. This frightened him, and he sensed an enveloping coldness. He thought of suicide. He was diverted from this gloom by a strange infatuation, low-keyed but impossible, with a thirteen-year-old girl. Her name was Magda. She was a niece of Madeleine, the little girl with whom he had flirted as a boy in Budapest eleven years before. He met Magda in January 1886, at a children's party:

> Since yesterday I am in love, presumably for a long time. I love a thirteen-year-old child. Magda . . . I went up to her longingly. A small big beautiful sweet little lady! I wanted to kiss her. She only turned her head . . . I looked at nothing but her, the sweet, sweet, sweet girl. Still short her little dress, the sweet body is undeveloped—but such a fine, distinguished, lovely face. This golden, golden hair! And the coiffure of a grown-up. . . . Later, when her hair fell loose and she stood before a lamp, I saw a halo around her small sweet face. . . .

Herzl envied the little boy who was permitted to dance with her. "I went out of my head completely. I had to force myself not to tell her, as to an adult, that I love her." He dreamed of her at night. He found out where she would be on the following day. "I restrained myself, with difficulty, from going to the ice-skating rink today, where she is." Two afternoons later he went there anyway, waited two hours for the child's arrival, and watched Magda from a distance. He did not dare approach. Five days later he went to the rink again, but Magda did not show up. He waited for hours in the cold. On the back of his ticket he wrote, in French: *

18.I.86

> J'y étais, le coeur gonflé d'amour. Elle ne vint pas, la douce, la chère. Et que ce soit un souvenir des heures tristement passées, d'une déception enfantine et douloureuse, je garde ce cachet pour les temps qui vont venir.
>
> Est-ce que, un jour, je pourrai montrer ce petit signe d'une tendresse cachée à cette bien-aimée?

> [I was there, my heart swollen with love. She did not come, the sweet, the dear. Let this be a souvenir of hours passed in sadness, of a childish and painful disappointment; I shall keep this ticket for the days to come.
>
> Perhaps one day I shall be able to show the beloved this little sign of hidden affection.]

---

* It was characteristic of Herzl that he often used the French language to express his feelings, or shyness, or a confusion in his thoughts.

Herzl went home in a daze. He resolved to marry Magda, "if she will have me." He was prepared to wait three years. He knew the whole thing was mad. Yet he was filled with an "immense happiness." The thought of little Magda did not leave him, at least for a few weeks.

A month later he fell in love with another girl. Her name was Julie Naschauer. Pretty, petite, blond, and blue-eyed, Julie was the eighteen-year-old daughter of a millionaire industrialist. She swept Herzl off his feet. It began with a furtive kiss, granted almost "in jest," behind the back of her stodgy papa. Herzl's diary reads:

> *February 28, 1886:* A sweet kiss from Julie. I am in . . . love. Unbelievable!

> *March 21, 1886:* Two more enchanting kisses from the same. After the first I immediately demand another. She says, "how immodest," but nevertheless grants it. . . . Meanwhile, two steps away the beloved's unbearable papa sits with two other men.

Two days later he retreated. He was entranced by this "drop of sweetness in the bitter cup of disconsolate unsuccessful careerism." But he was frightened of his own feelings, and of Julie's. He promised himself to end this "charming diversion." His fear of women was real and deep. It was vividly reflected in all the plays he wrote. His female characters were shrewd, bitchy women eager to indulge in wild sexual adventures with naïve males. Marriage was almost invariably portrayed as a speculative partnership of the greedy. With Herzl himself, narcissism alternated with its counterpart, self-disgust. His problem reached a crisis in his encounter with Julie. On April 20, he noted: "Repulsiveness everywhere." He was seized by a "wild nausea," so deep that he was "tempted to throw this empty life away. . . . A leap into nothingness is perhaps the best recourse."

Three weeks later, on May 1, he wrote: "She really loves me. She would be a sweet, gentle wife. But it cannot be. Therefore I shall have to cure her of me." Herzl resolved to deliberately hurt her, and did. He rudely turned his back to her at a party. She was shattered. "Pity, pity, pity," he noted. "It would have been better not to have begun this in the first place." But the following day the two lovers made up. "We are in love more than ever before."

He recoiled from Julie again, however, avoided her, and convinced himself it was over. He wrote, again in French: "C'est pourtant bien fini. N-i-ni. [It is, however, really over.]"

In July he left Vienna on a long journey. It took him through Basel and Paris to Normandy, where he remained until mid-August. From Normandy he sent a series of impressionistic travel articles to Viennese and Berlin newspapers for which he was now working regularly as a free-lancer. As he traveled through Dieppe and Rouen, his thoughts returned to Julie. He dreamed about her as he was lying on the beach. His feelings were confused. In his diary he noted, in French:

A l'attente de Julietta [Waiting for Julietta] . . . here I will lead her one day, when we shall be united, and I shall tell her . . . how I have always loved her, the dear, the sweet.

Le soir du neuf: J'y pense. . . .

Le soir du dix: J'y pense.

[Evening of the ninth: Thinking of her. . . . Evening of the tenth: Thinking of her.]

On his visiting card, under his name, he scribbled the title "Husband."

By mid-August the distractions of Normandy were helping to banish Julie from his thoughts. He played roulette and gambled at cards. He was satiated: "Seeing makes me unhappy. For whenever I see, I see something ugly or vulgar." Petulant, affected, he might have stepped out of the strained social tedium of one of his own unsalable plays.

He finished a new play, *Seine Hoheit* (*His Highness*), a satire on the power of money. The characters in *His Highness* resemble those of his other plays, men of brains and temperament but little soul and hardly any heart. Petty truths are concealed in shallow plots. The style is conversational, yet rather elaborate, like a Tiffany lampshade. His characters have no passions, only weaknesses. Love is sensuality or flirtation; marriage is a "speculative partnership," its aim, "capital gain." Youth is "a fairy tale invented by self-deluded old people." In October he took the manuscript of *His Highness* to Berlin, to try his luck with the prestigious Deutsches Theater. Again he was refused. Berlin was in the throes of the new realism of Ibsen and Strindberg. Herzl, with his tedious bourgeois problems and his stage full of refined aristocrats and vulgar *nouveaux riches*, was a decade behind his time. Ernst Hartmann, a leading actor at the Burgtheater, bluntly urged Herzl to study life as it really was:

"You undoubtedly have talent . . . [but] must create live models, not plaster-of-paris casts from a theater museum."

These were harsh words. Herzl's spells of depression became more severe. Together with the effects of overwork, they produced chronic headaches. He did not see Julie. In the winter of 1886–1887 he was tortured by a seemingly incurable pain in the nape of his neck. His parents were desolate and urged him to seek refuge again in travel. His mother suggested Italy for its warmer climate and the inspiration it had always given to German artists. When Herzl demurred, his father said, "Mother is right, as always! In Italy it is spring. The few hundred guldens it will cost, you will easily earn later."

Herzl left for Italy on February 26, 1887, and stayed for more than a month. His mood improved immediately; the pains in his neck gradually abated, although they did not disappear altogether. From Venice he informed Jakob and Jeannette of his improved physical and mental condition. "I must give up this wild, unnerving work method which I have followed for the past year and a half."

From Venice he traveled to Rome. Mornings he went sight-seeing. In the afternoons and evenings he wrote a series of *feuilletons*. A new tone was introduced in his work. The new *feuilletons* were more serious and mature than anything he had written before. There was a new power of observation and a gentle, melodious style suggestive of his later work. Herzl maintained his detachment as "the eternal passerby"—until his Jewishness struck him unexpectedly once more, this time in the musky lanes of the Trastevere quarter of Rome. He walked through the "frosty shadow" of the Via Rufa to the old Jewish ghetto.

> There is a vapor . . . in the dirty street. Is it dust, smoke, or fog? What a steaming in the air, what a street! Countless open doors and windows thronged with pallid and worn-out faces. The ghetto! With what base and malicious hatred these unfortunate people have been tortured and persecuted for the sole crime of loyalty to their faith. We have traveled a long way since. Nowadays Jews are harangued only for having crooked noses, or for being rich even when they are poor.

7

He returned to Vienna in April, a minor celebrity. His Italian travel pieces had created something of a stir in literary circles, or at least in the right cafés. Newspapers readily printed his reviews and *feuilletons*. Even the imperious *Neue Freie Presse*, Vienna's leading paper, opened its pages to him. The publisher, Dr. Edouard Bacher, a man more powerful in Austrian public life than many a cabinet minister, invited Herzl to contribute articles on a free-lance basis and held out a promise of permanent employment later. A Berlin theater notified Herzl that it would accept a rewritten version of *His Highness* for performance the next year, but the all-important Burgtheater still refused to produce his plays. It would take Herzl two more years to crash its gates.

The following autumn a collection of Herzl's earlier *feuilletons* was published in book form, under the somewhat titillating title *Neues von der Venus* (*News from Venus*). At first the title was misinterpreted, causing some consternation among puritanical circles. A German newspaper even refused to print an advertisement. The suspicion was of course unjustified; the book was harmless drawing-room entertainment. Its contents were well represented by the picture on the cover. Between two ornamental plants, leaning against a short column topped by a bust of Venus, stood an elegant dandy: blond, moustached, dapper, the perfect lady-killer, Herzl's ideal of masculinity.

The women he wrote about in the book likewise reflected his ideal of feminine beauty: blond, blue-eyed fairy-tale creatures. The single brunette in the collection was a deprived, lower-class waitress. Only a few hundred copies of the book were sold, but it helped to establish Herzl's reputation as a writer. The next spring (1888) he published another collection of essays, short stories, and moody travel pieces that were touched by the same peculiar melancholy first seen in his Italian sketches. It was entitled *Buch der Narrheit* (*Book of Folly*). The motto line came from Jonathan Swift's *Tale of a Tub*: "This is the sublime and refined point of felicity called the possession of being well deceived; the serene and peaceful state of being a *fool among knaves*." It revealed young Herzl's innermost conviction in a few words.

He had not seen Julie for over a year. In September 1887 the two had met again. The circumstances of their meeting are unknown. For Herzl the sudden reunion was decisive:

I have found my good Julie again—my last love.

She has always loved me. I shall marry her. I have told her so already. She is sweet, sweet, sweet.

However, a few menacing giants must be felled before I make the dear little princess mine.

Here, on the eve of his engagement, the twenty-seven-year-old was his mother's little boy again, the pampered and beloved only son: "*She has always loved me.*"

She did indeed. Juliette Naschauer (her name was pronounced Julie, with the French intonation) was popular, lively, emotional, quick-witted, willful, outgoing, and daringly elegant—she is said to have been the first woman in Vienna to paint her fingernails—and because of her father's great wealth, very much sought after. In the early days of their courtship, a friend of the Naschauer family remonstrated with her that there was no future in her relationship with Herzl. What would she gain from it? Julie's answer had been prompt and firm: "The *present.*"

It is astonishing that Herzl found his way to her in the first place. He disliked the life style of her opulent family. Julie's background was, nevertheless, similar to Herzl's own. Julie's father, Jacob Naschauer, was a Jewish oil millionaire, born in 1837 in Budapest. As a young man he had moved with his brother Wilhelm to Vienna, where they established a successful holding company, controlling factories, riverboats, and oil fields in Hungary. Herzl found Jacob Naschauer unbearable; there is little reason to assume that Naschauer was any fonder of his daughter's soulful suitor. But Julie was determined. Her willful impetuousness prevailed. The marriage was postponed until Herzl reached some measure of economic security as a playwright. He was still supported by his parents, with whom he lived, and was too proud to rely on his bride's fortune. Jacob Naschauer recognized Herzl's talent, but he was much too hard-boiled to underwrite his literary career.

In the following months, however, things finally began to look more promising. Herzl collaborated with a well-known Berlin producer to rewrite his comedy *His Highness*. The collaboration proved successful. *His Highness* was produced in February 1888 at the German playhouse in Prague. Herzl went to Prague for the premiere. For one so long frustrated by ignoble refusal, the acclaim of a packed playhouse crying "Author! Author!" was balm and honey. He beamed with pleasure as he bowed from the stage following the last curtain call. The reviews were good. A few weeks later the same play was given in Berlin, where "the applause was much greater than in Prague, although the acting was considerably worse." The Berlin reviews were less favorable. Herzl was mildly praised and moderately chastised. His friend Heinrich Kana congratulated him warmly. "I am so happy that the tall brown lad, who for so many years strode the world at my side disdainful and ill-tempered, has acquainted the Berlin public with his face from the high stage."

That summer Herzl was traveling again. Half a dozen editors were clamoring for his moody travel articles. He was also tiring of Vienna—"this droll, cute capital-village" of a run-down empire, its social system "based on envy," its politics on "fear." He passed through Germany to England. He liked England and stayed for over a month. He was deeply impressed by London's hustle and bustle, and by the gentleness of English manners, which appealed to his sense of style. England was so different in its understatement from his own Austria, and his German milieu. He wrote a series of articles and was pleased to see them published prominently in the *Neue Freie Presse*. For an aspiring Viennese writer there was no surer sign of arrival, no greater accolade than to be published by the *Neue Freie Presse*. Stefan Zweig said that a writer who appeared on the first page "had hewn his name in marble, as far as Vienna was concerned." It was as if, in Zweig's words, "Napoleon had pinned the Knight's Cross of the Legion of Honor upon a young sergeant on the battlefield."

In unusually high spirits, Herzl went to the Isle of Wight, which he found almost as charming as Amalfi. He witnessed the exciting spectacle of the Cowes Regatta. He missed Julie and his parents badly, and wrote them every day. From Ventnor on the Isle of Wight, he wrote his parents:

> When one is so much and so uninterruptedly alone, one naturally has the time and reason to do much thinking. I am a more serious and more thoughtful person today than ever before. My fondest thoughts however are for you, my beloved parents, and for the little one [Julie]. Whenever I receive and read your letters, and hers, my heart warms up.

In mid-August Herzl was traveling home through Germany, in a leisurely manner, as was his custom. On an overnight stop in Mainz he had an unpleasant encounter. He stopped in a cheap music hall for a nightcap; as he finished his beer and was making his way toward the door, a rude young fellow hurled a common anti-Semitic insult at him: "Hep! Hep!"* The affront was greeted all around by tumultuous laughter. For Herzl this was a new sensation. He had experienced intellectual anti-Semitism before, but for the first time in his life, he had been called a dirty Jew to his face, and the insult made him physically nauseous. He did not respond, but walked out stone-faced. He repressed the incident at the time. But another seed was planted, and he was to think back upon it at a later date.

Back in Vienna he renewed his assault on the stately gates of the Burgtheater. Collaboration had proved so successful in Prague and Berlin that Herzl decided to try it once more in Vienna. It was not easy for the proud, self-assured Herzl to coauthor a play with another man. But the bug of ambition was stronger. He approached Hugo Wittmann, the successful author and chief *feuilletoniste* of the *Neue Freie Presse*. Together they wrote the light comedy *Wilddiebe* (*Poachers*), a farce of seduction, jealousy, and divorce, which was promptly accepted by the Burgtheater. Under a joint pseudonym the play ran to packed houses for a long time. It was produced successfully later on a dozen stages throughout Germany as well.

In May 1889 *Der Flüchtling* (*The Refugee*), written in 1887, was finally staged by the Burgtheater under Herzl's full name. It won wide acclaim. He had finally reached his great goal. Thus established, he was able to face his bride's father with added assurance. Theodor Herzl and Julie Naschauer were married on June 25, 1889. The wedding took place at the fashionable resort of Reichenau. It was performed by Dr. Adolf Jellinek, the Chief Rabbi of Vienna, the very same man who in 1882 had received Leo Pinsker and had told the obscure doctor from Odessa that his plan of a Jewish state was insane. Here at Reichenau, with its magnificent villas and sumptuous hotels, it was an undoubtedly remote and forgotten incident.

The wedding was a spectacular affair. The bride's dowry amounted to 75,000 guldens. There was little reason to think that the young bridegroom, basking in his new glory as a playwright and husband of a pretty heiress, would soon step into the boots of the poor doctor from Odessa.

* The origin of the words "Hep! Hep!" is not clear. There are two suggestions, one that it is a corruption of *Heb*rew, the other that it is the acronym for the Latin *Hyrosolima est perdita* (Jerusalem is lost).

8

The young couple spent July and August on a honeymoon in Switzerland and France. Herzl was an experienced traveler with a feel for strange and distant places. He delighted in introducing his young bride to the haunts of his melancholy youth. But it was a mixed pleasure. Trouble between the two seems to have started on the honeymoon. It was partly Julie's fault. But it was already clear that Herzl was hardly cast for the role of ideal husband.

Herzl's marriage to Julie was a classic attraction of opposites; it also proved the cynic's old truth that marriage can be based on a mutual misunderstanding. Theodor was solemn, his manner grave and stately. Julie was effervescent, uncontrolled in her temper, tactless, given to fits of unjustified jealousy. Possibly her violent irritability stemmed from a history of hysterics in her family. Theodor was studious and hardworking. His literary interests, and later his political ambitions, filled his life. Julie was little interested in the arts and not at all in politics. He loved travel; she hated to leave the comforts of her home. He was reasonably well-to-do, but she was accustomed to the thoughtless spending of the very rich.

"If I ever get married, I am sure I'll cheat myself horribly," the twenty-three-year-old Herzl had written in 1883. Within weeks of his marriage it seemed to Herzl that this prediction had come true. While still on his honeymoon Herzl sadly wrote to Kana, his one and only confidant: "Once more I have become older, much, much, much older. Farewell and be happy!"

At the same time he started a new play, *Was Wird Man Sagen?* (*What Will People Say?*), an anti-feminist satire on marriage and the impossibility of communication between the sexes. Herzl himself referred to the play as "four acts of cruelty." The engagement of the protagonist, Heinrich, to Nelly, is compared to a visit to the dentist: "Would you like to get engaged with or without anaesthesia?" The history of the engagement is described thus:

Heinrich: The thing actually generated itself. Last winter . . . at a ball I saw her for the first time. We danced a waltz, then another one and another. I led her to the table (*in a tone of light regret*). So my happiness began. . . . As I was promenading with Nelly in the ballroom I heard two elderly ladies say, "What a nice couple!" We passed a mirror. I discovered they were right.

Heinrich cannot communicate with his bride. Where is she? "Oh, she—she is playing lawn tennis. . . ." But wouldn't the game soon be over? "No, not for Nelly. She is a child, she'll always be one. How could she know what slumbers deep in a manly soul? . . . If only I had the courage to desert—what a happy man I would now be!"

It was an odd play for a man to write barely six weeks after his wedding, and certainly an indication of his turmoil.

Julie's immediate pregnancy temporarily muted the inherent tensions. From the honeymoon the young couple returned to Reichenau to await completion of their new flat on the Mark-Aurelstrasse, in the inner city of Vienna. Here Herzl completed his new play. Julie went through the first stages of pregnancy. They were not without difficulties. Julie was irritable and given to violent outbursts of anger. Soon after their marriage she told Herzl that while she liked him, she also "hated and despised" him. There is evidence that even before her marriage she suffered from a nervous disorder, of which Herzl had not been aware. From the beginning she resented some of her husband's ways. She threatened suicide if he did not stop reading books in the evening. On three other occasions she threatened to hang herself or to take poison. There was an element of histrionics in these threats, but it seems that at least once Herzl pulled her back as she was about to jump from the window; on another occasion he cut her down from the curtain rod. In rage she once beat her pregnant belly and screamed, "Through your child I shall punish you!"

Not long after his marriage Herzl began to contemplate divorce. He was held back by a sense of bourgeois propriety and by the prospect of fatherhood. He was excited by the idea of having a son. From Reichenau he wrote on September 5, 1889, to Adolf Agai, a well-known Hungarian writer:

> . . . I hope that it will be a boy. What I'll do with him I don't exactly know at this moment. I won't let him study, and if he wants to write, I'll kill him. By the way, it will certainly be a girl, only because I want a boy. . . . And another thing. If it is a boy after all, I am convinced that world history will stand still and a new era will begin. Believe me! Perhaps I'll let him study after all. As I said, I am still undecided.

His daughter's birth in March gave Herzl days and weeks of complete bliss. He named her Pauline, after his beloved dead sister. He wrote again to Agai on May 3, 1890:

I kiss my good child, dazzled and with reverence, on her po-
po—my beard would hurt her face—and I pay homage to the
riddle of life. If you are well informed on this problem, please
let me know by return post. . . . What upheavals are caused by
a child . . . and how thoughtful one gets. I know I enter through
the gates of fatherhood into philosophy.

Kana, who knew the true state of the marriage, wrote Herzl
that Pauline would make the heavy burden easier to carry. She did,
but not for very long. The majority of Herzl's biographers have
tended to blame the problems on his wife, her short temper, her
incomprehension of his genius. Alex Bein was closer to the truth
when he said that Herzl was capable of being a good father and an
exceptional son; yet with all his protestations of manliness he
"never really became a man and husband." He addressed Julie as
"my dear child" and sometimes signed his letters to her "Your faithful Papa, Theodor."

A few months after Pauline's birth, the discord between them
grew again. As in past years, Herzl hid his turmoil behind a facade
of indifference. After the child's birth he asked Julie for a divorce.
She refused. *What Will People Say?* was produced in February in
Prague. To the producer, Heinrich Teweles, Herzl wrote an analysis of the play's leading character: "He doesn't give a damn for this
world, like you and me. He does not laugh sardonically, he smiles.
He says, like you and me, my dear Teweles, 'Je m'en moque pas
mal . . . je m'en fous. [I don't care at all . . . I don't give a damn].'"

To his parents, in June, he expressed, with exasperation, his
dire hope that Julie "will soon give peace." He sent Kana a photograph of himself with little Pauline, along with a letter pouring
forth his unhappiness. Kana answered, "My poor good Theodor, I
am deeply perturbed by your letters, even more so by the downright shocking expression on your face in the photograph. I know
that all words of consolation are in vain. . . ."

Jeannette Herzl did not make things any easier. The dislike
between mother and daughter-in-law was mutual and immediate.
Possessive, proud, and imperious, the strong, patrician mother
interjected herself between her beloved only son and his inexperienced young wife. She interfered in and controlled her son's household. Herzl often fled to relax in his parents' house. After one such
visit he wrote to thank them for the peace of their home, which had
made him feel "endlessly well." In his own house he had learned
not to protest. Herzl's mother refused to visit Theodor and Julie in

their home. In May 1890 Herzl resolved to seek a divorce unless Julie apologized to his mother. When she refused, he left her abruptly, and from Linz he wrote his parents on May 28, 1890: "I did not choose wisely. But she is after all my wife and the mother of my precious child. It is my duty to do everything to enable the continuation of our marriage." After a week of traveling alone in Upper Austria, he returned home to give Julie "one last chance."

The following February he was struck by a tremendous blow. Heinrich Kana shot himself in Berlin. Minutes before he took his life, Kana wrote Herzl, "My dear good Theodor, your old friend bids you good-bye before he dies. I thank you for your friendship and all your generosity . . . I kiss you."

Herzl was shattered. He had known of Kana's dejection over his failure as a writer, and of his abject poverty. Herzl had offered Kana financial aid, which Kana had angrily rejected. His suicide deepened Herzl's gloom. He was more than ever dismayed by his hapless married life. At home tension flared up. By February Herzl could no longer bear it. He ran away. With Julie in the fifth month of pregnancy, he left for Italy and the French Riviera. A year before, he would not have left his pregnant wife for a single day. His parents encouraged him to go. He announced his final decision to seek a divorce. Julie refused to agree. Herzl did not force the issue; his own family and Julie's abhorred the idea of a public scandal and the revelation in court of Julie's nervous state. He was expected to write for the *Neue Freie Presse*, but he resolved "to work on himself," sorting out his personal problems rather than entertaining his readers. From Milan he wrote his parents: "It's the same—life passes anyway, whether you fill it with great or small enterprises, heroic or ridiculous. The best in life is to watch it pass by thoughtfully, and not to let anything irritate you unduly."

He also wrote Julie in an effort to shore up his disintegrating marriage. These letters cannot be found, nor hers to him.° On February 20 Herzl wrote his parents from Nice: "I'm trying to find

° In the Herzl section of the Central Zionist Archive in Jerusalem there are about 165 empty envelopes addressed in Herzl's hand to his wife, but no letters. They were either lost, suppressed, or destroyed by Herzl's executors or his family. Alex Bein, the distinguished Herzl scholar and author of the first properly researched biography (1934), saw some letters in Vienna, but was not permitted to copy them. The letters were returned to Herzl's daughter, Trude, who at that time was in a mental hospital, where she remained until her deportation by the Nazis in 1942 to the concentration camp at Theresienstadt. She died the following year.

myself." They urged him not to return to Vienna, but to stay away at least until April. Herzl demurred. He had made his bargain, and for better or worse intended to stick to it. He was conscious above all of his responsibility to his daughter. Always the aesthete, he philosophized his predicament: "The performance of one's duty is one of the most refined delights invented by men." On February 26 he was "hurrying back home, as though the happiest family idyll awaits me there! . . . But the fault shall not be mine!"

On his return a halfhearted reconciliation was achieved. On June 10, 1891, a son, Hans, was born. Herzl cried as he received the news. He tore out a calendar page and scribbled in its margin: "At 3:45 A.M., my son Hans born. *In tears.*" The child was not circumcised—a reflection of Herzl's remoteness at the time from all things Jewish.* The improvement in Herzl's domestic situation did not last. In addition to the couple's temperamental differences, there were disagreements over money. As a playwright Herzl was modestly successful for a time. In 1890 his plays were performed at some seventeen theaters in Germany and Austria. But his income from royalties, derived from several sources, was sporadic. In October 1890 his fortunes took an abrupt turn for the worse. His curious play on marital convention, *What Will People Say?*, was a disastrous failure. Overnight, he was out of fashion; most theaters simply did not want anything to do with him. He was not poor. The interest from Julie's dowry alone produced a not inconsiderable income of approximately six thousand guldens a year. But the expanding household and Julie's expensive tastes required more.

9

In August, two months after his son's birth, Herzl ran away again. He could not love his wife, nor easily endure her company. He could not even turn her into literature. He went to Paris and from there to Bordeaux and the Pyrenees, intending to return only after his domestic situation was finally sorted out. He transferred his mailing address to his parents' home. Meanwhile, Julie's parents in Vienna were approached to explore terms of divorce. A lawyer representing the Herzl family called on Dr. Moritz Güdemann, the new Chief Rabbi of Vienna, and requested that he summon Julie's

---

* After Herzl's death, Hans, as an adolescent, underwent circumcision, apparently at the urging of Herzl's disciples.

father for a meeting. Güdemann refused. "My vocation," he told the lawyer, "is to perform marriages, not to negotiate divorce."

The matter did not rest there. Julie refused to legalize their separation; instead she bombarded Herzl with letters protesting her "helpless abandonment." Herzl wrote his parents on September 16, 1891, that Julie would never bring him back, "not through you, nor through the children." He still recoiled from the scandal of a public lawsuit, but Julie was adamant. She refused to settle out of court, or to permit Herzl to see the children.

Meanwhile, Herzl lingered on the beach at Arcachon in the Gironde. He toured Bayonne, Pau, and Lourdes. From there he wandered slowly through the Basque country on both sides of the French-Spanish border. To his parents, who expressed their concern that he might meet with an accident in the wild Pyrenees, he wrote, "You know well that on none of my journeys have I hurt myself as much as I did on the short stretch from the Stephaniestrasse [his parents' new home] to the Lillienbrungasse [home of the Naschauers]."

In his absence his parents were opening his mail. When he discovered this, there was a moment of annoyance, as brief as it was rare, with his prying mother. As the days went on, Herzl's restlessness and turmoil gradually died down. He took long walks through the forests. He was an accomplished horseman. In the early morning hours he charged through the steep river gulleys and wooded meadows of Saint-Jean-de-Luz in an aromatic cloud of myrtle, thyme, and dust. At breakfast each day, the lonely rider returned to his little hotel to spend the rest of the morning writing. He meditated on himself and on life. He read Schopenhauer and approvingly copied this observation: "At the very last we get to know ourselves, as completely different people than we thought we were. And then we are often frightened by what we discover."

He worked intensely on a series of travel sketches, which were published in the *Neue Freie Presse*. As they began appearing one by one, readers in distant Vienna were struck by a tone of genuine kindness, gentle understanding, and real beauty which contrasted with his previous penchant for wit and cleverness at all cost. Here and there his unresolved predicament echoed through—for example, in a snide reference to imperious women and to a feminine "thirst for power." Otherwise his descriptions of landscapes and people, mostly common people, were more penetrating, vivid, and humane than anything he had written before. From Saint-Jean-de-

Luz he wrote a little gem, in a tone of gentle, loving humor, sketch-
ing the barber ("When I say barber, I mean the postman who is
also the grocer") in his crowded little shop on the main square; the
smith standing at his bellows, a "Rembrandtesque glow, red in
black"; the town crier announcing the slaughter of a sick cow as a
large crowd watched ("before its departure the cow clearly sees the
vacancy it leaves behind"); the deep peace of the mountains; the
silent murmur of a pebbled brook.

The advent of autumn drove him farther south, to San Sebastián and Spain. He hoped to go to Madrid and spend the winter in
North Africa. He wrote to Hugo Wittmann (his collaborator on the
play *Poachers*) in Vienna to request an introduction to the Austrian
embassy in Madrid. He wanted to be "well received, and that is not
so simple when one is not a *Herr von*. Were I an English gentleman," he added bitterly, "the mere mention of my name would
suffice. This is quite humiliating for us all, but one bears what one
cannot change."

The memory of his dead friend Kana haunted him everywhere.
As he brooded over Kana's suicide he began a novel. His idea was
to remind the sheltered Jewish rich of the misfortunes and calami-
ties of the unprotected Jewish poor. "The rich feel nothing of anti-
Semitism, for which they in fact are principally responsible." Kana
was to be the central figure in the novel. Herzl hoped "to write
away his ghost."

His travel and writing schemes were interrupted by a cablegram from Vienna. The *Neue Freie Presse* was offering him the
coveted post of Paris correspondent at a thousand francs a month
plus eighty francs for each article. He accepted immediately, in a
simple two-word cable: "D'accord, Herzl [Agreed, Herzl]."

He owed his appointment to his superb travel sketches from
Saint-Jean, Lourdes, and Biarritz. Hugo Wittmann had been consulted by the editors on Herzl's appointment. "If he wants to, he
can do it very well indeed," Wittmann had answered. "The only
danger is his literary talent."

Herzl was in rapture. The cable had arrived during the night.
He could not fall asleep again. This was something he had dreamed
of for years.

San Sebastian, 2–3/ X /91
Night of appointment as Paris correspondent:
    I shall be wearing galoshes like a businessman.

A disillusioned man who suddenly sees himself recognized:
I cannot understand it! . . . has envy suddenly died out?

On the following morning he packed his bags. In his summer
clothing, without returning to Vienna, he proceeded directly to
Paris.

6

Fin de Siècle

ERZL'S FIRST DAYS in Paris were hectic and confused. To the fatigues of a long journey was added the anxiety over the unresolved crisis in his marriage. Moreover, Herzl had never held a steady job before. Now, at thirty-one, he had to adjust to a rigid daily routine of technical chores and responsibilities. He was sorry to abandon his novel, through which he had hoped to write himself free of Kana's ghost. But he was quickly engrossed in the new life. His burning ambition to succeed was intensified by his recent failures in the theater. It seemed to Herzl that he would never write another play.

Paris was in the heyday of the so-called *belle époque*. In later years Herzl sometimes thought that "everything he knew" he had learned there. In Paris there were more curiosity and debate than in Vienna. The arts were no substitute for politics, as in the semi-absolutist Austro-Hungarian monarchy. French politics was real, relevant, exuberant, and often savage. There was something in the air that stimulated experimentation, exaggeration, and flamboyance.

Paris in 1891 was the great European capital of culture, of elegance and daring innovation in the arts. It was a time of fabulous high living for the few, and of growing resentment among the many who struggled in abject poverty. In the words of the 1888 issue of the Baedecker travel guide, "In Paris luxury is raised to a science." The same might have been said of radicalism. The 1890s were also a period of great idealistic purposefulness. The Eiffel Tower had just been completed. Illuminated by the newly developed electric light, it celebrated a century of bourgeois progress through science and technology.

Later generations have looked back nostalgically on the *belle époque* as the good old days, a peaceful time before the great wars and revolutions. Through the tinted spectacles of sentimentalism, little more was seen than gentlemen in fine whiskers and frock coats crowding the stalls of the Moulin Rouge, or ladies in flowered bonnets floating gaily through the haze of Pissarro landscapes.

The real sensibility of the time was infinitely more complex. There is in fact a curious resemblance between Paris of the 1890s and our own time. As today, there was widespread disillusionment with the political and economic system, and much talk of a generation gap. The period saw drug addiction, student riots, a rash of anarchist bombings and political assassinations, a new cult of sex, a sudden fashion of occultism, and an art style that was wholly experimental.

Those who lived in the "gay nineties" often took a grim view of their time. Contemporaries referred to the period not as the *belle époque*, but as *fin de siècle*. The term bespoke restlessness, bleak pessimism, and distaste, all nourished by the imminent demise of culture and of man. The major symptoms were boredom and weariness—Huysmans' *dégoût* at "everything that surrounds me"; Barrès' *"génération dégoûtée* by many things, perhaps by all things save the toying with ideas"; Edouard Pailleron's play *The World in Which One Is Bored.* The *fin de siècle* mentality first became conscious in Paris, and there it was given its name, with that characteristic tendency of the French to ascribe their own moods to the century itself and to the world as a whole. It was seen by some as heralding a new world order, and denounced by others as "degenerate." The great exponent of the latter view was Herzl's acquaintance and colleague Max Nordau, who in a series of sensational international best sellers* decried *fin de siècle* Europe as a mire of corruption and decay. Like Herzl, Nordau was a Jew of Hungarian origin who lived in Paris as a German writer. Perhaps the most brilliant philistine of his day, Nordau was an enemy of all modernity in art. He preferred Italian operettas to modern music and Herzl's light comedies to Ibsen's dramas, which he denounced as degenerate along with the words of Tolstoi, Nietzsche, and the Impressionist painters. The young Freud had paid a visit to Nordau but was so bored by his hysterical strictures that he never came again.

Not so Herzl. Nordau was one of the first people he sought out

---

* *The Conventional Lies of Mankind*, 1883; *The Malady of the Century*, 1887; *Degeneration*, 1893.

after his arrival in Paris. He admired Nordau as a man and as a social analyst, and soon came under his influence. It was by no means a one-sided relationship, even though Nordau was ten years older, a world-famous man, and Herzl only a beginner. The two men had much in common. Both were conservatives, distrustful of modern culture; both were bewildered men, concerned about the future of civilization in a time of rapid change. Herzl shared many of Nordau's cultural prejudices. Nordau would soon find himself Herzl's chief lieutenant in the cause of Zionism.

To his parents Herzl wrote exuberantly: "[My post as] Paris correspondent is the springboard from which I shall leap high, to your joy, my dear beloved parents." It was indeed the golden age of the foreign correspondent. Herzl was fully conscious of his new power as a correspondent of the *Neue Freie Presse*. The paper reigned supreme as the most important arbiter of taste from Aachen in Germany to Zitovic in the Bukovina. The *Presse*—its editors were assimilated Jews—was a late flower of the Enlightenment; its style was witty and refined. In its columns the world of literature and the arts was valued as much as the world of politics, and sometimes even more. Among its regular non-German contributors were Anatole France, Shaw, Ibsen, Zola, and Strindberg. Its circulation was hardly more than 35,000, low even for its time, but its influence was spread over the entire German-speaking world. It was even widely read in the non-German provinces of the Austro-Hungarian Empire. A resident of Budapest would find more and better coverage of Hungarian parliamentary deliberations in the *Presse* than in his own Hungarian papers. There were people in the provinces who added, underneath their engraved names on their visiting cards, "Subscriber to the *Neue Freie Presse*."

The *Presse* was not intended, like the London *Times*, to inform the members of the house of parliament; parliamentary life was marginal in the semi-absolute monarchy. Its purpose was to reflect the views of the rising bourgeoisie. Pro-German in its orientation, it was liberal in its policies. For this reason it was especially popular among middle-class Jews, of whom it was said, "They do not keep the dietary laws, they do not keep the Sabbath. They keep the *Neue Freie Presse*." Innumerable anecdotes reflected or ridiculed the *Presse*'s hold on its readers. Hermann Bahr remembered that it was enviable to be acquainted even with a cousin of an editor or correspondent of the *Presse*.

2

Herzl was now a member of that august circle. For his parents in Vienna, his appointment was the cause of great pride. Meanwhile his marriage to Julie remained unsettled. Herzl lived in an uncomfortable hotel room on the rue Daunou, around the corner from the place de l'Opéra. It was now November; attempts at reconciliation, initiated by well-wishing relatives, continued throughout autumn and early winter. At first they were not successful. Although Vienna was merely an overnight train trip from Paris and Herzl missed his children, he avoided an unpleasant confrontation with his wife. He did not even go to Vienna for the premiere, on November 1, of the new play he had written in Spain during the summer.

But he corresponded with Julie. There was considerable bitterness in their letters. On November 10, 1891, Herzl passed on to his parents a letter from his wife "which I do not intend to answer." He added bitterly, "I send it along to you so that you might visit your grandchildren should you long to do so." On November 29 Julie, in a recalcitrant mood, implored Herzl to take her back "on indefinite probation." Herzl answered that if his parents agreed he would have her back on condition that she not share his bedroom.

At the same time Herzl strongly urged his parents to move to Paris to be with him permanently. He missed them even more than he missed his children; his parents were his only emotional support. Herzl never expressed his tender love of father and mother more intensely than during the first months of his stay in Paris. The letters he sent them in the winter of 1891–1892 are probably among the most stirring ever written by a son to his parents. He did not want them to live away from him under any circumstances. "My beloved good parents," he wrote,

> Whatever happens . . . move here you *must*. It would be sin and silliness if we shouldn't be together . . . everything I accomplish is yours; everything I am is due to you. Just as I owe you an infinite debt of gratitude for all and everything, so all the esteem I may gain in the eyes of people is yours as well. I shun any of life's pleasures which you do not share with me completely.

Herzl's parents still hesitated. In the meantime, another grudging reconciliation was achieved in January between Herzl and his wife. Julie came back to Herzl "on probation." Their love for each other had ended long ago; it could not be rekindled. But both adored their children. Julie loved them frantically—an overanxious, nervous, fretting mother. Herzl's love was philosophical in a languid sort of way: "Children are our grandest teaching masters. . . . The only lovely thing on earth—a baby. Only babies make life bearable, as heirs to our pains."

Common parental concern brought the couple together again, and in February Julie, the children, and their nurses arrived in Paris for a short visit. Tearfully, as on the day of Hans's birth, Herzl picked up his family at the gare de l'Est. He was overjoyed to see the children after the seven-month separation. Pauline was now two; little Hans, whom he had last seen as a baby of six weeks, was nine months old, a happy, smiling child with his father's dark and moody eyes.

"Life has an attraction for me again," Herzl wrote his parents on the following day. The only thing now missing to complete his happiness was that "you, my precious, precious [parents], would soon join me here." Julie was not told of their projected move. Her certain opposition to sharing her home with Herzl's parents might have wrecked the reconciliation that had been effected with so much difficulty. After a brief stay, Julie and the children returned to Vienna to await the completion of their new Paris flat. It was located at 8 rue de Monceau, in a fashionable district peopled by the new aristocracy of wealth. The flat was undoubtedly a concession to Julie's expensive tastes; the rent alone amounted to half of Herzl's salary.

Julie, waiting in Vienna, was still unaware of her in-laws' preparations to move to Paris. Wisely, Herzl's mother now made serious efforts to placate Julie's hurt feelings. Herzl was deeply moved by his mother's kindness. He wrote to thank her for the tact and good judgment she displayed toward the erratic Julie:

> For what you are and do, your richest reward is you yourself. There is nothing more exalting in life than to be, like you, every single moment rightly entitled to be satisfied with yourself. It is the noblest fulfillment of life.
>
>   . . . As for our beloved good Papa, he too is rewarded for all his sacrifices, all his efforts . . . by having such a wife, and a son who even when he is gray-haired will still be obedient, tender, and respectful as a child. My children too, if fate permits, shall grow up with this adoration and love for you. It shall be the best support of their character.

At first Julie balked at establishing a joint household with her
in-laws in Paris. She gave in to Herzl's insistent requests and the
intervention of her relatives. If the decision to set up a joint household was inevitable, given Herzl's emotional dependence on his
parents, it did not bode well for the future of his marriage. The
consequences were easily foreseeable. The decision undermined
whatever slim chances there were of rebuilding the marriage on a
surer foundation. Herzl was aware of this danger; but his attachment to his parents was so deep, and his devotion so real and so
complete, that he could hardly do otherwise. At the same time he
addressed a passionate appeal to his mother:

> . . . Your position is so strong, will always be so strong, that you
> can exercise it [vis-à-vis Julie] without dictatorship and didac-
> tics. Anything you say will of course be done. But I expect that
> with your wisdom and your love for me you will readily consult
> Julie, even when you don't need her advice, as a general who
> gives orders yet first asks his captain what he thinks. . . . I shall
> *ask* Julie not to be difficult. Of you, Mother, I *beg* the same.

3

Julie and the children returned to Paris in April; a few weeks
later they were joined by Herzl's parents. The marriage never resolved itself, but dragged on, through better times and through
worse, driven mostly by inertia and a common concern for the
children. The household was lavish, in a grander style than Herzl's
income allowed. The deficit was made up by Julie's dowry. Four
servants, two imported from Vienna, were employed. The older
couple resented Julie's extravagance. Their old-fashioned simplicity
was a cause of further tension.

An insight into these disagreements comes from an unexpected
source. Like other prominent foreigners, Herzl was spied on by
French police informers. According to one report preserved in the
French police archives, Herzl was said "to have considerable resources at his disposal," but his parents, "being great misers, reproach him for his extravagance."

If his home life remained unsettled, Herzl did not devote much
time to it. He threw himself into his new work with almost ferocious vigor. His schedule was hard and taxing. "I am not giving you
a birthday present," he told his father. This year's present would be

"in what I achieve." Herzl's workday began at 7:30 in the morning; it was rarely over before midnight. He dictated his first cable to his secretary at 9:00 A.M. In the afternoon he wrote his long dispatches and analyses, which sometimes filled three or four pages of the *Presse*.

As a correspondent he plunged into post-Boulangist France, a country torn by internal strife, violence, anarchy, economic depression, parliamentary crisis, and corruption in high places. The corruption was so widespread that only dedicated optimists could keep even a shred of confidence in the future of republicanism. Herzl was soon struck by the prevailing mood of impending social and political apocalypse. His first reaction had been to dismiss the negative signs; he still believed that science, technology, and rising living standards would reconcile the social extremes. Before long, however, he sensed a deeper malaise and his tone began to change. Reporting the farcical jury trials of anarchist bomb throwers, he observed: "A democracy which produces inadequate juries is already monarchistic in its nature. The only thing missing is a tyrant. He will be found."

Herzl was an instant success with his readers; shortly after his appointment he got a 20 percent raise in salary. It was well deserved; he had made an enormous effort to overcome the natural handicaps of inexperience and his earlier contempt for all politics. At first he had trouble keeping deadlines; the editor had to remind him that there was no point in cabling on Sundays since there was no newspaper. His German background was a slight handicap in a country still seething with the Germanophobia generated by France's defeat by Prussia in 1870. Nor was the *Neue Freie Presse* much liked in French official circles; as a pro-German paper it was often critical of France. But Edouard Bacher, the editor, wrote Herzl that he would "gladly permit him to be a shade more friendly to France," in order to establish and retain useful connections. On the other hand, Herzl was greatly helped by his wide knowledge and love of French culture. His perfect fluency in the language— always a shortcut to French hearts—and the natural grace of his personality, impressed men as different as Rodin, the sculptor; Clemenceau, the fiery parliamentarian; Alphonse Daudet, the writer; and Freycinet, the French Minister of War.

Yet Herzl grew only slowly into his new job. He came to politics from the sheltered republic of letters and the hothouse of the light theater. For many Viennese of Herzl's aesthetic temperament, the theater served as a substitute for politics; it was not easy for him to reverse the priorities. Herzl's experience of real life was limited; apart from his unsuccessful marriage, he had lived very little. As a foreign correspondent he was expected to brief his readers extensively on parliamentary debates, defense policy, and the latest fluctuations of the stock exchange. Since he was sometimes neurotically shy of famous personalities, he could not have been a very good reporter. But he was superb as an analyst, and as a surveyor of the general drift of events.

During the first few weeks, Herzl was still more interested in politicians than in politics; the setting for an event appeared more important than the event itself. As a parliamentary reporter, he succumbed to a playwright's feeling for dialogue, which sometimes came at the expense of substance. One of his earlier reports on the *Chambre des Députés* was turned down by Bacher with the admonition: "This treatment of a political theme is really too much in the style of an operetta." Herzl was still entrapped in his old pose of viewing the world in gloomy amusement, as an abode of the "dupes and the duped." When one views the world "from a proper distance," one realizes that it is nothing but a "play" staged to "amuse the gods who burst out in Homeric laughter."

But as the months went by he became more serious, less deliberately witty. The mocking essayist of "love" and bourgeois trivia, of distant and bizarre landscapes, became an astute political observer, coldly dissecting the body politic of France, concerned for the future of liberty, distrustful of formal institutions, gravely expecting a general collapse, even anticipating revolution: "The republicans are raising arms against one another again. Like their erstwhile kings they have learned nothing and forgotten nothing."

The superb plasticity of his style makes some of Herzl's Paris dispatches highly readable even today. An indifferent playwright, he suddenly found a profession in which he truly excelled. Once he abandoned his stilted pose, a reservoir of new energies was released. Unknown to him at the time, this awakening marked his first step toward a life of political action.

4

As a political analyst, he was greatly preoccupied with the sudden rash, in 1892, of anarchist violence. It was almost as if fate were offering him a primer course in direct political action. Before his eyes a fantastic shadow play was staged, in gross caricature and distortion. Until 1892 anarchist ideas had been confined to popular *chansons* and the brilliant journalism of magazines like *Père Peinard* and *La Révolte*. For more than a decade the radical press had been extolling the "beautiful deed" of political terror, "the bomb that cleanses," and had been calling for the knifing, strangling, shooting, and bombing of capitalists, judges, priests, generals, and related animals. Shortly after Herzl's arrival, the theory was put into practice; terror suddenly burst forth in an epidemic of bombings and political assassinations that rocked France for more than a decade.

The signal was given in February by the notorious Ravachol, a former thief, murderer, and grave robber, who had been converted to anarchism. He resorted to dynamite in order to force society "to look attentively at those who suffer." Herzl's daily reports convey the vivid picture of a city in the throes of fear and yet fascinated by the culprit. Herzl closely followed Ravachol's sensational trial. He was intrigued by the man's complicated personality. As Ravachol stood in the dock, Herzl would study his hard face for hours. He followed his every move and gesture; he was disturbed by Ravachol's apparent strength of character—"the individual in history"—and by his confused pattern of motive and design. Was Ravachol a hero or a criminal?

> A dreamer or a mean knave? A benefactor of the poor and wretched? . . . There is something impersonal in this man. He speaks calmly. Firmly, he says that the present state of affairs must be changed; but when he speaks of a better world, where the weak shall be protected by all, his voice softens. . . . He starts in evil and ends in goodness. He believes in himself and in his mission. He has become honest in his crimes. The ordinary murderer rushes into the brothel with his loot. *Ravachol has discovered another voluptuousness: the voluptuousness of a great idea and of martyrdom.*

The *voluptuous* pleasure of a great idea—here is a strong premonition of Herzl's later life. He did not, of course, condone Ravachol's crimes. "There is no good deed that excuses a bad one." He was appalled by the laxity of the jury and the recklessness of pseudointellectuals who enthused over anarchist crimes with: "*N'importe les victimes si le geste est beau*" (Never mind the victims if it is a beautiful gesture).* But the issue itself, and its prob-

---

* There is now considerable evidence that anarchist bombings were provoked deliberately from behind the scenes by the adventurer and czarist secret

lems, remained uppermost in his mind. Henceforth his thoughts were fixed on the prospect of a grand personal intervention in the course of history, through the flamboyant act of an individual—himself. We shall soon see how he proposed to go about it.

Meanwhile, the growing anti-Semitism was slowly pushing him in the same direction. The beginnings of "scientific" racism in France were described in a previous chapter. The poisonous plant now reached full bloom. Hard upon Ravachol's trial there followed a series of sensational anti-Semitic incidents. The deputy chairman of the French parliament brought a lawsuit against the notorious anti-Semite Edouard Drumont, who had accused him of being in the pay of the Jews. Then there was a series of duels between Jewish army officers and anti-Semitic rabble-rousers who had cast doubt on their patriotic loyalty.

The general commotion focused Herzl's attention on the situation of the Jews of France, the country that had first broken their shackles. He dealt with the problem in a tone of almost complete detachment. It did not seem to touch Herzl in any personal way. If he had encountered difficulties from bigoted Frenchmen, it was not because he was Jewish but because he was "German." Paris was not Mainz. In France, he said later, he was able to walk "unrecognized" through the crowds. He sensed that this word "unrecognized" constituted in itself a terrible reproach against the anti-Semites. But he did not show it.

Herzl covered Drumont's trial and wrote about it dispassionately. He graphically related the moving story of Captain Armand Mayer, the Jewish officer who crossed swords with the anti-Semitic playboy the Marquis de Morès. Mayer had trouble with his right arm but was too proud to admit it; after only three seconds he was stabbed to death. Later it became clear he hardly had the strength to lift the heavy *colichemarde*. Herzl walked in his funeral procession, which was attended by fifty thousand mourners. In front of the Palais Royal an anti-Semite yelled "Dirty Jews!" One of the mourners left the procession and slapped the fellow's face. The intruder fled the scene as the crowd moved forward to continue the chastisement.

Mayer's duel with Morès was the first of a series of similar

police agent Rachkovsky. "His motive in masterminding outrages in France and Belgium was to force a rapprochement between the French and Russian police as a first step toward a Franco-Russian military alliance on which he had set his heart, and which he did much to bring about." Norman Cohen, *Warrant for Genocide* (London, 1970), p. 87.

bloody skirmishes that greatly agitated French and foreign public opinion. Duels between political rivals were common in France. In the *opéra bouffe* atmosphere of the 1890s even authors and reviewers challenged one another to duels. "What a perplexity," Herzl wrote mockingly. "They want to cut each other's throats, but respectfully! They want to cleanse the earth of an individual whose death as a man of honor they will immediately mourn most deeply!"

The deadly convention, which induced mature men to meet at dawn in remote corners of the Bois to risk their lives, was now applied in the cause of racism. Bankers, officers, journalists, and politicians dueled with one another at the slightest suggestion of biological inferiority. Herzl's mockery of the duelers was a little strained. Perhaps it was self-irony. He himself would have readily dueled with any "man of honor" who disparaged his origins. He was obviously reaching a crisis point. In a long roundup of these events and of French anti-Semitism, he resorted to heavy sarcasm:

> Until recently, French anti-Semitism was quite good-natured; one might almost say charming . . . it was not directed solely against Jews. Where it struck Jews directly, no one . . . denied that Jews too were human beings. This is quite surprising for one who comes here from a certain other country.
>
> In France Jews have been accused primarily of being from Frankfurt. The injustice was obvious, for some come from Mainz, even from Speyer. Their money was resented only when they had some. . . . They are kindly treated, especially in death. When their splendid lives, for which they were so envied, are happily over, *Judenmenschen* are no longer discriminated against in France, but are buried alongside *Christenmenschen*, in the same cemeteries.
>
> Moreover, when a Jew, by his inborn cunning, goes as far as to sacrifice his life (like Captain Mayer) in a fine gesture of chivalry, his noble act is greeted with murmurs of approval. . . . (If Captain Mayer were not dead, he would surely be gratified now to hear his killer's eulogy of him.) The Marquis de Morès has said explicitly that he "deeply regrets the death of this man of honor." . . . That's really the pinnacle! No Jew, without being immodest, could truly ask for more.

For the first time Herzl now read Edouard Drumont's famous diatribe, *La France Juive* (*Judaized France*). Almost a million copies had been sold since its publication in 1885. The book was said to be the biggest best seller of the nineteenth century, and it put the blame for the decline and misfortune of France squarely on the Jews. Herzl was strangely fascinated by Drumont. He sensed the deeper causes of racial hatred stemming from a social structure for which the rich Jews were partly responsible. He even welcomed a discussion of the theme by serious men of letters and by artists like Drumont. It was better than letting the matter be thrashed out "by rabbis and monks."

Three years later Herzl would admit that Drumont had enabled him to view anti-Semitism open-mindedly, with "a new kind of freedom." Drumont helped him to understand anti-Semitism historically and even "to excuse it." But in June 1892, as he walked in poor Captain Mayer's funeral cortege through the thronged streets of Paris to the Montparnasse cemetery, he was not yet so "free," so deeply involved or concerned or "understanding." Anti-Semitism was still more than an anomaly in France, a "rendezvous of the malcontent," a kind of "salon for the rejected." As Herzl saw it, it did not yet touch the mass of the French people. For the time being, Herzl was reassured by the official condemnation of racism in the serious press and in parliament. He approvingly recorded an unusual newspaper interview with Pope Leo XII, in which the pontiff was decrying war and racism. "And the wars of religion, Holy Father?" asked the interviewer.

"Those two words are contradictory," the Pope answered.

"Well, race wars then?"

"Which races? All stem from Adam."

Charles Freycinet, the Minister of War, declared in parliament: "I solemnly announce that in the French army we recognize no Catholic, no Protestant, and no Jew; we recognize only French officers." Herzl, from his regular seat in the press gallery, noted Freycinet's speech and the "lively applause" that greeted it.

Interspersed with such reports were long dispatches on the arts, on books and exhibitions. In the leisured world of 1892 the turnout at the Longchamps races, headed by President Carnot, merited a cabled account of five hundred words, and a premiere at the Comédie Française, a report of over five thousand, with a full synopsis of each act and a detailed description of the acting. When Maupassant was committed to a lunatic asylum, Herzl felt a strong desire to visit him there and to "observe him as much as possible, unseen." In Herzl's drama reviews the disappointment at his own failure as a playwright was frequently evident, particularly in his disparaging remarks about the new realists.

5

Herzl's growing maturity was reflected in a remarkable exchange of letters with Arthur Schnitzler, the well-known Viennese novelist and playwright. The exchange started in the autumn of 1892 and continued sporadically for three years. It throws a light on both correspondents and their time. Schnitzler, two years younger, was beginning to achieve everything Herzl had tried unsuccessfully to do himself. Schnitzler was a rising figure in Austrian literature and theater. His most famous works, *Anatol, Der Reigen* (on which the film *La Ronde* was based), and *Der Grüne Kakadu*, came some three years later. But already he was the acknowledged spokesman of Young Vienna, a new wave of young, extremely gifted writers which included Hugo von Hofmannsthal and Richard Beer-Hofmann. In lyrics of sweet weariness the new school wrote of disillusionment and of death. Schnitzler wrote the swan song of Old Vienna; he captured the last gleams of its setting glory in works of rare poetic force and beauty. His worldly satires on human fate and vain eroticism anticipated in their subtlety some of Freud's psychoanalytical insights:

> Dreams are desires without courage,
> Insolent wishes which the light of day
> Chases back into the corners of our soul.
> Only at night they dare creep out.

> (Träume sind Begierden ohne Mut,
> Sind freche Wünsche, die das Licht des Tags
> Zurückjagt in die Winkel unsrer Seele.
> Daraus sie erst bei Nacht zu kriechen wagen.)

Like Freud, Schnitzler sensed that the sweetness and grace of Viennese life were only a surface phenomenon. His works were peopled by listless epicureans and skeptical sensualists. They knew too much of life to condemn or praise it. Life was a play, and men merely marionettes on gilded strings. Pleasure was not a goal; it ended in suffering. A child of his time and place—*fin de siècle* Vienna—Schnitzler dressed his protagonists in shrouds.

As artists, Schnitzler and Herzl had been nourished at the same moldy loaf. But where Schnitzler's melancholy was convincing, because it was so humane, Herzl's had merely been coquettish; and where Schnitzler, in his plays and novels, reflected the moral crisis and institutional failure of the liberal bourgeoisie, Herzl had merely ridiculed its drawing-room manners.

Herzl and Schnitzler had met as students at the University of Vienna. During a meeting of the academic debating society, they had "stared at each other contemptuously one evening." Later they had come to know one another personally, but they had never been friends. Herzl rather disliked Schnitzler and did not think much of him as a writer. But in July 1892 a colleague in Paris lent Herzl a copy of Schnitzler's new play, *Märchen* (*Fairy Tales*). Herzl was so impressed that he wrote Schnitzler a long letter full of remorse, modesty, and honest joy over Schnitzler's success where he himself had failed: "I wish I could write like you!" In his letter Herzl freely admitted that he had previously disliked Schnitzler and had belittled him as an artist.

> So stupid and unscrupulous is our judgment. Perhaps you have had a similar experience, perhaps even with me. I for one am filled with remorse for my frivolity. . . . But when I see a talent like yours coming into bloom, I rejoice as though I myself were not a *littérateur*, that is to say, not a narrow-minded, intolerant, envious, malicious wretch.

His own plays Herzl now called "my smeary scrawlings." He informed Schnitzler that he was through with the theater. "When I stop to reflect on my place in the world of German letters—and I do that very rarely—I feel I must laugh, and yet I must tell you that this does not embitter me in any way. Pain is always an education."

Schnitzler was pleasantly surprised at this unexpected outburst by someone not noted for modesty. He responded in warm, friendly tones. No, it was the other way around. It was he, Schnitzler, who should admire Herzl's work. It had always seemed to him that Herzl was "twenty paces ahead." He confessed the ambivalence of his own past attitude to Herzl, his envy of Herzl's dash, and the mild annoyance at his insolence. He reminded him of the evening when Herzl had shattered his self-confidence at a party by pointedly observing that his cravat was sloppily tied; and of the autumn night in Vienna when they were passing the shuttered Burgtheater and Herzl had imperiously pronounced, "I'll get in here one day." Schnitzler had been dining out on this story ever since. He was genuinely pleased about Herzl's appreciation of his work and assured him there were few people on earth whose judgment he valued so highly. Schnitzler asked about his current literary projects. Was Herzl working on a new play or novel? He would be thrilled to read any manuscript Herzl might care to send him. Schnitzler held out his hand for a friendship he hoped would be permanent.

Herzl answered despondently, but with a remarkable lack of bitterness. No, he was not twenty paces ahead of Schnitzler now, but in fact far behind, sitting on a milestone beside the road, "letting others pass me by." He urged Schnitzler not to fall victim to "Viennese *découragement* . . . I know it. It is cured by change of place."

No, he would not send any manuscript. "I am still vain enough not to be willing to be read for reciprocity's sake only," Herzl wrote. Schnitzler insisted. Again and again he repeated his request to see Herzl's manuscripts.

"My manuscripts!" Herzl answered. "I have forgotten them . . . only at certain lost hours am I homesick for art. Journalism takes its heavy toll!"

With astonishment Herzl watched the rise in distant Vienna of another marvelously gifted new poet, still hiding under the mysterious pseudonym Loris, who wielded a language so musical, ripe, and sensuous that people supposed the author must be a "titled diplomat" of fifty. He was in fact a boy of eighteen, Hugo von Hofmannsthal.

"Who is Loris? Who is Loris?" Herzl asked Schnitzler. Schnitzler, who had discovered the boy prodigy, urged Hofmannsthal to contact Herzl directly. Herzl's exchange with the young genius was not conducive to improving his flagging spirit. Hofmannsthal poured vinegar on his wounds. With all the insolence of youth, Hofmannsthal addressed Herzl condescendingly: ". . . by the way, I like your graceful style and think that you have taste . . . [but] I have a slight antipathy against your métier in spite of such colleagues as Heine and Anatole France."

6

As a journalist Herzl continued to pursue "the métier which the charming little Hofmannsthal so despises," as conscientiously as he could. "It is a difficult job . . . but it trains one in cool reflection and fast action." He was busier than ever. His brilliant dispatches were the talk of Vienna. There was no lack of exciting themes. In the wake of the anarchist bombings and the duels between anti-

Semites and Jews, the terrible Panama Canal scandal broke over
France. The seedy revelations of bribes, slush funds, and the sale of
influence rocked the foundations of the state. Deputies and ministers were implicated directly or by association. "Stupidities and
crimes repeat themselves. Memories arise," Herzl wrote on December 31, 1892. "So it was a hundred years ago. . . . Death knells are
ringing: 1793."

Under the impact of it all, Herzl concluded, in a letter to
Schnitzler early in 1893: "There will be a revolution here this year.
If I don't escape in good time to Brussels, I'll probably be shot as a
German spy, as a bourgeois, as a Jew, or as a financier, whereas I
am really just a worn-out, used-up trapeze artist."

As the reputation of the republic sank, so anti-Semitism flour-
ished. It was no longer the "rendezvous of a few malcontents," but
the reflection of a social and political crisis of ever-growing mag-
nitude. The bankruptcy of the Panama Canal Company wiped out
overnight the savings of innumerable small investors. Although
there were no Jews among the defunct company's directors, whose
greed and incompetence had precipitated the disaster, two Jews,
Cornelius Herz and Baron de Reinach, were implicated in the
shady dealings that followed its collapse. The public's fury fell on
their heads, and indirectly on all Jews. They were held responsible
for everything that had gone wrong. In the Panama Canal scandal
the medieval canard of Jewish ritual murder was reincarnated in a
new, economic version.

At one stormy mass meeting Herzl heard, for the first time, the
sickening yells of "A mort! A mort les Juifs!" What was this? A sort
of blood bank where people came for infusions? Herzl began to
ponder the curious "phenomenon of the mob"; he was fascinated
by its manipulation and control.

Thoughts of a possible political career briefly crossed Herzl's
mind. He regarded his present work as intensive political training.
"Is this [journalistic] exercise of any further value for me? Certainly not," he wrote Hugo Wittmann on March 30, 1893, unless he
were to go into politics. "But I, a Jew, in Austria?"

His reports from the troubled Paris scene were still very bal-
anced; but as he saw France slowly withdrawing into barbarism, a
certain bitterness seeped through. To his French acquaintances he
spoke his mind freely. In April 1893 Herzl's name appeared on the
official list of "suspect foreigners" submitted to the Minister of the
Interior by the Quatrième Bureau of the police.

The French parliament frequently erupted in ugly scenes,

Herzl's mother, Jeannette, was enamored of German *Kultur*. Strong-willed and possessive, she was convinced that her only son was born to greatness.

Herzl's father, Jakob, was a wealthy businessman, "assimilated" but too proud, or perhaps too inert, to cross the line into Christianity.

It was a time of rising expectations in Budapest, even more than elsewhere on the continent, before the rise of nationalism and racism in the multinational Austro-Hungarian Empire. Herzl's birthplace on the Tabakgasse.

Theodor Herzl at the age of 7 with his sister, Pauline. In the shock of her sudden death at 18, the Herzls abruptly cut their roots and moved to Vienna.

Herzl as a dashing young law student at the University of Vienna. No man was more Viennese and less Viennese at the same time.

Herzl (far right) as a member of the German nationalist student fraternity *Albia*. He resigned in protest against the fraternity's tacit identification with anti-Semitism.

Herzl's wife, Julie, as a young bride. A psychotic from early infancy (at the time of the marriage Herzl had not been aware of this), she was tied to Herzl in a disastrous marriage and bitterly resented his politics.

Baron Maurice von Hirsch, railroad king
and philanthropist. Herzl, in fact, offered
him a crown. Hirsch dismissed him as an
amusing dreamer.

Herzl's colleague Arthur Schnitzler, the
well-known Viennese novelist and playwright. He urged Herzl to be not only
bold but also defiant: "It is not true that
in the ghetto all Jews ran about depressed
or inwardly sordid."

Baron Edmond de Rothschild, the great Jewish financier who sponsored the first Jewish colonies in Palestine "as an experiment." Like all Jewish plutocrats, he resented Herzl's scheme and regarded him as a "dangerous adventurer."

Colonel Albert Goldsmid, professional British army officer. A Jewish General Gordon, his dream was to be the Joshua of the New Exodus.

Grand Duke Friedrich of Baden, one of the architects of German unification and Herzl's first royal sponsor. Entranced by his persuasive force, he introduced Herzl to the German Kaiser.

Herzl's first Viennese committee meets in the back room of a popular café.

Julie Herzl in 1904. Shortly before his death Herzl and his wife achieved the reconciliation that had escaped them throughout their married life.

Herzl in 1896, shortly before the publication of *The Jewish State*.

The Basel Municipal Casino, where the first Zionist congress met in 1897.

occasioned by debates on the so-called Jewish "question." A decade earlier such debates would have been unthinkable. Herzl brooded over this development constantly. In his agitation he devised a fantastic plan, the first of a series that would preoccupy him over the next two years.

The plan called for his personal intervention to force the issue to a head, and then to a resolution. If necessary he would sacrifice his life. He envisioned a scenario of flamboyant heroes and sensational effects. Karl Lueger, Prince Alois Liechtenstein, and Georg von Schönerer were the great leaders of Austrian anti-Semitism. He, Herzl, would challenge one or all three to a duel. It would be by pistols, and fought to the death. Herzl was undoubtedly inspired —or shamed—by Captain Mayer's example, probably also by the anarchist Ravachol. The idea was to create a stir and so catch the conscience of the world.

Herzl thought his plan out carefully, to the last dramatic detail. A magnificent *coup de théâtre*, he hoped, would compel men to serious thought. Before the duel he would write a letter fully explaining his motives. If Lueger should shoot him, "The letter would tell the world that I fell victim to this most unjust movement. Thus my death might at least improve the minds and hearts of men."

But if he shot Lueger, or Schönerer, or Prince Liechtenstein, he would turn his prosecution in court into a show trial against anti-Semitism. He would deliver a magnificent address; first he would express regrets at the "death of an honorable man," in the manner of Morès, who had stabbed Captain Mayer and eulogized him afterward. Then he would present the court with a detailed analysis of the Jewish tragedy. It would be a "powerful speech" in the manner of Lassalle. It would impress world opinion, shake the court, move the jury, inspire respect, and lead to his acquittal. This would not be the end of the affair. The Jews of Austria would undoubtedly now offer to elect him to parliament. But he would decline, for he could not build a political career as a people's representative "over the dead body of a man."

It is not clear why he never carried out this plan. The flamboyant, as well as the suicidal, element was entirely in character. In a diary entry over two years later, he referred to it as a dream he had had during his "period of uncertainty."

He was groping in the dark for an idea, a dramatist's plot, a happy stage effect that would instantly, as in Greek tragedy, result in cathartic release. He had no faith in conventional committees, formed to combat this or that evil. In their inefficacy they were comparable to charitable societies created after great floods or earthquakes.

In January 1893 the founder of just such a committee approached Herzl to request his collaboration on a planned magazine. The Viennese Society to Combat Anti-Semitism had been founded in 1890. It was led by Berta von Suttner, the well-known pacifist and future Nobel Prize winner, and her husband, Gundaccar; Professor Hermann Nothnagel, a famous stomach specialist; Johann Strauss, the Waltz King; and Baron Friedrich Leitenberger, a leading industrialist. The origin of the Society to Combat Anti-Semitism was characteristically Austrian. The Austrian poet Peter Rosegger, one of the founders, originally suggested naming it "Society to Combat *Nationalism*." But Professor Nothnagel had objected, "Let us stick to anti-Semitism. This is a disease that can still be healed. The nationalist malady is incurable."

Herzl's answer to Baron Leitenberger's invitation to participate in the society's work was evasive. Another little magazine preaching to the converted would achieve little. On the other hand, he told Leitenberger, "half a dozen duels might raise the social position and prestige of the Jews immensely." Furthermore, Jews simply must cast off all these "peculiarities for which they are rightly resented." The only real solution would be the complete disappearance of Jews through conversion and intermarriage.

Leitenberger was annoyed by this response. Herzl's suggestion that Jews should engage their detractors in duels—or convert *en masse* to Christianity—was all right for "charming chatterers" making conversation at a party; as a practical policy it was essentially irresponsible. Those seriously concerned with combating the poison of racism, Leitenberger wrote, could not even consider such "coquettishness."

He could not have struck a more sensitive spot. Herzl reacted as though he had been bitten. "Coquettishness? Only an idle chatterer? Your judgment is hard. But is it true?" he wrote Leitenberger in the longest letter he ever wrote, before or since. It took four days to compose. On twenty-two tense pages, scribbled in his fine, clear handwriting, he poured out his heart as he tried to clarify, to himself as well, a position still considerably confused. Several drafts of this letter exist in his files. He wrote and rewrote again and again.

I observe the Jewish problem from many sides. What would you say, for example, if I did not deny there are good aspects of anti-Semitism? I say that anti-Semitism will educate the Jews. In fifty years, if we still have the same social order, it will have brought forth a fine and presentable generation of Jews, endowed with a delicate, *extremely sensitive* feeling for honor and the like.

I myself would never convert, yet I am in favor of conversion. For me the matter is closed, but it bothers me greatly for my son Hans. I ask myself if I have the right to sour and blacken his life as mine has been soured and blackened. . . . When he grows up I hope he will be too proud to abjure his faith, though evidently he will have as little of it as I.

Therefore one must baptize Jewish boys before they must account for themselves, before they are able to act against it, and before conversion can be construed as a weakness on their part. They must disappear into the crowd.

Don't think that I carry coquettishness so far as to judge all Jews too harshly. On the contrary, considering their long oppression, they still cut an astonishingly good figure. . . . There is much to excuse in the Jew, who, after all, is living perpetually in enemy territory. . . .

Here was a new thought almost casually thrown out: *enemy territory*. Herzl proposed to change sides and join the victor. There must be an end to every calvary. In a subsequent letter Herzl informed Leitenberger that he was "pregnant with a new idea." Discarding his plan to shoot or be shot in a duel with Lueger, he concocted a second scheme, even more fantastic and theatrical than the first.

Herzl's new scheme was an extravaganza with a cast of millions. It would start in Rome. Herzl would go to the Pope and say to him, "Help us against anti-Semitism. In return I shall initiate a great mass movement for the free and honorable conversion of all Jews to Christianity." It would be a "diplomatic peace treaty, concluded behind closed doors." But its sequel would be public.

The mass conversion of all Jews, or most, would take place in a series of magnificent pageants staged in broad daylight. In Vienna the pageants would take place on Sunday at noon, in St. Stephen's, the city's main cathedral, where each year on Corpus Christi, the aged Emperor Franz Josef himself led his nation in prayer. The festive procession of converting Jews would enter the vast Gothic vaults amid the pealing of bells. Not in shame, as individual Jews had converted until now, "but with proud gestures," the great mass would flock to the cross. The leaders of the movement—Herzl in particular—would not themselves enter the cathedral, but would remain the last Jews on earth, or at least in Austria. As the last of the Jews, free and honorable, they would propagate conversion to the faith of the majority. By escorting the people only to the threshold of the church while themselves remaining outside, they would elevate the entire performance with a touch of righteousness and candor.

As was his custom, he thought out the entire scenario down to its most minute details. He already saw himself arriving solemnly at the cathedral square in frock coat, marching at a measured step, the heavy peal of bells resounding in his ears. He heard himself in discourse with the Archbishop of Vienna. In his imagination he stood before the Pope. Both the Archbishop and the Pope would be sorry that Herzl did not take the crucial step, but would merely press the cross into his people's hands and send his conversion message flying across the world.

On May 20, 1893, Julie Herzl gave birth to a third child, a girl named Trude (Margarethe). Her birth reaffirmed Herzl in his resolve to spare his children the agony of their parents. He set out to win the publishers of the Neue Freie Presse to his great plan. He hoped that the influential newspaper, which for so many Austro-Hungarian Jews was a bible of enlightened citizenship, would propagate the idea. An opportunity to approach the publishers presented itself in June 1893, when Herzl took his family home to Austria for a summer vacation.

Edouard Bacher and Moritz Benedikt, copublishers of the Neue Freie Presse, met his proposal with derision and weighty counterarguments. Bacher appreciated Herzl as a charming feuilletoniste, a darling of the Viennese reading public, and a boon to the newspaper's circulation; but he did not take him very seriously as a political strategist. It was not the first time that he rejected Herzl's political advice. The previous December Herzl had suggested that the Presse revive the flagging cause of Austrian liberalism (and take the wind out of the Socialists' sail) by demanding universal suffrage. Bacher had rejected that proposal, as he now derided Herzl's new one.

Benedikt was much more sympathetic and forthcoming. He was a heavyset man of sharp intelligence, a native of Moravia and a brilliant editorialist who, it was said, "combined the pathos of liberalism with that of a chief rabbi." Benedikt heard Herzl out. He too rejected the plan as frivolous and impractical. "Besides," he added, "the Pope would not even receive you!" Herzl argued in vain. But one thing in Benedikt's response struck him as being true.

"For a hundred generations your line has preserved itself within the field of Judaism," Benedikt said. "Now you propose to set yourself up as the terminal point in this process. This is audacious. You cannot do it. You have no right."

7

Disappointed, Herzl returned to Paris. He was sure of himself as a would-be savior, but only half-sure of his ideas. He returned to his regular work, commenting on the daily news and the people who made it. Love, or social distraction, sometimes compensates the disappointed man of ambition; such rewards were denied to this luckless husband, who disliked social events.

The French political crisis, meanwhile, was mounting steadily. It seemed to be a crisis of civilization as a whole. For many observers the tone was set by Renan, who, when asked by Paul Déroulède to join the League of Patriots, gave this characteristic answer: "Young man, France is dying. Do not trouble her in her agony." The persistent mood of despondency was enhanced by a swift succession of new financial scandals, more anarchist terror, corruption and incompetence in official quarters, and the violence of party factions.

Groping his way through the bewildering uncertainties, Herzl saw himself as a "David Copperfield" who had "mastered the terrible secret of stenography . . . night after night I write down prophecies that never materialize, confessions of faith that are never acted upon, declarations that only lead to nowhere." There was no relaxation in his obsession with the Jewish tragedy. He realized now the naïve innocence of his conversion scheme of only months before. Clearly, the problem was not really religious. "Gone are the days when people slaughtered one another over forms of the Lord's Supper. Today it is a question of the people's daily bread at lunch. The Jewish problem is neither national nor religious, but social."

On the eve of the French general elections of 1893 he made an extensive tour of the provinces. The elections were overshadowed by incredible scandals of corruption. In Lille, a citadel of French socialism, Herzl attended a rally featuring Paul Lafargue, Karl

Marx's erratic son-in-law. Lafargue entered the hall and shook
hands with the local police chief, "a fat man with a gold watch
chain," who attended the meeting in his official capacity. The irony
of their friendly handshake did not escape Herzl. "There will come a
day when one will probably have the other jailed or executed."
Lafargue opened his speech with an assault on the Jews, to thunderous applause. Herzl was appalled. He was seized by deep pity
for the audience of workers, and also by a "physical realization of
their latent power." They were hardworking and miserable, the
first unlucky generation of the new machine age. Could their difficult lot be changed? "Their fate is similar to that of Jews who
happen to be living in an anti-Semitic age," Herzl wrote. "Jews of a
later generation will see happier days. Those alive now are just
badly off."

In October he went to Toulon to cover a ceremonial visit of
the Russian fleet. The spectacular pageant marked the growing
rapprochement between republican France and the most backward
regime in Europe. Large crowds lined the streets of Toulon to
cheer the Russian admiral. The instant euphoria generated by the
visiting Russians prompted Herzl once more to ponder "the phenomenon of the masses": the apparent ease by which they were
manipulated by the state, "held together, and their feelings
whipped up" by cleverly concocted symbols.

While in Toulon he contracted a severe fever, which was diagnosed as malaria. His medical treatment was inadequate. An injection of quinine produced swelling abscesses on his thighs, which
required surgery. The abscesses reappeared and had to be operated
on once again. Herzl was bedridden for weeks, and for some time
thereafter had to walk on crutches. He suffered great pain.
Whether the rash of abscesses was the result of quinine injections
delivered by an inept doctor, or the recurrent venereal infection of
his youth, cannot now be determined. Much remains unclear about
this illness and the circumstances of the treatment. It is enough to
say that whatever struck Herzl at Toulon, he was never to be
wholly cured of it. His heart may have been permanently damaged.
His subsequent fits of fainting, his listlessness, and frequent spells
of fever and of brain anemia have been attributed by those who
knew him to his days at Toulon.

His recovery was difficult and prolonged. During the period of
enforced idleness he returned to writing for the theater, a vocation
that a year before he had abjured for all time. He wrote *Die Glosee*
(*The Comment*), a play in verse set in thirteenth-century Bologna.

Dedicated to "my dear parents," the play was another comment on the difficulties of marriage. He wrote it in eight bedridden days of feverish excitement. It was Herzl's final effort at pure poetry, and he convinced himself that it marked his breakthrough to artistic perfection and maturity.

"In a few years the theaters will be looking for *The Comment* and produce it everywhere," Herzl wrote an acquaintance. But the Vienna Burgtheater promptly rejected it. At the same time Herzl was surprised to learn from Max Burckhardt, the director, that the Burgtheater now wanted to produce his old farce, *Tabarin.* Herzl had written it as a student ten years before and had "completely forgotten" it.

The decision did not increase Herzl's faith in the sagacity and good taste of theater directors, but he took it in stride. "When a theater director makes a promise and still keeps it afterward, fall on your knees and kiss the seam of his coat in grateful ardor."

That summer (1894) he returned to Austria to spend his vacation at Alt-Aussee, in the company of Arthur Schnitzler, Hugo von Hofmannsthal, and Richard Beer-Hofmann. The mountains and cool lakes soothed his spirit and body, weakened by prolonged illness and subsequent hard work.

The company was both stimulating and depressing. The men of Young Vienna, already on the threshold of great fame, combined the melancholy of Werther with the precocious aestheticism of Dorian Gray. In lyrics of sweet weariness and playlets overloaded with sad introspection, they were the self-appointed heralds of an impending apocalypse. The twenty-year-old prodigy Hofmannsthal, in particular, exemplified the utopian attempt to evade the crisis of the time by retreating into the world of language—"fired only by his intellect, for his heart remained cold."

Hofmannsthal was Old Austria incarnate. His Polish Jewish great-grandfather had been knighted in 1827. His grandfather had converted to Catholicism and married an Italian countess. His mother was a German of peasant stock. Poland, Italy, Judaism, Germany, Catholicism, the nobility, and the peasantry were all part of his makeup. For all who loved the universalism of Old Vienna, Hofmannsthal was the ideal Viennese. Some considered his meteoric appearance as heralding a new dawn. It really portended the end.

On Whitsunday of 1894, only a few weeks before he met Herzl in Alt-Aussee, Hofmannsthal had noted in his diary: "How strange it all is, that in Vienna we are perhaps the last thinking men; the very last men of soul; that afterward there will probably come a great barbarism."

Herzl spent many hours in the company of Schnitzler and Hofmannsthal, conversing and debating, and taking long walks together in the woods. He felt alternately intrigued, envious, and embarrassed by their talent. On one occasion the company took a boat ride on the lake. Herzl decided to read them his new verse play, *The Comment*. Beer-Hofmann grumbled: "Now he starts reading it, when one can't get off." The play was not greeted with any enthusiasm. Herzl was made to feel that as a playwright he might really be bankrupt. His manner did not enhance his standing with the company. Even Schnitzler—more attached to Herzl than the others and warmly seeking his friendship—was put off by Herzl's insistence on "dominating the conversation."

From Alt-Aussee, Herzl went to Baden to join his parents at their summer resort. Here, at the favorite watering place for wealthy Viennese Jews, the air was strained. The talk was of anti-Semitism. Almost daily, the newspapers carried reports from Vienna, Berlin, Paris, and Prague of anti-Semitic incidents and violence in the streets. A well-known Jewish sculptor had been struck down with a stick by a politician on the Vienna Naschmarkt: "You *Saujud* [Jewish pig], you probably wanted to pick my pocket!"

The harassment of Professor Nothnagel, head of the Society to Combat Anti-Semitism, by rabble-rousing students at the University of Vienna brought forth this editorial in the *Neue Freie Presse*: "Nothnagel stands so exalted, the sewer of anti-Semitism does not even touch the soles of his feet. He needs no defense, but the reputation of the university must be protected." But the student riots continued.

Under the depressing impact of these events, Herzl drove out to the neighboring village of Hinterbrühl, to visit Ludwig Speidel, his colleague on the *Neue Freie Presse* and a well-known theater and music critic. As the two men walked over the green meadows of Hinterbrühl, they naturally got to talking of the "problem." Herzl has left a record of the conversation.

I understand what anti-Semitism is about [Herzl said]. Through no fault of our own we Jews have retained ourselves as a foreign body among the various nations. In the ghetto we took on a number of antisocial qualities. We cling to money because [in the Middle Ages] they flung us onto it. . . . Our character has been corrupted by oppression. It must be restored

through some other kind of pressure. Actually, anti-Semitism is
a consequence of the emancipation of the Jews. But peoples
who lack historical understanding—that is, all of them—do not
see us as the historical product of cruelty. . . . Still, anti-Semitism
might be useful to the Jewish character. Education is accomplished only through hard knocks. A Darwinian mimicry will
set in. The Jews will adapt themselves. They are like seals, cast
by an accident of nature into water. . . . Once they return to dry
land and are allowed to remain there for a few generations,
their fins will become feet again.

Speidel only shrugged his shoulders and replied, "This is a
universal-history concept." He was more concerned for the immediate here-and-now than for the overall historical view.

Herzl then said good-bye and drove off into the gathering
darkness back to his parents' house in Baden. As he sat in his
carriage, slumped and huddled in thought, two young officer cadets
yelled in at him: "*Saujud!*" Herzl was stung with rage. He whirled
around in his seat, but the two men were already far behind. A
moment later his impulse to fight vanished. He consoled himself
with the thought that the insult had not been directed at him
personally but merely at his "Jewish" nose and beard, which they
had glimpsed in the semi-darkness.

As the carriage sped on, Herzl breathed heavily. "What a curious aftermath," he thought, to his just-concluded sermon on universal history. "World history is of no use in such a situation." Nor
Darwin; one's feet remained heavy as clay fins.

8

"It is of no use." Was there nothing to be done? Returning to
Paris in October, Herzl searched his mind. He sensed he had a
rendezvous with fate. He groped with the shadows. He was driven
by a sense of urgency, even stronger than before. He conceived a
new plan; he would tackle the problem journalistically. He would
prepare a world survey of the "Jewish condition" fashioned after
Heine's celebrated analysis of France under Louis Philippe,
Französische Zustände (*French Conditions*). He would visit and
describe the different places where the accidents of history had
scattered communities of Jews. He wanted particularly to see the
great house of Jewish bondage in czarist Russia, Galicia, and

Romania. Later he would go to the Orient. And finally he would analyze the failure of emancipation in the free countries of Western Europe. He would use his newly acquired skills as a political reporter to expose the Jews' undeserved misfortunes.

He also planned to visit the dozen or so new Jewish colonies that had been established in Palestine since 1882 by young enthusiasts from Russia and Romania in a Jewish version of the Russian back-to-the-people, back-to-nature movement. He did not as yet contemplate a national solution. On the contrary, he still felt that there was no point in leading the Jews back to their historic homeland in Palestine. For if they really "returned home one day, they would discover the very next day that they are no longer one people. For centuries they have been rooted in diverse cultures and nationalisms, different from each other, group by group."

His worldwide survey, then, would be mainly an appeal to the world's conscience. Herzl hastened to prepare for it. He told his publishers that he was tiring of his Paris post and would like to leave it. The publishers were reluctant, but he insisted. The crisis now came to a head. On October 19, 1894, Herzl was sitting in the Paris studio of the Austrian sculptor Friedrich Beer, who was doing a model of his head. Inevitably the conversation turned to the problem weighing so heavily on Herzl's heart. Herzl spoke heatedly. He shouted at Beer: "It does a Jew no good to be an artist like you! As an artist you have freed yourself from the taint of money. You are not a usurer! Nor a stock-exchange Jew! But the curse still clings! We cannot get out of the ghetto!"

Beer was sympathetic but felt that Herzl was grossly exaggerating. Herzl insisted that in Austria especially, the position of Jews was becoming untenable. He worked himself into a frenzy; his face glowered. He might translate his ideas into the language of the theater, he said. Yes, he would write a political play! His play would both shock and arouse. "Beer," he shouted, "if I weren't a hired laborer I would run off to Ravello and finish that play in two weeks!"

Beer made a dubious face and Herzl took his leave. Down in the cold rue Descombes, his excitement still glowed within him. Yes, he would write a political play. He quickened his pace. He felt as though he were in a dream. One dramatic sequence after another shot through him "like blocks of basalt stone." Before he reached the nearby place Péreire, the plot of the new play was clearly outlined in his mind.

On the following day he skipped his daily session with the

sculptor; he kept Beer waiting until the middle of the next month. In "three blissful weeks of frenzied glow and labor, tears and laughter," he finished the play. Herzl at first called it *The Ghetto*, later *The New Ghetto*. He dedicated it "in hearty friendship" to Max Nordau, the leading prophet of *fin de siècle* doom. Nordau's sensational new best-selling book, *Degeneration*, with its violent attack on all modernity—from Ibsen to Zola and Manet, and from Tolstoi to Dr. Jaeger's woolen clothing—was just then stirring up controversy everywhere. The dedication of Herzl's play to the reactionary Nordau is of some significance, but Herzl was not *fighting* modernity; he meant to reform it. He intended his drama to be "a piece of Jewish politics"; the emphasis was on politics, not on drama. The main point of the play was that new, invisible ramparts had replaced the ghetto walls of old. The best Jews were making vain attempts to break out. But the world was still deaf to their suffering.

The New Ghetto, Herzl's first departure from pure art or light comedy, is probably the best play he ever wrote. To a modern reader the plot might seem melodramatic, but it is not really more so than those of his contemporary George Bernard Shaw. The main characters and some of the dialogue, taken from Herzl's own life, are sketched with great skill and feeling. The play's tragic hero, Dr. Jakob Samuel, is a high-minded Jewish lawyer, a combination of Herzl and Kana. Samuel's wife, Hermine, like Julie, is blond, spoiled, the extravagant daughter of rich, vulgar "stock-exchange" Jews; like Julie she does not understand her husband.

Samuel, like Herzl, vainly attempts to break out of the moral and social Jewish ghetto, and is killed in the process by an anti-Semitic aristocrat. Samuel's traumatic memory of a duel engagement he had been unable to keep in his youth, because of his father's illness, seems contrived until one remembers that it happened to Herzl himself. In the last scene he does keep a duel engagement to defend his honor as a Jew, and is killed. His death was meant to serve as a warning that the situation of the Jews in the "enlightened" West was untenable.

As a period piece, the play still makes for fascinating reading; as a landmark in the development of a politician, it suggests the inner motivations of a future leader of men. It shows Herzl's childhood traumas, the frustration of his energies in the confines of family life, and his main inner motive—wounded pride. A modern reader is likely to be embarrassed by some of Herzl's caricatures of gross, materialistic Jews, even rabbis who talk of nothing but the stock exchange; but just as he castigates Jews for the faults they developed under persecution, so he attacks Gentiles for their brutality and prejudice. In a period heavy with embarrassed Jewish apologetics, Herzl's *New Ghetto* offered refreshing candor. In the final scene, the dying Samuel cries, "Jews, my brothers, there'll come a time when they'll let you live—*when you know how to die. . . . (Murmurs:)* I want to get out. . . . (*With all his strength:*) *Out! Out-of-the-Ghetto!*"

Herzl hoped that through the frenzy of "this dramatic eruption," which had preoccupied him for seventeen days, he would also write himself "free of the subject matter." On the contrary, he only found himself more deeply involved with it. For the first time, apparently, since his childhood, he went to a synagogue. He visited the Jewish temple in the rue de la Victoire. It was not religion he sought, for he had none; he wanted human contact.

He found the service festive and moving. Many things reminded him of his childhood and the temple next door to his birthplace on the Tabakgasse in Budapest. He looked at the men crowded in the aisles and thought he "recognized a family likeness in their faces: bold, misshapen noses; shy and cunning eyes." A year ago, he would have recoiled at such comparisons; two months before, he had still thought Jews had no common traits. He now realized that what might be lacking in comparison to other peoples was amply compensated for by the existential anguish generated by a common enemy. He said to himself, "I must do something for the Jews."

There was, first, his new play. Herzl knew it would be difficult to sell. He decided to "hide and bury" himself under the pseudonym Albert Schnabel. In order to keep the secret, he even abandoned his original plan to read the play to Max Nordau. Schnitzler was the only man in whom he confided, and to Schnitzler he also explained his decision to hide under a pseudonym: "It is arrogance, cowardice, or shame, or whatever you want. But so it is . . . in the special case of this play I intend to hide my private parts even more than is usual." He devised an elaborate plan whereby Schnitzler would anonymously submit the play to German and Austrian theater directors.

Schnitzler went along with the subterfuge, but he voiced some serious reservations. In his opinion, *The New Ghetto* was too harsh and unfair. Were Jews really as unsympathetic as Herzl portrayed them in his play? Was it fair to say that *they do not know how to die*?

[*Schnitzler to Herzl, November 17, 1894:*] There was a time when Jews were burned by the thousands at the stake. In this respect your drama . . . slips off course. Nor is it true that in the ghetto . . . all Jews ran about oppressed or inwardly sordid. There are other Jews—and these are the ones most hated by the anti-Semites. Something like this ought to be said in the play too. Your play is bold—I should like it to be defiant as well.

[*Herzl to Schnitzler, December 17, 1894:*] I do not think there are too few "sympathetic" [Jewish] figures. And even if there are too few, should I falsify my misanthropy? Just where no one will believe me, shall I present a show of wonderful, noble people? . . . . The play is not intended to defend the Jews, or to save them, but merely to pose the question for discussion . . . if it only gets onto the stage. I don't care about the rest.

[*Schnitzler to Herzl, December 19, 1894:*] . . . about the sympathetic characters. I didn't disapprove of them for theatrical reasons. But simply on the grounds of truth. There are more sympathetic characters even in the milieu depicted by the author.

[*Herzl to Schnitzler, January 1895:*] I'll continue on my way. My new way! There is something blissful in this too.

Despite his reservations, Schnitzler did his best to have the play produced. He tried half a dozen theaters in Vienna, Berlin, and Prague. He met with complete failure everywhere. Jewish directors were shocked by the play's impertinence. Non-Jewish directors were afraid it might be misunderstood. Nobody as yet knew who the author was. Schnitzler, with a deep feeling for Herzl, continued to press his case. But his efforts were spent in vain. Schnitzler's loyalty and perseverance moved Herzl deeply; the episode brought the two men closer than ever before.

Herzl was very lonely and needed friendship badly. In November his tense relations with Julie had led to a new separation. Julie and the children returned to Vienna to stay with her parents. The luxurious household was dissolved, and Herzl moved to a hotel on the rue Cambon. In his loneliness Herzl clung to Schnitzler. He begged to be shown the manuscript of Schnitzler's latest play, *Liebelei*. Schnitzler apparently hesitated. In his dejection Herzl cried out (February 16, 1895):

Why don't you send me your play? Have I not come close enough to you in our secret conspiracy of recent months? I have a great need for a good friendship. I almost feel like advertising in the newspapers: "Man in prime of life seeks friend in whom he can confide all his weaknesses and stupidities." . . . Am I too shy or suspicious? Or are my eyes too sharp? I can't find anyone among my acquaintances here.

Schnitzler's reply to this outcry has not been preserved. Every theater to which he had dutifully submitted Herzl's play under the pseudonym of Albert Schnabel had refused it point-blank. Herzl now instructed Schnitzler to reveal his identity, yet even this was of no avail. It pained Schnitzler to tell Herzl the bad news, for fear of depressing him even further. At Herzl's insistence he finally came out with the truth. Dejected, Herzl wrote back, "Perhaps the play is really that bad . . . Perhaps you haven't criticized enough. . . . Should I break my miserable pen?"

9

In the two months that Herzl was sitting on the edge, nervously expecting *The New Ghetto* to be produced somewhere, another, real-life drama began to unfold before his eyes. In October 1894, while Herzl was still in the "blissful glow" of work on *The New Ghetto*, French army Captain Alfred Dreyfus, a Jew, was arrested on a trumped-up charge of high treason. Dreyfus' arrest and conviction in secret trial began an *affaire* so sordid that all the preceding scandals seemed minor by comparison.

The celebrated affair, which would bedevil France for almost a decade, is so well known that only its impact on Herzl need be mentioned here. The leading characters, as Hannah Arendt has observed, could have stepped from a Balzac novel. Alfred Dreyfus came from a distinguished upper-middle-class family of Jewish civil servants, scientists, and businessmen. He was captain of artillery assigned to the General Staff. A man of medium height and intelligence, his stiff carriage, thin lips, moustache, and monacle made him resemble an anarchist's caricature of the abominable militarist. In his prison on Devil's Island, and even to the very end of his life, this staunch soldier and blind patriot did not understand what the *affaire* was all about, that it was not merely a judicial error but a deliberate frame-up by anti-Semites in search of a scapegoat. Dreyfus incarnated the whole tragedy of emancipated Jewry, trapped in Herzl's "new ghetto," robbed of inner freedom.

Anatole France said Dreyfus was "the same type as the officers who condemned him. In their shoes he would have condemned himself." Only his closest relatives believed in his innocence. The Jewish bourgeoisie of France was too frightened, or deluded, to rally to his cause. Anxious to assimilate, eager to conform, many adopted their own frivolous brand of anti-Semitism. Bernard Lazare, the great defender of Dreyfus, complained that for the three dozen or so men in France who were ready to defend Dreyfus, thousands of French Jews were ready to stand guard on Devil's Island.

Legend has it that Dreyfus' trial and degradation convinced Herzl of the necessity of a Jewish exodus from Europe and planted in his mind the need for an independent Jewish state. The truth is that the Dreyfus affair was merely the last straw.

Like most people, Herzl at first believed in Dreyfus' guilt. Two days after the first announcement of Dreyfus' arrest, Herzl wrote: ". . . the fact that the arrest of this General Staff captain has been *admitted* and that the matter was submitted today by the War Minister to the cabinet, indicates that Dreyfus has really committed the ignominious act." For two more weeks Herzl's cables reflected a tacit assumption of Dreyfus' guilt. The Vienna-based editorial writer of the *Neue Freie Presse* was more circumspect. An editorial entitled "Sniffing for Spies" (November 17, 1894) complained that in France, as in Austria, there was a tendency to be "hasty in the arrest of alleged spies."

By mid-December the first notes of doubt cropped up in Herzl's daily dispatches. His reports did not reflect everything that was happening to him, or in Paris. For by now the howl of the Paris mob on the place de la Concorde, screaming "Down with the Jews!" like dogs baying at the moon, was rising almost daily into Herzl's hotel window in the nearby rue Cambon. He described the chilling memory of that experience a few years later to a Zionist audience. One Jew an alleged traitor, and down with all Jews? "Where? In republican, modern, civilized France, one hundred years after the Declaration of the Rights of Man!" What was to be expected of less civilized countries?

As he watched the demonstrations, he sensed a kind of evil-smelling fog rise from the massed crowd, only to redescend on it like poisoned vapor. He thoroughly disliked Dreyfus as a man, but he decided that for psychological reasons Dreyfus simply could not be guilty.

He argued this point with Colonel Pannizardi, the Italian military attaché in Paris. Pannizardi believed in Dreyfus' guilt because, in his view, it seemed inconceivable that seven military men of honor would conspire to falsely condemn a fellow officer. Herzl disagreed. Jews were not better than other people, he said; but a *Jewish officer* of Dreyfus' particular background and mentality was a special case. As Herzl saw it, Dreyfus was so obsessed with notions of honor, so anxious to be 100 percent French, that he was psychologically incapable of being a German spy. Moreover, Dreyfus was independently wealthy; only ambition had driven him to a military career. He was not likely to risk his own honor by committing an act of treason.

Herzl was in the crammed courtroom when Dreyfus was pronounced guilty and sentenced to life imprisonment. A heavy, relieved "Ahhh" swept through the audience. One man shouted, *"Vive la Patrie!"* Two weeks later Herzl attended the convict's public degradation. An icy wind swept through the vast courtyard of the École Militaire. A great crowd of spectators waited outside the École to see the degraded man led away in chains. Only officers and a few journalists, Herzl among them, were admitted to the courtyard.

Herzl stood huddled in a heavy coat. The sky was low and dark gray. Across the wet expanse of stone, Dreyfus raised his right hand and cried, "I swear and declare that you are degrading an innocent man. *Vive la France!"* The last word was drowned by the rumble of drums. Then Dreyfus was stripped of his insignia. His sword was broken and thrown at his feet. Dreyfus stood without moving an eyebrow. Herzl, across the yard, was impressed by his firm demeanor. In Herzl's eyes the scene was symbolic in a wider sense: the degraded man symbolized the Jew in modern society, conforming to its ways, speaking its language, thinking its thoughts, sewing its insignia onto his shoulders only to have them violently torn off on a gray winter morning to the ominous sound of drums. Dreyfus represented a stronghold, for which European Jews had fought, and were still fighting, but "which—let us not delude ourselves—is a lost one."

After his degradation, the convict was paraded before the troops. He passed a group of officers who screamed, "Judas! Traitor!" Dreyfus cried back, "I forbid you to insult me!" He was then handcuffed and handed over to ordinary gendarmes. As he passed the group of journalists he called, "You will tell all France that I am innocent." Some of the journalists threw back insults. The mob, surging at the iron gates, growled, "Death to the Jews." Herzl walked home in a state of "strange agitation" to write his dispatch for the day. In Vienna, that evening, his editors censored his story. "Death to the Jews" was changed to read "Death to the traitors." Bacher and Benedikt felt there was little need to breed more anti-Semitism in Vienna, which had so much already. The chilling howl could not, however, be erased from Herzl's consciousness.

10

On the following morning, the conservative French press glee-fully mocked Dreyfus' dignified protestations of innocence as a further example of Jewish cunning and duplicity. Léon Daudet, in *Le Figaro*, wrote that "the wretch was not a Frenchman. We all understood it from his deed, his demeanor, and from his face."

Herzl now finally made up his mind to lead a worldwide action on behalf of the Jews. Events elsewhere strengthened his determination. As he looked up from the humdrum of his daily work to view the world at large, it seemed to him that the whole of Western Europe, with the exception of England, was being seized by a veritable paroxysm of anti-Semitism. In the Lower Austrian Diet the anti-Semitic factions were approaching majority status. There were demands in February for the expulsion of all Jews from Austria and for confiscation of their property.

> *Representative Schneider:* We feed in Austria four million Jews who don't work. . . . Out with the Jews, I say, so Austria will be *wunderschön* again, and good. . . . Why shouldn't this people, this God-damned rabble, be exterminated from the face of the earth? (*Applause and sneering laughter among the anti-Semites, cries of indignation on the left.*)

In the Vienna municipal elections the anti-Semites more than doubled their strength. The council was now composed of seventy-one liberals and fifty-six anti-Semites, led by Karl Lueger, whom Herzl had once planned to challenge to a duel. Herzl was in Vienna in March during the elections attempting to sort out his family problems. He reached another reconciliation of sorts with Julie, and also arranged his transfer the following August back to Vienna as the new literary editor of the *Neue Freie Presse*. Everywhere he went in Vienna the talk was of Lueger. Bacher and Benedikt were gloomy. Lueger's rise to power was thought inevitable; Vienna would soon be the first European metropolis with an avowed anti-Semitic administration.

In the French National Assembly too the strength of the anti-Semites was growing. There were motions to ban all Jews from public service. The move was rejected, but only by 268 votes to 208. At the same time, in Russia the Czar's counsel and head of the Holy Synod, Konstantin Pobedonostsev, announced his solution to the Jewish problem: a third of the Jews would die out, a third would emigrate, and a third would convert. In Germany as well there were skirmishes in the *Reichstag*, where the anti-Semitic faction had increased its strength. All these events confirmed Herzl in his conviction that some drastic action on behalf of the Jews of Europe was urgently needed.

The French secret police was now intercepting his private mail. On March 21, 1895, a police report on Herzl noted his "hostility to France." He still moved through the sophisticated salons of Paris, which Proust later described, and "where Jews were regarded, like homosexuals, with sophisticated curiosity." But he wearily drew up a bitter balance.

He confessed his still vague plans to Alphonse Daudet, the writer. Daudet was an avowed anti-Semite, although less virulent than his son, Léon, the future fascist. Herzl appreciated Alphonse Daudet's frank admission of his prejudice. "I want to write a book for and on the Jews," said Herzl.

"A novel?"

"No, I would rather write a book for men."

"You are wrong," said Daudet. "A novel can reach farther. Think of *Uncle Tom's Cabin*."

Herzl went on talking with great passion. The Jews must take their fate into their own hands. Daudet was very moved: *"Comme c'est beau, comme c'est beau!"* he exclaimed.

But Daudet had put enough doubts in Herzl's mind, and he again thought of the "Jewish" novel which he had planned long ago in the Pyrenees, in order to write himself free of Heinrich Kana's ghost. But now Herzl himself, not Kana, would be the central figure. The hero of his novel would set out to find a new promised land where the wretched of the earth would find peace.

How Herzl later passed back from the idea of an earthshaking novel to a practical program of political action is unclear. It was a mystery to Herzl himself, as he wrote only a few weeks afterward. Herzl was one of many writers and artists in Paris who, before the Dreyfus affair, had maintained a pose of world-weariness and precocious detachment—and then, as a result of the affair, became passionately involved.*

In Herzl's case it quickly became evident that he had been miscast in his earlier role as a creative recluse and passive observer of events. Herzl's ecstatic awakening as a man of action was in fact tapping the darkest, innermost resources of his soul, resources for which Herzl the artist had groped in vain. Politically his life had gone full circle twice—from German nationalism to cosmopolitanism and from cosmopolitanism to a belief in a Jewish exodus from Europe.

Having finally made up his mind, he felt elated. He was sure he had broken through the nets of prejudice and reached a real, higher "understanding" of anti-Semitism. Anti-Semitism, as he now saw it, was in fact inevitable, a force of nature and of history, like the class struggle. But how, like Marx, would he harness the evil to produce good? His answer was that one must break the vicious circle that tied victims and culprits to each other in a mutually harmful embrace. First and foremost, a suitable territory must be found somewhere, and Jewish sovereignty over it properly negotiated. Emigration to the new territory must under no circumstances be furtive or clandestine but organized openly on a vast scale, with the full consent of the present host countries. There should be no haphazard or sporadic emigration, as there had been to Australia or America. Everything must be done with modern efficiency. The Jewish exodus from Europe would be a well-planned scientific operation. By the time the emigrants arrived at their destination, everything would be ready—housing, employment, educational facilities. The exodus would be financed by a worldwide Jewish national loan, but European governments, pleased to have solved their Jewish problem, would also willingly subscribe. It would be a blessing for all, and Herzl would enter history as one of the great benefactors of mankind. Confidently, he wrote, "They will pray for me in the synagogues, and in the churches as well."

His first step was to look for powerful allies. One potential ally was in Paris, living close by: the Jewish railroad king and philanthropist, Baron Maurice von Hirsch, one of the richest men in the world. In the last days of April 1895, Herzl wrote Hirsch the following letter.

---

* Emile Zola led the *Dreyfusards* with his famous *J'Accuse.* After Zola's death, the plan for a Zionist novel, which he apparently wrote in the aftermath of the *affaire,* was found among his papers.

Dear Sir:

When may I have the honor of calling on you? I should like to discuss the Jewish question with you. This is not to be an interview, nor a masked or open money matter. There are so many claims on your time that one cannot guard soon enough against suspicions of unsavory designs. I simply wish to discuss Jewish politics with you. Our discussion may have an effect on future times that neither you nor I will live to see.

Therefore I would ask you to arrange our meeting on a day when you can devote an uninterrupted hour or two to the matter. What I have in mind will interest you. But even though I am not telling you much by saying this, I should not want you to show this letter to the people around you. . . . Please treat it confidentially. Perhaps my name is not unknown to you. In any case, you know the newspaper which I represent here.

> Respectfully yours,
> Dr. Herzl
> Correspondent of
> the *Neue Freie Presse*

He put the letter aside and considered it for two weeks. When, after this interval, the letter still did not seem ridiculous, he mailed it. It marked the opening of Herzl's unusual political career. Herzl's greatest fear remained that Hirsch might see it as a journalistic extortion trick. But his mind was made up. Hirsch, the multimillionaire playmate of kings, should finance and head the new exodus as a new Moses, cast in gilt-edged securities. Herzl, in effect, was offering him a crown.

7

First Skirmishes

BARON MAURICE VON HIRSCH AUF GEREUTH was one of the more arresting characters of his time. Herzl was attracted by his enormous wealth, his philanthropy, and his alleged political power, which Herzl, like most contemporaries, overestimated.

Hirsch was a Bavarian nobleman who lived mostly in his French châteaus, on his vast estates in Hungary and Moravia, or in London. A man of pleasure, financier, sportsman, and amateur politician of surprisingly progressive views, he felt at home everywhere and nowhere. He was successively a citizen of Bavaria, Belgium, France, and Austria. His real passport was his money. He personified the "international financier" in an age before private entrepreneurs were dwarfed by the power of corporate conglomerates.

On both his mother's and father's sides Hirsch was descended from German court Jews, who had overcome their civic disabilities by padding the pockets of kings. His paternal grandfather had been knighted by the King of Bavaria in 1818 for services rendered in the Napoleonic Wars. Maurice von Hirsch was a tall, slim man of fine bearing. His jovial face was cut horizontally by an oversized handlebar moustache. He subscribed to socialist views but secretly financed the French and Spanish monarchists in order to enhance his standing with the old aristocracy. His fortune was estimated variously at 500 to 700 million francs. He was popularly known as "Turkish Hirsch" because he had first come into prominence as a builder of railroads in the Orient. He was richer than most Rothschilds, but unlike them he was never assimilated into Gentile society, except in England. There was something pathetic in this restless migrant's desperate attempts to "belong." He was a friend of the King of Bulgaria, the Prince of Wales, and the Austrian Crown Prince Rudolph, but in Vienna he was blackballed, as a Jew, by the Jockey Club and was never received in court.

His character was an extraordinary mixture of egotism and magnanimity. Conscious of his power, he was also afraid of it. He was one of the few rich men of his day who felt duty bound to share his wealth with the poor. If his wealth, like that of the Rothschilds, nurtured the anti-Semitic myth of Jewish world power, Hirsch in his own way felt guilty about it. His philanthropic enterprises were on a scale unheard of in his time. Having no legal heir—his only surviving son was illegitimate—he spent the largest part of his fortune helping poor Jews. It was estimated he spent some 400 million francs on Jewish charities alone. He intended above all to retrain the downtrodden Jews of Russia in agriculture and handicrafts. To this purpose he endowed a system of broad social aid and vocational training. When the Russian Czarevitch, the future Nicholas II, visited his English cousins at Sandringham in 1894, he was bewildered by the company; along with turf enthusiasts, there was Baron Hirsch, who on this occasion "was less interested in horses or even in railroad contracts than in philanthropic plans to succor the oppressed Russian Jews." Hirsch offered 50 million francs to the Russian government as a donation to finance vocational training of Jews. The Russian government refused his offer.

Despairing of the possibility of helping Russian Jews in their own country, he devised an ambitious plan to resettle hundreds of thousands as farmers in overseas territories. He harbored vague hopes of future Jewish sovereignty in these territories. At one point he had even considered Palestine, but as he noted in an 1891 memorandum, Palestine was too close to Europe and was likely sooner or later to be overrun by Russia, the archenemy of all Jews. He finally chose Argentina as the most suitable territory. He established the Jewish Colonial Association (JCA) with a capital of 180 million francs. Yet by 1895 only about six thousand Jews had emigrated to Hirsch's Argentine colonies.

This was the man Herzl approached in May 1895. Hirsch's first reaction to Herzl's letter was evasive. He was besieged by too many beggars and impostors to grant his time readily to hear yet another scheme. Hirsch answered Herzl through a secretary, pleading lack of time. He asked Herzl to submit his thoughts in writing.

Just as he received Hirsch's letter, news reached Herzl that the anti-Semite Karl Lueger had finally been elected lord mayor of

Vienna. He answered Hirsch in an irritated mood, but promised to prepare a written memorandum "as soon as I find the time." And he added pointedly: "What you have undertaken up till now has been as magnanimous as it has been misapplied, as costly as it has been pointless. Until now you have been only a philanthropist, a Peabody. I will show you how to become more."

This last remark apparently hit home. Reluctance gave way to curiosity, and Hirsch suddenly found time in his crowded schedule. He asked Herzl to visit him on the following Sunday. Herzl was gratified that he had judged the man correctly. In preparation for the interview, he made extensive notes, which have survived.

On Sunday he dressed with discreet care. "The day before, I had purposely broken in a new pair of gloves so that they might look new but not fresh from the shop. Rich people must not be shown too much deference." He always felt shy in the company of great or famous men. Now, on the threshold of his public career, he was more overwrought than ever. He had even prepared an answer in case Hirsch should offer him a job. "In your service? No! In that of the Jews? Yes!"

Hirsch's residence on the rue de l'Élysée—overlooking the palace of his hunting companion, the President of France—was only three blocks away from Herzl's hotel on the rue Cambon. Self-consciously, Herzl chose to drive up in a rented carriage. As he entered the palatial home—Hirsch had acquired it from the Bonaparte family for 2.3 million francs—he was stunned by its wealth and exquisite beauty. He had resolved not to let himself be impressed, but could not help it. He fought his intimidation by telling himself, "Wealth affects me only in the guise of beauty." He took in the grand stairway, the old paintings, the muted Gobelins hanging on the marble walls. "Donnerwetter," he thought to himself, "the Baron must be employing somebody in charge of good taste." A little "dazed," Herzl let himself be handed from one liveried valet to the next. He had just arrived in the billiard room when Hirsch emerged from his adjacent study. The Baron shook hands with him absentmindedly, asked him to wait, and disappeared once more.

His offhand manner certainly didn't make Herzl any less ill at ease. Through Hirsch's door Herzl recognized the voices of two Viennese gentlemen he knew, employees of one of Hirsch's charitable organizations. He was annoyed by the possibility that they might see him here, waiting in the anteroom like some miserable pleader. He suspected that Hirsch had arranged it on purpose. When the Baron finally reemerged, Herzl spoke brusquely: "Have you a full hour for me? If it isn't at least an hour, I would rather not start at all. I need at least that much time, only to hint at how much I have to say!"

"Just go ahead," the Baron smiled. "Just go ahead."

Herzl pulled out his notes. They were arranged under three headings: Introduction, Improvement of the Jewish Race, Emigration. He began a long speech: "Some things I say you will find too simple, and others too fantastic." Hirsch frowned. "But men are ruled by the simple and fantastic. It is astonishing, and commonly known, how unintelligently the world is ruled. . . . Through our two-thousand-year dispersion we Jews have been left without a unified political leadership. This is our greatest misfortune. It has done us more harm than all the persecutions, and has led us inwardly to rack and ruin."

He had hardly spoken for five minutes in this vein when the telephone rang. Herzl was sure that it had been prearranged. He was ready to tell Hirsch right away that he need not have himself called away on imaginary business; let him say outright whether he was willing to talk. But Hirsch gave orders over the telephone that he was not at home to anybody. Herzl was relieved by this unexpected turn. He was fencing all the time, and he took Hirsch's order as proof that he had gripped the man: "I knew . . . that he had let his guard down."

The interview, however, was not a success. It can be fairly reconstructed from Herzl's notes and diaries. Herzl's nervousness handicapped his every move. The would-be kingmaker was too anxious to convince Hirsch that he was not job hunting. Just as, the day before, he had bought a new pair of gloves and carefully crumpled them, so he now tried to outsnob the snob in his brocade-lined study. He did not present his case well. He shouted and lost the thread of his argument. Instead of speaking practically to this man of action, he spun generalities: "If only we had a united political leadership!" He forgot to say how this might be achieved, although he had outlined it in his notes. He knew little of the Baron's real thinking, but felt he had to straighten him out. He had only a vague idea of Hirsch's work so far, but bluntly told him that everything he had done was wrong.

"You are breeding *schnorrers* [beggars]," Herzl cried. "It is symptomatic that no people produces so much charity and so many paupers as the Jews. Charity debases the national character."

With this Hirsch readily agreed. But then Herzl lashed out

against Hirsch's experiments in Argentina. The results were poor, or nonexistent. Hirsch spoke up to contradict him, but Herzl insisted that he finish first.

"I hear that your Argentine Jews are debauched. One item rather shocked me—the first house you built was one of ill repute."

"Not true," Hirsch interjected. "That house wasn't built by my colonists."

"Never mind," said Herzl. "In any case, you should have started the whole thing differently. You drag these farm Jews overseas. They must think they will be supported by you forever. This does not promote eagerness to work. Whatever such an exported Jew may cost you, he isn't worth it. Anyway, how many such specimens could you transport? Fifteen, twenty thousand? There are many more than that on one single street of the Viennese Leopoldstadt." He raised his voice: direct means were utterly unsuitable to move masses of people, only indirect means were effective.

Hirsch smiled ironically. He was becoming annoyed. "Enough of this criticism," Herzl said wearily. What was to be done? First of all, whether they emigrate or not, the race must be improved on the spot. "It must be made strong for war, eager to work, virtuous." One cannot buy people on a retail basis, as Hirsch had tried to do. The mass must be seized by appeals to the imagination, by shining symbols, as in religion. With nations one must speak in a childish language, with flags, medals, songs. They can be led by hope and indefinite promises; by great rewards for courage, virtue, and achievements in the arts and sciences. In this way the world will learn there are good Jews too—so many of them. Thus also the moral level will be raised. . . .

"No, no, no!" Hirsch cried. "I don't want to raise the general level at all. All our misery comes from Jews who want to climb too high. We have too many intellectuals. I want to prevent Jews from pushing ahead too much. They should not make such great strides!"

Herzl froze. He was suddenly seized by the utter uselessness of this talk. Hirsch admonished him: the Argentine colonies were not that bad at all, except in the beginning. Now there were many decent people there. He would soon charter a fine English vessel and invite a hundred newspaper correspondents to see for themselves. "I am inviting you right now . . . the world will see that Jews make good farmers after all. As a result, maybe, they will be allowed to till the fields of Russia as well."

Herzl's patience was running out. "I did not interrupt you

although I hadn't finished. I was interested to hear just what you had in mind. But I realize it would be useless to present any further ideas to you."

Hirsch said patronizingly: "I do notice that you are an intelligent man." To Herzl this sounded as though he were being considered for a position in the Baron's bank. Hirsch also felt that he may have gone too far, and quickly added, "But you have such fantastic brain waves!"

Herzl rose. "Well, didn't I tell you before that it would seem either too simple or too imaginative to you?"

"Emigration would be the only solution," Hirsch said. "There are enough countries for sale."

Herzl shouted, "Who told you that I don't want to emigrate? It is all here in these notes! I shall go to the German Kaiser. He will understand me. He has been trained to be a judge of great things. . . ."

Hirsch blinked. Herzl put his notes in his pocket and concluded, "I'll tell the German Kaiser, 'Let our people go! We are strangers here!' He will understand our simple call. We want to go home! The German Reich, too, was born of dreams."

"Where will you get the money?" Hirsch asked mockingly. "Rothschild will subscribe five hundred francs."

"The money?" Herzl laughed. "I'll raise a Jewish national loan of ten million marks."

"A fantasy," said the Baron. "The rich Jews will give nothing. The rich are mean and care nothing for the sufferings of the poor."

"You talk like a socialist, Baron Hirsch."

"I am a socialist. I am ready to give away everything, but the others must do likewise."

Herzl did not take this charming suggestion any more seriously than it was intended. Herzl's time was up. As they shook hands, Hirsch said that this was not their last talk. "As soon as I come over from London again, you'll hear from me."

Herzl was calmer now. He said, "Whenever you wish." He descended the beautiful staircase again. It was clear to him that he had approached the Baron from the worst possible angle. Herzl, the intellectual Jew, and Hirsch, the rich and powerful Jew, had, in fact, much more in common than both then thought. The record of their meeting is fascinating for the curious student of the past. The initial presentation of a revolutionary program, destined ultimately to succeed, could not have been more badly staged and formulated than it was by Herzl in his conversation with Hirsch. Hirsch might have saved Herzl a host of subsequent troubles and perhaps have accelerated the success of Zionism by decades, long before the advent of Arab nationalism. His vast fortune might have bought the Zionists a Turkish charter for the colonization of Palestine at a time when such transactions were still possible, indeed not uncommon.

Later historians have chastised Hirsch for his shortsightedness; he "had immortality within his grasp." But Herzl had not really whetted his appetite. He managed to get through only six of his twenty-two pages of prepared notes. He never reached the point in his notes where he had intended to ask Hirsch to summon an international Jewish congress. The congress was to plan the establishment of a Jewish state under Hirsch's initial leadership. Herzl never found time to tell Hirsch that the congress would issue a proclamation to all Jews: "You are pariahs! Let us move out! The promised land is something we can take with us. We will build ourselves a new world. (I do not know yet where, perhaps in Argentina.) What? You love your cruel homelands? We will give them back to you, more beautiful, over there. We will build our own Paris, Rome, Vienna—whatever we like."

Herzl had had no time to say all this. He had also intended to add that a project like Hirsch's Argentine colonies was indeed necessary, only on a much vaster and political scale. The aim was attainable through diplomatic moves; it was possible to sway great masses by means of political dogma. But in his excitement he had not found time to say all this.

The liveried doorman opened the heavy gate. Outside, Paris was bathed in sunshine. Herzl was not disappointed, but rather stimulated and intrigued. He rushed home and immediately sat down at his writing desk.

2

Then and there he began the first volume of his political diaries. In the remaining nine years of his life the diaries mirrored his innermost thoughts, hesitations, and most secret plans. Their style is lucid, devoid of any self-indulgent pose or ornament; they remain fresh, immediate, and readable today. Herzl instinctively felt he was writing for posterity, and yet the diaries are marked by an honesty rare in modern political literature. They are the best record of his work—a confirmation of Dr. Johnson's dictum that every man's life could best be written by himself.*

On the first page Herzl inscribed the title, *Book One of the Jewish Cause*. The date is noteworthy. "Begun around Whitsunday, 1895." He was still so remote from Judaism that even as he was rallying to its cause, his calendar still observed the Christian holidays.

His new diary was radically different from the fragmentary, disjointed notes he had kept as a young man. He devoted it entirely to the cause, which already engrossed him almost totally. Herzl was in a kind of ecstasy, not unlike the mystic conversion of a Loyola, or the abrupt awakening of a Frantz Fanon: "For some time past I have been working on a task of infinite grandeur. I do not know today whether I shall carry it out. It looks like a mighty dream. But for days and weeks it possesses me beyond the limits of consciousness . . . it disturbs and intoxicates me."

It was another "volcanic eruption" shooting up within him, similar to the mood that had produced *The New Ghetto*. He wrote himself free of ideas that rose "like bubbles in a retort, which would burst if they found no outlet." The political thinker often shares with the artist an obsession with his own authentic sensations. There was now in Herzl that combination of man of action and man of letters that the historian with a psychological bent finds utterly fascinating—along with a humane candor likely to disarm the most cynical critic. As he watched and recorded his transformation from moody aesthete to man of fanatic, unbending will, he was alarmed; he even wondered, in writing, if he might be "insane."

The diary mirrors his loftiest dreams and his most bizarre ambitions with unabashed openness. Other historical figures have harbored similar fantasies; it is rare to find one admitting them so candidly. No better record exists to trace the growth of a political mind. Herzl informs us of his severe headaches, his sleepless nights, his royal ambitions for his son. He paints the detailed scenery, the ups and downs of his feverish moods. He describes the music he

---

* An abridged and censored version of the diaries was published in 1922. The censored version omitted Herzl's innermost thoughts, intimate prejudices, and personal ambitions. An uncensored English translation was first published in America in 1960; it has not been published in Israel. This biography is based on the complete, uncorrected German text preserved in Herzl's handwriting in the Zionist Archive, Jerusalem.

drank in to dispel his doubts, and the tears he shed while writing. He was perfectly aware that much of what he wrote was wild, even megalomaniacal. But he refrained from self-censorship so as not to hamper his inspiration. Aware that he might appear ridiculous, he recorded his fantasies with something like narcissist pleasure, and also with unswerving respect for the truth. For Herzl this was as much an artistic endeavor as it was political. "I think that for me life has ended and world history has begun . . . I shall be counted among the greatest benefactors of mankind. Or is this belief already megalomania?"

With great detail he outlined the principles and the *mise-en-scène* of the planned exodus into still undefined new territory. Theatrical ideas and political ideas overlapped: "Actually, in all this I am still the dramatist. I pick poor people in rags off the street. I put them in gorgeous costumes and have them perform for all the world a wonderful pageant which I compose."

First he wrote a long letter to Hirsch. He would soon come to regret its haughty tone, but it faithfully reflected his impetuousness in the aftermath of the interview. "Because of your impatience you heard only the beginning. Where and how my idea blossoms you did not get to hear." But no matter! The plan did not depend on Hirsch alone! "I would have liked to *use you* as a known and available force . . . but there are other forces." One was Herzl's pen. He promised Hirsch that he would soon be convinced of its tremendous power. Hirsch's desire to "lower" the Jews' general level was utterly wrong:

> Do you realize that you are pursuing a terribly reactionary policy—worse than that of the most absolutist autocracy? Fortunately your resources won't suffice. Your intentions are good. Heavens, I know that well. *That is why I should like to direct your will.* Do not be prejudiced because I am a younger man. In France, men of thirty-five are ministers of state, and Napoleon was Emperor. . . .
>
> I have already drawn up . . . the entire plan. I know all it involves: money, money, and more money; means of transportation, provisions for the multitudes . . . organization . . . treaties with heads of state . . . the construction of new, splendid sites. And before all that, a tremendous propaganda . . . pictures, songs . . . a flag. You might ask mockingly: "A flag? What's that? A stick with a rag on it?" No sir, a flag is much

more. With a flag you lead men . . . for a flag, men live and die.
In fact it is the only thing for which they are ready to die in
masses, if you train them for it.

Believe me, the politics of an entire people—especially a
people scattered all over the earth—can be manipulated only
through imponderables that float in thin air. Do you know what
went into the making of the German Empire? Dreams and
songs, reveries of black, red, and gold banners, all in a very
short time. Bismarck merely shook the tree that the vision-
aries had planted.

In practical terms, the exodus to the promised land constitutes an enormous feat of transportation, unprecedented in the
modern world. . . . I am going to raise a Jewish national loan.
Will you pledge fifty million marks after I raise the first hundred million? In return, I shall make you the top man.

During the next two or three weeks Herzl neglected his job
and closeted himself in his hotel room. He outlined the economic
and legal character of the exodus and the constitution of the new
state. He wrote day and night, standing, sitting at his desk, walking
along the street, at dinner, in bed, strolling in the park. For hours
he tramped about the Bois de Boulogne and the Tuileries "to dispel
the pangs of new trains of thought." The hot June air inflamed his
body. His days passed in a state of feverish exaltation. At night the
idea crept into his sleepy consciousness, and he would awake with
a start, unable to fall asleep again.

For inspiration and to dispel occasional doubts, Herzl turned
to Wagnerian music. He was enraptured by the music of the great
anti-Semite, whose memorial rites had been the occasion of his first
personal encounter with racism, in 1883. Herzl faithfully attended
every performance of Wagner at the Paris Opéra. "Only on those
nights when no Wagner was performed did I have any doubts about
the correctness of my idea." Such nights he spent brooding at home
in a state of nervous dejection.

At a performance of *Tannhäuser* on June 5, he resolved that as
soon as possible the new Jewish state must construct auditoriums as
splendid as the Paris Opéra. "Yes, I want to make use of the Jewish
love of luxury, in addition to other resources. The gentlemen [will
be] in full tails, the ladies dressed as lavishly as possible." The
opera made him think again of the "phenomenon of the crowd:
There they sit for hours, tightly packed, motionless, physically uncomfortable. And for what? For imponderables, the kind Hirsch

does not understand! For sounds! For music and vivid images!"
And he added, "I shall also cultivate majestic processions on great
festive occasions."

On the following day he wrote Teweles in Prague that he was
prey to the "mood of a Savonarola." Like Savonarola, in Lenau's
poem, he felt possessed:

> Lightning strikes, I am God's Knight,
> The solemn bond shall stand forever.

Teweles was taken aback. "The harmlessly joking Viennese
feuilletoniste . . . had suddenly become a fighter, a proselytizer, a
kind of prophet."

On June 6 he wrote down his order of procedure. The new
exodus "compares to that of Moses as a Shrove Tuesday play to a
Wagnerian opera." The plan entailed:

1. Fund raising.
2. Beginning of publicity. (It will cost nothing. The anti-
   Semitic press will be happy to help; the liberal press will
   be broken by threats of competition.)
3. Surveyors to begin looking for a suitable land.
4. Further publicity, on a vast scale. Let Europe laugh, swear
   —but let them talk of it.
5. Negotiations for possession of the new Zion and purchase
   of land.
6. Issuance of land priorities.
7. Purchase and construction of ships.
8. Continuous enlistment of *all* recruits, their assignment and
   training.
9. Beginning of publicity for the big subscription (the national
   loan).
10. Expedition to take possession of the land. News reports in
    all the newspapers.
11. Demarcation of provinces in the new land, and selection of
    sites for new cities.
12. The construction of embarkation centers, in the meantime,
    by workers from Russia, on the Italian or Dutch coast (de-
    pending on the site of the new territory).
13. Fare and freight contracts with the railroad companies. We
    must make a big profit on transportation.
14. To the German Kaiser. (Request privileges from him!)

A week earlier Hirsch had still been the cornerstone of his plans; now the Baron mattered very little. In his thoughts Herzl even felt "magnanimous" toward Hirsch. He might make him "vice-president." He laid down plans for an aristocratic constitution fashioned after that of medieval Venice, to be headed by an elected doge. He outlined a program for education, a seven-hour workday, and plans for mass entertainment ("as soon as possible—German and international theater, circuses, café-concerts, a Champs Élysées, a new Louvre"). Entire Jewish centers should be dug out and transplanted from the old world to the new; these would be entire environments where Jews were now feeling comfortable, and which they should be able to enjoy in the new territory as well.

He had very definite ideas on town planning. Everything must be very rational and carefully thought out, unlike the chaotic development of the European metropolis. "First dig the canals, sewage systems, etc.—then build roads and houses"; also "construct something like Palais Royal or the Venice Piazza San Marco." He passed feverishly from the particulars to the general, and back again to the details. "The ship of coffins! We take our dead with us."

As he was spinning such plans, his thoughts focused on his own future role. "A lot of toasts will be drunk to me." He would lead the movement, but would ask nothing for himself. "If the Rothschilds join with us, the first doge will be a Rothschild. I myself will never be a doge, for I wish to secure the state beyond the term of my own life." But he would appoint his beloved father as "first senator" and he hoped to be able one day to crown his son Hans as doge.

The details of the coronation ceremony occurred to him at Longchamps, while he was attending the Grand Prix horse races. Watching the President of France, Carnot, surrounded by the *Garde Républicaine* on horseback, Herzl devised a detailed ceremonial program, which he jotted down on his way back to town:

> The procession which starts at the doge's palace will be opened by *Herzl-Cuirassiers*. Then come the artillery and infantry . . . while all are marching in gold-studded gala uniforms, the high priests under canopies, the doge himself will wear the garb of shame of a medieval ghetto Jew: the pointed hat, the yellow badge. . . . Only, inside the temple we wrap a princely cloak about his shoulders and place the crown on his head. This will mean: "To us you are but a poor Jew. Never forget what we

have suffered. But in the eyes of the world you are our resplendent prince."

... When I thought that someday I might crown [my son]
Hans as doge ... and address him in the Temple in the presence of the great men of the land ... I had tears in my eyes.

With his playwright's sense of drama and an eye for vivid
images, he already saw himself placing the crown on his son's head.
He even decided on the exact text of the formal greeting he would
utter on this occasion. He would say, "Your Highness—my beloved
son!"

The following morning (June 10) was Hans's fourth birthday.
"I sent him a telegram to Vienna. 'Gentle kisses to my *Vaterkönig*
[father-king].'* That is what my mother calls him. And I think of
my dream."

He was conscious of a great task awaiting him, and knew the
dangers he might possibly have to face. "My personal security," he
noted, "will be the concern of a well-run secret police." Pausing one
day in the Tuileries, before Gambetta's statue, he noted, "I hope
the Jews will put up a more artistic one for me." The same day,
back in his room, he ruminated among old papers and came upon
the little note ("I'll be wearing galoshes like a businessman") that
he had written in San Sebastián on the eve of his move to Paris. He
felt that already in San Sebastián he had had premonitions of what
would come to pass. Referring to the note, he added, "Today I say,
'I shall associate with the lords of the universe as their equal.'" He
pictured himself dealing with the German Kaiser. The Kaiser
would say, "'I shall be grateful to you if you lead these unas-
similable people out.' This will lend me authority. It will make a
big impression on Jews."

And a few days later there was this remarkable reflection:

I should still be able to dazzle and divert myself—I will have
the opportunity for it as few men have.

But I shall no longer live only for myself. This I think is
now over. Just as [the Emperor] Franz Josef took leave of his
youth as he sadly mounted the throne.

I have a spiritual throne.

There's not much happiness up there. I already foresee
that.

---

* A mystifying term. Perhaps a family joke. Perhaps it echoes *Avinu-
Malkenu* (in Hebrew, "our father-king"), the appellation of God in the Hebrew
prayer.

3

Such flights of fancy must not be taken too seriously, except as an indication of Herzl's feverish excitement. They disappeared without trace as soon as he passed from planning to direct political action. Bolder conceits than his are more common than we realize in the history of political inspirations; Herzl simply had the courage to record his reveries. The borderline between politics and art was still blurred. The dramatic fantasies were accompanied by a keen political realism that was surprising under the circumstances.

He soon regretted his haughty letter to Hirsch and berated himself for his rashness. He had been stupid to write that at thirty-five Napoleon had been Emperor of France. Herzl knew well it "smacked of megalomania. What I really meant was that I too have the maturity of a statesman." In his subsequent letters to Hirsch he did his best to make amends. He proved correct in foreseeing the coming catastrophe and in his blunt assertion that a "Jewish state is a world necessity." Subsequent history has fully vindicated his insight, even though he may have reached it indirectly and through flights of egoistic fancy.

In the final analysis the roots of human action always remain mysterious. Herzl's unhappy marriage may have been an important factor in his development. All the starved passions in his nature suddenly came to life and made his new project an obsession that swept aside every scruple and regret. He was strangely aware of this himself. Thus, in a note he inserted at about this time among the pages of his diary, he wrote, "Tragicomedy: the woman who causes the discovery of America (by tormenting)." And in another: "How one learns to say no: a good boy . . . always taken in. Then he gets a nasty wife. From her he learns it."

In his ecstasy he kept admonishing himself: "I must above all keep *myself* under control." After one more fanciful outburst, he noted, "My God, after this confession Lombroso* might think I am mad. And my friend Nordau will conceal from me the apprehension I am causing him. But they are wrong. I know that two and two are four."

Reassured by this thought, Herzl turned to his next step. He decided to engage the powerful Rothschilds in his scheme. A "Society of Jews" should be set up to negotiate the purchase of a

---

* Cesare Lombroso (1836–1909) was an Italian criminologist who claimed there was an affinity among genius, lunacy, and epilepsy. He inspired Max Nordau's strictures against the "degeneracy" of modern art. See p. 98.

country and organize the mass transfer of emigrants. It would be the nucleus of the new government. The Rothschilds must contribute their prestige and connections by pledging the first billion francs to the proposed national loan. In return the first elected doge of the republic would be a Rothschild.

In mid-June Herzl asked a colleague to replace him temporarily at his job. He wrote a long memorandum entitled *Speech to the Rothschilds*; its sixty-eight tightly scribbled pages have survived. Herzl hoped to be able shortly to deliver the speech to the assembled members of the Rothschild family. The memorandum is one of the first systematic expositions of his views; parts of it were later incorporated into his book *The Jewish State*.

The draft is a remarkable document in more than one way. Expressed in threatening terms, it opens with the curt announcement that hereafter Herzl could only be the Rothschilds' friend or enemy, for the power of an idea lay in the fact that there could be no escape from it. "You will think 'We have invited an unpleasant visitor!' But it would not have changed the situation had you not sent for me. . . . You are rich enough, gentlemen, to further this plan. You are not rich enough to prevent it. Because, simply, I cannot be bought."

In his memorandum Herzl developed an alarmist theory that the vast Rothschild fortune was "a danger for you, for the countries in which you are established, yes, even for the entire world." Therefore, sooner or later, it would be expropriated, either from below— by revolution—or from above—by reactionary anti-Semites. The Rothschilds, like all Jews, would be expelled from some countries, "and in those where we seek refuge, they will kill us."

"I bring you the salvation." It was an ancient, very famous, very proven maneuver but in a different, modern, more refined form: "The exodus from *Misraim* [Egypt]." The new exodus would employ strictly scientific methods. There was no place for sentimentalism or nostalgia in the choice of the new territory. Palestine was probably unsuitable. It was too close to Europe; for the first twenty-five years at least, it would be necessary to insulate the new state from the military and social entanglements of Europe. There was also the fact that most Jews were no longer Orientals and had become accustomed to a different climate. There were enough countries for sale, and the promised land would be chosen by a committee of geographers and social scientists. After the territory was purchased, a series of international treaties would guarantee the Jews' right to dispose of their current property, through the society, and to depart to settle in the new state. The momentous transition would come with exquisite ease. Herzl foresaw no cultural, political, economic, military, or absorption difficulties; it was all a problem of proper stage direction. In his *Speech to the Rothschilds* he outlined his ideas on the economic system of the new state, its mode of government, its army, labor laws, social security, culture. He warned the Rothschilds not to expect great riches in the new state. The Rothschilds' alarming concentration of wealth would not be tolerated even "if you go with us." But they would have ample moral compensations.

The new country would not be a theocracy. "Faith holds us together; science makes us free." Its language would not be Hebrew, for how many Jews could still order a railroad ticket in that language? The main language would probably be German, because of its affinity to Yiddish. Even now, as a Jewish nationalist, Herzl considered himself a German: "I am a German Jew from Hungary, and I can never be anything but a German. At present I am not recognized as a German. That will come soon, once we are over there!"

"The promised land is within us, where nobody has looked for it." He ended with a passionate plea: "Let us all move there under the bright banner which we fashion for ourselves."

While he was composing this text—and at the same time jotting down hundreds of random notes on how his plan was to be executed—he addressed a series of passionate appeals to Dr. Moritz Güdemann, the Chief Rabbi of Vienna, the same man who had refused, in 1891, to mediate his divorce from Julie.

The spiritual leader of the Jewish community of Vienna, Güdemann also enjoyed great esteem as a scholar. Herzl knew him only vaguely, but Güdemann was of course familiar with Herzl's work as a newspaperman and playwright. Herzl informed Güdemann on June 11 of his decision "to place myself at the head of an action on behalf of the Jews." He asked Güdemann to meet him, on June 18, halfway between Paris and Vienna, at Caux, a little resort above the Lake of Geneva. He should bring along the Viennese philanthropist Salo Cohn, whose "worldly advice" would complement Herzl's and Güdemann's "spiritual views." Conscious as always of the importance of the proper setting, Herzl looked to the magnificent scenery of Caux, and its associations with Rousseau, to lift Güdemann and Cohn above their "everyday, narrow, restricted concepts. At Caux they will see a victory of mind over matter."

Güdemann was surprised. He had not expected the dandy

ironist, the assimilated litterateur, who never went to synagogue and had not even bothered to circumcise his son, to take any interest in "our cause." He was also mystified, for in his letter Herzl had divulged no details. Güdemann cabled back: "Trip impossible. Salo at North Cape. Letter follows."

Herzl was incensed by this telegram. Here he was, trying to save the Jews, and that Rabbi was not even ready to make a short journey by rail. Wasn't Güdemann aware how desperately serious the situation was? Güdemann's subsequent letter reassured him. Güdemann wrote that he was ready to help but wanted more details. Herzl informed Güdemann by return post not to be surprised at his warm interest in Jewish affairs. "At the moment you cannot even suspect the degree of heat which this interest has generated. ... My Judaism until now was indifferent, but just as anti-Semitism is forcing the halfhearted, cowardly, and self-seeking Jews into the arms of Christianity, so it powerfully forced my Jewishness to the surface. This has nothing to do with false piety." Again Herzl divulged no details but announced mysteriously: "I have the solution to the Jewish question. I know it sounds mad. But I have it."

He told Güdemann that his *Speech to the Rothschilds* would be ready within three days. He asked the Rabbi to immediately contact Albert von Rothschild, head of the Viennese branch of the family, and request an urgent meeting. "For your first mission, dear doctor, is to read this speech to Albert Rothschild. Don't give it to him to read. You read it to him. ... He must make himself free for an entire day. He will be just as shaken and as happy as you yourself. For I have been told that he is a serious, good Jew. He will immediately come to Paris to see me."

Herzl had tears in his eyes as he wrote this letter, and he told Güdemann so. The admission was remarkable in a man whose obsession with "manliness" normally excluded any such confessions to a virtual stranger. It is difficult to see how Herzl could have seriously hoped that Güdemann, who had a reputation to uphold, would promptly contact Rothschild to arrange for the reading of a speech of whose contents he was totally ignorant. Herzl was clearly in a state of crisis.

A reliable eyewitness account of the state of Herzl's nerves at this point is available in the testimony of Dr. Emil Schiff, a physician by training, but working as the Paris correspondent of a German news agency. In mid-June Herzl urgently summoned Schiff by letter to come to see him. The letter was couched in mysterious terms and indicated that Herzl needed Schiff's advice on

a matter of grave importance. Schiff, as he later recalled the incident, thought that Herzl wanted to talk of marriage difficulties. He
was not prepared for what followed. "Herzl himself opened the
door. The look in his face frightened me. In the few days that I had
not seen him his face had changed into that of a sick man, suffering
from a long disease. There was something strange and mysterious
in his eyes. His hair and clothes were unkempt."

Schiff could not believe his eyes; he later recorded his amaze-
ment in a memoir. Before he could open his mouth Herzl whispered, "Listen, my good friend, during the past two weeks I have
evaded all my acquaintances, I have hardly slept or eaten. . . . I
have written a book, I am almost sick from the exertion and excitement. At the moment I do not know its full meaning, but I know
that my fate is inextricably tied to it." He asked Schiff to give him
a few hours. "I will read you the manuscript. Please don't interrupt
until I am finished. Then tell me everything you think."

Herzl, in a shaking voice, read Schiff his *Speech to the Rothschilds*. Schiff listened silently. Even as Herzl was reading, Schiff
decided, "This man is sick. He has gone mad." According to Herzl's
cursory report of the meeting, Schiff broke down in tears when the
reading was over. He quickly realized to his consternation that
Schiff was crying for his sanity. "With this project you will either
make yourself ridiculous or tragic." Schiff remembered taking Herzl
by his arms. "My dear friend, there is something wrong with your
nerves. This book is a product of sickness. You must see a doctor."

Schiff *was* a doctor. He immediately checked Herzl's pulse.
"The pulse was not normal. [It raced] as in a state of delirium. I
felt very sorry for my friend."

Schiff told Herzl that Rothschild, being a reasonable man,
would not even hear him out. Rothschild would ring for his butler
and order him to deliver Herzl either to the police or to an asylum.
In the eighteenth century, Schiff argued, a false messiah named
Sabbatai Zevi* had tried that very same thing. He had ended very
badly, first in an Ottoman jail, then as a convert to Islam.

"Yes," answered Herzl, "in the eighteenth century it was not
possible. But now it is possible to do it—because we have machines."

In Schiff's opinion the only salvation for modern Jews was in
socialism. He was shocked to hear that Herzl had already written to

* Sabbatai Zevi actually lived in the seventeenth century. Herzl, recording
this conversation in his diary, was unaware of this. It may well have been the
first time he had heard of Zevi.

Güdemann. He decided to secretly cable the Vienna post office (in Herzl's name) and ask that the letter be returned to the sender. He warned Herzl that Güdemann would certainly say, "Completely cracked! The poor family!" and rush to Herzl's parents to console them over their son's sudden mental breakdown. Herzl's parents would be heartbroken. As a parting counsel Schiff advised, "Burn that manuscript."

Herzl passed a difficult night. The thought of upsetting his parents disturbed him greatly. In the first flush of excitement he had been sure that the project would "gild my dear parents' old age." His deep filial love and devotion was boundless; if there was still anything more important to Herzl than his cause, it was his parents' happiness and peace of mind. Was he not putting that in jeopardy? He tossed in his bed, unable to sleep.

Next morning Herzl left the hotel early, seeking solace in the Tuileries. He was strained with thought and worry, and tired from his sleepless night. Nervously he paced up and down the pebbled walks. It was a bright and pleasant day in June, children were floating their little boats in the lily-studded pond, and a light breeze swept over the bowl-shaped green lawn. Resting his feverish eyes on the white statues around him—especially "Coustou's charming 'Runners' (1712)"—Herzl slowly recuperated, or so he thought. Outdoor art always gave him much satisfaction. He resolved that in the new state Coustou's " 'Runners' should be copied without delay."

Schiff returned in the afternoon and resumed the attack with added vigor. The two men went for a walk in the Tuileries, arguing as they strolled along. The pleasant park now cast its spell in vain; Schiff finally convinced Herzl that he must desist. Herzl was swayed by the persistent argument that he would become either a tragic figure or ridiculous. Herzl did not mind being a tragic figure, but he realized that by being "ridiculous" he would ruin not himself, but the cause.

Herzl went home alone. "Schiff . . . has 'cured' me," he noted in his diary. Rashly, for he would soon regret it, he decided he must have a clean slate. He wrote Baron Hirsch a despondent, almost apologetic letter:

Paris, 18 June 1895

Dear Sir:
My last letter requires a postscript. Here it is. I have given

the matter up. Why? My plan would more likely be wrecked by
poor Jews than by rich.

You told me as much on Whitsunday. It is true. But I was
in no position to believe you, for you had not let me finish what
I had to say. . . .

For the present there is no helping the Jews. If someone
were to show them the promised land, they would mock him.
For they are demoralized. . . .

I cannot break that wall. Not with my head alone. Therefore I am giving it up.

As a practical proposition I am done with the matter.
Theoretically I still cherish it highly. Perhaps this shows that I
too am only a demoralized Jew. A Gentile would go through
thick and thin with an idea of such power. What would you
have me do? I do not want to be a Don Quixote . . . I am no
Sancho Panza either,

but your respectfully faithful,
Dr. Th. Herzl

Yet he was already too involved to extricate himself easily with
a witticism. After a good night's sleep he attacked the issue from a
new angle. If Jews were too petty to understand, he told himself,
he would turn to a powerful Gentile, like Bismarck, the idol of his
youth. "He is big enough to understand me or cure me." He drafted
a letter to the retired Chancellor. Then he was seized by new
doubts. "But will Bismarck understand me? Napoleon did not
understand the steamboat, and he was younger, more accessible to
new ideas." On the other hand, "Napoleon was the sick Superman,
Bismarck is the healthy one."

He was still tormented by fears that he might hurt or sadden
his beloved parents. In this almost suicidal mood, he was delighted
to receive a sign of encouragement from his mother. The encouragement was not intended to be taken in this context, for although
Herzl exchanged almost daily letters with his parents in Vienna, he
had not yet divulged his secret to them. On June 21 Jeannette
Herzl read in the *Neue Freie Presse* a poem by the late Betti Paoli
and liked it so much that she copied and sent it immediately to her
son in Paris. The poem extolled the sacred duties of "committed
men," whom nature has endowed with great gifts. Such men give
"target and direction" to the masses; they are stars in the dark
firmament of time. But in return the chosen man is duty bound to

judge himself severely. Let him not bend his head to mean temptation, for

> Weaknesses are easily forgiven to the crowd.
> To you, their leader, they are not allowed!
>
> (Die Schwächen leicht verziehn der dunklen Menge.
> Dir, ihrem Führer, sind sie nicht erlaubt.)

Herzl took it as an omen. "From my good Mama who copied it
for me and sent it," he scribbled in the margin, "while I was working on the plan! As if mother-heart divined it!"*
He now dispatched his letter to Bismarck. It is the dialogue of
a lonely man with himself. Herzl did not hesitate to tell Bismarck
that his plan had already been dismissed as impracticable by one
"very rich" man and as insane by one "poor, but educated" man.

> I appeal to your Highness. Allow me to present my plan to you
> . . . as a last court of appeal. At worst it is a utopia, of a kind
> often written, from Thomas More to Bellamy. A utopia is more
> amusing the farther it strays from the world of reason. I daresay
> that in any case I shall present you with a new utopia and
> therefore an entertaining one.
>
> It will be an easy matter for your Highness to make in-
> quiries in Hamburg, Vienna, or Berlin as to whether I have in
> the past been considered a sensible man—*bien que ça n'en-
> gagerait pas l'avenir* [even though that says nothing about the
> future]—and whether it would be all right to admit me to a
> room. But as I imagine Prince Bismarck, you will need no in-
> quiries after reading this letter. A man who reads the faces and
> guts of men the way you do, will also understand the inner
> meaning of these lines.

At the same time he wrote Schnitzler: "I no longer think of
death but of a life full of manly deeds." The suicidal mood of a few
days before was gone. Yet he did not preclude any eventuality. He
informed Schnitzler that he had deposited his notes in the "*Comp-
toir d'Escompte* bank, strongbox six, compartment number two. To
open, each of the three buttons must be pushed seven times toward
the right. Someone must know this, in case I disappear overnight.

---

* On her own copy Jeannette later added: "I suspected my dear son's
great task. May God keep him in good health. Amen."

That one is you! Do I seem excited to you? I am not. I was never in a higher, happier mood."

4

With his letter to Bismarck, Herzl considered that his scheme had "logically entered a new stage." He began a new volume of his diary. The first already comprised more than two hundred pages. He decided to approach the German Kaiser through a high-ranking German diplomat acquaintance.

He was proceeding like an old-fashioned conservative. Even though he hoped, ultimately, to affect the lives of millions of people, he felt he was no demogogue and so had nothing to say to the masses, Christian or Jewish. He would speak only to kings, ministers, and multimillionaires in their palaces. "Democracy is political nonsense," he told his diary. "It can only be decided upon by an incensed mob in the excitement of a revolution." True statesmanship, as he saw it, was the art of making lonely decisions, far removed from the glare of publicity. Democratic publicity merely eroded the "respect which is necessary for [good] government."

At the same time he was concerned that he might be reproached for acting "without, i.e., against, the consent of the Jews." Hence he decided that before approaching the Kaiser, "it might be useful, after all, to notify Albert Rothschild." On June 28 he wrote Rothschild about his memorandum to the German Kaiser. "The memorandum is not a fatuous and querulous complaint . . . but a comprehensive plan for self-help on the part of Jews of all countries." The memorandum would bear only Herzl's signature. "But since I am taking up the cause of the Jews, I owe them some proof of my good intentions, and for this purpose I need a few reputable and independent witnesses. Mind you, witnesses, not guarantors or bosses! Do you want to be one of the witnesses? I am having some trouble finding serviceable men." He asked Albert Rothschild to grant him an uninterrupted half-day. Herzl would go anywhere, anytime, to present his case.

Rothschild never answered this letter. There was no reply from Bismarck either. Bismarck was said later to have decried Herzl's scheme as a danger to both Germany and the Jews.

Herzl was not dismayed. He consoled himself that he had not been too humbly courteous in his letter to Rothschild. He was profoundly Viennese in his tendency to observe the negative and expect the worst—in Nestroy's refrain, "The world's bound quite soon to go under"—but he refused to give in, and continued tenaciously with his notes, drafts, and urgent letters. He resumed his daily journalistic chores. In the Chamber he got into an argument on democracy with Leo Franckel, the Hungarian Jewish anarchist who had played a role in the Paris Commune of 1871. Later that day, he observed Moritz Wahrmann, the son of a Jewish Hungarian politician, driving by on the Champs Élysées, looking vigorous but bored. "Such fellows, with their splendid unused energies, would be excellent material for us," he thought. "How beautiful is my scheme in which such Franckels and young Wahrmanns would find room for their development."

He gave up his seclusion, frequented the cafés, and dined with friends, whom he had anxiously evaded for the past three weeks. He even allowed himself a brief respite in the country and spent a happy day lying on the grass at Enghien-les-Bains, thinking of his children. He looked forward to spending the summer vacation with them at Aussee in the Austrian mountains. He wrote Julie that he was at work on a marvelous new task. He did not tell her what it was, only that "it is a splendid, great romance." He planned to finish his work at Aussee, if she would let him. He was very much hoping she would. There would be time enough for everything—"play with the dear children and, if she be lovely, tickle my beautiful wife's most pleasant little neck."

He started to go out again into society. At dinner in Nordau's home he decided that "it has been a lucky thing for me that I haven't had a real social life here. I would have spent myself producing *bons mots* at dinner parties." In the Taverne Royal, "over a cassoulet," as he was jotting down his notes on the political system best suited to his scheme, he was joined by two Austrian Jews he knew, an architect and a scientist. Herzl deliberately turned the conversation to the virulent state of anti-Semitism in Vienna. All agreed that things were getting increasingly worse. The architect expressed his pleasure that the Emperor had suspended the City Council in order to block Lueger's election as mayor.

Herzl disagreed vehemently. "Suspending the City Council is like suspending the constitution," he said. "Together with the constitution, equal rights for Jews will be thrown out too."

Then the scientist said, "There will be no other course left but to assign us a state of our own." Herzl was inwardly delighted, since he was badly in need of moral support, but he did not divulge his plans.

In the Austrian Bierhaus in Paris, two weeks later, he fell into a similar discussion with Max Nordau. The two men were of one mind. "I have never been so perfectly attuned with Nordau." Both men admitted they were freethinkers; they agreed that "only anti-Semitism has made Jews out of us."

Nordau said, "What is the tragedy of Jewry? That this most conservative of peoples, which yearns to be rooted in some soil, has had no home for the last two thousand years."

Tense and happy, Herzl already thought that Nordau was secretly harboring a scheme similar to his own. But Nordau arrived at a different conclusion. "The Jews," he said, "will be compelled by anti-Semitism to destroy the idea of patriotism everywhere." Not necessarily, Herzl thought to himself. "They might become patriots in their own country."

As the day of his departure from Paris drew near, he turned his thoughts to the uses and delusions of his journalistic craft. In a thoughtful piece entitled "School of Journalism" he summed up his five years as a foreign correspondent. There was little point in being a political journalist for long, he felt, except as preparation for a life of political action. Indeed, nowhere in Europe could men of ambition so easily exchange a seat in the press gallery for one on the main floor as they could in the French parliament, which Herzl had covered regularly over the past five years. Now he was tired of journalism. It was "a life of dreams begun, of half-baked ideas, unutilized moods. Is there no way to put one's life to better use?"*

In mid-July 1895 the streets of Vienna erupted in more anti-Jewish riots. "These are but trifles," Herzl wrote Güdemann on July 15. "Things are going to get worse and more violent all the time . . . we must think of the poor and decent Jews. They are the majority (not the mean cowards or those made arrogant by their money). We are not a chosen people, but not a base one either. This is why I am holding on."

He had another argument with Schiff. "The Jews must turn socialist," Schiff said obstinately, commenting on the Vienna riots.

"How wrong you are! This would do even less good in Austria than in Germany," Herzl argued. He failed to convince Schiff, who stuck to his view that Herzl was wrong and ruining himself with his "crazy" plan.

* A few years later he rationalized his years as a journalist as the direct consequence of his being a Jew. "What is left for talented Jews who are not interested in commerce? I would have been a minister of state long ago if I were not a Jew."

Güdemann, on the other hand, pleased Herzl immensely with a prompt and sympathetic answer. The Chief Rabbi of Vienna was distressed by the latest street riots and even more embittered by the feeble and cowardly reaction of the rich community leaders, on whose good will and energy he was so dependent. There was a need for courageous new leaders, a new Moses, a new David. The hint was unintentional, but struck the proper note.

"My dear friend," Herzl worte Güdemann on July 21. "Permit me to address you so, after receiving your letter. Your letter delights me! I was not deceived when I saw in you one of the right people that I need." Herzl again suggested a conference, somewhere in Switzerland, to discuss the contents of his memorandum to the German Kaiser. He asked Güdemann to bring along the Berlin philanthropist Heinrich Meyer-Cohn to the meeting. "I don't need rich Jews, but I need men! Damn it, they are hard to find! I am sure you were very surprised [when I first approached you] that the fellow who writes light comedies and *feuilletons* wishes to speak of serious matters. Do you believe me now? Don't you sense from my every word that I have important things to say?"

But Güdemann was not yet ready for a meeting. He preached Herzl a little sermon, reminding him that politics might jeopardize his position on the *Neue Freie Presse*. Herzl had a duty to his wife and children, Güdemann wrote, and concluded his letter with a liberal sprinkling of pious citations and Bible quotations. Herzl reiterated his proposal for a conference. He complained that Güdemann was flirting with him "like a woman who charms and then withdraws."

The correspondence between the two men, by letter and cable, continued for some time. Elaborate negotiations were needed before a meeting with Güdemann and Meyer-Cohn was finally arranged. Meanwhile, Herzl continued to work on his proliferous notes. He seriously believed that the exodus he was planning would take place within a very short time, perhaps a year, or two years at most. As usual, he was thinking in vivid images and often dwelling on minor details. "In the process of transplantation, lovingly respect all local customs. *Salzstangel*,* coffee, beer, customary meat, etc., are not indifferent matters. Moses forgot to take along the fleshpots of Egypt. We will remember them."

He drew up plans for the "capital city, our own little treasure trove." It would be an improved Vienna. "Its location, protected by

---

* A popular Viennese roll, flavored with salt and caraway seeds.

mountains (fortresses on the highest ridges), a beautiful river, with forests nearby. Take care that the site is protected from the wind, but no sun bowl; guarded by mountains, but not too small. Prevent urban sprawl through protected green belts and forests." Clearly he was a man of tremendous visual imagination. In his diary he penned one pictorial detail after another until the reader sees the scene rising before his eyes: the ships sailing, the cities ready to receive the passengers, the secularized mystique of Herzl's elaborate public ceremonies.

Herzl left Paris on July 27 and traveled directly to Upper Austria to join his family at Aussee. The small summer resort—popular among artists—nestled along a small lake set in the rocky, wooded mountains. He relaxed, took long walks, and swam. One day he found himself in a bathing cabin on the lake front; its walls were covered by anti-Semitic graffiti. Many were crossed out, Herzl noted, "or answered by upset Jewish boys." One inscription Herzl copied into his notebook:

> Oh God, return Moses to this land,
> To take his Jews all by the hand
> And lead them to their promised land.
> And when the whole bad lot's afloat
> In the middle of the sea,
> Then, Good Lord, just sink the boat,
> And all good Christians will be free.

While at Aussee Herzl divulged none of his plans to his wife and parents, who assumed he was working on a novel. He spent the next two weeks carefully probing acquaintances, outlining to them his premises but not his conclusions. He noticed, not without satisfaction, that he had a power to stir people, a kind of magnetism projected by his eyes and voice, of which he had not been aware before. "I feel their souls emitting sparks whenever I strike them."

Güdemann was still being difficult. When Herzl refused to reveal his plans by letter, Güdemann mockingly compared Herzl's reticence to "the secret war plans of an operetta general." Many more letters and cablegrams were necessary to fix the desired rendezvous with Güdemann and Meyer-Cohn. It finally took place on a Sabbath, August 17, in Munich, at the elegant Vier Jahreszeiten Hotel.

Herzl arrived in Munich early on the morning of the meeting.

He was unhappy at the choice of place; he would have preferred
the more inspiring scenery of Caux. The pretentious hotel was not a
place that would suggest the desired "victory of mind over matter,"
but he had to make do.

He met Güdemann in the hotel lobby. The Rabbi looked fresh
and cheerful; his smooth skin and ruddy cheeks made him seem
much younger than his age. The two men went upstairs to Meyer-
Cohn's room. From the moment they entered the room, everything
seemed to go wrong. Meyer-Cohn had arrived a few moments earlier and was just washing up. A short man of simple bearing, he
spun a long dull tale on "parliamentary" doings in the Berlin Jewish
community. Herzl disliked him at first sight. "He is a small man in
outward appearance, and inwardly he is just as petty," Herzl complained to Güdemann as they left, fifteen minutes later.

The three men reassembled for lunch in Jochberg's kosher restaurant, a site Herzl found even less appropriate than the hotel.
The stuffy little side room and the heavy meal were in no way
conducive to the spirit of elation Herzl had hoped for. The conference opened rather heavily with an exchange of views on God
and theology. Over the coffee Herzl finally brought out the manuscript of his *Speech to the Rothschilds*.

Güdemann listened tensely, visibly moved, with shining eyes.
Meyer-Cohn was disruptive and carped at details in a petty way,
ignoring the grand sweep of Herzl's plan. As a democrat he resented Herzl's proposals for an aristocratic constitution. "Very
well," said Herzl, "let's drop the aristocracy." He lost his temper
while rebutting Meyer-Cohn's objections. "There is time to debate
such issues later," he said; meanwhile the important thing was that
"we be Jews . . . let us first get over there, and then split up into
aristocrats and democrats."

Herzl had barely finished the first thirteen of his sixty-eight
pages of text, when the reading was broken off because Meyer-
Cohn had to rush off to another engagement. Herzl and Güdemann
walked back to the hotel. Güdemann said with great feeling: "If
you are right, all the views I have held until now simply break
down. Nevertheless I very much hope that you may be right. I
thought until now that we are not a nation, that is, that we are
more than a mere nation. I thought we had a historic mission to
propagate the idea of humanism among all nations, and that for
this reason we are more than a territorial people."

Herzl answered, "Nothing stops us from being and remaining

what we are on our home soil as well. To propagate universal understanding we do not actually have to continue to reside among the nations that hate and despise us."

At six that evening the three men met again, this time in Herzl's small hotel room. Again it was hardly the ambience Herzl might have wished. There were only two chairs, and Herzl sat on the edge of his bed to continue the reading. Meyer-Cohn went on carping at various aspects he considered utopian, but Güdemann was swayed once more. Herzl again did not reach the end; after two and a half hours they broke off for supper. As they were about to leave for Jochberg's restaurant, the Chief Rabbi fixed his beautiful large eyes on Herzl's face and said, "You remind me of Moses!"

Herzl laughed. He was completely sincere in his rejection of the compliment. "Come, come," he said. "As I see it, it is a very simple idea, a skillful and rational device, even though it deals with great masses. As a pure idea the plan is not really grand. In abstract terms, two plus two equal four is just as great as two trillions plus two trillions equal four trillions."

No, no, Güdemann protested. "For myself, I am quite dazed. I feel like one who has been invited to receive a piece of news, and instead, when he arrives, is shown two beautiful, big horses."

Herzl liked this vivid simile. ("It made me realize the plasticity of my idea.") At the restaurant Herzl read out the conclusion. When he had finished there was a silence. Even Meyer-Cohn, who disagreed on the principle, was a bit awed. He and Güdemann agreed that Herzl must by no means waste his speech on the Rothschilds. Güdemann said it had been a terrible narrishkayt* on Herzl's part to write Albert Rothschild in the first place. The Rothschilds were mean people, base and selfish. "I did not know he was such a bastard," Herzl retorted.

Güdemann said, "You must carry the idea to the people, in the form of a novel!" The people might understand; the novel might lead to the creation of a great mass movement.

Herzl said that premature publicity might spoil his plan, but he also felt that he must comply. "I cannot carry it out all by myself. I must believe you when you say that the 'big Jews' will have nothing to do with it."

He took Güdemann to the station. As they were parting, the Chief Rabbi said with solemn enthusiasm: "Remain as you are. Perhaps you are the one called of God."

* Yiddish for "foolishness."

The train whistled and they said good-bye. The air was thick with the smell of steam and burning coal. The scene remained imprinted in Herzl's mind. He described it with much feeling in his diary. "There was a strange gleam in Güdemann's beautiful eyes as he reached out once more, through the compartment window, to firmly squeeze my hand." Herzl did not know that that same night Güdemann had written a postcard to his wife: "Herzl is a poet. His plan, however interesting, is not feasible."

8

Burning Bridges

Early in September 1895, after an absence of five years, Herzl resettled in Vienna. He assumed his new post as literary editor of the *Neue Freie Presse*. The Munich meeting with Güdemann and Meyer-Cohn had been inconclusive, but Herzl was more determined than ever. At thirty-five he was still a would-be leader without a people; the would-be founder of a state that as yet had no locale. With his pale face and silky blue-black beard he looked (to his cousin Raoul Auernheimer) like "an insulted Arab sheik." If the issue at stake had been less serious, he might have seemed a character in some comic opera, but it was grave and he approached it with a desperate earnestness.

His every encounter seemed to confirm his worst fears. In the autumn of 1895 Vienna was seething with anti-Semitism, social strife, and mob violence. Freud later wrote that the autumn of 1895 had given him his "first glimpse into the abyss of instinctual life . . . I saw things calculated to sober and even to frighten me."

Herzl renewed his acquaintance with Hermann Bahr, his former fraternity brother in *Albia*, whose anti-Semitic speech had caused Herzl's resignation. Bahr, who had since become an avid philo-Semite, had just published an international survey of anti-Semitism. His conclusion was that anti-Semitism, "a new madness," was an opiate designed to amuse modern man, to restore his "wilted nerves." "The rich resort to morphine and hashish. Those who cannot afford drugs become anti-Semites." To use reason against anti-Semitism "is useless," for anti-Semitism could not be cured, except "through a nobler ecstasy." With this, Herzl readily agreed. Of all his former friends and colleagues Bahr was the most sympathetic to his new cause.

A few days after Herzl's arrival the anti-Semites, under Lueger, won another victory at the polls. In the previous six months they had increased their strength by 50 percent and were now in full control of City Hall. Lueger was reelected mayor, although the aging Emperor once more refused to ratify his appointment. But in the streets Lueger reigned supreme; he was the darling of the masses, swept along on mounting waves of social dissatisfaction and race hatred. "These Jews" cried Lueger, "they are robbing us of everything we hold sacred! Fatherland! Nationality! And finally our property too!"

On election day, Herzl went out into the teeming streets. In Vienna he was not able, as in Paris, to move "unrecognized" through the crowd. Everywhere he went he seemed to encounter "looks of hatred." He watched the tense mob outside the polling station. Lueger came out into the square and a tremendous cheer went up. Women were waving white kerchiefs from the windows. The police held the crowd back. A man standing next to Herzl said calmly: "This is our *Führer.*"

Herzl trembled. The man's calm voice frightened him more than the screams of the mob. His "tender warmth and quiet tone," more than the heated declamations and angry words of abuse, convinced Herzl "how deeply rooted anti-Semitism is in the hearts of these people."

Most Viennese Jews rejoiced in the Emperor's refusal to confirm Lueger's election as mayor. Freud gave expression to his joy by permitting "himself an extra ration of cigars that day." The irony in the situation was blatant, for Viennese Jews, erstwhile champions of representative government, now put their trust in a tottering coalition of feudal and clericalist forces buttressed by imperial dictates. Herzl was one of the few Jews who deplored the Emperor's decision. The suspension of Lueger did not suspend race hatred, but strengthened it. The Emperor was bound to give in sooner or later to Lueger's massively growing popular support; meanwhile he was merely helping to increase it. In November Herzl had a confidential talk with Count Badeni, the Imperial Prime Minister. He surprised the Prime Minister by advising him that it was in the Emperor's interest to ratify Lueger's election.

There were still immense reserves of loyalty to the crown, in Vienna no less than in the remotest provinces of the empire. But the affection was more for the person of the venerable old Franz Josef than for the supranational or multinational principle he symbolized. In the tottering arch that was Austria-Hungary, the

Emperor himself was the keystone. He had been Emperor for almost half a century, a lonely, naïve, unimaginative man, bewildered and embittered by a long succession of defeats and family disasters. His only son had committed suicide with his young mistress, his brother had been executed in Mexico, and he was estranged from his wife —within three years she would be killed by an anarchist. It was widely assumed that upon his death his realm would collapse.

As the poet Rainer Maria Rilke wrote in a celebrated line, "The kings of the world are old and shall have no sons." The old traditions seemed to be tearing apart, and it was though tomorrow would not link itself with today. Max Nordau observed in *Degeneration*: "Things as they are totter and plunge. They are allowed to reel and fall because man is *weary*."

An instinctive anxiety resided in the collective subconscious. It was a real force, not merely the irrational prejudice of the reactionaries of Nordau's world. Freud sensed it; the writers and artists in the vanguard of Viennese culture sensed it. It is important to understand this awareness of universal decay and cultural pessimism in order to appreciate Herzl's apocalyptic temperament and desperate sense of urgency.

Herzl's Zionism coincided with the twilight of Old Austria, its tragedy as a *failing* experiment in pluralism, its search for solutions and its incapacity to find them. In Austria, insecurity came hand in hand with relentless self-criticism. Vienna at the turn of the century was a place where, just before the advent of barbarism, many cultural currents of great vigor and originality were fused in a baroque synthesis. The best minds searched for clarity. Freud sought it through psychoanalysis, Wittgenstein through logical positivism, and others through art. As literary editor of the *Neue Freie Presse*, Herzl was particularly attuned to the artistic quest. Viennese art had changed since Makart's days; the new school excelled in a peculiar, harrowing, almost hallucinatory treatment of shadowy light and ominous darkness.

In the Belvedere Museum of Austrian Art in Vienna the student of Herzl's life finds one key to the central sensibility of the time. Take, for example, the figures of Anton Romako, a precursor of Kokoschka, drawn in macabre colors with distorted features and insane eyes, that express unfathomable dread. Or Gustav Klimt's melancholy landscapes of perennial autumn, decayed trees, dried-up roses, and pearls strung like worms. And Egon Schiele's figures —twisted as by pain, huddling together for safety, maimed, shaken by ecstatic spasms. In Klimt's landscapes and Schiele's portraits, Old Austria was taking its leave. The morbidity heralded Austria's death and that of old Europe as well.

2

This was the Vienna Herzl returned to in the autumn of 1895, and where he would pursue the "mission" that totally preoccupied him for the remaining nine years of his life. He had left the city in 1891 as an effete litterateur, content to observe, reflect, and sometimes sigh. He returned a transformed man. "Every man of action is a *tragic* figure," he had written as a young man in 1882. He had reason now to suspect that, as a man of action, he might also appear *comic*. In the sophisticated milieu of a great metropolis there is always something disconcerting about a man with a "mission."

Within weeks Herzl's circle was swarming with jokes about his mad scheme. It was said that he planned to evacuate the Jewish habitués of Vienna's celebrated cafés to a new chain of similar establishments in Argentina or in the Orient. A common rejoinder among Jews was: "I'm all in favor of a Jewish state provided they appoint me as ambassador to Vienna." Others spoke of Herzl as "the new Mahdi from the Pelikangasse."*

The amazing transformation of this once hypersensitive man can be seen in the cool composure with which he faced such ridicule. "Not everyone who is first considered insane is correct thirty years later. But in order to be proved right in thirty years, one has to be prepared in the first few weeks to be considered a madman."

Arthur Schnitzler was one of the few to take Herzl's plan seriously. Herzl's first words to the playwright on his return to Vienna were: "I have solved the Jewish problem!" He outlined his program to Schnitzler as the crowning achievement of "this century of inventions." Schnitzler's first reaction was enthusiastic, and Herzl promptly promised to appoint him director of the national theater in the new Jewish state.

He confided his plan for the first time to his beloved parents. They did not fully understand it, but trusted him implicitly and in the beginning provided Herzl's only real moral support. Jakob

* The name of the street on which Herzl lived.

Herzl made a careful study of the draft of the *Speech to the Roth-schilds* and wrote Theodor a long letter. He disagreed with his son's basic tenet that anti-Semitism would inevitably grow. The old Herzl believed that even in Vienna, despite the latest election results, the movement would soon be "dammed up, if not arrested completely." But even if this might prove a delusion, Jakob told his son, he was wrong to pin his hopes on the Rothschilds and other millionaires. Address yourself to the large public by writing a book, he said. He also advised Herzl not to sacrifice his own material interest and that of his family for the sake of a public career.

If Herzl was successful in winning his parents' slightly bewildered approval, he failed completely with his wife. His marriage to Julie had been patched together again after a separation of almost a year. Julie met his plan with complete incomprehension, adding a new burden to the unhappy marriage. In the words of a contemporary, who knew them both, "Julie liked society, not public life. The crowd of poor Jews who soon came to her door to beg and petition the new leader did not enhance her interest in a cause for which she had no natural emotion."

She gave Herzl no support and no sympathy in his new task. Herzl, in turn, had even less time for her now than before. (Nor, from all we know, for any other woman.) He lived in the kind of physical and intellectual celibacy that has often been observed in "charismatic" leaders. His entire life was taken up by his new mission ("At night it burns within me when my eyes are closed; I cannot hide from it") and by his editorial work, which he pursued as best he could to make a living.

Within weeks after his return to Vienna he developed a vast correspondence with interested people all over the world. He took his father's advice and prepared an appeal to the masses, not without some reluctance, for it ran counter to his conservative nature. He rewrote his Rothschild speech in the form of a political pamphlet. And he tried very hard to win over the two publishers of the *Neue Freie Presse*.

Bacher and Benedikt were fond of Herzl. They wavered between incredulity and bewilderment at their star correspondent's fantastic scheme. Herzl first broached the subject to Bacher, to whom he was especially attached, but Bacher was totally unreceptive. He made it clear that he would fight tooth and nail against Herzl's ideas. Herzl did not give up. He indicated that he might leave the *Neue Freie Presse* unless the newspaper permitted him to

publicize his plan. His negotiating position was briefly strengthened by a totally unexpected offer from Count Badeni, the Austro-Hungarian Prime Minister, to be editor-in-chief of a new
pro-government newspaper.

Herzl had a long talk with Badeni (in French) but did not
commit himself. He was as reluctant to leave the *Presse* as Bacher
and Benedikt were to lose him. A few days after his talk with
Badeni he approached Benedikt, the *Presse*'s senior publisher, with
his plan. Benedikt, one of the most influential men in Austria, married to a Gentile woman, was the embodiment of Jewish pan-
Germanism.* A man of great erudition, with an exceptionally keen
mind, his editorials resounded from one end of the empire to another. Unlike Bacher, he realized how serious Herzl was, and he
feared that the newspaper might lose one of its stars. Benedikt and
Herzl took a long walk in the country. For three hours they argued
back and forth, talking and walking themselves to exhaustion.

Herzl said he would like best to be able to launch his plan "in
and with" the newspaper, but he would launch it even if they
refused.

"You are confronting us with a monstrous choice," Benedikt
said. "The entire newspaper would take on a different complexion.
We have always been considered a Jewish newspaper. But we have
never admitted it. Now we are supposed to suddenly remove our
cover."

"But you won't need that cover anymore," said Herzl. "The
very moment my idea is publicized, the entire Jewish question is
solved honestly. After all, we can stay in all those countries that
accept our good citizenship and loyalty to the fatherland. Only
where they do not want us shall we move away."

Herzl asked Benedikt to place a Sunday edition of the newspaper at his disposal. On the front page would be printed *The
Solution to the Jewish Question, by Dr. Theodor Herzl.* Herzl would
invite all of Jewry to contribute questions and comments; the ensuing debate would be more interesting than anything ever pub-

---

* At his death in 1920, the London *Times*, not normally critical in its
obituary columns, wrote, "[As a pan-German] Benedikt . . . was unscrupled,
fanatical, untiring and a menace. . . . He employed his influence almost without exception against those men and movements who wanted to save Austria
from the disaster which was the inevitable result of its subordination to German
policy . . . his memory and example will long remind the lands of German
tongue what a journalist ought not to be."

lished by a newspaper. "The responsibility will be mine alone. You can preface my outline with a disclaimer on the part of the newspaper."

"No, that would be cowardly," Benedikt said. "If we publish, we accept joint responsibility. Your idea is like a powerful machine gun, which could also backfire." It might well trigger more anti-Semitic outrages, confiscation of property, even bloodshed. The Jews could lose their present homelands even before they gained a new one of their own, which he very much doubted they would. For the newspaper this was too dangerous a bombshell. Benedikt urged Herzl to launch his idea—if launch it he must—through an outside organization, some charitable society or study group. He promised to personally help him find the right people.

Herzl was gloomy, but he also felt that he had finally crossed a bridge from the realm of dream to the realm of action. "This was a historic walk," he told Benedikt on their ride back to town. By placing his own career in jeopardy he was setting *himself* in motion. "Action has begun, because I will have the *Presse* either with me or against me."

Aware that he had reached a decisive turning point, he recorded the talk in his diary and concluded with the remark: "I shall be the Parnell of the Jews." He could not have made a truer observation. Both men stood with feet in two camps; both reacted from a deep sense of wounded pride. Parnell too had begun on the "other side." The feudal landlords of Ireland felt he was betraying their cause, just as powerful assimilated Jews like Benedikt were sure that Herzl was undermining theirs. Both men overestimated the positive power of modern technology. "Electricity was not invented to illuminate the salons of a few rich snobs," Herzl noted a few days later. "It was invented so that in its light we might solve the Jewish question."

For about a week Herzl continued to carry on negotiations both with his publishers and with the Prime Minister's aides who wanted to start a new newspaper. There were moments of tension when Herzl asked Bacher to excuse him from work as long as the issue was undecided. He did not really want to leave the *Presse*, and he disliked the Prime Minister's men with whom he was negotiating. They were not aware of Herzl's Jewish scheme. Herzl told Bacher he could not bear the thought of losing his friendship. Bacher was delighted to hear that. He said that despite all their disagreements, Herzl had a better chance of realizing his idea through the *Presse* than through Badeni's newspaper. Herzl con-

tinued to pressure the *Presse* to print his plan. Finally a compromise was reached. The *Presse* would not launch Herzl's scheme
but would print a review of his political pamphlet. It was characteristic of Herzl's strict sense of propriety that he asked Bacher for
a letter confirming, on his word of honor, that Herzl had not used
Badeni's offer as leverage to increase his pay. He went back to the
Prime Minister, gave him Bacher's letter, and said he regretted he
was unable to accept his offer.

But Bacher and Benedikt did not keep their promise. As soon
as Herzl had shown that he would not weaken the *Presse* by joining
a rival newspaper, he became a mere employee again. Benedikt
suddenly had no time to discuss the proposed study group, nor did
he make good on his offer to introduce Herzl to men of influence
who might aid his cause. Bacher claimed he knew no such persons.
Instead he pointedly asked Herzl for his next contribution to the
newspaper.

Güdemann, whom Herzl had consulted throughout his negotiations, also let him down. His ardor had cooled since Munich,
where he had proclaimed Herzl another Moses. Güdemann had
first urged Herzl not to quit the *Presse*. After Herzl took his advice,
Güdemann complained that it was a pity he had not left the newspaper, for he might then have had "the ear of the Prime Minister."
Herzl deplored Güdemann's weak-mindedness: "Of a man he has
only the beard and the voice." He would soon have more serious
cause to deplore Güdemann's treachery.

Meanwhile he fell back on his old, well-tried remedy against
depression: foreign travel. On November 11 he departed for Paris.
As he rode to the station the streets of Vienna were once more the
scene of violence, for on the previous day the Emperor had again
refused to ratify Lueger's election as mayor.

On the following day Herzl arrived in Paris. Nostalgically he
booked into the same hotel room on the rue Cambon where he had
had his first inspiration the previous May. He had three long talks
with Zadok Kahn, the Chief Rabbi of France, to whom Güdemann
—not without repeated prodding by Herzl—had consented to
recommend him. In his four years in Paris Herzl had never bothered to meet Kahn, although Kahn played a prominent role in the
affairs of European Jewry. He was a confidant of Edmond de Rothschild, who since 1882 had been subsidizing a small number of
Jewish farm communities in Ottoman-ruled Palestine. Sympathetic
to Herzl's plan, Kahn now introduced Herzl to a number of French
Jewish intellectuals. These introductions opened up a world Herzl

had ignored in his four years in France. One man stressed his French nationality.

"What?" cried Herzl. "Don't you and I belong to the same nation? Why did you wince when Lueger was elected? Why did I suffer when Captain Dreyfus was accused of high treason?"

But another man, a young rabbi, Kahn's son-in-law said, "I am going with you."

Herzl remained in Paris for almost a week, placating the angry Bacher in Vienna by cabling an occasional feature for the newspaper. The fact that he had to do it depressed and humiliated him. He longed to be free but knew that his hands were tied by banal material needs.

The high point of the visit was his reunion with the peripatetic Nordau. Like Benedikt, Nordau immediately understood the implications of Herzl's plan. Unlike Benedikt, Nordau converted unreservedly to the cause. He clutched Herzl in his arms and cried excitedly, "If you are insane, we are insane together!"

The world-famous author, who in his books had ridiculed the "conventional lies" of mankind, from marriage and religion to nationalism and the state, was swept off his feet by Herzl. He too had been traumatized by the Dreyfus trial. The worldwide growth of anti-Semitism was driving him back to the Judaism which, like Herzl, he had tried to forget. The elaborate intellectual constructions of this lover of clever paradox, this enemy of the irrational and the amorphous, collapsed like a house of cards.

Herzl rejoiced at his conquest of a man of great international repute whose politics and tastes were as conservative as his—"my easiest conquest and possibly the most valuable to date." He decided that Nordau might be an excellent minister of education in the new Jewish state.

Nordau still wondered whether Jews were fit "anthropologically" to form a nation. "It may take three hundred years," he said, but he would work for it anyway.

Herzl said, "No more than thirty, if the idea catches on."

The two men parted in high spirits. Nordau advised Herzl to go to London, where, he felt, Herzl could probably make important converts.

Herzl left for London the very next day, although he did not know a single soul in England. Arriving in a blizzard, armed with only an introduction by Nordau, he rode in a fog through endless streets to Kilburn, to visit Israel Zangwill, a well-known Anglo-Jewish writer, whom Nordau had met a few weeks before at a party given by the publisher William Heinemann. In his best-known book, *Children of the Ghetto* (1892), Zangwill had drawn a lively portrait of the Jewish East End of London. His humor and warmth appealed to the English romantic love for the exotic and the picturesque; he had evoked much sympathy for the Jewish refugees from czarist persecution who had found a haven in England.

Zangwill was a short man. His olive-skinned face was topped by a shock of curly, deep black hair. Sitting huddled by an open fire, he gave Herzl the impression of "a shivering southerner who has been cast up on the shores of ultima Thule." Zangwill readily agreed with Herzl's main theme. He was in favor of an independent Jewish state, but from a racial point of view. This Herzl could not accept. He jokingly contrasted Zangwill's almost Negroid features with his own Central European face. "We are a historical unit, a nation with anthropological diversities," said Herzl. "But this also suffices for a Jewish state. No nation has uniformity of race."

The two men soon got down to practical points. Zangwill undertook to introduce Herzl to several suitable men. He arranged an invitation for Herzl to address the next banquet of the Maccabeans, a club of Anglo-Jewish intellectuals and civil servants. Zangwill was tremendously impressed by Herzl. His brother Louis later remembered that after Herzl's visit, "things were never the same for us. Something had entered into the mind, fermenting, reshaping. A new era had begun."

During the next few days, Herzl met, through Zangwill, some of the leading figures in the London Jewish community. Almost everywhere he was received with sympathy. In England the ground had been prepared for Herzl's work by the "Zionist" programs of Lord Shaftesbury, Palmerston, the men of the Palestine Exploration Society, biblical scholars, and the novelist George Eliot. In her well-known book *Daniel Deronda*, Eliot had told the story of a young man who, upon discovering his Jewish parentage, returned to Judaism to work for the creation of a national home for Jews. In England, Zionism was romantically fashionable. Pious English Fundamentalists propagated the restoration of Jews in Palestine in the hope that it would bring about the second coming of Christ. Moreover, the Jewish community was small and well sheltered from abuse in a country where overt anti-Semitism was almost unknown. The easy, unproblematic self-assurance among the free Jews of England touched Herzl deeply; the contrast to Vienna was stupendous.

Herzl lunched with Sir Samuel Montagu, an Orthodox Jew,

prominent banker, and Liberal member of Parliament. After a kosher meal served by three liveried footmen, Herzl expounded his case, to which Montagu responded with enthusiasm. As early as 1892, Montagu told Herzl, he had petitioned the Turkish Sultan to grant 250,000 acres east of the River Jordan for the purpose of Jewish colonization. The plan was said to have been supported by Gladstone but "was blue-penciled out of existence by Lord Roth-schild." Montagu confessed to Herzl "in confidence" that he felt himself more an Israelite than an Englishman. "I will settle in Palestine with all my family," he said. Herzl mentioned Argentina as a possible alternative, but Montagu would not hear of it. He promised his support, political and financial, for the acquisition of Palestine only. It was possible, he thought, to buy the country for two million pounds sterling.

Herzl's speech at the Maccabean Club was the first public exposure of his plan. He received a standing ovation and was unanimously elected an honorary member. His speech was forceful and he evinced a magnetism even in a foreign language that he spoke only haltingly. He was gratified by the discovery and at the same time slightly frightened.

The emotional high point of his visit came the next day. Zangwill sent him to see Colonel Albert Edward Williamson Goldsmid. Goldsmid was a professional army officer, scion of an old military family. In the past he had supported Baron Hirsch's abortive project to settle Jews in Argentina, but only as "a nursing ground for Palestine." His dream was to be the Joshua of the new exodus. At one time Goldsmid had suggested the establishment of a Jewish armed force to charter ships and reconquer Palestine. A militarist who found solace in the Bible and in mysticism—a kind of Jewish General Gordon—he was the first eccentric romantic (a very common breed in Victorian England) to rally enthusiastically to Herzl's cause.

Herzl traveled to Cardiff, where Goldsmid was Colonel-in-Command of a Welsh regiment. The Colonel met him at the station on horseback and in uniform, and said cheerfully, "We shall work for the liberation of Palestine."

In the afternoon Herzl read Goldsmid his plan. The exposition dragged, for the Colonel did not understand much German. But he said, "This is the idea of my life." He declared his readiness to leave the British army and enter the Jewish serivce. After dinner, while the ladies and another English colonel in the party were in the drawing room, Goldsmid closeted himself with Herzl in the smoking room. And then came a remarkable story.

"I am Daniel Deronda," Goldsmid said. "I was born a Christian. Father and Mother were baptized Jews. As a young man in India I discovered this and decided to return to the ancestral fold. I was a lieutenant when I embraced Judaism. My family was furious. I eloped with a girl who was also Christian of Jewish descent, and after her conversion we were married in a synagogue. I am an Orthodox Jew. It hasn't harmed me in England. My children, Rachel and Carmel, have had a strict religious upbringing and learned Hebrew at an early age."

To Herzl the story sounded like a novel. "With Goldsmid I suddenly find myself in a different world," he wrote in his diary. He was charmed by the graceful bearing of the Colonel's daughters. He pictured the two young women as model aristocratic ladies of the future Jewish state. As he took leave of Goldsmid next morning, he wrote, "I feel close to him in my heart, like a brother."

Herzl's English visit revealed potential support, both emotional and financial, that he had not expected to find. He did not stay long enough to discover that tapping that potential was more difficult than it seemed. He was impatient to return home to finish his pamphlet, which he was sure would convert that potential into a real force. He had run around so much in the wet weather and the cold, that he left England with a bronchial catarrh.

"A prophet must have good lungs," said Nordau as he welcomed Herzl in Paris on his way home.

Herzl pointed to his light overcoat and laughed. "With such a winter coat one cannot be a prophet." Tired, coughing, brimming with new ideas, he took the train for Vienna.

3

He went to work immediately on the pamphlet. It was a revised, expanded version of his *Speech to the Rothschilds*, more cogent, factual, and persuasive, but with none of the graphic, theatrical details of the original draft. Warned by his first skirmishes with the cynics, Herzl was anxious to avoid the impression of a utopian romance, or a political science-fiction novel. The 1890s had been inundated with popular utopian romances: Edward Bellamy's portrait of a model society, *Looking Backward* (1888);

William Morris' version of ideal life, *News from Nowhere* (1891);
Theodor Hertzka's novel, *Freeland* (1890), the blueprint of a utopian state in equatorial Africa. Herzl was especially afraid that he
might be compared to Hertzka, who, like Herzl, was a Viennese
journalist, and moreover a former economic editor of the *Neue
Freie Presse*. Hertzka's African exploits had been derided in the
popular press for some time.

Herzl believed that Hertzka and the other utopians had designed complicated pieces of machinery, with many cogs and
wheels but no proof that they could be set in motion, whereas his
own plan would utilize a "force of nature." What was this force?
"The distress of the Jews! Who dares deny that this force exists?"

To avoid all suspicion of frivolity or romance, he phrased his
pamphlet in dry, laconic, matter-of-fact terms. For a time he
thought that his mission would end with the publication of the
book. The cause might be pursued by others, and he would be able
to return to his literary avocation.

While he was working on the book he saw few people. On
December 24 Güdemann came to visit, just as Herzl was lighting
the Christmas tree for his children. The Chief Rabbi was upset by
this "Christian" practice in the home of the self-appointed savior of
the Jews. But Herzl was not dismayed. "I will not let myself be
pressured! But I don't mind calling it the Hanukkah tree—or
winter solstice."

The eighty-six-page booklet was now ready for printing. He
called it *The Jewish State: An Attempt at a Modern Solution of the
Jewish Question*. To stress the break with his literary past, he
signed it, "By Theodor Herzl, Doctor of Law."

We are a *people, one* people.

We have everywhere tried honestly to integrate with the
national communities surrounding us and to retain only our
faith. We are not permitted to do so . . . in vain do we exert
ourselves to increase the glory of our fatherlands by achievements in art and in science, and their wealth by our contributions to commerce . . . we are denounced as strangers. . . . If
they would only leave us in peace. . . . But I do not think they
will.

The heart of Herzl's little book was a request that sovereignty
be granted the Jews over a land large enough to satisfy the reasonable requirements of a nation. Palestine or Argentina? The Jews

would take what was offered, and what Jewish public opinion would approve.

No reputable publisher wanted to touch the book. Herzl's regular publishers, Dunckner and Humboldt of Leipzig, would have nothing to do with it. A similar refusal came from the Jewish-owned publishing firm Cronbach of Berlin. "I do not agree that anti-Semitism is increasing," Siegfried Cronbach wrote Herzl. "In the past hundred years we Jews have seen our political and social situation improve steadily." Herzl finally signed with M. Breitenstein, a small, non-Jewish Viennese bookseller who liked the book, although he had little confidence in its commercial success.

A short excerpt was published on January 17, 1896, in the London *Jewish Chronicle*. In an accompanying editorial the *Chronicle* pondered the present phase of Austrian anti-Semitism which "must be grave indeed if such heroic remedies suggest themselves as not only advisable but also as practicable." News of this first publication was carried to Vienna by the wire services. Bacher and Benedikt were alarmed, for Herzl had been identified in the *Chronicle* as a responsible editor of the *Neue Freie Presse*. Theodor Lieben, secretary of the Jewish Community of Vienna, received an inquiry from London asking whether Herzl was really the author. His answer was no—for he knew Herzl "as a sensible man." But Güdemann, who read the first proofs, wrote Herzl enthusiastically: "This is a bombshell—it will work wonders."

Bacher and Benedikt, ignoring their gentlemen's agreement of the month before, pressured Herzl to withdraw the book. Benedikt appealed to him not as an employer, but as a friend, "personally," for Herzl's own good. He offered him money if he would withdraw. Bacher warned, "You are burning your bridges behind you." Herzl resolved to remain "hard and firm. I will agree to no procrastinations, accept no more promises."

"No individual," said Benedikt, "has the right to take upon himself the tremendous moral responsibility of setting this avalanche in motion. We shall lose our present country before we get a Jewish state. The pamphlet is unripe for publication. There is also a personal danger for you. You are risking your literary reputation."

"My honor is pledged," Herzl replied. "I have already published the idea in the *Jewish Chronicle*. It no longer belongs to me, but to all Jews. If I keep silent now, I endanger my reputation all the more."

Benedikt begged Herzl to think it over once more. His insistence bordered on hysteria. From a distance of so many years, all this excitement seems odd, but this was a time and a civilization that took the written word with deadly seriousness and saw a book as a major power in human affairs. Benedikt resorted to thinly veiled threats; he mused about the many gifted young men capable of replacing Herzl on the newspaper. He appealed to Herzl's vanity. "It is not a matter of indifference if a Dr. Theodor Herzl publishes such a book. You are one of our best collaborators, an integral part of the *Neue Freie Presse*. . . . At least you shouldn't put your name to it."

"That would be cowardice, and what's more, needless cowardice," Herzl answered. Benedikt asked him to delay for a few months and volunteered to help Herzl with the necessary rewriting.

"When?"

"This summer, when I go on vacation."

To this Herzl laughed. The confrontation continued for about two weeks. Herzl lay awake for hours in the night weighing his alternatives and the dangers to his family in the event that he should lose his employment. The excitement affected his health; he suffered from heart palpitations and shortness of breath.

In mid-February the first five hundred copies of the booklet were delivered to his home. Herzl was shaken: "This package of pamphlets constitutes the decision in a tangible form." His father rushed over to tell him that the booklet was already on display in Breitenstein's window. His parents were his only moral support; others were either against him or cautiously biding their time. "At my side I feel no one but my dear old man," wrote Herzl. "He stands firm as a tree."

4

For the next few weeks he was on pins and needles as the booklet created a stir. It is fascinating in retrospect to trace its varied impact. Few books have changed the world, and even fewer have created nations. Herzl's own newspaper maintained an icy silence. Benedikt broke his promise to publish a review and sent down an order that under no circumstances would the book or the issue be so much as mentioned in the *Presse*'s columns. Herzl reflected sardonically in his diary that the same newspaper for years had ignored the existence of socialism in the hope of silencing it out of existence.

The booklet was briefly the talk of Vienna. The first reaction, with few notable exceptions, was shock. In his memoirs, Stefan Zweig remembered the "general astonishment and annoyance of the bourgeois Jewish circles of Vienna" at the publication of "this piece of nonsense, this obtuse tract." What had happened, they wondered, to this otherwise intelligent, witty, and cultivated man?

Next there was contempt. "No man in Vienna was so derided as Herzl was," wrote Zweig, "except perhaps Sigmund Freud, his great brother in fate who also tried, single-handedly, to create a grand world concept." Quickly, through the grapevine, the derision reached Herzl's ears. In cafés and literary circles, the current retort was: "We Jews have waited two thousand years for the Jewish state, and it had to happen to me?"

An office colleague told Herzl: "You are the Jewish Jules Verne." As he entered the theater, people giggled and a murmur went around—"Herzl the King," or "His Majesty has arrived." Alexander Scharf, publisher of a Viennese weekly, when asked what he was prepared to do for Herzl's cause, replied, "If Herzl should be taken to the lunatic asylum, I shall be glad to put my carriage at his disposal." A friendly editor asked Herzl if it were true that he had gone out of his mind. Another man accosted him in the press club: "What would you like to be in your Jewish state? Prime minister? Or president of the assembly?"

To this Herzl answered, "Anyone who undertakes this sort of thing must naturally be prepared to have street urchins like you on his heels in the beginning."

Bacher warned Herzl that he risked becoming the darling of the anti-Semites. The first printed reaction—a most positive one— came in a provincial newspaper from the pen of an anti-Semitic member of parliament, Ivan von Simonyi, a notorious rabble-rouser. If Herzl was crying in the desert, there were at least a few hyenas responding.

"My warmest supporter to date," Herzl noted in his diary on March 3, "Simonyi bombards me with flattering editorials and sends me two copies of each."

Hermann Bahr told Herzl that the city's elegant literary salons were aghast. The metropolitan papers—with the exception of Herzl's own, which remained silent—soon began their attacks. In the *Wiener Allgemeine Zeitung*, Herzl's boyhood friend Julius Ludassy denounced his pamphlet as "madness born of desperation. Away with such chimeras!" Zionists were "escaping Maccabees." In *Die Zeit*, Herzl was savagely attacked by the well-known philosopher Theodor Gompertz, who admitted he had not read the book.

In a Munich newspaper the book was attacked as "an imbecilic prospectus for a Jewish Switzerland on the installment plan," the drunken dream of a *feuilletonist* whose mind had come unhinged from Jewish enthusiasm. The *Berliner Tagblatt* suggested that Herzl was an "English agent."

In political circles—except among the anti-Semites—the reaction was equally bewildered and unfavorable. Herzl sent a copy of his pamphlet to Badeni. The Prime Minister told Leon von Bilinsky, the Austrian Minister of Finance, that Zionism was an issue likely to attract "weak-minded chatterboxes." He was annoyed with Herzl anyway, for having turned down his offer of an editorship. The aging Emperor Franz Josef was revolted by Jewish nationalism as much as by any other. He told Bilinsky: "There are some people who cannot see a green meadow without trampling on it. What would have become of this ungrateful Herzl had there not been equality of rights for Jews? A curse on all these nationalist movements, for they have only strife and torment at their roots."

Bilinsky was a Pole, loyal to the monarch. His rejection of Herzl's plan was confirmed when Schönerer, the anti-Semitic leader, informed him that Herzl was right. "He can be proud of his loyal friends," Bilinsky said bitterly. Bilinsky even pointed to similarities in language between the anti-Semite and the Zionist. Schönerer was everywhere proclaiming the unification of all Germans as a "world need. Therefore it will come about." In his tract Herzl wrote, "The Jewish state is a world need. Therefore it will come about." Bismarck told an American newspaperman that Herzl's ideas were "melancholy reveries."

In spite of all the vitriol that met the publication of his pamphlet, Herzl kept steadily at his correspondence and made almost daily notations in his diary. Schnitzler, who had first voiced enthusiasm, expressed his doubts after *The Jewish State* appeared in print.

"Are you coming with us?" Herzl asked him. Schnitzler, whose *Liebelei* had just been produced at the Burgtheater, wondered if Herzl himself would emigrate; Herzl assured him that in Palestine his plays would be better produced.

"In which language?" asked Schnitzler.

"In all civilized languages," Herzl answered enthusiastically. Herzl did not intend to develop a national culture and language, but to transplant the best of Europe to the new territory, there to strike roots. But Schnitzler was a cosmopolitan. "Trees have roots, men have legs; as a poet I have wings," he exclaimed. The words became the slogan of intellectual opposition to Herzl's Zionism for decades.

Richard Beer-Hofmann, however, whose poetry celebrated the neo-romantic revival of Jewish myths and biblical heroes, was deeply moved by Herzl's tract. He wrote Herzl: "At long last, here is a man who carries his Judaism not like a burden, or as disaster, in resignation, but as the legitimate legacy of an ancient civilization." The rabbinical establishment in the West—both Orthodox and Reformed—took a different view. Güdemann, frightened by the opposition of the rich, abruptly withdrew his support following publication of Herzl's tract. In the German-Jewish press Herzl was viciously attacked as an irresponsible demagogue and fake. The representatives of five hundred Austro-Hungarian Jewish communities petitioned the Emperor to outlaw Herzl's Zionism as a godless movement. The Orthodox argument was well expressed by the father of young Julius Braunthal, the future Social Democrat, who dispelled the boy's brief infatuation with Herzl in the following words: "Surely the Jewish people will one day return to Palestine. But it will be led there by the grace of God and the Messiah, not by Herr Doctor Herzl of the *Neue Freie Presse*."

On the other hand, there were welcoming sounds in England, where Herzl had struck a note that others, including Disraeli, had sounded earlier. Holman Hunt, the great Victorian landscape painter and member of the Pre-Raphaelite school, publicly claimed priority for the idea, and for a Jewish Palestine, which he supported wholeheartedly. Hunt was probably the first who addressed himself to the problem of the present Arab population of Palestine, which he knew well from his extended visits to the Holy Land. "The Arabs are nothing more than hewers of wood and drawers of water," he said, echoing Joshua (9:12). "They don't even have to be dispossessed, for they would render the Jews very useful services." This was an aspect that did not bother anybody at this early stage.

Sir Samuel Montagu told the *Daily Chronicle* that Palestine could be acquired for two million pounds. Such concrete ideas were to Herzl's liking.

In Vienna too he had his supporters. Most important for him was the spontaneous support of the Jewish student fraternities at the University of Vienna which Herzl, with his pan-German tendencies, had shunned thirteen years before. He received numerous requests to address student groups, but turned down most of them. "Speaking to enthusiastic friends like you would only make me vain," he wrote the fraternity of *Gamalah* on February 28. "I prefer to address opponents, in the hope of moving their hearts."

He was besieged by veteran Zionists of all ages, mostly of East European origin, who came to vow their undying support for an idea they had already begun to despair of. Herzl was amazed to discover that he had precursors in this cause, which since the 1860s had been espoused by a few isolated enthusiasts, mostly in the East European hotbed of nationalism and in czarist Russia, which Lenin was later to call the great prison of nations. For the first time Herzl now read Leo Pinsker's *Auto-Emancipation** and was baffled by the similarity to his own analysis and remedy. "It is a pity I did not read this work before I wrote my own. On the other hand, it is a good thing I did not, or perhaps I would have abandoned my own undertaking."

Seldom has a movement owed more to the fact that its founder was totally ignorant of his predecessors. Pinsker was only one of a half-dozen writers who had advocated similar schemes in the past. Several rival sects of liberal Zionists and socialist Zionists had even sprouted up in Eastern Europe and in some Western universities. The so-called Lovers of Zion movement, a loose network of peripatetic clubs, was already engaged in the support of a few isolated Jewish colonies in Palestine.

The adherents of various Zionist policies now flocked to Herzl's door whenever they came through Vienna. Almost without exception they were East European–born. Julie was shocked by their strange manner and their occasional wildness. Poor, ill-clad, intense, passionately argumentative, they intruded on the elegant household and did not enhance the understanding between Herzl and his wife.

There was, first and foremost, Nathan Birnbaum, the inventor three years earlier of the term "Zionism." One afternoon late in February 1896, Birnbaum and a few of his Zionist disciples were sitting in a Viennese café when a friend rushed in breathlessly to announce that the famous Dr. Herzl of the *Neue Freie Presse* had just published a pro-Zionist tract. The company was electrified; it was as if a revolutionary cell in London had been informed that a senior editor of the conservative *Times* had just written a communist pamphlet. None of them had known that Herzl was interested in the subject, or even that he was a Jew. It was decided immediately to dispatch a delegation to him.

* See p. 59.

In 1893 Birnbaum had written his own little tract, which few people read, entitled *The National Rebirth of the Jewish People in Its Own Country, as a Means to Resolve the Jewish Question. An Appeal to All Noble-Minded Men of Good Will.* He was a man of sharp critical intelligence and pronounced socialist leanings. He was desperately poor; his mother had sold her little shop to enable him to publish an obscure fortnightly magazine, *Self-emancipation*, which advocated a Jewish state in Palestine, in application of Pinsker's ideas. With his fiery voice, his unruly beard and hair, Birnbaum was a wild sort of man with a quick temper. He immediately asked Herzl for money and attempted to involve him in the spiderly infighting of his little sect.

March 1: The Zionists Birnbaum, Kohn, and Landau paid me a joint visit and wrangled among themselves.

Kohn is against Landau. . . . Birnbaum wants agitation to be confined to scholarly weeklies, Landau wants to agitate everywhere, Kohn only in Vienna. It is downright disheartening to watch their rank hostility toward one another.

Birnbaum is unmistakably jealous of me.

March 4: Dr. Birnbaum today wrote me a letter in which he bemoans his financial straits. I gave him twenty gulden, which I record here, because I am certain he is hostile to me and will grow more so. Landau writes that Birnbaum wants to become the socialist leader in Palestine. We haven't got a country yet, and already they are tearing it apart.

5

At the same time the lonely veterans of the cause inevitably became suspicious of Herzl's sudden intrusion into their affairs. Who was this latter-day prophet? Why was he so indifferent to Jewish culture and so patronizing to the Hebrew language, which they held so dear? Was he serious? Or an impostor? Was he really without knowledge of his predecessors? Or did he merely pretend to be ignorant, in the hope of "usurping" the leadership of their little "movement"? The writer Arthur Levysohn, Herzl's Berlin acquaintance, warned him that those he wanted to help would be the first to "nail him to the cross." In the first few months it often seemed that this prediction would come true. Nahum Sokolow, later Herzl's faithful stalwart, lashed out against Herzl's tract in the pro-Zionist Hebrew weekly *Hazephira*, published in Warsaw. The headline itself was sarcastic: "Wonderful Rumors About the Establishment of a Jewish State Originating from the Mind of a Dr. Herzl."

Sokolow derided the Viennese *"feuilletonist* who dabbles in diplomacy." He surmised that Herzl's activity might harm the Palestine colonies and warned Herzl to control his prophetic energy. Otherwise, he wrote, *Hazephira* might be forced to denounce "this honorable dreamer as the spokesman of his own private vision, not that of his people."

But these were isolated cases, not surprising under the circumstances. In the East—Galicia, Romania, and czarist Russia—the "message" of Herzl's book fell like a torch on dry straw. The book itself was available to few people because of czarist censorship, but its reputation spread quickly; its very vagueness enhanced the popular notion of a great and wondrous event. David Ben-Gurion, later the first Prime Minister of Israel (1948–1963), was a ten-year-old boy in the little Jewish *shtetl* of Plonsk when Herzl's tract was published in Vienna. Ben-Gurion later recalled a rumor spreading suddenly "that the Messiah had arrived—a tall, handsome man, a learned man of Vienna, a doctor no less—Theodor Herzl."

Here, in an area roughly corresponding to present-day Romania, Poland, and the Soviet republics of the Ukraine, Byelorussia, Latvia, and Lithuania, was the Jews' great house of bondage. Some six million Jews eked out a meager, dreary existence. About five million of the most miserable lived, like Ben-Gurion, under czarist rule, forced to reside, like the Bantus of twentieth-century South Africa, in restricted areas, the so-called Pale of Settlement. Their situation was radically different from that of the assimilated, or semi-assimilated Western Jews with whom Herzl was familiar. The Jews of Eastern Europe were wedged in as aliens between Poles and Lithuanians, Russians and Ukrainians, Letts, Magyars, Germans, and Slovaks, a multitude of diverse people whose separate national aspirations were beginning to rock the foundations of two great multinational empires. The Jews of the East, unlike those of the West, were a cohesive ethnic group, separate and distinct in almost every way. They spoke their own Yiddish language. They lived in tight, semi-urban clusters (little towns where they often constituted a near majority), a people among peoples, clinging tenaciously to their own traditions, liturgy, diet, and even dress. They were the only people on earth who had succeeded in retaining their national identity without a national territory. But the cost to themselves was grim. They were exposed to brutal, discriminatory legislation and to periodic spurts of violence, arson, and looting.

Here, long before Herzl's tract, the message of liberal European nationalism, as enunciated by Mazzini, had fallen on receptive ears: "Without a country of your own you have neither name, nor rights, nor admission as brothers into the fellowship of peoples. You are the bastards of humanity."

Here, rather than among Jews of the West, Herzl's clarion call—"We are a *people, one* people!"—echoed with particular vigor from one corner of the Pale to another. Here, fourteen years before Herzl's emergence, a small but devoted number of Jewish intellectuals had agitated for the settlement of Palestine by young Jewish university students retrained as farmers, a back-to-the-land, back-to-the-people movement inspired partly by Tolstoi, partly by the age-old messianic hope of Zion redeemed in justice. It was by no means a mass movement. For every Jew who migrated to Palestine, tens of thousands went to America. But as Machiavelli had said, before a man could become Moses, there must first be children of Israel who want to leave Egypt. The radical difference between Eastern Jews and those of Herzl's West was that the former wanted to get out and the Western Jews wanted to remain.

From the massive contemporary evidence it is not difficult to reconstruct the enthusiasm that Herzl's tract generated among the poor and oppressed of the East. In their hearts there always vibrated the fear of pogroms. Herzl's appearance was probably more significant than his tract, which few were able to read. The very fact that Herzl was an outsider, an assimilated, free Jew, with a foot, like Moses, in Pharaoh's camp, added to his magical appeal. "The credibility of strangers is always greater than that of one's own people. This is one reason for the success of impostors," Herzl himself had written, in a totally different context, in 1890. The response to his tract in Russia surpassed his most optimistic expectations.

The enthusiasm generated in the East by Herzl's appearance quickly spilled over to the Jewish Russian student colonies in universities in the West. The Russian-born Chaim Weizmann (first President of Israel, 1948–1953) was a second-year student at the University of Berlin, active there in a small cell of Russian Zionist students. Herzl's tract struck Weizmann and his friends "like a bolt from the blue." Herzl's ideas were not new. Weizmann and his

friends had adopted them a long time before. They were enthralled, not by the ideas, but, as Weizmann later wrote, "by the
personality which stood behind them. Here was daring, clarity, and
energy. The very fact that this Westerner came to us unencum-
bered by our own preconceptions had its appeal. We were right in
our instinctive appreciation that what had emerged from the tract
was less a concept than a historic personality."

Herzl was surprised by the resonance of his tract in the East;
he had expected it to strike hardest in the assimilated West, not in
the East, which he regarded as backward, even primitive.

His fatigue from all the excitement, meanwhile, gave way to
illness. By mid-March his heart palpitations grew worse. His worried parents insisted on a thorough medical examination. The family
physician diagnosed "a heart ailment caused by agitation." The
doctor could not understand why Herzl concerned himself so much
with the Jewish cause; among the Jews he associated with, he
claimed, no one understood it either. He strongly recommended a
prolonged rest.

But within less than five days Herzl was again rushing about,
meeting students, supervising the English translation of his tract,
negotiating with the banker Adolf Dessauer* about a loan of one
million guldens for the creation of a national pro-Zionist daily newspaper. He was swamped with letters of support, from all sorts of
remote places, especially in the East. A man from his father's birthplace wrote that all Semlin Jews were ready to emigrate en masse
as soon as the Society of Jews was formed. A Hassidic leader in
Poland wrote that three million *Hassidim* were ready to join Herzl's
movement.** At a mass meeting in Sofia, presided over by the
Chief Rabbi, Herzl was proclaimed the Messiah. On April 8 he
wrote, "I already have my reward. The poor regard me as their
friend. From Russia, Galicia, Romania, Bulgaria, I receive fervent
expressions of support. The academic youth is with me. In England
the matter is treated with utmost seriousness."

His list of countries is significant in terms of those left out.
Within weeks of the German publication of his tract, authorized
translations were being prepared in English, Russian, Yiddish,
Hebrew, Spanish, French, and Romanian. The English translation
was greeted by the London *Daily Chronicle* with a whimsical review: "To your tents, O Israel! For another Moses has arisen in the

* See p. 71.
** Herzl, characteristically, responded that the participation of Orthodox
Jews was most welcome—"but we are not going to have a theocracy."

person of Dr. Th. Herzl. . . . We do not remember to have read a more elaborate or amusing effort of the scientific imagination."

Other British newspapers ignored Herzl's tract, and only about a hundred English copies were sold. Meanwhile, undaunted, Herzl continued his efforts. As a result of his constant writing, his right hand was cramped and nearly incapacitated for weeks. The daily schedule of this lonely man was a curious mixture of the serious and the bizarre. He was visited by his strange supporter, the anti-Semitic rabble-rouser Ivan von Simonyi. The loquacious sexagenarian surprised Herzl with his "astonishing amount of sympathy for Jews." However, Simonyi told Herzl that he was absolutely convinced Jews were in fact murdering little Christian babies for ritual purposes. "But along with this, Simonyi has the brightest, most modern ideas. He loves me!"

In May he was visited by a different sort of man, a timber merchant from Cologne by the name of David Wolffsohn. The meeting had important consequences. Wolffsohn soon became his closest collaborator, and after Herzl's death in 1904, took over as president of the Zionist movement. Wolffsohn, son of poor Lithuanian parents, had emigrated to Germany as a youngster. He was a self-made man of considerable wealth. Deeply rooted in Jewish culture and the Jewish traditions of the East—of which Herzl knew so little—he was a man of great human warmth and loving concern for his less fortunate coreligionists. He was active in the Lovers of Zion movement in Germany. This eminently practical man, whose nature would so well complement Herzl's impatient flamboyance, traveled to Vienna expressly to meet the author of the booklet that had left him "a thoroughly changed man." Wolffsohn expected to meet a clean-shaven, corpulent "Viennese type." He was astounded to encounter instead "Herzl's imposing figure. From the first moment on I was tremendously impressed by his majestic appearance."

Wolffsohn placed himself at Herzl's disposal "unreservedly, with all that I am and all that I have." He was surprised to hear Herzl's strange notions of the Eastern Jews. Herzl, on the other hand, was astonished to discover that Wolffsohn was a "Russian Jew" and that Russians were "Europeans." Thus far he had considered Russian Jews as primitive people, a passive mass to be transferred to the new land.

He knew very little of the Jewish East. Yet strangely, he derived strength and courage from his ignorance. The Russian Zionist agitator Menachem Ussishkin came to see him later in the year.

Ussishkin was a fierce, imperious, arrogant man who believed in deeds, not in words, and regarded Herzl as a superficial theoretician. Ussishkin was a Jewish populist who might have stepped out of a Russian revolutionary novel. He would cause endless trouble in the future as the head of a vociferous opposition to Herzl's leadership. Upon leaving Herzl's house after his first visit, he remarked, "His greatest deficiency will be his most useful asset. He does not know the first thing about Jews. Therefore he believes there are only external obstacles to Zionism, no internal ones. *We should not open his eyes to the facts of life, so that his faith remains potent.*"

Herzl was not impressed by Ussishkin. He did not yet believe in mass agitation or the need for a well-organized political machine. He aimed at an "aristocratic" solution from above. He still turned down offers to address mass meetings. "Great things need no solid foundations," he wrote on May 12. "An apple must be put on the table so that it will not fall. The earth floats in mid-air. Similarly I may be able to found and stabilize the Jewish state without any firm support. The secret lies in motion."

He looked around for a grand diplomatic opening which might resolve his problem in one stroke. Quite unexpectedly, it walked through his door one day in the person of a long-bearded, eccentric English parson.

9

Princes, Pashas, and Millionaires

"HERE I AM!" cried the Reverend William Hechler, Chaplain to the British embassy in Vienna, as he rushed excitedly into Herzl's study.

"That I can see," Herzl answered cheerfully. "But who are you?"

"You are puzzled," Hechler said, "but, you see, as long ago as 1882 I predicted your Coming to the Grand Duke of Baden. Now I am going to help you."

Herzl blinked at his unusual visitor. The Reverend William Hechler was a fifty-year-old man, short, with delicate limbs and blazing eyes. His high and furrowed forehead descended on a pair of heavy, bushy eyebrows. The "long gray beard of a prophet," in Herzl's words, came with the winning smile of a True Believer.

"I have prepared the ground for you," Hechler announced triumphantly. He told Herzl that he regarded his new Zionist movement as a "prophetic crisis" which Hechler himself had foretold years before. On the basis of a prophecy dating from the reign of the Caliph Omar (637–638), he had calculated that following forty-two "prophetic months," that is, 1,260 years, Palestine would be restored to the Jews. This would make it in 1897 or 1898. Hechler presented Herzl with a copy of a booklet he had published in 1893 announcing his discovery, entitled *The Restoration of the Jews to Palestine according to the Prophecy.* Hechler had accidentally discovered Herzl's pamphlet in a bookshop and was astounded at the coincidence. It had to be divinely inspired. As Chaplain to

the British embassy, he had immediately rushed with his discovery
to his ambassador, Edmond Monson, and told him: "The fore-
ordained movement is here! He lives among us—incognito—the
King of the Jews!"

Hechler told Herzl that as the former tutor at the court of the
Grand Duke of Baden, he was on intimate terms with his nephew,
the German Emperor Wilhelm. "Did you intend to fulfill a prophecy when you wrote your book?" Hechler asked hopefully.

"I am not a theologian," Herzl answered evasively. "I arrive
rationally at all my conclusions."

"In any event," said Hechler, "I will help you. I shall arrange
an audience for you with the German Kaiser, to whom I shall
highly recommend your plan." The Kaiser, he said, would lead the
Jews back to their promised land.

Herzl did not know what to make of this peculiar man: "Next
to Colonel Goldsmid he is the oddest person I have met in this
movement so far." As British embassy Chaplain, Hechler occupied
a position in "official" Viennese society. His reputation, though controversial, was considerable. In a lecture he had given in 1891
("Ancient History in the Light of Recent Researches") he had
"proved scientifically" to an astounded Viennese audience that the
Patriarchs had indeed lived for hundreds and hundreds of years.
He had also calculated the exact date of the Flood. Some people in
Vienna considered Hechler a hypocrite. Herzl's impression of Hechler's oddness was strengthened a few days later when he paid
Hechler a return visit at the British embassy. Even as he climbed
the stairs to Hechler's fourth-floor apartment,

> I heard the sound of organ music.
> The room I entered is lined with books on every side, from
> floor to ceiling:
> Nothing but Bibles.

Hechler showed Herzl his sacred treasures. He then spread out
a huge British military ordnance map of Palestine. Its four sheets
covered the entire floor. Herzl was fully conscious of the bizarre-
ness of the scene, as he and Hechler, surrounded on all sides by
Bibles, knelt on the rustling paper and crawled up and down the
promised land. Hechler showed Herzl the exact spot where, according to his calculations, "our new Temple must be built. At Bethel,
for that is the geographic center of the country." Next he showed
Herzl models of the ancient temple. "You see! We have prepared

the ground for you!" Hechler exclaimed triumphantly again and again.

They were interrupted by the visit of two pious English ladies, to whom Hechler showed his map once more, along with his Bibles, souvenirs, and other knickknacks, while Herzl grew very bored. Hechler played a Zionist hymn of his own composition on the organ. Herzl was very glad to see the two ladies finally leave.

The two men then returned to practical matters. Hechler declared that he was prepared to go to Karlsruhe and Berlin to arrange audiences for Herzl with the Grand Duke of Baden and the Kaiser.

"I have only one scruple," Hechler said, "namely, that as mortals we must not contribute anything to the fulfillment of the prophecy. But even this scruple is dispelled, for you began your work without me and you will complete it without me."

A trip to Berlin would cost money. Hechler was an impecunious prophet, living on a meager salary. "Would you be willing to give me the travel expenses?"

Herzl assured him at once of his support. "It will come to a few hundred guldens, a considerable sacrifice in my circumstances," he reasoned to himself, "but I will risk it on the slight chance that I might speak to the Kaiser."

He realized that Hechler, whom he did not really know at all, could well be a "penniless clergyman fond of travel. Perhaps he will come back and say that it was impossible to reach the Kaiser."

Viewed through the eyes of a seasoned, skeptical Viennese newspaperman, Hechler certainly was a highly "improbable figure." But, Herzl told himself, the Grand Duke and the Kaiser might see Hechler in a different light. Experience had taught Herzl that great offices are often filled by little men: "Highly placed persons do not reason any more broadly or see any more clearly than the rest of us." The Grand Duke and the Kaiser were just as likely to be charmed by Hechler's naïve fancies as to laugh at them. Herzl accepted Hechler as a naïve visionary, a charming, likable man with the quirks of a collector. As he pondered the pros and cons, a little surprised with himself, he decided that, even as a fake, Hechler might well render an important service.

As Herzl was leaving, Hechler assured him that their departure for Jerusalem was quite imminent, in fact less than two years away. With winning exuberance he even showed Herzl the coat pocket in which he would carry his big map when the two of them rode up and down the Holy Land together. This last gesture struck Herzl as

Hechler's "most naïve, but also his most *convincing*, touch." A
little dazed, but hopeful, he then went home, where he found one
of his wife's relatives who had come to report the snide gossip then
current about his Zionist quixotism. "The same Jews who now poke
fun at me," he told his wife's brother-in-law, "will later derogate me
as a shrewd speculator, when success has come."

A few weeks went by before Hechler's connections began to
play a role. During this interval, on April 14, the German Kaiser
came to Vienna for a short visit. Herzl spent an evening at the
opera in a box diagonally across from the imperial loge, studying
the Kaiser's every movement. That same evening, he arrived home
to find that Hechler had been patiently waiting for him for over an
hour. Hechler told him that he was leaving for Karlsruhe early in
the morning to arrange Herzl's audience. The clergyman's eyes
shone brightly. Softly, he repeated over and over, in English: "To
fulfill prophecy!" He asked Herzl for a photograph, apparently so
he could show his royal friends that Herzl was no "shabby Jew."

Herzl was still a little incredulous. Next morning he went to
Hechler's residence to inquire after him, for the whole affair still
appeared highly improbable. But Hechler had really gone. On the
following day he cabled: "Everyone enthusiastic. Hold yourself in
readiness. Hechler. Circle 2."* Herzl remained skeptical. His
thoughts wandered back to Baron Hirsch. As so often in the past
year, he was remorseful about his blunders with Hirsch in their one
and only meeting in Paris. Why had he told him, "Everything you
do is wrong," without properly outlining his own plan? He sat
down and wrote Max Nordau in Paris, asking him to put out another feeler. "If Hirsch will withdraw from [his] Argentina [plan],
and come with us—for today it is clear that the masses want nothing but Palestine—we might win within the foreseeable future. We
need a few millions for propaganda and a few more for *baksheesh*
in Turkey." An hour after he dispatched this letter, Herzl learned
that Hirsch had died the previous night on his estate in Hungary.

Sensitive as always to dramatic coincidence, Herzl was dumbfounded by Hirsch's sudden death: "The pamphlet has been finished for months. I gave it to everyone but Hirsch. The minute I
decide to do so, he dies. His participation might have helped our
cause to succeed tremendously quickly." Why hadn't he written to
Hirsch earlier? He was shaken out of this mood of self-accusation
by another cable from Hechler. The bizarre clergyman was no fake

---

* This may have been an astrological reference.

after all. The cable summoned Herzl to an audience with the Emperor's uncle, the Grand Duke Friedrich of Baden. "A curious day," Herzl wrote. "Hirsch dies and I make contact with princes."

Early next morning he left for Karlsruhe, the capital of the Grand Duke's little principality. Throughout the long journey his thoughts turned again and again to the late Baron Hirsch. He felt he was finally beginning to pass from dream to reality. "The Jews have lost Hirsch, but they have me," he wrote in a shaking hand as the train roared through the lovely countryside of the upper Rhine valley. "And after me they will have someone else. Things *must* get better."

2

Meanwhile, at Karlsruhe, Hechler was preparing his royal hosts for Herzl's visit. To a roomful of courtiers and princes he delivered a sermon in which he announced that the restoration of the Jews to their ancient homeland was imminent. He unfolded his "prophetic charts." They apparently made a deep impression, especially on the aged Grand Duke. The Kaiser himself was more interested in Hechler's British ordnance map of Palestine. He greeted the clergyman with the words "Hello, Hechler! I hear that you want to become a minister in the Jewish state!"

Nonplussed, Hechler replied in English, against etiquette, that he had no personal ambitions, except to fulfill prophecy, whereupon the Kaiser continued in English: "Is not Rothschild behind all this?"

Hechler vehemently denied that. He knew well that so far Herzl had met nothing but obstacles among the rich Jews. Hechler told the Kaiser that Herzl's support came from the downtrodden and poor whom the Lord had blessed, for theirs was the kingdom of heaven. The Kaiser, he suggested, might help, as a first step, to restore the temporal Jerusalem.

Wilhelm II did not reject the matter out of hand, and so Hechler had another talk with him. The Kaiser was interested, but noncommittal. The discussion seemed to have ended there.

Hechler had much more luck with the Grand Duke. The old man spoke to him of his son, the late Prince Ludwig, whose tutor Hechler had been. He wept freely; Hechler comforted him and read him a psalm that mentioned Zion, and the two men prayed together.

This put the Grand Duke in a more receptive frame of mind. The restoration of the Jews in Zion! The Grand Duke, still weeping, asked Hechler: "What could I actually do for this worthwhile cause?"

"Your Royal Highness has made history once," Hechler said. "What if you were to do it again? You were the first among the German princes at Versailles who pronounced King Wilhelm as Emperor of the new German Reich. What if you were to participate in the second great state-founding of this century as well? For, believe me, the Jews will be a *grande nation!*" He was not a prophet, Hechler stressed, nor the son of a prophet, but "only a humble student of divinity watching the signs of the time. . . . It does seem to me that the forty-two prophetic months mentioned in Revelation eleven, verse twelve, are coming to an end in 1897 or 1898. Your Royal Highness—the Second Coming of Christ is near."

The little speech impressed the pious Grand Duke very much. He ordered Hechler to summon Herzl so that he could discuss the matter with him directly.

All this Hechler related to Herzl when he met him at the station, overflowing with joy and good tidings. Herzl was swept along by Hechler's enthusiasm. The Emperor had unfortunately left the previous day, but the Grand Duke would receive him in the afternoon.

Herzl made nervous preparations for the audience. He fussed over his clothes.

Hechler asked, "Don't you want to wear tails?"

"No," said Herzl, "too formal an attire might appear tactless. The Grand Duke wishes to speak to me incognito."

He decided on a dark, conservative Prince Albert suit: "Externals increase in importance the higher one climbs. Up there, everything becomes symbolic." At the same time he admonished himself: "I must not be dizzy on these heights. I shall think of death. I shall be earnest, cool, calm, firm, modest, but determined, and speak the same way."

All this fret and fuss over an audience with the ruler of a petty German principality may seem strange and exaggerated unless one remembers that grand dukes like Friedrich of Baden, in 1896, still moved about in public like demigods. Friedrich, the uncle of the German Emperor and a cousin by marriage of the Czar, was said to be influential with both monarchs.

Despite his resolve, Herzl was "breathless" with excitement as he entered the ducal castle. The cheerful Hechler sensed his confusion. He "chattered without break" to dispel Herzl's shyness. "Don't be frightened," he said. "The Grand Duke is only a man, like you and me." Once more the marvelous quality of total candor in Herzl's diaries is both remarkable and endearing. He was terribly self-conscious. The Duke ignored his outstretched hand as he came into the room, but shook Hechler's. Herzl's chair was uncomfortable; he noted with dismay that it directly faced the light.

The interview, however, was a tremendous personal success. It lasted two and a half hours. The Grand Duke was swept away by Herzl's persuasive force. A man of great humanity, he genuinely sympathized with the travails of Jews in the liberal West and with their oppression in the autocratic realm of his Russian cousin. With all the good-natured benevolence of the ruler of a prosperous, liberal little fairy-tale principality, he pronounced himself ready to help. Herzl not only charmed the old man, with great shrewdness he appealed to both his humanitarian instincts and to his fear of revolution. He said that a Jewish state would be a benefit to all concerned; those Jews who settled there would find a new dignity, and those who remained in their present host countries would assimilate more quickly and probably disappear without trace. Moreover, Zionism might divert young Jewish idealists from the revolutionary parties.

"I wish it were so," the Grand Duke murmured, "I wish it were so. I think it will be a blessing for many people!" His single concern was that his support of Herzl could be misinterpreted by his own Jewish subjects; they might think he wanted to drive them out of the country.

"Only those Jews who want to will go," Herzl explained. "Since the Jews of Baden are content under your Royal Highness's liberal reign, they will not emigrate, and rightly so." He asked the Grand Duke to use his good offices with the Kaiser.

The Grand Duke smiled. "I advise him, but he does what he wants."

Herzl added, "I would like to make an effort myself to explain the merits of the plan to the Kaiser. If he consented to receive me, it would remain as secret as this conversation."

The Duke did not reject this request. Within a few weeks, in fact, he warmly recommended Herzl to the Kaiser. During their meeting, however, he urged that Herzl first create his Society of Jews, as a representative body. "Then one shall see whether one can deal with it." He wondered whether it would not be better to first send a few hundred thousand Jews to Palestine and later raise the question with the Sultan of Turkey and the great powers.

"That I am against," Herzl said with great determination. "It would amount to sneaking in. . . . I want to do everything openly, aboveboard, fully within the law."

Throughout their long talk, Herzl carefully dissociated himself from Hechler's metaphysical, "prophetic" approach to the issue. He argued from a rational, political point of view. When, toward the end, Hechler took the floor and discoursed on the imminent fulfillment of divine prophecy, the Duke swallowed his every word and listened "silently and magnificently in his faith, with a strikingly calm look in his fine, steady eyes."

"I should like to see it come about," he said again. Herzl and Hechler took their leave. Now the Duke warmly shook Herzl's hand "and held it for a very long time."

"I hope very much you will achieve your goal," said the Duke, adding many kind words of farewell.

The audience was over. A little dazed, Herzl walked past the lackeys and the guards, who seemed to wonder at the unusual length of the audience. He could hardly speak. To Hechler, he simply said, "He is a wonderful person."

Outside, the castle park was bathed in the lovely light of a clear evening. The spring air was fresh and peaceful. Herzl walked Hechler back to his lodgings in an annex of the palace. The exuberant clergyman was anxious to cable his Revivalist friends in London that "two European sovereigns" had been won over to the cause, that the fulfillment of prophecy was imminent. Herzl urged him not to do anything so rash. For the moment he was content to enjoy the discreet aspects of his success; for the moment he was a very happy man.

3

On the train back to Vienna Hechler spread his Palestine map on the floor of their compartment and lectured Herzl for hours on the geography of the Holy Land. The restored Jewish state should stretch from the Suez Canal in the south to the Taurus Mountains (Turkey) in the north: "Just as in the days of David and Solomon!"

Herzl arrived home in high spirits. He wrote Nordau: "I do not think I am in error when I say, 'The matter is getting serious.' " On

Whitsunday he recorded in his diary the first anniversary of his visit to Baron Hirsch. "If, during the coming year, I make relatively the same progress as I did from the zero point of last year to the achievements of today, then we shall be *leshanah habah bi-Jerushalayim* [next year in Jerusalem]!"

His optimism was reinforced by another coincidental meeting. While he was plotting with Hechler, Herzl had found himself an even stranger ally, Count Philip Michael de Nevlinski, to whom he was introduced by a Viennese friend. Nevlinski was a Polish nobleman of dubious repute, a free-lancing diplomatic agent who promised to smooth Herzl's way into the Turkish Sultan's court. He was the publisher of a little newsletter in Vienna called *Correspondance de l'Est*. Newsletters of this kind were not uncommon political instruments of the time; through them governments floated trial balloons or spread rumors and reports for which they did not care to be held responsible.

Nevlinski was a mysterious man, amazingly well connected in the Balkan countries and especially in Constantinople. He was an intimate of the Turkish Sultan and enjoyed the unique privilege of being able to see him at almost any time. He was carefully shadowed by the secret services of at least three European powers. He was a diplomatic mercenary, successively or simultaneously in the pay of the Austrian, French, Russian, Bulgarian, Turkish, Italian, and Serbian governments. If he had any real personal commitment, it was that of an exiled Polish patriot, who would have liked to disrupt the European balance of power that had led to the partition of his Polish fatherland.

As a young man of twenty-two he had joined in the Polish mutiny of 1863 against Russia; as a result his family's estates at Volhynia had been confiscated by the czarist government. He was a wry and disillusioned man of considerable culture, charm, and versatility, with a sense of humor to match. He held all governments in disdain and liked to present his friends with birthday gifts of genuine medals which he had succeeded in wangling out of the various sovereigns of his acquaintance. To a modern observer he resembles a character from a Graham Greene novel. He treated politics as a fine art of sly intrigue. He told Herzl he admired Bismarck "the way a musician listens to Rubinstein playing the piano."

This likable, complex, disillusioned Pole cannot be dismissed as a mere "adventurer." His life was overcast by the tragedy of exile. "Since I cannot shape the politics of my own Polish nation, I don't give a damn for anything," he told Herzl. "I go on artistic *tournées* in diplomacy, like a pianist—that is all." Herzl, noting that Nevlinski was a devout, practicing Catholic who yet worked for the Jewish cause, was convinced that his scheme heralded the true reconciliation between Judaism and Christianity.

When Herzl first met him in March 1896, Nevlinski's fortunes were low; the Austrian government had cut his retainer, on the suspicion, undoubtedly justified, that he was a double agent. A contemporary Austrian intelligence report preserved in the Austrian archives stated, "Herr von Nevlinski is a thoroughly unreliable man, in the pay of our opponents."

Herzl was very much taken by Nevlinski's romantic allure, just as Nevlinski was taken by his. Herzl hoped to purchase Palestine from the Turkish Sultan, much as Disraeli had bought Cyprus from the Turks in 1878. He convinced himself that Nevlinski could be the proper intermediary. Nevlinski himself was not so sure. Although he was normally ready to serve almost any cause for money, it took Herzl some weeks to engage his services, for Nevlinski had been warned that Herzl was "not serious"; he also knew of his lack of funds. Herzl finally succeeded in hiring him for a pittance, compared to Nevlinski's going rates. There is some reason to believe that Nevlinski was excited by the very audacity of Herzl's undertaking, which he may have hoped the Poles might emulate one day; Herzl was possibly the only employer whom Nevlinski never consciously cheated.

A contemporary claimed that Herzl "never wholly believed, never wholly distrusted" his strange agent. As with Hechler, he felt it worthwhile to take the chance. The position of "secret" or "unofficial" agent was not as disreputable in the nineteenth century as it would soon become in our own less individualistic era. Nevlinski's "diplomacy by agents" was the obverse of "government by gentlemen"; it afforded scope for many efforts that could be repudiated by the "gentlemen" in power if occasion demanded.

This, then, was the man Herzl hoped would open for him the *Sublime Porte* of Turkey that led to his coveted goal. In his conversation with the Grand Duke of Baden, Herzl had already mentioned the exchange he planned to offer the Sultan (through Nevlinski): the Jews of Europe would "regulate" the Sultan's finances and take over the huge national debt. This would relieve Turkey of its humiliating subservience to French and British creditors. In return, Palestine—"not a very valuable territory"—would be leased to the Jews either as an independent state or as a vassal territory. The Grand Duke had very much warmed to the idea. Early in May, Nevlinski reported to Herzl that he had spoken of the plan to the Sultan. The Sultan seemed to have had only one objection: Jerusalem, as a holy place for Islam, was not negotiable. Herzl was not daunted. "We can easily get around this difficulty," he told Nevlinski. "Jerusalem will be extraterritorial. It will belong to nobody, and to all—a holy place in the joint possession of all believers. The great condominium of culture and morality."

After some weeks of talk back and forth, during which some money apparently changed hands, Nevlinski finally agreed to accompany Herzl to Constantinople. They set out on their journey on June 15. Nevlinski began to prove his usefulness on the train by introducing Herzl to a number of fellow-traveling Turkish statesmen and diplomats, with whom he was clearly on an intimate footing. The journey took two days. In a series of long conversations in the restaurant car, Herzl's plan was discussed, criticized, but not dismissed by the Turks.

"It is against our principles to sell any territory," Ziad Pasha, a leading Turkish statesman, told Herzl.

"But why?" Herzl replied. "It has happened in history countless times."

"Only recently England relinquished Helgoland to Germany," Nevlinski interjected.

"Under no circumstances will you get Palestine as an independent state," Ziad persisted, "but perhaps you will get it as a vassal."

This was really enough for Herzl, although he did not say so in order to retain a bargaining position. As they approached their destination, his hopes soared. His spirits were further raised by the moving scene that awaited him at Sofia. News of his passage had preceded him. When the train stopped at the station an enormous crowd of Bulgarian Jews hailed the author of *The Jewish State* as their long-awaited savior. The crowd included old and young; men, women, and children. Herzl was completely surprised. One gray-bearded patriarch in a fur coat reminded him of his late grandfather.

The other passengers looked on in astonishment at the scene. A bouquet was presented, and in speeches delivered in French and German, Herzl was proclaimed "leader," "the heart of Israel," and its hope. As the train began to move, there was considerable commotion. People were waving their hats and crying, "Next year in Jerusalem!" and "Long live Herzl! Long live the Jews!"

They reached Constantinople on June 17. At the hotel Herzl

took nothing less than the royal suite. The experienced Nevlinski insisted on this to enhance Herzl's standing as the spokesman of a nation and the representative of vast (though as yet nonexistent) financial resources. From Herzl's windows a magnificent panorama of mosques and minarets extended over the green hills that crowned the Golden Horn. In the dazzling sun, the dilapidated splendor of Constantinople—grass growing between the stones— struck Herzl, as "though nature were slowly recapturing this crumbling town."

Next morning he awoke in a fine mood. Outside, in the gardens, light filtered through the silver leaves of olive trees, and the bright air was full of damp freshness and the odor of charcoal smoke. Herzl's eyes feasted on the "astonishingly beautiful, dirty city." He was elated by the view of the Bosporus, lined with white palaces shining in the morning sun.

But his mind soon reeled at the labyrinthine convolutions of negotiating with inscrutable Turkish officials. Herzl felt like Alice in Wonderland. But he was pleased with Nevlinski, who seemed to be as well connected as he had claimed. He had intended to use Nevlinski "only as an instrument. Yet now I am at the point where I esteem and love him."

His first major appointment was with the Grand Vizier, Khalil Rifat Pasha. The Grand Vizier received Herzl in a large salon at the palace of the *Sublime Porte*. He was a tall, stooped old man; his wrinkled, withered face was encased in a fine, long white beard. Through an interpreter Herzl expounded his proposed trade. We shall free Turkey, he told the Grand Vizier, free her from the clutches of her foreign creditors who had seized the bankrupt state's revenues. Moreover, the Jews were ready to pay Turkey an annual tribute as well, in return for the ceding of Palestine.

The Grand Vizier listened. His face remained expressionless, his half-shut eyes turned downward to his fine fingers, which ticked off slowly, one by one, a long string of worry beads. He said, "Palestine is large. Which part of it do you have in mind?"

"That will have to be weighed against the benefits that we offer. For more land we shall make greater sacrifices."

The Grand Vizier inquired about the terms. Herzl begged his pardon, but he could not go into details. "I could state the exact scope of our proposals only directly to his Majesty the Sultan. If they are accepted in principle, Sir Samuel Montagu of London would present our financial program."

At that time there was nothing very remarkable in Herzl's

proposal. In the nineteenth century, territories were exchanged, leased, and purchased with apparent ease. Asia was considered by most, if not all, Europeans as a political vacuum. The attitude of the imperialists was shared by most liberals and socialists. Karl Marx had considered China and India as ahistorical countries. In 1882 Friedrich Engels had welcomed the British occupation of Egypt (nominally a Turkish vassal) as being in the interests of human progress.

Turkey was generally regarded as the "sick man of Europe." The Sultan was viewed as a bloody tyrant, the murderer of Armenians and Greeks. The dissolution of his backward, bankrupt, and corrupt realm was widely considered as imminent and desirable. Why should not the Jews—the only people without a territory of their own—share in the general redistribution of his sparsely populated and often deserted territories? An offer to lease Palestine from the Turks in return for good services and an annual tribute was fair and equitable. Only eighteen years earlier, England had leased Cyprus from the Turks for an "annual tribute of 92,000 pounds and 4,166,220 okes of salt."

Although Herzl had originally thought of Argentina, he now preferred Palestine, not only because the veteran Zionists wanted it, but also because he thought it was possible to deal with the Turks. He would never "infiltrate" the country, as some Zionists were doing, but was determined to wait for a transaction, openly arrived at by legal covenant. In his negotiations with Turkey he expected to be helped by those countries that were embarrassed by their Jewish "problem." After all, even his compatriot the Viennese journalist Theodor Hertzka,* had been supported in his Kenyan "Freeland" by the Austrian government, and had received supplies of Austrian army surpluses, including rifles.

And yet the audacity of Herzl's undertaking was never as evident as at this very early stage of his complicated, drawn-out negotiations with the Turks. Here he was, the self-appointed spokesman of a people, as yet without an organization or any clear or binding mandate from anyone, and with no money at all, promising to release Turkey from the fetters of an international indebtedness that amounted nominally to almost one hundred million pounds sterling. He hinted at "Jewish money power." Perhaps he himself believed in what even then was at best a gross exaggeration and at worst a dangerous illusion. Even if there were a few Jewish multi-

* See p. 174.

millionaires, as bankers they were as little interested in politics as their Christian colleagues, and in Jewish politics not at all. Hirsch was dead; the Rothschilds refused even to speak to Herzl; Sir Samuel Montagu had made no firm commitment. Herzl had no certainty whatsoever that Montagu would not leave him in the lurch at the last moment.

It is not clear whether Herzl was fully aware of the trapeze act he was performing. His courage derived from an unbounded, simple faith in the rightness and urgency of his case. He may have told himself that if the rich Jews at present were opposed to his scheme, this was only temporary, or because a pariah people always loses faith in itself. All this could change overnight as the result of a successful arrangement between himself and the Turks.

The Grand Vizier, however, remained noncommittal. Another meeting was scheduled for later in the week. But Herzl's plan was welcomed enthusiastically by the next Turkish statesman he met, Mehmet Nuri Bey, Secretary-General of the Foreign Ministry.

"*C'est superbe,*" he said when Herzl announced his intention to free Turkey from the foreign debt control commission. Nuri Bey was "delighted and won over completely." As the son of a Circassian mother and a French father who had converted to Islam, Palestine meant little to him, and he was ready to relinquish it in return for Turkish economic independence. He had some minor reservations regarding the future of the Holy Places; but these were quickly dispelled by Herzl's explanations, as well as, it seems, by the hint of a lavish *baksheesh.*

In the meantime, Nevlinski was closeted in private audience with the Sultan. He was less successful. He returned from the palace in the evening in a gloomy mood and ordered "only *half* a bottle of champagne—as a sign of mourning." He said, "Nothing doing. The Great Lord won't hear of it." Herzl took the blow stoically. In Nevlinski's words:

> The Sultan said, "If Herr Herzl is as much your friend as you are mine, advise him not to take another step in this matter. I cannot relinquish a square foot of land, for it does not belong to me but to my people. My people have conquered and fortified this empire with their blood. . . . The Jews should save their billions. When my empire is partitioned, perhaps they will get Palestine for nothing. But only our dead body will be divided. [As long as we are alive] I will not permit a vivisection."

Herzl's brightest hopes were shattered by this news, but he refused to lose heart. On the contrary, he was moved by the Sultan's "truly lofty words" and by the "tragic beauty of his fatalism." Nevlinski was surprised; he had expected a fit of depression. But Herzl immediately thought up a new approach. He would offer the Sultan in advance "proof of devotion." He asked Nevlinski to do his utmost to arrange an audience with the Sultan after all. He needed that audience very badly, even if nothing should come of it, in order to keep his movement going, and to keep faith in himself as leader. An audience was now more important than before. If the Sultan had agreed to his Palestine plan, he might have returned home triumphantly even without a personal audience. But with a "no" and not even an audience, people would think it was all a crazy dream. Nevlinski admired Herzl's acumen and promised to do his best.

To his wife, Herzl wrote,

> My dear child,
> These are great days that I am passing here. Of course I cannot as yet foresee the results. I deal with the government; yesterday I had a long audience with the Grand Vizier and spent three hours with sundry excellencies. In the evening I am completely exhausted. I trust that you and the children are in good health. . . .

On the following morning, a Friday, Herzl had his first glimpse of Sultan Abdul-Hamid and his resplendent court—from a distance. He attended the magnificent ceremony of the *salamlik*. In the forecourt of the white Yildiz mosque, Herzl's eyes feasted on the dreamlike pageant. Pashas in fairy-tale uniforms, majestic eunuchs, mounted guards, heavily veiled harem ladies passed in procession, while from a nearby minaret the muezzin's call for prayer was accompanied by military music. In the background was the gleaming Bosporus. The *feuilletonist* in him burst forth as he described the scene in glowing terms in his diary. But his impression of the Sultan was far from edifying:

> He is a slight, sickly man, with a large hook nose and a middle-sized beard, dyed brown. As he passes the terrace on which we stand he stares sharply at Nevlinski, and at me . . . as he passes us the second time he gives me another hardened look.

A scramble of officers running up the hill behind his carriage. Then the splendid fairy-tale picture fades away.

During the next few days Herzl had another round of meetings with the Grand Vizier, Foreign Ministry officials, and a succession of pashas and imperial chamberlains who alternately encouraged and discouraged him. At the Foreign Ministry, Nuri Bey was "fire and flame" for Herzl's scheme. Izzet Bey, the Sultan's secretary and future Vizier, was interested and sympathetic.

"Herzl is an *inspiré*," Izzet told Nevlinski. Izzet was the son of a noble Arab family of Damascus and one of the most powerful officials in the empire. Izzet encouraged Herzl to pursue his quest. He believed it was in the interest of both Turks and Jews, and in his own interest as well, for he was notorious as an extractor of enormous bribes from all possible sources. Izzet suggested that Herzl and his Jews first acquire another territory somewhere in the Near East and then trade it for Palestine with additional payment. Believing that Izzet spoke in the Sultan's name, Herzl immediately thought of Cyprus. He decided that the Sultan's refusal to relinquish Palestine was not a matter of sacred principle but one of face-saving.

Others gave Herzl hope by advising him to wait. The empire was in such dire straits financially that within six months he might get Palestine for a pittance.

The key lay in the Sultan's hand. He did not receive Herzl, but Nevlinski had three more private talks with him. Nevlinski told the Sultan that Herzl had not resented his principled refusal; on the contrary he had much admired his "sublime response." Herzl is a friend of Turkey, Nevlinski added; he wishes to serve his Majesty. The Sultan, according to Nevlinski, said that he would happily receive Herzl "as a friend," but Herzl must first render him a service. Could not Herzl use his influence with the international press to treat Turkey more kindly, especially as regarded the Armenians?"

"I am a much misunderstood man," the Sultan said. "To me, all my peoples are like children I might have had by different wives. They may differ among themselves, but not with me." Let Herzl induce the exiled Armenians to submit directly to him instead of agitating against Turkey in the European press; he would make all sorts of concessions to them.

Nevlinski recounted this conversation to Herzl as they were sitting in the great noonday heat, under a tree, in a garden café on the Bosporus. Herzl immediately declared his readiness to throw himself "into battle" for the Sultan. "Of course, my efforts would be greatly facilitated if the Sultan right now consented to receive me." He needed an audience as proof that he had at least managed "to drive in the first stake"—as a sign that all was not yet lost.

But the Sultan continued to hedge. On the following day he sent word to Herzl not to leave Constantinople; he might still have something important to say to him. Nothing much of consequence happened in the next forty-eight hours. Herzl and Nevlinski were besieged by assorted agents, contact men, and alleged favorites of this or that pasha, ready to offer their services for money. Between one bizarre negotiation and another, Nevlinski entertained Herzl with stories from Yildiz Kiosk:

> Dreams play an important part. There is Lufti Aga, the Sultan's valet, a great dreamer. Lufti Aga hovers around the Sultan all day, waits on him personally, has great influence. If Lufti Aga says, "I've had such and such a dream," it makes an impression on the Sultan. If Lufti Aga were to say one day, "I have dreamt that the Jews are returning to Palestine," this would be worth more than all the "steps" taken by the entire diplomatic corps. It sounds like a fairy tale [Herzl concluded], but I have unlimited confidence in Nevlinski.

On June 26 the Sultan, of his own accord, spoke again to Nevlinski of Herzl. He reproached Nevlinski for having submitted Herzl's scheme in a thoughtless way. With his experience in Turkish affairs, Nevlinski ought to have known that Palestine was not "for sale." But now he had heard that Herzl and his friends were thinking of a possible exchange. In the Sultan's view this was a much more plausible idea. His trusted secretary Izzet Bey, who liked Herzl's scheme, had planted the idea in the Sultan's mind. Nevlinski advised the Sultan to broach this possibility directly to Herzl, "whose most ardent desire is to be received by your Majesty."

"I shall see," the Sultan said. "In any case I shall receive Mr. Herzl—sooner or later." He told Nevlinski that he had already been approached by one of the great powers regarding his attitude to Herzl's scheme. "Must the Jews have Palestine at all costs? Why can't they settle in another province?"

"Palestine is their cradle," Nevlinski said grandly. "That is where they wish to return."

"But Palestine is the cradle of other religions too," the Sultan argued.

Nevlinski, already deep into Herzl's role, shrewdly rejoined, "If the Jews cannot have Palestine they will simply have to go to Argentina." In such case Turkey would lose the proposed financial support and remain shackled forever to the foreign debt commission. After this perspicacious hint, the Sultan and Izzet, who was also present, talked at great length in Turkish. Nevlinski understood only the repeated recurrence of Herzl's name.

There the matter stood. Nevlinski urged Herzl not to lose hope. "I am convinced the Turks want to give us Palestine," he said. "The Sultan is just like a woman, willing to surrender but coy about it. I say she's a whore," Nevlinski announced in his broken, Polish-accented German. "I don't know why. I just feel she's a whore."

But whatever the morals of the lady, Herzl was to have no rendezvous with the Sultan. Over a week had passed since his arrival in Constantinople. His own talks with various officials, as well as Nevlinski's, convinced Herzl that a deal with the Turks was possible, even if at a high price in bribes. It was a question of money and of time. But what now? Could he go back to face his friends in Vienna and London empty-handed? Wouldn't the entire movement lose its momentum? He needed at least token proof of the Sultan's sympathy.

With great reluctance and a deep sense of "secret shame," Herzl swallowed his pride and asked Nevlinski to at least get him a high Turkish decoration. "I implore you not to take me for a medal hunter," he said with great emotion, "but for my people in London I need a sign of favor from the Sultan."

Nevlinski immediately wrote Izzet Bey, the Sultan's secretary. While still awaiting word, Herzl went on a tour of inspection of the imperial palaces along the Bosporus, to which he had been officially invited. "The Sultan today showed me a rare favor," Herzl wrote his wife in a short letter describing the tour. In the Sultan's own caïque, rowed by eight sturdy oarsmen in resplendent uniforms, he floated up and down the Bosporus in "a sultry Oriental dream." The Sultan's adjutant showed him the sights and replied to each question with, "*Oui, mon Excellence.*"

On his return to the hotel, hot and tired, he found the corpulent Nevlinski in their stifling suite, stripped to his underwear, writing letters. "He sends you this," Nevlinski said casually, and flipped him a box containing the Commander's Cross of the Ottoman Medjidiye Order.

4

After the customary distribution of gold coins to the doormen and valets of the pashas with whom they had negotiated for the past week, Herzl and Nevlinski left for Vienna. On the train to Sofia, Nevlinski related his farewell conversation with the Sultan. It had been a good talk and quite encouraging. "The Sultan said that he would have given you a decoration even if I had not asked for one," Nevlinski claimed. "But he could not receive you on this visit because your plan was no longer a secret."

The Sultan had been embarrassed by all the commotion, said Nevlinski. "Since he was obliged to reject your proposal in its *present* form, he did not care to talk about it at all. But he told me: 'The Jews are intelligent. They will soon find a form that will be acceptable.' This proves that the Sultan merely wants to save face, and I think in the end he will accept."

It was Herzl's view too. On balance, he regarded the trip as a "brilliant success." In addition to the political connections he had established, his visit to Turkey proved an important personal education. His inborn trepidation before the high and mighty was beginning to wane. "The great of the earth are composed only of the respect that we hold for them," he scribbled in his diary as the train sped across the plains of Thrace on its way toward the Bulgarian border.

In Sofia he was treated to another massive welcome. His drive through the center of town caused such a sensation that Herzl asked his friends to call off a scheduled parade. People rushed to kiss his hand, and in the synagogue he was placed by the altar. He did not know how to face the crowd without turning his back to the holy Torah. But a man called out: "It is all right for you to turn your back to the altar. You are holier than the Torah!" Once more he sensed his mysterious power to arouse a crowd and hold it in his sway.

In Vienna he took cordial leave of Nevlinski, of whom he had become very fond. He promised Nevlinski "friendship for life." In his diary he resolved that if "through him we obtain Palestine we shall present him with a fine estate in Galicia as an honorific reward."

The Turkish visit had cost him a small fortune out of his own pocket, close to two thousand dollars. But he was a driven man, and he believed that with tenacity and perseverance he might reach his goal before the year was out. He stopped only a few hours in Vienna and rushed on to London and Paris to seek financial backing for the next round of negotiations with the Turks.

Herzl arrived in London on July 4. He planned to assemble a syndicate of Jewish bankers who might accompany him on his next trip to Turkey. The syndicate would offer the Sultan an annual tribute of one million pounds for a Jewish principality in Palestine under the Sultan's suzerainty. He was also scheduled to address a meeting in East London.

But no sooner did he drop initial hints than he suffered his first setback. Sir Samuel Montagu, the banker and key figure in his scheme, who had been so forthcoming on his previous visit, was at first too busy to see Herzl. When they finally met later in the week, Montagu was reserved and refused to assume any responsibility. Three months earlier he had glibly asserted in public that Palestine could be bought from the Turks for a mere two million pounds. Now he set down three conditions for his public adherence to Herzl's cause:

1. He would need the prior consent of the great powers.
2. The foundation of the late Baron Hirsch would have to lend its support, to the extent of ten million pounds.
3. He would require the participation of Edmond de Rothschild of Paris (whose philanthropy currently supported a few hundred Jewish colonists in Palestine).

Clearly Montagu was hesitant, and perhaps anxious to back off. Herzl had apparently also "offended his religious scruples by writing him a postcard dated on the Sabbath."

Herzl fared no better with other members of the Anglo-Jewish aristocracy. Claude Montefiore, president of the powerful Anglo-Jewish Association, and Frederic Mocatta, an important financier, called on him at his hotel. Herzl presented them with a very moderate program: the establishment of a "Society of Jews" for the purpose of acquiring, under international law, a territory for those Jews unable to assimilate in their present host countries. Montefiore and Mocatta asked for time to think this over. After a few hours they came back with an emphatic no. They advised Herzl to stay away from the contemplated meeting in his honor in East London. This was Montagu's parliamentary constituency, and it was felt that Herzl's appearance would merely excite the masses.

After some hesitation Herzl rejected this demand. "I don't want a demagogic movement," he told Montagu, "but if the aristocrats prove too aristocratic and aloof, I will set the masses in motion." This was not received very graciously. Herzl was also asked for fuller accounts of his interviews with the Grand Duke and the Turkish leaders. But since both in Karlsruhe and in Constantinople Herzl had promised utmost secrecy, he could not fulfill this request either. His veiled hints didn't satisfy the reluctant financiers.

Yet the major objection of most Anglo-Jewish aristocrats, save a handful of romantics like Colonel Goldsmid, remained one of principle. However strong their Jewish pride—and it was stronger here than among the rich Jews of Germany and Austria—the idea of a Jewish restoration in Palestine was infinitely more popular in England among upper-class Protestants than among upper-class Jews. Zionist historians have customarily portrayed the Montefiores and Mocattas as cowards. But in 1896 they hoped for the ultimate triumph of reason and tolerance in England and were unwilling to jeopardize a satisfactory status quo for an adventure in statecraft nurtured in the feverish mind of a Viennese man of letters.

Such objections were less evident among the poor Jews of East London, most of whom had escaped from the lands of persecution —Russia and Romania—in the last decade. On July 12 Herzl addressed an excited crowd in the Jewish Workingman's Club of Whitechapel; the meeting had been called by its young organizers in defiance of the existing communal leadership. Only a fraction of the huge, sweltering crowd gained admission to the hall. As in Sofia, the sheer glamour of Herzl's presence and the magic appeal of his simple message—"We are a *people, one* people"—electrified an audience already excited by their exuberant leaders.

With his magnificent beard, his glowing eyes, his proud frame, and fine, simple gestures, Herzl stood on the stage, looking "as kings wish to look but seldom do." He spoke calmly, but the huge audience was ready to applaud every word and suggestion. At one point he said, almost in passing, "The East is ours," referring to East London's Whitechapel. But the mesmerized audience took it to mean the Near East—Palestine—and exploded in tumultuous cheers. Herzl was effusively hailed by the other speakers. One man compared him to Moses; another said he was the new Columbus.

While the cheering continued, Herzl sat stiffly on the platform. He experienced the strangest sensations: "I saw and heard my legend being born. The people are sentimental; the masses do not see clearly. I think that even now they no longer have a clear perception of me. A light fog is mounting around me, which could become the cloud in which I walk."

An introspective man of little humor, he had an almost baroque facility for double perspective. The hero of his own drama, he observed himself in a kind of play within a play:

> Of course, they would probably display the same love to some clever deceiver and impostor as they do to me, by whom they are not deceived. This is perhaps the most interesting thing I inscribe in these diaries: *how my legend is born.* While I sat on the stage and listened to the emphatic speeches and to the cheers of my supporters, I resolved to be even worthier of their trust and their affection.

Thus, even though the rich were disappointing him, Herzl was satisfied with the results of his trip. "My dear child," he wrote his wife on July 12, "I am very tired . . . but I have accomplished something very great, and with this I must comfort myself. . . . Your faithful Papa Theodor."

He had reached a point where the decision to emerge as a popular leader was his alone. He was being urged by young enthusiasts in London to pressure the reluctant aristocrats by organizing a mass movement among the poor. After his meetings with Montagu and other rich and lukewarm Jews, the young Zionist journalist Jacob de Haas took Herzl aside: "You have been utterly defeated here. I know these people. But I will show you a way to victory if you are willing to talk things over." Herzl was cheerfully responsive and appointed the enthusiastic de Haas as his London "honorary secretary." At the same time Herzl still preferred an "aristocratic" solution from above and hoped to find it in some banker's elegant drawing room.

He decided to make one last effort with Edmond de Rothschild in Paris. On July 16 he sailed for France, where Nordau welcomed him warmly. He assured Herzl that despite all setbacks, he had already accomplished a near miracle. Nordau was astonished at Herzl's audacity and his marvelous luck thus far, especially in his negotiations with the Turks: "Didn't these people ask, 'With whom are we negotiating? Who has the money?' "

It was an eminently sensible, practical question. Montagu was the only man with money, and even his lukewarm support was conditional on the participation of Edmond de Rothschild, who had already intimated that he regarded Herzl as a dangerous adventurer. Undaunted, Herzl immediately applied to Rothschild for an interview. It was not an easy thing for him to do, since the

Rothschilds had rebuffed all his previous approaches and Edmond, only a few weeks before, had reacted coolly to Nordau's entreaties. But Herzl had already gone too far to turn back. To his surprise, Rothschild received him almost immediately. Their meeting was a turning point in Herzl's career.

Edmond de Rothschild was one of the lesser-known scions of the famous family of financiers, but foremost among them in his charitable support of Jewish and other causes. A tall, slim man in his mid-forties, Rothschild was a dandy and an art lover. He was inclined to leave the making of money to his brothers and cousins, preferring to spend it as he saw fit for good and useful ends. The main beneficiaries of his generosity were the Louvre and the new Jewish colonies in Palestine. He had rescued the latter from bankruptcy in 1883 with huge investments in land and equipment, guaranteeing the colonists a minimum income. He was said to be the richest man in France. For a Jew, his social prominence was unique; Clemenceau referred to him derisively as "the friend of the entire anti-Semitic nobility." He was venerated by masses of poor and oppressed Jews who vicariously rejoiced in his opulence and enjoyed his full acceptance in Gentile society.

At the time Herzl came to see him, the two dozen or so colonies established by Rothschild in Palestine included about three thousand people and were already achieving a relative degree of prosperity. The colonies were managed by the Baron's French administration on a paternalistic basis; their vineyards produced a Bordeaux-type wine. The official language in the colonies was French, but in the village schools Hebrew was taught. Some of the younger colonists already spoke Hebrew as their everyday language.

Rothschild's colonies, in fact, were already the budding cells of a new Jewish society in Palestine. But this was not as apparent then as it is in retrospect today, either to Herzl or to Rothschild. When Herzl came to see him, Rothschild was not a Zionist. His philanthropy was of the paternalistic kind common in the nineteenth century. A few weeks before Herzl's visit he had angrily told Nordau: "These are my colonies and I shall do what I like with them."

In his colonies he followed a humanitarian aim. He was not seeking a national revival, rather he was conducting a nonpolitical experiment to see whether it was possible to rehabilitate poor Eastern European city Jews as farmers in Palestine. Although Palestine was the Jewish historic homeland, the idea of a Jewish state was anathema to him. He was strongly opposed to Herzl's political activity, fearing that Herzl's Zionism might expose French Jews like himself to accusations of disloyalty to France. By arousing Turkish suspicions, Herzl might even harm the colonies in Palestine.

This was the man who, in Herzl's words, was the kingpin of the entire plan he had agreed upon with Sir Samuel Montagu. It would take a miracle now to save that plan. But such was Herzl's tenacity and unbounded faith in the rightness of his cause that even now he thought it might work. He convinced himself that he could "purchase Rothschild's enrollment with my own withdrawal."

He let it be known in advance that his agreement to call on Rothschild was in itself a concession on his part, for he was embittered by Rothschild's treatment of Nordau a few weeks earlier. Rothschild responded in kind. He received Herzl not in his home, but in his office on the rue Laffitte, where so many humble pleaders for Rothschild's benevolence had been received before. Herzl was as self-conscious as ever in the company of the very rich; as with Hirsch, he could not help expressing his resentment by being short-tempered and aggressive.

As he was waiting in the anteroom, one of the Baron's aides assured him that Rothschild "is a human being like ourselves." The information did not amaze Herzl, but the servility it reflected merely increased his annoyance. The Baron came in soon after. He impressed Herzl as an "aging youth, his movements quick and yet shy . . . with a long nose and an ugly, large mouth. He wore a red necktie and a white waistcoat that flapped about his thin body." Two aides were present. It seemed to Herzl that Rothschild wanted them there for his protection "in case I turned out to be an anarchist." Rothschild himself later admitted that he had asked his aides to stay as witnesses so that Herzl would not be able to spread lies about their conversation. He was a generous man but had all the petty suspicions that sometimes characterize great philanthropists.

"To what extent are you familiar with my plan?" Herzl began.

"I have heard that you are a new *Bernard l'hermite*," the Baron said. He lost himself in a disjointed refutation of Herzl's program which he knew only through hearsay. His two aides nodded emphatically at his every word.

After five minutes Herzl interrupted Rothschild, who was not used to such bluntness. "You don't know what it is all about. Let me explain it to you first. A colony is a small state; a state is a big colony. You want a small state; I want to build a big colony."

Once more, as so many times in the past, he unfolded his plan for consolidating the Turkish national debt in return for a Jewish vassal state in Palestine. He told Rothschild he did not have to make up his mind immediately. He asked only for Rothschild's conditional agreement. Only in the case of success would Rothschild be asked to place himself at the head of the movement, at which time he, Herzl, would voluntarily withdraw. If it proved impossible to conclude a transaction with the Turks, there would be no movement and no need for his leadership and support.

Rothschild listened attentively, at times with surprise. Occasionally Herzl thought he even detected admiration in the Baron's eyes. But he was wrong. Rothschild quickly made clear that he wanted nothing to do with the project. First, he had no faith whatsoever in the promises of the Turks. Second, even if he did believe in them, he still would not engage in such an undertaking. His reasoning was simple; it echoed a philanthropist's practical concerns, not a politician's vision. "It would be impossible to control the influx of the masses into Palestine," he said. "The first to arrive would be a hundred fifty thousand beggars. They would have to be fed, presumably by me. I don't feel up to that—but perhaps you do!" he added sarcastically. Rothschild could not assume such a responsibility. There could be unforeseen mishaps.

"Are there none now?" Herzl cried. "Is anti-Semitism not a permanent mishap, with loss of honor, life, and property?" But his ardor was of no avail. The Baron had not read Herzl's pamphlet, in which he had carefully outlined the mechanism of emigration, his detailed blueprint of an organization that would process the exodus at all points of departure, and the meticulous preparation for the arrival, designed to preclude mishaps and accelerate absorption in the new country. Herzl repeated his favorite argument that modern science and technology permitted a system of colonization infinitely more rational and humane than the chaotic settlement of Australia and America.

Rothschild was merely piqued by this observation. "I have not waited for you to come along and tell me that we now have machines at our disposal."

"I had no intention to enlighten you," Herzl answered, not a little piqued himself.

The battle of words continued for about two hours. At one point, Rothschild asked, "And what in heaven's name do you want me to do?"

Herzl answered brusquely, "I beg your pardon, Baron. You did not understand me. I want absolutely nothing from you. I am only inviting you to lend your conditional adherence."

But Rothschild would hear nothing of it. He was not interested in political action. Twice he repeated a proverb, which Herzl took as the expression of his deepest philosophical insight: *Il ne faut pas avoir les yeux plus gros que le ventre* (It does not do to have eyes bigger than one's stomach). His aides dutifully echoed whatever line Rothschild took, and obligingly provided him with arguments. When Rothschild said that there would be no curbing of the masses, one aide said darkly, "Yes, just what happened at Chodinko," referring to a plain outside Moscow where a frightened mass of Jewish refugees from a czarist pogrom had recently suffered great hardship.

If Rothschild considered Herzl a megalomaniac, Herzl for his part considered Rothschild a narrow-minded coward. Though decent and good-hearted, his philanthropic efforts were of no use at all; in twelve years only a few hundred families had been resettled. But in Eastern Europe millions were waiting to be helped.

"You were the keystone of the entire combination," Herzl said bitterly as he turned to leave. "If you refuse, everything I have fashioned so far will collapse. I shall then be obliged to do it in a different way. I shall start a mass agitation. And," he added threateningly, "that way it will be even harder to keep the masses under control. I was going to turn the direction of the entire project over to you. . . . You think it would be a disaster to operate with such great masses. Consider whether the misfortune would not be greater if your refusal forces me to set the masses in motion by uncontrollable agitation."

But Rothschild was obdurate. Herzl took his leave. He saw the entire intricate web collapse because of the unimaginativeness of one millionaire. "And the fate of millions is to hang on such men. . . . I believe he is already aghast at having gotten himself involved in Palestine in the first place. Perhaps he will now run to [his brother] Alphonse and say, 'You were right. I should have gone in for racing horses rather than resettling Jews.'"

5

Thinking back on his negotiations with the Turks, Herzl realized with a shock that had the Sultan said, "Yes, it is a deal," he would have stood there like a fool, lacking even a fraction of the money needed to back up his ambitious offer. Apparently this fact had never occurred to him in Constantinople, or before going there.

But he was not discouraged. He reassured himself that all the Jews put together could accumulate more money than Rothschild. On the following morning he wrote de Haas in London, "There is only one answer. Organize our masses at once. Let us get them ready to go or to stand by for a word of command. As a means of agitation I suggest the flag with seven gold stars . . . here is my design for it:

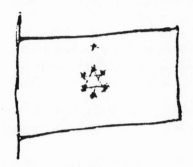

"Our flag—white field—seven gold stars"

To strengthen his resolve, he turned once more to Nordau. Herzl urged him to join the Paris committee "as chief of the movement in France." Nordau demurred over the title of chief but accepted the post. Before he left Paris Herzl addressed a meeting of Jewish students in the Paris suburb of Gobelin. The hall was filled to overflowing with the sons and daughters of poor Jewish refugees who had escaped to France from persecution in Eastern Europe. Among those present was Bernard Lazare, a well-known anarchist-socialist, and a prominent figure in the Dreyfus-is-innocent movement. Lazare had just published (in Brussels) his scathing *La Vérité sur l'affaire Dreyfus*. He was called "Chief of Staff of the Dreyfus Army" and was credited with having mobilized Clemenceau, Jaurès, and Zola in the battle to defend Dreyfus. Lazare was an instant convert to Herzl's movement; his adherence proved that among the young and enthusiastic, Zionism appealed as much to left-wing radicals as to conservative nationalists.

Herzl gave a rousing speech, concluding with the words, "*Je ne vous dis pas encore, marchons—je dis seulement, la jeunesse, debout!*" (I am not as yet saying to you, Forward march—I say only, Youth, to your feet!)

He left for home the next morning, passing through Karlsbad, where the faithful Nevlinski had arranged an audience with King

Ferdinand I of Bulgaria. Nevlinski was greatly discouraged by
Herzl's failure with Rothschild. "I did not know your troops are
that bad," he said. Herzl had a very friendly meeting with the King
under rather strange circumstances. They met behind a bush in the
park of the Karlsbad watering spa; as they conferred, the King
accidentally stepped on Herzl's foot and recoiled with an emphatic
"*Pardon!*" Ferdinand's entourage remained at a respectful distance
as the King and Herzl strolled on their long walk. The King quickly
warmed up to Herzl's cause.

"It is a marvelous idea," he said. "No one has ever talked to me
of the Jewish question in this way. But what you say has often
occurred to me. Actually I was raised by Jews. I spent my youth
with Baron Hirsch. Your idea has my full sympathy. What can I do
on your behalf?"

"I should like to ask your Royal Highness to prepare the Czar
of Russia for my plan, and if possible to obtain an audience for
me."

"That is very difficult," the Catholic-born sovereign of Orthodox Bulgaria said doubtfully. "It is a matter that involves religion.
As it is I do not stand well with the Russian Orthodox. There are
delicate matters here in which I often must subordinate my convic-
tions to political necessities."

As he said this, he drew himself up and looked down at Herzl
in a grand manner, his head thrown back regally. But Ferdinand
promised to intervene with the Grand Duke Vladimir, the Czar's
cousin. "All others [in the court of the Czar] speak of the Jews as
though they were not human." The King also promised to dissemi-
nate Herzl's pamphlet, on the condition that their relationship
remain secret.

With this Herzl returned home. There was little time to relax,
or care for his wife and children. Herzl spent most of his days and
nights in conference or writing. He sent a stream of letters to Paris,
Berlin, Cologne, Sofia, Galicia, Russia, and England, reporting his
failure with Rothschild and urging his disciples to organize cadres
everywhere. Within a relatively short time he produced a new
phenomenon in European politics, an international national movement, which, despite its inner divisiveness and personal rivalries,
soon became a political instrument of some import.

He wrote David Wolffsohn in Cologne on August 1 that he
intended to call a "conference of Zionists" from all European countries. Wolffsohn responded enthusiastically. In his reply he re-

minded Herzl of Moses' device in the battle with the Amalekites: "Keep your fists up! Fight to the finish!"

To de Haas, Herzl wrote urging contacts with the Jewish community in the United States. To all, he added, "Organize! Organize!"

He immediately applied the same admonition to himself. Offices were rented, manned by a small staff to coordinate the international effort. Until now the Zionists had managed their affairs at weekly meetings in the back room of a Viennese café. Circulars were printed and dispatched, and preparations were begun for the publication of a magazine. The bulk of financing came from Herzl's own pocket. He now readily agreed to address public meetings that a few months ago he had still shunned.

The organization slowly begun to take form. All over Europe Herzl's newly won adherents were calling the multitude into action. Riper issues, handled by more experienced men, have "seldom sped forward so rapidly." David Wolffsohn, the timber merchant of Cologne, took charge of Germany. He was aided by Max Bodenheimer, a well-known Cologne lawyer. In Paris there was Max Nordau; in Sofia, Dr. Reuben Bierer, a physician by training. From London the young Jacob de Haas, imaginative, brimming with energy, extended the scope of his work to North America. In Russia, Professor Max Emanuel Mandelstamm of Kiev, an eye specialist and veteran Jewish activist, led the way. There were a dozen others in Galicia, Romania, Holland, and Belgium. And in Vienna itself, the lawyer Dr. Ozer Kokesch; the engineer Johann Kremenezky, a pioneer of the Austrian electrical industry; Oscar Marmorek, an architect; and Professor Leon Kellner, a philologist and Shakespearean scholar, became Herzl's faithful adjutants, a *corps d'élite* that followed his every command. He prodded and bullied them constantly, and continually complained that the bulk of the work was left to him alone.

He received visitors from all parts of the world. For many eager to settle in the new Jewish colonies in Palestine, the road from Europe to Palestine went through Herzl's book-lined study at Berggasse 6. A short distance down the narrow street, at number 19, Sigmund Freud was just beginning his epoch-making psychoanalytic practice. At this time both Freud and Herzl were considered charlatans, if not madmen, by a good many of their peers. As the two men met, almost daily, in the street, there must have been a flash of mutual recognition in their eyes.

Herzl also continued his daily work at the *Neue Freie Presse*. His growing expenses made him more dependent on it than ever. It was still difficult for his colleagues to take him seriously in his new role. On his first day back from Turkey and England he had a "brief and vigorous" clash with Bacher. "Aren't you going to write us a *feuilleton* on Constantinople?" Bacher asked.

"No," said Herzl. "In Constantinople I only had historical experiences, not *feuilletonist* ones."

Bacher laughed.

"You don't believe me?" Herzl asked.

"No, I don't."

"You'll believe, all right!" Herzl cried.

A few weeks later Bacher accosted Nevlinski in a park: "What on earth are you doing with Herzl?"

Nevlinski replied that he was helping Herzl arrange for the Jewish colonization of Palestine by negotiating with the Turkish government. Bacher shrugged his shoulders. "Herzl is such a *schmuck!*"

Turkey's continued financial difficulties enabled Herzl to pursue his contacts with the Sultan's government through Nedim Pasha, the Turkish ambassador in Vienna. Nedim Pasha, in fact, was sympathetic to Herzl's renewed offer of an exchange; but the diplomatic correspondent of the *Presse* (perhaps at Bacher's instigation) advised the ambassador not to take Herzl seriously—he was "a madman."

Not only in Vienna was Herzl so handicapped. In September he was shocked to learn that certain "Jewish circles" were intriguing against him in the Sultan's court at Constantinople. Suspecting that Edmond de Rothschild was behind these intrigues, Herzl sent him a strong cablegram: "If this was [the work of] one of your overzealous underlings, he has made *you* seriously responsible. I hope this is not so. We must understand one another." Rothschild never answered.

Even within Herzl's own social circle, there were rumors that he was really in the pay of English bankers. It was said that English and French real-estate speculators were using him as a middleman for shady dealings with corrupt Turkish politicians. Herzl took such slander in his stride; he believed it proved merely the general demoralization of people who refused to believe that "a person would do something out of conviction."

It was harder for Herzl to sustain his equanimity when, on

another occasion, the slander threatened his integrity as a senior editor of the *Neue Freie Presse*. Early in October Herzl was urgently summoned to Bacher's office.

"What kind of business dealings have you made for the *Neue Freie Presse* in Constantinople?" Bacher bluntly demanded.

"Dealings? None whatsoever."

"But you were down there with Nevlinski?"

"Yes. But that is common knowledge."

"He took you around to see various ministers?"

"Yes indeed."

Bacher informed Herzl that Baron Ludwig Doczy of the Austrian foreign ministry had passed on to him, confidentially, a diplomatic dispatch from Constantinople. According to this secret report, Herzl had demanded and received for the *Neue Freie Presse* a bribe of three thousand pounds from the Turkish government.

"And you actually believed this, even for a single moment?" Herzl asked icily. "Don't you know me by now? I should think you ought to at least take me for a gentleman."

Bacher immediately backed down. He only suspected that the disreputable Nevlinski had played a dirty trick "behind your back and ours. He must have used your presence to take money from the Turks."

Herzl doubted this, but he promised to pursue the rumor to its end. He assured Bacher that during his visit in Turkey he had consistently drawn a very clear line between his responsibilities as an editor and his role as a representative of the Jewish cause. But Bacher clumsily pursued the interrogation:

"Tell me everything! With whom did you speak?"

"With the Grand Vizier . . ." Herzl began, but he immediately stopped short and cried, "I shan't tell you! You are an opponent of my movement. Let me write about it in the *Neue Freie Presse*, and I'll tell everything in public."

"That I shall never permit!" Bacher shouted. "I don't accept your point of view. There is no Jewish problem, there is only a human problem!"

The shouting match continued for some time. Herzl, terribly shocked by the affront, decided to challenge Doczy to a duel. He asked Karl von Vincenti, a colleague on the newspaper, to serve as his second. Vincenti excused himself on the pretext of an urgent journey, but induced Herzl to tell him the entire story of the rumored bribe, which he gleefully repeated to everybody in the

Presse's newsroom. By evening the whole staff was happily discussing the affair. Bacher again summoned Herzl and furiously took him to task.

"Sir, you ought to have your head examined," he cried. "You have committed an act of disloyalty to the newspaper."

"Disloyalty?"

"Yes, by spreading this story around. Doczy could lose his position at the foreign ministry for having leaked the gist of a confidential report to the *Presse*. He might even be accused of breaching the official secrecy act."

"It was not my fault," Herzl said, but the indiscreet Vincenti's. Vincenti came in, embarrassed and apologetic for having caused the commotion. Herzl agreed to drop his challenge, whereupon Bacher calmed down. He even gave Herzl his hand in a reluctant truce. Still, Herzl went away with the distinct impression that he would soon be squeezed out of the newspaper. In order to kill the rumor of a Turkish deal, the *Neue Freie Presse* promptly published two furiously anti-Turkish editorials, even demanding the immediate dismemberment of the Ottoman Empire.

Once again Herzl briefly toyed with the idea of founding a new daily newspaper in order to win his independence and gain a reputable platform for his ideas. As in the year before, the Prime Minister, Badeni, notified Herzl that he was very anxious to see a rival newspaper established; his emissary hinted that in return, the government might support Herzl's Jewish scheme. Herzl was able to raise 400,000 guldens of his own and from his parents (his wife's family refused their support), but another million was needed. The entire project floundered and Herzl was despondent. "One single million guldens! Because it is unavailable for my purpose now, we may miss the historic moment to resolve the Jewish problem."

In Eastern Europe, and to a lesser extent in England, Austria, and Germany, his movement was rapidly growing, as was his personal legend. But Herzl was dissatisfied with his followers. He was a prophet in a hurry, and he criticized them constantly for their languor. In his apocalyptic frame of mind, he feared he might miss the last opportunity before the disaster. On October 13 he noted in his diary: "I must frankly confess it to myself. I am demoralized. No help from anyone, attacks from all sides. . . . All the well-off Jews are against me. So much so that I am beginning to feel entitled to be the biggest of all anti-Semites."

The fact that some Jewish bankers in London and Paris were moving to help Turkey in her current financial difficulties, without opening up Palestine for Jewish colonization, added to Herzl's dismay. The wry Nevlinski told Herzl ironically: "I seem to be your only supporter." In his diary Herzl noted on December 20: "I feel I am getting tired. More frequently than ever before, I now believe that my movement is at its end. I am fully convinced of its feasibility, but I cannot overcome the initial difficulties."

He ushered in the new year, 1897, sarcastically, as "one of the *critical* years of my friend Hechler." His depression was not fully justified, for even as he bemoaned his lack of a major, spectacular breakthrough, the movement, under his steady guidance, was gaining ground almost everywhere in the East, and in some parts of the West as well. An international Zionist congress was scheduled for the coming August. Herzl had begun to prepare for it immediately after his row with Rothschild. The purpose of the congress was to institutionalize the movement and create representative governing bodies. Herzl intended to evoke the vision of a parliament, a political center, the constituent assembly of a nation on the march—to the future Jewish state.

His depression was deepened by further disagreements with his wife and by the worrisome state of his health. His heart palpitations continued. He had occasional bouts of anemia and difficulties in breathing. As in his student days, he was plagued by recurring thoughts of death. On February 12 he felt impelled, for the first time in his life, to draw up a will. It contained two parts. The first, entitled "My Literary Testament," called for the immediate publication of his political diaries and, if possible, also the collection of his theater writings and *feuilletons.*

> It is proper to be prepared for death.
> I do not wish to use empty phrases.
> What I was for the Jews, future generations will judge better than the contemporary masses. . . . My name will grow after my death. Therefore I believe that it will be possible to find a publisher for all my works.
> I am conscious today, as I have always been, that as a writer, I was an honorable man. I never sold my pen, never used it for mean ends, never even made it the instrument for the promotion of friendship. This Last Will may be published. Even after my death no one will be able to call me a liar.

The second document, "My Last Testament," was not intended for publication. It covered his personal and financial affairs and shed a gloomy light on the sorry state of his family life. After thanking his good parents for everything, he expressed the hope that after his death the value of his literary works would increase, thus enabling "the full replenishment of my wife's dowry, which was spent in recent years on the growing household. This was not my fault, but my wife's. . . . Whenever I suggested that we economize she resisted, in a harsh manner and with wounding words. . . . I have preferred to circumvent *at least* this point of contention between us."

Herzl denied his wife any rights in the upbringing of his children, appointing his parents as their legal guardians. He admonished his mother and father to protect his children from his wife's evil influence. Their inheritance should be safeguarded from "any possible interference by my wife or her relatives. No relative of my wife may ever receive powers of guardianship over my children." His son, Hans, must under no circumstances remain in Julie's hands. "She does not love him, and might spoil and ruin his happiness by her tormenting." Hans must be moved to his grandparents' house or a boarding school abroad.

For better or worse, my daughters, Pauline and Trude, will probably have to remain in their mother's house, but may my wife be prompted, by the seriousness of my death, to introspective reflection. Even if she has not been a good wife to me, let her at least try to be a good mother to her daughters, a model of decency and frugality.

10

Creating the Mood

BUT IF HE WAS dejected and contemplated death, he told no one. In his tremendous correspondence he remained hopeful, and in his personal dealings with friend and foe he displayed an assuredness all the more remarkable when one considers the morose tone of his private notes.

He often discussed his cause with Benedikt. A few days before Christmas Benedikt asked Herzl to suggest a good subject for a holiday article. "Certainly," Herzl said jestingly. "Write about the solution of the Jewish question through the colonization of Palestine. And how such a solution would also settle the Oriental problem through the restoration of Turkish finances."

"A fine article," Benedikt agreed, "and a popular one too. But I can no longer write it because your pamphlet is already available, in which you speak of a 'Jewish nation.' "

"All right," said Herzl, "so you don't write the article *this* year. You will perhaps write it for Christmas next year. We can wait."

From London the faithful de Haas complained that the rich and influential Jews were still as cautious as before: "Everybody is waiting to see how the cat will jump." But Herzl was not dismayed. He comforted de Haas and urged him to continue his mass agitation on an ever larger scale. Although "the Upper Jews are miserable scoundrels," there was hope in the poor and the young. He flooded de Haas with orders, including a suggestion to establish Zionist boys' clubs and a society of women. At the same time he retained a sense of proportion about himself and his own role as self-appointed leader. He rebuked young de Haas for propagating *Herzlism* instead of Zionism:

... Let us guard against turning the national movement into a personal one. Nothing could hurt us more. . . . The movement must be and should remain impersonal. That is a fundamental principle, from which we should not be swayed. Raising one individual on our shield would be to forge a weapon in the hands of our enemies. We must think of the future. The movement must not rest on two eyes. The idea must not die with me.

I hope, my dear de Haas, that you will act henceforth precisely within these, my intentions.

Throughout these weeks, the possibility of a French financial settlement with the Turks hovered like a dark cloud over Herzl's scheme. Nevlinski reassured him that no matter how much money the Turks might receive from the French, it would soon be squandered, or disappear into the pockets of various pashas. In a few months' time, he said, Turkey would be as desperate as before, only more resentful of its old rapacious creditors. Nevertheless, Herzl was furious that some Jewish bankers, even while turning a deaf ear to his pleas, were involved in these negotiations. But he kept up his own spirits, and those of his lieutenants, by bombarding the Turkish ambassador in Vienna with new offers of large-scale Jewish financial aid, and by continuing to hope for some unexpected turn of events. To Gustav Cohen, the Hamburg banker, he wrote:

From Constantinople, where I am well remembered, I had good news a few days ago. The transaction can probably be made in such a manner as to surprise the world with a *fait accompli*. Then I will ask [the rich Jews]: "Who is joining us?" It is a giant's task, for which I will first be ridiculed, then scorned, and later reap only ingratitude. But I am firm in my own mind. And I do it, in fact, only because conscience dictates it.

On a gloomy winter day in February, he noted wistfully in his diary: "In Palestine the oranges are now blooming. Everything is possible in that country!" But how, and when? To Professor Kellner, a Shakespearean scholar who had joined his Viennese committee, he exclaimed, "My dear friend, if we do not get there with black beards, we shall most certainly with white ones!"

Kellner, and many others, urged him to run for a seat in the Austrian parliament. Less than a year after the publication of his pamphlet, Herzl's name had become a household term in thousands of Jewish homes throughout the eastern regions of the Austro-Hungarian Empire. He was told that his election was certain in either of two legislative districts in Galicia. But Herzl declined; he feared people might say that his entire Zionist scheme was only the basis for a career in Austrian politics. "I think that if I had relented [and run for office], the same people who tried to persuade me would have inwardly despised me."

There was work enough without the additional burdensome mandate in a parliament paralyzed by party strife. Early in March he held a conference in Vienna to prepare for the international Zionist congress which was to take place in August in Zurich. Eleven prominent activists from Germany, Austria, and Romania attended. They included Herzl's Viennese aides, Kellner, Kokesch, and Kremenezky. Others, notably Dr. Willi Bambus of Berlin, a prominent German-Jewish social worker, and Isaac Turow of Breslau, a popular Jewish journalist, had been active in promoting small-scale Jewish colonization in Palestine long before Herzl had appeared on the scene. They were still inclined to view Herzl as a Johnny-come-lately, whom they might permit, under certain conditions, to aid the little "movement" they thought they were still leading. Nevertheless, they responded to Herzl's call.

But the seeds of many a future discord were already beginning to germinate at the Vienna meeting. Bambus and his friends were loath to convene a worldwide national Jewish meeting. They were interested mostly in consolidating the various existing little clubs and charitable societies that now promoted small-scale settlements in Palestine. Herzl was solidly opposed to all such attempts. He shared none of the romantic notions of resurrecting the "historical Hebrew peasant" on Palestinian soil. His own scheme aimed at a sophisticated modern industrial society of technicians and scholars. Moreover, he regarded the present "infiltration" of Palestine by a few hundred souls a year as useless—even dangerous, because it lacked proper political guarantees recognized in international law. Perhaps he darkly sensed the future avalanche of Arab hatred, for he argued that "infiltration" without a political charter would simply transplant anti-Semitism from Europe to the promised land.

Despite their differences in principle, all participants at the preparatory conference were impressed by Herzl's calm resolve and his dignified, aristicratic demeanor. Herzl, little versed in matters of Jewish life and tradition, was the most un-Jewish Jew they had ever met. He mesmerized them more by his style than by his thoughts.

In the end, differences were somehow bridged, or at least swept under the rug.

It was decided to convene the international congress not in Switzerland but in Germany. Zionism was illegal in Russia; Switzerland, with its cells of Russian "nihilists" and exiled revolutionaries, might frighten the Russian delegates, who already had enough trouble with the czarist tyranny. A congress in Munich would appear less suspect; also, there were kosher restaurants in Munich. "Well then," Herzl noted a bit sardonically, "we shall meet at Jochberg's once again, where, in August 1895, I began my discussions with Güdemann and Meyer-Cohn. How big the movement has grown since!"

Herzl took charge of all the preparations. The stream of letters now increased. There was hardly an organization or dignitary Herzl did not approach, except Edmond de Rothschild in Paris and the men of his Palestine administration. His study, overlooking a little old garden on the Berggasse, was crowded with visitors, well-wishers, and givers of gratuitous advice. It was not easy to hold them off, and Herzl saw them all. In addition, there were continued consultations with Hechler and Nevlinski and an assortment of other agents, fortune hunters, crackpots, schemers, and charlatans who came to his door. Within the family, his parents were still his only moral support. Julie resented all the intrusions on her privacy; her constant nagging added to the strain.

The ten other members of the committee readily offered advice, and then tended to resign or secede at the slightest provocation. Herzl wrote until his fingers were cramped; the pain was so severe that it interfered with his regular work at the newspaper. He sometimes fell asleep from fatigue while still at his desk; the milkman rattling his cart down the cobbled street early in the morning would rouse the lonely activist at his desk. A quick breakfast prepared him for his day at the *Neue Freie Presse*. Herzl liked to ride downtown on a bicycle, believing the exercise good for his failing health. In fact, it may well have aggravated his heart condition.

Early in April he sent out a first, carefully worded announcement on behalf of the congress's preparatory committee. Organizations and individuals were invited to register for participation in the congress. The provisional agenda took up five major points:

1. The economic, political, and social condition of Jews in various countries

2. Colonization, its achievements thus far, and its future prospects
3. The tasks of Jewish charity in Palestine
4. Finances
5. The Jewish question and the next diplomatic congress of the great powers

This last point, to be introduced by Herzl himself, echoed his desire to achieve his goal through some grand diplomatic coup. The announcement went on to say that the congress might, if so decided, establish an "executive committee" to lead Jewish affairs on a worldwide basis. This committee would seek "to establish a permanent and secure national home for those Jews who cannot or will not assimilate into their present homes."

The physical effort involved in Herzl's self-imposed task was considerable. He suffered from heart palpitations and from chronic headaches and fatigue, but he was gratified to see that his labors were not in vain. The impact of the circular letter, particularly in the East, was as electrifying as the publication of his pamphlet the year before. The real meaning behind the careful wording of Herzl's announcement was not lost. This was no invitation to a conference of charitable organizations, but a call to form a national assembly—a government in exile. It harked back to the French Revolution, to the American Continental Congress in Philadelphia. Throughout the nineteenth century many "congresses" had been convened by subject peoples to mark the beginning of their self-determination. The participants in such congresses were regarded not as individuals but as the instruments of a collective will, who rose above their own limited circumstances to serve universal historical forces.

The idea of a Jewish congress was not new; it had been expressed by others before Herzl, but no one had had the energy and authority to see it through to fruition. In the tenements and little hamlets of the Russian Pale of Settlement, Zionists responded to Herzl's call with an enthusiasm that few would-be leaders have ever inspired. Young agitators went from one Jewish town to another to explain what a "congress" was, what Herzl wanted to accomplish, what a Jewish state meant, and how it could become a reality. A slogan passed from mouth to mouth: "If we will it, it is no legend."

Chaim Weizmann, the future President of Israel, remembered

a friend named Buchmill who spent the spring of 1897 traveling from one little Jewish *shtetl* to the next.

> I accompanied Buchmill on several occasions. He traveled fourth class, because there was no fifth. He traveled by night and made speeches by day. I remember how we once arrived in a little town near Pinsk, and spoke to a handful of Jews there very early in the morning. I asked one man, who was still half-asleep: "Tell me, did you really understand what I was talking about?" He replied, "No, but I do understand one thing. If what you are talking about is not true, you would not have come here." This was the atmosphere . . . and everybody waited impatiently for the day of the congress. . . . I myself was not present at the first congress for the simple reason that I could not pay the fare.

2

To weld a people so vague and disparate, so demoralized by persecution, so inarticulate and confused, into a political body capable of mass action—this was the task Herzl set himself. The official spokesmen of Jews everywhere, rabbis and millionaires, saw it—and Herzl—as a menace. They regarded any *public* discussion of the Jewish question, on an international basis, as unthinkable. It was something only the anti-Semites had ever done. They believed that Jews must not explore their own internal problems publicly, for fear of giving the anti-Semites a powerful weapon.

Moreover, to enunciate a doctrine of nationhood was a denial of the Jews' "moral mission" on earth; it could undermine the great liberal hopes so carefully built up since emancipation. In Herzl's view, emancipation was a house of cards, but the Jewish establishment, both pious and secular, did not allow itself to think so.

In Berlin, the Rabbinical Council of Germany went into emergency session; five prominent rabbis argued into the night and published a vehement protest against Herzl's congress.

> The aspirations of the so-called Zionists to establish a national Jewish state in Palestine contradict the messianic promises of Judaism as enunciated in the holy scripture and later religious canons. . . . Judaism obliges its adherents to serve the *fatherland to which they belong* with utmost devotion and to further its national interests with all their heart and strength.

A similar resolution in New York deprecated any "formation of a Jewish state in Palestine in such a manner as may be construed as casting a doubt upon the citizenship, patriotism, and loyalty of Jews in whatever country they reside."

The rabbis had not counted on Herzl's sharp pen. He hit back mercilessly, below the belt. "The latest vogue in Jewry is the Protest Rabbi," Herzl wrote. "These are people who sit in a safe boat using their oars to beat the heads of drowning men who try to hang on to the sides." In Herzl's eyes the German rabbis were guilty of a petty act of denunciation; the weakness of their position was revealed by the very language of their statement. They claimed to be German, but "a German would never have written the *fatherland to which I belong. He would say, my fatherland, your fatherland,* or *their fatherland. You do not belong* to a *fatherland*; it belongs to you. When your *fatherland* does not belong to you, you are in bad shape." The pious claim of a Jewish "mission" on earth was "sheer arrogance," Herzl argued. "The civilized world would and should resent being missionarized by us. If there has ever been a Jewish mission, it was Christianity, which is no longer in need of the honorable Protest Rabbis."

More painful to Herzl was his sudden betrayal by Moritz Güdemann, the Chief Rabbi of Vienna. Eighteen months before, in Munich, Herzl had first confided his plan to Güdemann. At that time Güdemann had exclaimed, "You remind me of Moses. . . . Remain as you are. Perhaps you are the one called of God." Later on, under pressure from the rich, Güdemann had vacillated, but nevertheless responded kindly when Herzl sent him the proof sheets prior to the publication of *The Jewish State*. Güdemann had warmly approved the text: "I have read every single word and I find nothing at all to criticize."

But in April 1897 Güdemann suddenly published a scathing attack on Zionism. Without mentioning Herzl by name, and in vague, sanctimonious language, he sought to prove that Judaism and nationalism were irreconcilable. "A malicious counterpamphlet," Herzl noted on April 17. He resolved to answer Güdemann, "following the Machiavellian precept, i.e., devastatingly." Herzl was convinced that the weak clergyman had written his pamphlet at the behest of the Viennese "Upper Jews." As soon as it appeared in print, the Viennese Rothschild had sent for thirty copies.

Herzl's troubles increased within the movement as well. The Zionists were plagued by all the infighting and schisms that seem to mark the beginnings of most revolutionary enterprises. It is difficult today to disentangle the purely personal, temperamental differences from those that were ideological. No sooner had Herzl's first circular on behalf of the congress's preparatory commission gone out, than it was publicly attacked and disowned by one of its members, Willi Bambus, who resigned from the commission, maintaining that he had never intended to go beyond a conventional conference on colonization. Bambus criticized Herzl's "futuristic plans," which he regarded as "dangerous." Again Herzl suspected the intrigues of the Rothschilds and other rich Jews behind Bambus' "perfidious" disavowal. He wrote Bambus that his treachery would be of no avail. "The congress shall take place in any case."

Among the English Zionists, too, trouble was brewing. The eccentric Colonel Goldsmid had changed his mind again, and now urged Herzl and his "hotheads" to call off their congress. Since the great philanthropists, headed by Rothschild, did not want a congress, Herzl would better serve the cause by avoiding a schism. Herzl would hear nothing of it. "I have waited long enough," he wrote Goldsmid on April 4, 1897.

> In August it will be two years. . . . I was willing to do everything on a higher level, without arousing the masses. . . . I was neither understood nor supported. I went ahead alone. At the Munich congress I shall call upon the masses to serve themselves, since no one is willing to help them. . . .
>
> Today we might already have [Palestine as a Turkish vassal state], had my proposals in London and Paris last July been accepted. Do you realize my wrath and impatience?

Even within Herzl's own Viennese *corps d'élite*, disagreements were rampant. Romanticists resented Herzl's rejection of Hebrew. He wanted the new state to adopt a ready-made modern language, German or English, rather than struggle to revive what he regarded as a dead tongue. Some of his collaborators also disliked his essentially rationalist but negative definition of Jewish nationalism as a reaction to anti-Semitic pressures. Herzl said, "The enemy makes us *one*, against our will." Some members sought more positive virtues; in their view every nation was endowed with its own "soul." Martin Buber resented Herzl's loose usage of the term "promised land," the way he was ready to apply it to whatever territory he might eventually get, even Argentina. There was no such thing as an unspecified promised land, Buber complained; only Palestine was "promised." Much time, as well as energy and nerves, was spent, or in Herzl's view, wasted, in heated discussions of this kind.

There were personal clashes as well. A movement such as Herzl's naturally attracted a great variety of people. He had little patience for fools and cantankerous busybodies. Steeped in his self-appointed role as leader, he demanded discipline and was a particularly exacting taskmaster. He was almost physically repelled by praise, but also could bear little or no dissent; and he disliked men of strong and independent minds. "I am proud of you," he wrote one of his coworkers. "I feel *you* have learned something from *me*." In his relationships with others he was handicapped by his pride and self-consciousness.

He was not capable of friendship on an equal footing. In a weak moment (Paris, 1895) he had confided to Arthur Schnitzler a deep need for companionship, which Schnitzler was eager to reciprocate. But after his return to Vienna Herzl did little or nothing about it. Schnitzler complained that Herzl's condescension made friendship impossible, and they rarely saw one another. One day Herzl met Schnitzler in the street. "You ought to write something for us," Herzl said. "It might be good for you too."

Schnitzler was affronted by this afterthought. "Such a remark," Schnitzler's wife wrote later, prevented Schnitzler "from complying with Herzl's wish, much as he wanted to."

Having rejected men of strong character, Herzl complained, not surprisingly, that he was surrounded by windbags. His coworkers were expected to follow his lead blindly. But even the hand-picked members of his Viennese "action committee" grew restless under his "one-man rule." Every second week his establishment was shaken by a little palace revolution. Kellner and Kokesch complained, "We do not care to be the privy counselors of an absolute monarch," though they invariably were. On the other hand, with all their enthusiasm for the common cause, his coworkers were rarely prepared to shoulder the physical burden or the expense of the daily work. No one sacrificed his entire free time or risked his livelihood as did Herzl, although there was a permanent scramble for honorary titles and positions.

In his diary Herzl constantly complained of rivalries and intrigues. Now and again he recorded brief moments of joy. Gladstone, in England, twice came out publicly in favor of Herzl's scheme. In Paris, Alphonse Daudet, after reading the French translation of Herzl's tract, wrote Herzl that it was "*un très beau poème*. If I am still standing on my feet I will come to the Jewish state to give readings."

There were some amusing moments too. In April Herzl at-

tended a particularly heated discussion, during which everyone
present changed his mind at least once, and one man previously
slandered and denigrated by all the participants was in the end
selected for the committee. "A veritable scene from a comedy,"
Herzl noted. "The first pleasurable day I have had since I started in
Zionism. Otherwise all it has given me thus far is heart palpitations,
annoyance, and shock." Here was an august Jewish committee,
supposed to create illusions for the public, and which, itself, had no
illusions at all! The situation appealed to the playwright in him. He
concluded that, Jewish life being what it was, the first great literary
form in his new state "will probably be light comedy—no matter
what the language."

3

The *Neue Freie Presse* continued to ignore Zionism, as it had
ignored socialism for over twenty years. A strict order of the publishers forbade any allusion to the existence of Herzl's tract, or to
his growing movement and the forthcoming congress. Stifled by his
own newspaper and thwarted in his attempts to found a rival daily,
Herzl decided early in May to establish a political weekly. He
called it *Die ✡ Welt* (*The ✡ World*); within the star of David was
a globe with Palestine as its center. Dedicated solely to the cause
and reflecting Herzl's point of view, the weekly considerably
strengthened his position within the movement and without. The
decision to publish came abruptly, almost overnight. Herzl decided
to finance it himself, from his own dwindling resources, with some
help from his father. Kellner and Kokesch marveled at his drive.
Kellner said, "You astound people by the speed of your march—
you are a veritable Moltke." To Nordau, whom he informed of his
decision, Herzl admitted, "The *Neue Freie Presse* is my legal wife.
With *Die Welt* I am buying myself a mistress, who I hope shall
not ruin me."

The first issue appeared early in June. Herzl wrote it almost
entirely himself. Since his coworkers were busy elsewhere, he attended to every detail. He made up the columns, read the proofs,
and solicited advertisements. Although it started slowly, *Die Welt*
soon became a success, and within the year its circulation had
reached ten thousand. *Die Welt* was a new turn in "parochial"
Jewish journalism in the West; aggressive, polemical, belligerent,
witty, it dared to discuss Jewish problems and travails openly, with

uncommon candor. The front page was bright yellow, the color of the badge of shame that Jews had been forced to display prominently on their coats in the Middle Ages (and that the Nazis would revive forty years later). In Herzl's words the "stain of our shame shall become the sheen of our glory—

> Our weekly is a Jew Paper.
>
> We take this word, which is supposed to be a term of calumny, and wish to make it a word of honor.
>
> *Die Welt* is a newspaper for Jews. Which Jews? Not the strong, who are being helped anyway, and do not need any support.
>
> *Die Welt* is a newspaper of the poor, the weak, the young, and of all those who without being persecuted themselves have found the way home to their ancestry.
>
> [Our aim is] to create a homeland secured by public law for those Jews who cannot, or prefer not to, assimilate in the lands in which they reside.
>
> We are variously and simultaneously attacked as reactionaries and revolutionaries, whereas all we wish is measured, healthy progress. *Die Welt* will be the organ of those men who wish to lead Jewry out of these times into a better era.
>
> Vienna, June 3, 1897

As the first issue began to roll off the presses, Herzl was completely exhausted. But he was aglow with satisfaction and proudly dedicated the first copy to his parents. At the *Neue Freie Presse* the publication of *Die Welt* caused a renewal of the war between Herzl and his two publishers. Benedikt was furious. He had more or less reconciled himself to Herzl's strange forays into statesmanship, which he did not take too seriously, but this venture into publishing was too much. He urged Herzl to close *Die Welt*. Furious harangues alternated with friendly cajoling.

"Be a *bon garçon*," said Benedikt. "Don't be obstinate. *Soyez bon prince*. What do you get out of *Die Welt*? You are only doing yourself harm. I feel sorry for you. On the *Neue Freie Presse* you can make a great career . . . you are causing us the greatest embarrassment. [Because of you] we appear as a Jewish sheet. . . . Give it up, it will not be to your disadvantage."

A few days later Benedikt resorted to threats, telling Herzl there could be no compromise. *Die Welt* must cease publication; Herzl must not go on summer holiday without agreeing to this. But

Herzl remained inflexible, though he expected to be fired from the *Neue Freie Presse* within a matter of days. Julie was aghast. An ugly, enervating scene ensued between Herzl and his wife. But his mind was made up. Calmly he faced the possibility of losing his job. "My heart is pounding, to be sure. But this is only a weakness of the muscle, not of my will. Should the *Neue Freie Presse* drive me out, and I lose the position I have acquired through twenty years of hard work, it shall be in a manner of which I need not be ashamed."

June 10 was his son Hans's sixth birthday. He was so tired and distraught that he congratulated him on his "seventh."

But soon after their last exchange Benedikt became more amiable. Herzl could not make up his mind whether he was won over, or shrewdly preparing another assault. Meanwhile, a different kind of trouble was afoot. The Bavarian government had tacitly agreed to the Munich congress, but in a sharply worded statement the Jews of Munich gave notice of their opposition to having the congress in their city. The community elders, in a letter to Herzl, announced that he was "virtually endangering" their safety, for as they saw it, the congress might reflect on their patriotism as Germans. They denounced Herzl's scheme as a "fantasy created by sick circumstances and which will vanish as soon as these circumstances change." Herzl did not try to persuade them. He promptly made arrangements to move the congress to Basel, Switzerland. The sudden change added to the burden of his work. In the words of a collaborator, "we advised and we decided. Then we went back to our various occupations. The congress, however, was made by Herzl. He alone, with his own money and his work."

As the congress drew near, Herzl took a short leave in the country with his wife and children. His final conversation with Benedikt was calmer than he had expected.

"With your permission I shall now go on leave. I know now your point of view regarding *Die Welt*, and will send you my answer by the first of July."

Benedikt quickly said, "No, no, no, don't write! I am convinced you will do as I say. I speak as your true friend, and in my own interest too, of course, but not without considering yours. You only do yourself harm by standing up as a Jew."

"Harm?" Herzl retorted. "One only harms oneself by committing some mischief."

"We two certainly need not argue about character," Benedikt replied. "No one will ever cast any doubt on yours."

"Well, I must go on leave now," Herzl concluded. "These arguments with you have excited me too much."

"Me too. Heed my friendly advice, then! Promise me that you will close down *Die Welt!*"

Herzl shook his head mutely; he did not promise anything. Instead, he cleaned out his desk and cheerfully packed his files, "as a good housewife would hang up her keys before she lies down in agony." He clearly realized the meaning of his clash with the *Neue Freie Presse*. His much-envied position on the newspaper was recognized as the top literary post in Vienna. Without that position, he might overnight become a has-been, *déclassé*.

He faced that possibility with equanimity. On a little loose leaf, he jotted down a single line: "The greatest happiness: to be able to be what one really is." He had little interest now in his previous literary activity. To his first biographer, Reuben Brainin, then already at work, he wrote on May 24: "I do not want to say anything about my plays and literary creations. I wish they were dead and forgotten." At the same time he wrote the editors of *Kürschner's Who's Who in German Literature* and asked that all references to his literary works be removed from his listing, save the pamphlet *The Jewish State* and his collection of French political reports, *Palais Bourbon*.

The brief vacation at Ischl gave him little rest. He initiated an internal competition for the text of a Jewish national anthem. Much of the vacation was spent sending out a final stream of letters and memoranda and in endless arguments with his wife, who refused to accompany him to the Basel congress. She disapproved of his political activities even more than Benedikt; she had married a writer, an elegant man-about-town, not the harassed leader of an ethnic cause she could not share. In the margin of a manuscript a little note in Herzl's hand has been found: "While my wife is making me a scene." He was a very lonely man.

In the train on his way to Basel, Herzl reflected on the turbulent events of the past few months. He wavered between exultation and melancholy. The congress would be the high point of his public career; its worldwide resonance might arouse the interest of the great powers, who might finally take the matter under consideration. Herzl's hopes ran high; he might actually be *offered* a territory, or else his movement could benefit from current designs to dismember the Ottoman Empire. The German Kaiser might send for him. If there should be such a positive response, "I shall keep on working. If not, and if the moneyed Jews also show no readiness to carry forward the movement that I have brought to this stage at such great personal and material sacrifice—I shall retire." Concerning the true strength of the movement he had built, he had few illusions. How much of it was real? How much was make-believe? "The fact is—which I conceal from everybody—I have only an army of *schnorrers* [beggars]. I am at the head of boys, beggars, and *schmucks*."

Most of the threads he had spun to date would converge in Basel. The world press would be there, the diplomatic corps, the Sultan's representatives, Reverend Hechler, and Count Nevlinski. Herzl feared they would all lose faith when they saw how flimsily the present structure was built, or when they met his colleagues.

He arrived in Basel four days before the congress was to begin; the city was sweltering in the August heat. Herzl took rooms at the Hotel Trois Rois overlooking the misty Rhine. He rushed to inspect the offices that the city had placed at the disposal of the congress. Here he had his first shock. The offices were located in an old tailor's shop that had just been vacated. To forestall any obvious flippant comments, he called for a piece of cloth to cover the shop's sign and hide it from view. He knew that at this first national convocation of a pariah people, every detail would weigh heavily; the borderline between the lofty and the ridiculous was thin.

Next he inspected the assembly hall. There he received his second shock. Herzl's Swiss collaborator, the Zurich lawyer Dr. David Farbstein, had rented the cheap *Burgvogtei*, a large beer cellar with a music-hall stage and a silly backdrop for gymnastic performances. Herzl promptly canceled the lease and rented the more austere Basel Municipal Casino. With its severe facade and somber interior, the casino was more suitable for the serious deliberations Herzl was planning for his congress. Over the entrance a large blue and white banner was hung. This was Wolffsohn's idea. In his quest for a suitable flag, Wolffsohn had suddenly had a brainstorm: "But we do have a flag! It is blue and white, the color of our prayer shawls. Let us unfold it in full view of the entire world!" He ordered a blue and white flag inscribed with a star of David. "This is how our national flag was born," Wolffsohn remembered later, "and no one wondered how or from where it developed."

With every train, delegates were now arriving in Basel, caked with coal, sweaty from their long journeys across the continent— most had traveled third class. They trooped into Herzl's office to collect their delegate cards, which were imprinted with the picture of a farmer sowing long furrows that converged on the Wailing Wall. The delegates came from every part of Europe, some from overseas, Palestine, North Africa, and America. The majority were young men from the East. Fervent but impecunious, they had been equipped by their worried mothers with satchels of food for the long journey, and had begun the first of the congress's interminable discussions in heated caucuses on the train.

The narrow streets of Basel were alive with a strange assortment of people. Students from Kiev, Stockholm, Montpellier, and Berlin, with proud duel slashes across their cheeks. Pious, bearded rabbinical scholars with earlocks mingled with scions of long-assimilated or even baptized families of the West and publishers of obscure little newspapers appearing in Warsaw and Odessa. Neurotic Hebrew poets, who wrote for audiences of a few hundred readers, or spent their lives translating Shakespeare, Goethe, and Homer into Hebrew, came in the hope of reviving their ancient national tongue. There were Romanian and Hungarian businessmen, university professors from Heidelberg and Sofia, a Kiev occulist, doctors, engineers, a small sallow Polish shopkeeper, a yellow-bearded Swede, a bespectacled French intellectual, a stiff Dutch banker, a courtly Viennese lawyer, and many journalists from all over the Jewish world, for whom Zionism was the great and sacred work of their lives. Absent were Sir Samuel Montagu of London, and Colonel Goldsmid, who stayed away despite Herzl's urgent pleas, as did the Chief Rabbi of France, Zadok Kahn, who deferred to Rothschild's wishes. Kahn nevertheless cabled the congress a carefully worded greeting. But Willi Bambus of Berlin, who had roused Herzl's bitter ire first by resigning from the preparatory commission and then by protesting against the congress, showed up in hopes of breaking Herzl's hold on the delegates—or, as he put it, to prevent the worst. And there was Nordau, of course. Breezy, gray-haired, Nordau was Herzl's chief deputy, the only man of international fame among all the delegates. They were a fascinating potpourri of faces and types, scurrying to and fro, from office to hall to Braanschweiger's kosher restaurant (where, as Herzl complained, the food was bad), and tempers as well as intrigues were always running high. All were wearing small blue, seven-cornered shields embossed with twelve red and gold stars and bearing the legend, in German, "The only solution to the Jewish question is the establishment of a Jewish state."

More intoxicated than capable, what the delegates lacked in

eminence and experience they made up in zeal and unending argument. The Russian contingent immediately went into a caucus lasting through the day and into the night, conferring (Herzl noted) "about I don't know what." The unexpected appearance of Bambus and his friends confused Herzl and aroused his suspicions. From the very first day he suspected what he called "enemies" everywhere, and men "full of designs," most against himself, especially when they assured him of their esteem. His truculence amounted almost to paranoia. Confusing argument with indiscipline and divisiveness, and criticism with disloyalty, he saw himself surrounded by "rascals" and "bastards," by "jealousy" and "slyness," and by cunning opportunists whom he believed would betray him as soon as some little career opened up for them elsewhere.

Among the delegates who had answered his call, Herzl was probably the only one who knew precisely what he wanted. The others thought in terms of ideas; Herzl thought in terms of power. He now set out to win it with inflexible determination; everything else ceased to exist. He believed he had to assume responsibility for everything. He paid formal calls to the Swiss federal and city officials, like a visiting head of state, a courtly, suave figure in formal, dark attire. In the afternoons he received various delegations in audience.

On one occasion seven stern rabbis called on Herzl at the hotel; they left beaming with satisfaction. Stupefied, one of Herzl's young aides inquired of them, "What happened? Has he promised to keep the Sabbath and eat only kosher food?"

"On the contrary," said their spokesman. "That would have worried us a great deal. If he had suddenly become pious and observant, we could not have joined his movement for fear that we would have to accept him as the Messiah." Such light moments were rare. Herzl left his mark everywhere by his serious, solemn tone, and his critics were stunned into silence, both by his shrewd maneuvers and by his regal manner.

His acute sense of ritual and decorum was especially evident in the *mise-en-scène*. In his addiction to form and ceremony, he was the true Viennese—the species who, according to Schiller (in his drama *Piccolomini*), is ready to forgive everything except being cheated of a spectacle. As a man of the theater, Herzl was thoroughly familiar with the magic of props, lighting, and costume, and so from the first moment of his arrival in Basel he personally supervised every detail. There is an element of theater in all politics; the convergence of the two has rarely been as evident as at this moment in Herzl's life. In Basel he was almost back at the Burgthe-ater; but here he was not only playwright, but also the director, stage manager, and leading actor.

The delegates lived through a kind of psychodrama. Under Herzl's direction a theory of liberty and of history was acted out by the delegates on a small, yet perfect, stage; no one could ignore the superb theatrical impact. Herzl put it this way: "Guiding intellects must simply put on the hat and lead the way, then the others will follow along with admiration and devotion. Do they admire the in-tellect? [No!] They admire the *hat* and the courage it took to put it on!"

Shrewdly calculating the effect it would have on the religious delegates, Herzl visited a Basel synagogue on the Sabbath. He took Nordau with him. It was the first time in many years that the two men had gone to "pray." A few hours before, Herzl had been drilled by an aide in the text of the benediction. When he was called up to the Torah, he found that the few Hebrew words of the benediction were causing him more anxiety than all the speeches he had delivered, more than the entire direction of the congress. How-ever, he managed to get through without making a mistake. For Nordau, the avowed atheist, the visit was especially trying. When his own turn came to read a portion of the Law, he "refused and fled the synagogue in confusion."

Herzl left nothing to chance. He insisted on a very rigid agenda and imposed a definite time limit on all speeches. For Herzl's ebullient Eastern European disciples, this was an unheard-of procedure, but he fought for it and in the end won. There were no impromptu addresses; all speeches had to be submitted in writ-ing to the chairmen of the various committees.

He was acutely conscious of the role of costume. The dele-gates' cards bore this warning: "Black formal attire and white neck-tie must be worn at the festive opening session." There was a run on rental shops. The injunction was not easy to enforce. Max Nor-dau tried to rebel against the formal attire, which after all was one of those "fashionable lies" of modern civilization against which he had always fought so vigorously. He showed up in an ordinary frock coat and simply refused to change. He would not wear anything more formal, certainly not at ten in the morning. Herzl drew him aside. "Today the presidium of the Zionist congress is nothing at all," he said. "We still must establish everything. People should get accustomed to seeing the congress as a most solemn and exalted thing." Nordau grudgingly relented and returned fifteen minutes later in formal dress. Overwhelmed with gratitude, Herzl embraced him warmly.

The choice of dress was not snobbishness, but a political impresario's shrewd device, carefully thought out months before, to give the proceedings an air of importance and restraint. Stiffness would "give rise immediately to a sedate tone, one they might not assume in light-colored summer suits, or travel clothes." The congress, as Herzl saw it, was a pariah people's "rudimentary form of self-determination." Even more than to impress the outside world, Herzl wanted to impress the delegates themselves with their own importance.

He was eminently successful. When the congress formally opened on Sunday morning, August 29, everybody was keyed to the highest expectations. Present were 208 delegates from 16 countries, and some 26 special correspondents of major European newspapers, although Herzl's own *Neue Freie Presse* boycotted the event. There was not enough space in the galleries for the several hundred onlookers, including many Swiss Gentiles who were intrigued by the spectacle of a "Jew Congress." The overflow had to be accommodated on the main floor behind the delegates' cane chairs. The platform was draped in green and flanked by tables for newsmen and stenographers. Although Herzl had designed it all himself, he was so moved when he entered the oblong hall from the rear that "I quickly walked out again so as not to lose my composure."

The proceedings were opened by the senior delegate, Dr. Karl Lippe of Romania, a veteran of the old Lovers of Zion movement. He spoke too long, thirty minutes instead of the ten Herzl had allocated, ignoring four nervous pleas and a final threat by Herzl to cut him short. But when, in a shaky voice, the venerable old man pronounced the traditional Hebrew prayer of thanksgiving, "Blessed be Thou, our Lord, for having let us live this day," a quiver of emotion swept the crowded hall and some wept. As he turned the gavel over to Herzl with the challenging words, "The only thing we need is a fatherland," the audience rose to its feet in a tumultuous roar of applause.

The scene has been described by many eyewitnesses. Herzl slowly strode to the rostrum, walking stiffly through the roaring crowd. Poised and erect, he looked more regal than ever, with his proud carriage, blue-black beard, and the steady look of his dark, velvety eyes. Amid the mounting roar and the stomping of feet and sticks on the wooden floor, in the flutter of handkerchiefs, men reached out to kiss his hand while others wept and embraced. He reached the rostrum but could not begin his speech. Each time he opened his mouth, the roar of applause mounted again. The cheers continued for some fifteen minutes. The Hebrew writer Ben Ami was overcome by a "powerful wish, an irresistible inner compulsion to cry through these stormy waves of cheers: *'Yechi Hamelech!'* [Long live the King!]"

Herzl had come a long way. His models were Bismarck, Disraeli, Gambetta, and Parnell. A tall and picturesque figure at the rostrum, he drew himself up and did not acknowledge the cheers. "I intentionally refrained from bowing, so as to keep [it] from turning into a cheap performance, or mere showmanship." Ben Ami's cry "Long live the King!" was taken up by others and echoed through the hall. Herzl made a slight, suave movement with his hand. In the midst of the tremendous uproar he remained (outwardly) serene. His face was pale; the features appeared embossed as if on wax. His eyes glowed. He threw back his head and opened his mouth to speak. The roar continued, and he folded his arms on his chest. At once the person and the actor, the real person and the model merged until, in one supreme moment, Herzl was almost mimicking himself.

When the cheers finally abated Herzl delivered his address. He read the prepared text like a formal speech from a throne. It was not a rousing "nationalist" or emotional speech, but eminently practical and matter-of-fact. Yet he possessed that vehemence which, on a profound level, seldom fails to persuade:

> We want to lay the cornerstone of the edifice that is one day to house the Jewish nation. The task is so great that we should speak of it in none but the simplest terms. . . . In our day . . . so progressive in most respects, we see and feel ourselves surrounded by the old hatred. . . . The first impression anti-Semitism made on the Jews of today was one of astonishment; astonishment gave way to pain and resentment. Perhaps our enemies are quite unaware of how deeply they wounded our sensibilities. That very part of Jewry which is modern, cultured, and had outgrown the ghetto and lost the habit of petty trading, was pierced to the heart.
>
> . . . From time immemorial the world has been misinformed about us. That clannishness for which we have been reproached so often and so bitterly was in the process of disintegration just as we were attacked by anti-Semitism. Anti-

Semitism has served to strengthen it anew. We have come
home, as it were. Zionism is our return to Judaism even before
our return to the Jewish land. . . . We have not the least intention of yielding an iota of our acquired culture. On the contrary,
we aim toward a broader culture such as the increase of knowledge brings with it.

He made no reference to his pamphlet. The purpose of the
congress was to set up an organization and to seek agreement with
the great powers, notably with the Ottoman Empire, for large-scale
Jewish settlement in Palestine. Any agreement must be "based on
rights, not on toleration. Surely we have had enough experience
with [the kind of] protection that can be revoked at any time." He
took sharp issue with the present small-scale infiltration of Palestine
by Jewish settlers. Colonization must not be furtive, as now, but
open and anchored in international law. "If anyone thinks that the
Jews can steal into the land of their fathers, he is deceiving either
himself or others. Nowhere is the coming of the Jews so promptly
noticed as in their historic home, for the very reason that it *is* their
historic home. Nor would it be in our interest to go there prematurely." An arrangement with the Turkish Sultan would not only
afford the necessary legal guarantees, but also considerably benefit
his realm. The purpose of the congress was to create a new type of
Jew, he said. "A people can only help itself. If it cannot, that people
cannot be helped at all."

When he finished there was a brief hush, then another storm of
applause broke loose. He received "the hosannas of a king, and
men climbed over one another to congratulate him." All order collapsed; in the general excitement tables and chairs were overturned, a lady fainted in the gallery, others waved their handkerchiefs, crying "*Heddad*" (Hebrew for "Hurrah"). Even the cynical
Nevlinski was impressed. "My dear friend," he said, "your speech was
a masterpiece." Nordau too, who had often decried "increased ex-
citability" as a "debilitating nervous disease," succumbed to the
general fervor and embraced Herzl warmly.

Herzl was elected president by acclamation, with Nordau as
his first deputy. One of his first reactions was proudly to send
congress postcards to his parents, his wife, and each of his children,
a "childishness" for which he quickly scolded himself. Soon there
were more serious matters. It was Herzl's constant concern during
the three days of the congress to make Nordau forget that he was
taking second place; Herzl thought Nordau's self-esteem was "visi-

Herzl at 11:00 A.M. walking from his hotel to the congress. At his insistence, black formal attire was made mandatory: "I hounded them into the mood for a State. I worked them up to feel *they* were its national assembly."

Herzl greeted by delegates to the congress.

A contemporary artist's impression of the congress. "At Basel I founded the Jewish State. If I said this aloud today I would be answered by universal laughter. Perhaps in five years, certainly in fifty, everyone will agree."

Facing page: Herzl and his three children, Hans, Pauline, and Trude. Hans and Pauline committed suicide. Trude, after a near lifetime in a psychiatric clinic, died in a Nazi concentration camp. The direct line ended when her only son, Peter Theodor, committed suicide in 1946.

Herzl in his study with his father: "He stands beside me like a rock."

Herzl and his mother: "Weakness is easily forgiven to the crowd. To you, the leader, it is not allowed."

Max Nordau, the iconoclastic author of *The Conventional Lies of Mankind* and other worldwide best sellers, was one of the first who rallied enthusiastically to Herzl's cause.

The Reverend William Hechler, a Protestant clergyman who accompanied his friend the German Kaiser to Palestine in Arab attire. No man of stranger charm ever assisted at the birth of a national movement.

David Wolffsohn of Cologne, Herzl's closest collaborator and successor. An eminently practical man: "Herzl tends to loose the ground under his feet. My job is to stand him up again."

Sultan Abdul-Hamid of Turkey, ruler o Palestine. Herzl offered to relieve Turke of her crushing indebtedness to Frenc creditors in return for a tribute-payin Jewish vassal state in Palestine under th Sultan's rule.

Herzl and his colleagues on the banks of the Suez canal on the way to Palestine.

erzl and his colleagues on board a freighter on their way from Egypt to Palestine to meet the German Kaiser.

At 7:00 A.M. the first pale, barren bit of land was sighted.

Herzl and the Jewish deputation in Jerusalem shortly before the meeting with the German Kaiser

bly suffering." He used every possible occasion to assure Nordau that his own election as president was for purely technical reasons, because of his acquaintance with the people and the details. "Next year you will be president of the congress and I shall head the executive committee."

But if Nordau was disappointed, he did not show it in his speech, which followed next on the agenda. Nordau's very presence on the dais was in itself important for the public image of the congress. He was the world-renowned guardian of "normalcy," a fanatic about mental health, and a merciless critic of all "imbecile romanticism." By his presence he attested to Herzl's soundness of mind. In his "state of the nation" speech, Nordau sounded a jeremiad on the modern Jewish condition. In the "free" West, Jews suffered from moral distress; in the illiberal East, the burden was legal, political, and economic. In both the East and the West, Nordau said, the plight of Jews was peculiar; they suffered not as *men* but as Jews. In most cases they would have been freed from suffering had they been anything but Jews. Those nations that had emancipated their Jews had succumbed to a self-delusion as to their own true feelings about Jews. There was a single exception, Nordau noted: England. In England the emancipation of the Jews was a true one, not merely written on paper, but effective in real life. Yet how many Jews were there in England? Would not a mass influx from the East into England produce reactions similar to those in Germany and France? Nordau was accorded a reception only a little less royal than Herzl's. Herzl afterward went up to him and said, "*Monumentum aere perennius*" (A monument more enduring than bronze).

From then on the passion *to act* grew. The assembly broke up into various commissions. A general debate took place, and Herzl was an efficient if ruthless chairman, consciously emulating the niceties and refinements of the French parliament which he had covered for four years as a correspondent. He delighted in coining witty *mots présidentiels*; affable but energetic, he ruled with an iron hand. On one occasion he remained in the chair for almost twenty-one hours to sustain his personal control. "I felt as if I were playing thirty-two games of chess simultaneously." A motion to limit his powers by the appointment of a secretary-general, elected directly and paid by the congress, was ignominiously rejected. It was not the only discordant note, but Herzl was able to squash dissent with authoritarian rulings from the chair. One must remember the natural skepticism of any assembly of Jewish intellectuals in order to appreciate Herzl's charismatic hold, for he seems to have gotten away with the most undemocratic measures, including an improper counting of votes on one occasion.

On the third day the resolutions drafted in committee were passed in congress. One resolution finally established a worldwide Zionist organization, with an "actions committee" in Vienna under Herzl's authority. It was necessary in this instance to remain vague, for "international organizations" were forbidden in most countries and in some they were equated with nihilism. Another resolution established a form of voluntary taxation (the *shekel*, or one franc a year), and a representative system of elections. At the next congress there would be only delegates elected by members who had paid their *shekel*. Each one hundred contributors would elect one delegate.

Another resolution spelled out the official program of the Zionist movement. By its vagueness it reconciled the opposing views and also avoided international complications. Drafted by Nordau, after much argument in committee, the Basel Program (as it was commonly called afterward) was a masterpiece in subterfuge: "The aim of Zionism is to create for the Jewish people a *homestead* [*Heimstätte*] in Palestine secured by *public law.*"

The wording was elastic and open to many interpretations. Nordau supplied the nonpolitical, almost sentimental term "homestead," for Palestine was under Turkish rule and any other term might have struck the Sultan as subversion. "I knew what I was doing," Nordau explained a few years later. "The wording contains everything. You only have to interpret it. But the masses will understand." Many delegates wanted to secure the proposed homestead by *international* law. Herzl convinced the congress to say "public law," for the Sultan would have read "international law" as a call to dismember his empire. "Do not burden the executive in the fulfillment of its task by imposing a term that is perhaps too precise," Herzl begged delegates who demanded stronger language. When de Haas complained to Herzl that the wording might be all right for German jurists, but was clumsy and difficult to translate into English, Herzl's answer was: "No need to worry. The people will read it as the Jewish state anyway."

In order to achieve its goal, the congress envisaged the following means:

1. The settlement in Palestine of farmers, artisans, and laborers in *such a manner as serves the purpose* (Herzl insisted on this

qualification to express his opposition to small-scale infiltration without political guarantees)

2. The organization and union of the whole of Jewry in suitable local and general bodies, in accordance with the laws of their respective countries
3. The strengthening of Jewish national feeling and national consciousness
4. Preparatory steps to obtain governmental consent necessary to achieve the goals of Zionism (this was a mandate for Herzl to continue his diplomatic quest)

At the end of the third day everybody was thoroughly exhausted. Herzl had slept hardly more than twelve hours in five days. The technical arrangements, the interminable debates over matters of principle and ideology, the personal clashes brought him to the end of his strength. Everything revolved around him. "Four or five people are always talking to me at the same time, an enormous mental strain since they all have to be given a definite decision." He fretted nervously over every word uttered in public for it was common knowledge that there were czarist police spies in the audience as well as agents of the Turkish Sultan. The slightest indiscretion might have compromised the colonists in Palestine or caused further harassment of the oppressed Jews of Russia. His own position as an editor of the *Neue Freie Presse* was another source of concern. Herzl wanted to avoid giving Benedikt a pretext for easing him out. It was like "dancing among eggs, all of which are invisible," Herzl wrote.

The closing session, at night, brought more emotional scenes. The congress was given the pleasure—always gratifying to an ideological movement—of hearing a former heretic's mournful recantation of his errors. The Chief Rabbi of Basel, Dr. Cohn, mounted the rostrum. He admitted that like most rabbis he had opposed Zionism and only a few weeks earlier had criticized Herzl from his pulpit. The speeches at this congress had caused him to change his mind. His only remaining concern, he said, was that in the new Jewish state the Sabbath and all the other tenets of the Jewish religion be faithfully kept. If the president could reassure him on this matter, he was prepared to dedicate his life to the noble cause.

Herzl was grave, almost imperial, in his reply from the chair. Judaism, he said, had nothing to fear from the Jewish state. But he made it equally clear that there was more than one school of thought in Judaism, and that Cohn's Orthodox line was not the only one. He was greeted with stormy applause; the majority of delegates were secularized Jews.

Herzl now closed the proceedings. He apologized for any harshness he may have been guilty of as chairman of the congress. "My intentions were good, and we have achieved something." A vote of thanks followed. Then Herzl announced, "The first Zionist congress is now closed," but his words were drowned in the applause. A scene now took place which even *Die Welt* later admitted was hard to describe. It lasted for almost an hour. The minutes refer to "thunderous cries of 'hail!'" Men stamped on the floor, embraced, and kissed; women waved handkerchiefs. Some of the delegates began to sing, while others jumped onto chairs and tables to dance and cheer Herzl and his colleagues, who slowly withdrew into a back room. From all over the teeming hall came shouts of "Next year in Jerusalem!"

4

The congress was the first authoritative assembly of the Jewish people since their dispersion under the Roman Empire. It was as if a fossil had suddenly raised its head and bitten its detractor in the heel. It is not easy today to fully appreciate its impact on the participants. Herzl thought they would soon constitute an aristocracy, like the Puritan founding fathers who had traveled to America on the *Mayflower*. "For us the first congress was a crisis that changed our fate," wrote Leib Jaffe, a delegate to the congress. "It revolutionized our entire world and divided the history of our exile in two parts, the first before the congress and the second the part that came after." Israel Zangwill, a mocking skeptic at most times, wrote, "By the rivers of Babylon we sat down and wept as we remembered Zion. By the river of Basel we sat down resolved to weep no more!" From distant Odessa, Chaim Nachman Bialik, the first national poet in the reviving Hebrew tongue, followed the congress and wrote:

> Your memory in dark hours shall rest
> A never-fading sun to the oppressed.

It is interesting to trace the impact of Herzl's congress on the confidential diplomatic records of the time. The Austrian legation in Berne insinuated revolutionary undercover activities and reported to Vienna that the idea of a Jewish national state in Palestine was the intellectual product of radical German socialists. The French consul in Basel ironically reported a "rampant dream to restore the kingdom of Zion" in Palestine, which, despite the grand publicity it had been given, did not appear to be as important as it claimed, nor was it likely ever to achieve its goals, for "it was prompted and is being supported mainly by *les Juifs du journalisme*. . . ."

The German legation in Berne dispatched the longest, most thoroughly detailed report on the deliberations of the congress. In the margin of this report the Kaiser scribbled the remark: "I am all in favor of the *kikes* going to Palestine. The sooner they take off the better. I shan't put any obstacles in their way."

In the demented minds of some anti-Semites, the Basel congress tended to feed the most lethal myths of Jewish world domination. In later years, the first Basel congress often figured in anti-Semitic literature as a meeting of Jewish bankers plotting the final take-over of the world by the Jews. The notorious *Protocols of the Elders of Zion* were said by their Russian editor, the forger Sergei Nilus, to have first been presented in Basel in 1897 to the Council of Elders by Theodor Herzl, the prince of the Exile.

The strange conclusions that Gentiles sometimes draw about Jews were evident even in the good-natured reaction of Mark Twain. "I am not the Sultan, and I am not objecting," Twain wrote of the congress, "but if that concentration of the cunningest brains in the world was going to be made in a free country (bar Scotland), I think it would be politic to stop it. It will not be well to let that race find its strength. If horses knew theirs we should not ride anymore."

The delegates gave Herzl a rousing farewell. A student choir intoned a Zionist adaptation of a patriotic German song:

> There where the cedar kisses the sky,
> And where the Jordan quickly flows by,
> There where the ashes of my father lie,
> In that exalted Reich, on sea and sand,
> Is my beloved, true Fatherland.

> (Dort wo die Ceder schlank die Wolken küsst
> Und wo die schnelle Jordanquelle fliesst,
> Dort wo die Asche meiner Vater ruht,
> Das hehre Reich am blauen Meerestrand,
> Es ist mein liebes trautes Vaterland.)

Herzl beamed. "The man who brought to Basel the daydreams he had had in the Tuileries gardens two years before," he told himself, "that man may yet sail the Mediterranean Sea as a Jew returning home."

He returned to Vienna in a state of total exhaustion. The long hours in the train went by in half-conscious reveries, and before his eyes there passed once more the strangely varied procession of the delegates. The Russian Jews had left the deepest impact. Warm-hearted, soulful, eminently practical, deeply steeped in folk tradition, which in the East was still very much alive, they had none of the identity problems of the Western Jew, none of his sense of alienation. Herzl had previously thought of them as poor, oppressed candidates for relief, living in a "primitive" East; it took the congress to open his eyes.

> How ashamed we felt, we who had thought that we were superior to them.
>
> Even more impressive was that they possess an inner integrity that most European Jews have lost. They feel like national Jews but without narrow and intolerant conceit. . . . They are not tormented by the need to assimilate. Their nature is simple and unbroken . . . they are upright and genuine, and yet they are ghetto Jews, the only ghetto Jews of our time. By looking at them we understood what gave our forefathers the strength to endure the most difficult times. They confronted us with our history. I had often been told in the beginning, "The only Jews you'll win will be the Russian Jews." Today I say, "They would be enough!"

The next morning Herzl was back in Vienna. In the city room of the *Neue Freie Presse* he was greeted with derision, as though he had just participated in some childish folly. "The President! Make way for the President, ha, ha!" Herzl put on a good face. The *Neue Freie Presse* had completely ignored the Basel congress, while at the same time giving extensive coverage to a convention of trouser-makers at Oxford who were deliberating about whether lady cyclists should wear crinoline skirts or knickerbocker pantaloons.

Bacher received him with an uncertain smile. "I don't want to hear one word about that business," he said. But even as Bacher spoke, Herzl noticed a thick batch of Swiss press clippings bulging from his side pocket.

Herzl still owed his editors an answer to their request that he

close down his Zionist weekly *Die Welt*. But after all the shouting
and threats of the last summer, Bacher and Benedikt no longer
pressed the issue. Herzl compromised by writing in *Die Welt* only
under a pseudonym. Despite this, Bacher and Benedikt made certain that not a single word of Herzl's project would appear in their
own newspaper, then or in the future. The rest of the world press,
which had covered the Basel convention, reported Herzl's continued activities. In England the *Pall Mall Gazette* and *Daily
Chronicle* proposed a conference of the European powers to settle
the Jewish question. And of course, in Jewish newspapers all over
the world Herzl's congress was the subject of heated discussion.

In his diary, a few days after his return to Vienna, he wrote
with no little prescience:

> Were I to sum up the Basel congress in a few words—which I
> must guard against uttering publicly—it would be this: In Basel
> I founded the Jewish state. If I said this aloud today, I would
> be answered by universal laughter. Perhaps in five years, and
> certainly in *fifty*, everyone will agree. The state is already
> founded, in essence, in the will of the people to be a state; yes,
> even in the will of a sufficiently powerful individual (*l'État c'est
> moi*, Louis XIV). Territory is only the material basis. The state,
> even where it possesses territory, is always something abstract.
> The church state exists without territory. . . .
>
> At Basel, then, I created this abstraction, which as such is
> still invisible to most people. And with what infinitesimal
> means! I gradually hounded them into the mood for a state. I
> worked them up to feel *they* were its national assembly.

11

Noise and Clamor

FROM MOOD to accomplishment the road was still long and arduous. The mood was strong enough, however, to arouse immediate apprehensions in some quarters, among them the Vatican. Reconciled for centuries to the Moslem reconquest of Jerusalem, the Holy See could not bear the idea of a Holy Land governed by Jews. Shortly after the congress, the Pope was reported in the press as preparing an encyclical to protest the "proposed seizing of the Holy Places by the Jews." After summoning Monsignor Bonetti, the apostolic representative in Constantinople, to consult on measures to be taken against the Zionists, the Pope was said to have turned to France, as the "protector" of Christians in the East.

An ancient feud seemed to rear its ugly head again. Herzl, deeply concerned, wrote to Emigidius Taliani, the apostolic nuncio in Vienna, requesting an interview. Taliani refused to see him. In his opinion all Jews were rich anyway and had no reason to complain. "Have you ever seen a poor Jew?" he once asked one of Herzl's colleagues, Dr. Sigmund Münz, the political correspondent of the *Neue Freie Presse*. When, after many months of waiting, Herzl was finally admitted to his presence, he assured Taliani there was no question of seizing any Holy Places. Jerusalem and Bethlehem would be extraterritorialized, and the capital of the Jewish state established on a completely new site farther north. Taliani said that personally he was not opposed to Herzl's scheme, but there was little change in the basic position of the Holy See. Taliani smoothly assured Herzl that the church "had always been well disposed toward the Jews." When they had been "locked up in ghettos, it was only to protect them against the mob."

"There have been interruptions in this benevolent tradition,"

Herzl remarked sarcastically. There was little else he could do, and there the matter rested for the time being. The Vatican's antagonism to Herzl's cause has survived to our day.

Herzl's communications with the Turkish government had been interrupted a few months earlier. After his return from the congress he set out with added vigor to renew his contacts. His main link was still the mysterious Nevlinski, who traveled back and forth to Constantinople and whom he now paid a modest subsidy of two hundred guldens a month. For the first time the money came not solely from Herzl's pocket, but from the new organization's little treasury of *shekels*. Nevlinski was Herzl's chief of protocol: "He tells me the hundred and one petty details of diplomatic etiquette, e.g., that letters to the Sultan are to be sealed with five seals but should bear no inscription." Together they drafted another appeal to the Sultan asking for a vassal state in Palestine in exchange for the liquidation of the Turkish foreign debt by the Jews. The letter to the Sultan was delivered through Nuri Bey, Secretary-General of the Turkish Foreign Ministry. During their last encounter Nuri had been "fire and flame" for Herzl's scheme; he now asked for an advance bribe of "some twenty thousand francs." For a movement which, in Herzl's words, still consisted largely of "beggars with dreams," this was a high price to pay for the delivery of one letter, but what choice was there? The auspices seemed propitious.

Nevlinski sustained Herzl's faith with endless stories on the bad state of Turkish finances. "The Turkish ambassadors abroad can no longer pay their butcher bills," Nevlinski said. Some had been forced to leave their posts because they had not been paid salaries for a year; the Turkish ambassador in Vienna was living on beans, which he cooked himself.

Herzl had three long conferences with the Turkish ambassador to Berlin (and future Grand Vizier), the powerful Ahmed Tewfik Pasha, on the eve of Tewfik's appointment as Foreign Minister. Tewfik agreed to permit Jewish immigrants into Turkey, where they would be given a "friendly reception, but no territorial autonomy." Even for this the Jews would have to pay enormous sums of money. "That is no solution," Herzl said. The Jews had no desire to become the "new Armenians." "We will have to wait until Turkey is even worse off." But to himself he reflected bitterly that "perhaps Tewfik reasons also, and it would not be stupid: 'We Turks must wait until the Jews are even worse off.'" On their third meeting Tewfik became a bit more amenable. Herzl flattered the

Turk's vanity, and with his great gift for words he built up before
Tewfik's eyes a fabulous Turkey of the future, free, strong, and
prosperous, under Tewfik's leadership.

"When you, Excellency, are Grand Vizier, you will invite me to
Constantinople and I will rebuild it for you." For a moment Herzl
had the distinct feeling that he had won Tewfik over, and he decided that Nevlinski had been right, "one ought to live with these
Turks, render them services for which they will be very grateful,
and gradually bring them to love us."

This last conversation with Tewfik took place over dinner in
Berlin, where Herzl had gone to deliver a speech and seek an
audience with the Kaiser. He visited Friedrich Karl von Lucanus,
chief of the Kaiser's Privy Council. "The Emperor is acquainted
with the matter," Lucanus said. In Lucanus' opinion it was something fine and great, but he understood that "the Israelites are not
too eager."

"You are telling me!" Herzl rejoined. Lucanus, however, promised to pursue the case further and to convey a copy of Herzl's
pamphlet to the Emperor.

At the same time Herzl devoted every free moment to consolidating the new organization. In an article in *Die Welt* he launched
another project, a Jewish Colonial Bank, to finance the proposed
exodus by a consolidation of all available popular resources. "The
national movement must be independent of the mercy of philanthropists." Herzl made preparations to establish the bank in London, with an initial capital of two million pounds sterling. Meanwhile he often felt ill and was troubled by his heart. "I am as tired
as an old man," he complained on October 27, 1897. But he did not
spare himself.

Another stream of letters went out to his followers all over the
world. He harnessed his newly created Zionist executive to the task
of creating the new bank by cajoling and begging them to sell
shares. Many of his colleagues were skeptical. Ozer Kokesch said,
"To the likes of us, nobody is going to lend as much as ten thousand guldens"—let alone two million pounds sterling. But Herzl
was persistent. If all the poor Jews could only pull together, they
would have more money than even the Rothschilds; surely it was
not ludicrous to seek two million pounds by popular subscription.

Since David Wolffsohn of Cologne was the only man with
some experience in banking and finance, he was charged with practical arrangements. During the next few months the faithful Wolffsohn wandered over half of Europe in search of underwriters and

subscribers. He was almost totally unsuccessful with the rich. "We are like soldiers of the French Revolution who went into battle without shoes and stockings," Herzl noted. Sir Edward Sassoon in London and the private bankers M. Warburg of Hamburg, Oppenheim of Cologne, and Seligman of Frankfurt turned Wolffsohn down; the "Zionist" Sir Samuel Montagu of London did not want to hear of Herzl's latest adventure in international banking. The only financial body ready to underwrite the issuing of shares was the non-Jewish German banking firm of Schaffhausen.

Behind these refusals Herzl suspected the fine hand of the House of Rothschild. He worked himself up into a veritable Rothschild phobia. They were mean "scoundrels and malefactors. . . . Sooner or later," he wrote on September 23, "I shall have to start a campaign against the Rothschilds . . . the world menace that this octopus constitutes." In a public statement he threatened the Rothschilds with the international boycott of the Jewish middle classes. When Montagu let his opposition be known, Herzl swore terrible "revenge on these big-time bankers . . . it will be well deserved."

He went so far as to vent his growing resentment in a rare act of invective. His sketch *"Mauschel"* ("Kike") appeared in the second October issue of *Die Welt*; it reads like a piece of anti-Semitic horror propaganda. Herzl vilified all those Jews who were opposed to Zionism, calling them a degenerate racial strain—objects of physical "disgust," "selfish," "dirty," and "mean," in short—"kikes."

> Kike is anti-Zionist. We have known him for a long time. We have always been disgusted whenever we looked at his face . . . in a kind of romantic tenderness we tried to help him because he was a scamp. Whenever he committed an act of meanness we tried to hush it up. . . .
>
> As a type, my dear friends, *Mauschel* has always been the dreadful companion of the Jew, and so inseparable from him that they were always confused. The Jew is a man like all others, no better, no worse . . . but *Mauschel* is a distortion of the human character, unspeakably mean and repellent. Where the Jew experiences pain or pride, *Mauschel* only feels miserable fear, or faces you with a sneering grin . . . impudent and arrogant. The Jew aspires to higher levels of culture; *Mauschel* pursues only his own dirty business. . . . Even the arts and sciences he pursues only for mean profit . . . he hides behind subversive opposition movements and urges them on, secretly, whenever he is dissatisfied with the existing order; or he escapes

into police protection and squeals whenever he becomes frightened of revolt. . . . It is as if in a dark moment of our history some mean strain intruded into and was mixed with our unfortunate nation. . . . In times of anti-Semitism *Mauschel* shrugs his shoulders. Honor? Who needs it, if business is good?

He finished his diatribe with a threat: the Zionists, like William Tell, are holding a second arrow in reserve. Should they miss the first shot, the second arrow will serve for vengeance. "*Mauschel*, take care! Friends, Zionism's second arrow is aimed at *Mauschel's* breast."

Herzl had little patience, either, for his Viennese colleagues, whom he dubbed "members of my *in*action committee." They were too slow, too timid, too *gemütlich*. His colleagues, with their careers and various personal interests which they would not and could not jeopardize, had only limited time for the cause. Although he held his men under a constant spell, Herzl's own autocratic manner did not help to produce very much individual initiative. He was tough and sometimes gruff and offensive toward his aides. In his postcongress statements he employed the royal "we" and in his diary he referred to his aides as "my Nordau," "my young Schalit," "my good Schnirer." He preferred yes-men, like the servile and adoring Wolffsohn, who even imitated "his tone of voice, posture, and that characteristic gesture of the right hand, with closed fingers."

The new organization was handicapped by his haughty attitude and his authoritarianism. "You take advice with difficulty, and criticism even harder," wrote Kellner, whom Herzl dubbed his best friend. "You are a very, very great man, but you look down on the rest of the world. You are also very suspicious. . . . I have spent wonderful hours in your company, but do you know what I often tell myself? I tell myself that to serve this man, to help him, is pure joy. To be his true, sincere friend is difficult."

That winter, for the first time, no Christmas tree was set up at the Herzl home at Berggasse 6. Instead Herzl solemnly lit a nine-armed Hanukkah candelabra and lectured the children on the Maccabean revolt and the miracle of lights. At Basel he had announced, "Zionism is our return to Judaism even before our return to the Jewish land." The substitution of a menorah for the Christmas tree reflected his search for roots in a tradition he had thus far ignored and often disparaged. The name "menorah" pleased his ear, especially as it came back to him from the mouths of the children. In a charming little autobiographical tale, "The Menorah," he traced the intellectual consequences of this decision.

> There was a man who felt deep in his heart the distress of being a Jew. His outward circumstances were not unsatisfactory. He had a sufficient income and a pleasant, creative profession. . . . He was an artist. He had long ignored his Jewish origin. Then the old hatred rose again, disguised under a fashionable new title. Like many others he believed that the trend would soon disappear. But it grew worse. He personally was not struck, but the mounting assault pained him all the more until his soul was one bleeding wound. And it came to pass that through these inner muted passions he was led to their source, to his Judaism. In pleasanter days he might never have been able to find it, for he was already so far removed. Now he began to love it fervently. . . . Out of dark feelings grew clear thoughts; he uttered them aloud: . . . the one way out of the misery of being Jewish is to return to Jewishness.

The man's own generation, raised in another culture, was perhaps incapable of achieving this return, but at least his children might. So, at Hanukkah time that man acquired a menorah. The eyes of the children glistened. He likened the spreading light to the slow awakening of a people.

> First one candle is lit. It is still dark and that one candle looks sad. Then another joins in, one more, and more. The darkness must yield. First the young and poor are enkindled, then gradually others . . . when all the candles burn there is astonishment and great happiness over the accomplished task. *And no task affords more happiness than to be the servant of light.*

From such distractions he returned to the daily humdrum of work. To further his bank, he now kept company with the very people he had shunned in the past, financiers and stockbrokers. He received Israel Poznanski, owner of huge textile mills in Lodz, said to be the richest Jew in Poland and a notorious exploiter of child labor. Poznanski was ready to join the syndicate which would guarantee the subscription of shares for Herzl's bank. Herzl wrote Nordau that Poznanski was "completely sold on the cause," but his involvement turned out to be a rich man's passing fancy. In the end nothing came of it. Money is a good thing, Herzl told himself, but people have spoiled it.

Early in January 1898, there was another brief distraction in his life. His old play, *The New Ghetto*, which he had written in Paris just as the Dreyfus scandal was breaking out, was finally produced on the Vienna stage. In the past three years the play had been regarded as too risky, and no producer had been found. The popular Viennese producer Franz von Jauner was now willing to take the risk, also apparently hoping to cash in on the author's new reputation as a "modern Moses." The play was staged at the Carl-Theater, next door to the Herzl family's former home on the Praterstrasse. Bacher and Benedikt were enraged at this further exposure of their star in a controversial "Jew play." The ensuing quarrel with them caused Herzl more cardiac pain, but he refused to have the play withdrawn.

The Viennese police censor was also concerned and demanded savage cuts because the streets of Vienna had recently been the scene of further violent demonstrations. The censor ruled: "At this time, so rife with national and religious conflicts, it does not appear opportune to treat the Jewish problem on the stage in such a topical manner." The censor's decision was overruled by Count Kielmannsegg, the Governor of Lower Austria, to whom Herzl and Jauner had appealed. The only restriction was that the unsympathetic rabbi in Herzl's play should not wear rabbinical dress on the stage.

The production itself was an anticlimax. There was little excitement: "Nobody felt insulted, nobody protested, and nobody was enthused." The political reputation Herzl had acquired in the past three years was no substitute, in the eyes of a highly discriminating Viennese audience, for real dramatic tension, which the play still lacked. The reviews were restrained, and Herzl complained of the bad treatment he was receiving from the "Viennese newspaper-Jews." The *Neue Freie Presse* praised the play but, ludicrously, failed to mention its theme—the Jewish problem!

After a short run in Vienna, the play moved to Berlin. Here it was mercilessly slaughtered by the critics. The defeat, coupled with the continuing difficulties of his banking scheme, threw Herzl into deep depression. A week after Berlin, he asked Nordau to assume the leadership of the movement as of the next congress. "I am very weary. I must start thinking of my own affairs again. I have not had a chance to do so in the last few years. And life runs out."

Nordau was not willing. He was an ardent Zionist, ready to deliver one or two rousing speeches annually, but he shunned the daily responsibility of the job and pleaded all kinds of excuses. Paris was not a suitable headquarters; his telephone, because of his reputation as an ardent *Dreyfusard*, was tapped by the French police. Finally, the fact that he was married to a non-Jewish woman might be resented by the more Orthodox elements in the Zionist movement. Herzl pleaded for an interim regime at least, one year's respite. But Nordau remained adamant.

2

The movement, meanwhile, was growing daily. If there were still difficulties in launching the bank, Herzl's organization was gaining ground among Jews everywhere. Zionist federations and branch offices were springing up in most European countries, in the United States, in South Africa, even in Australia. In Galicia alone 120 Zionist groups had been formed in the months after the conference. "Night after night, in a hundred European cities, propagandists argued and opponents disputed." *Die Welt* continued to swallow considerable amounts of money—Herzl's own, his father's, his wife's dowry—but the newspaper's circulation reached ten thousand by mid-May. At the *Neue Freie Presse* he was now treated with a kind of grudging, hesitant respect, which is so often the reward of those persistent enough in their obsession. Bacher was amiable; Benedikt the sharper of the two, was cordial, and in the habit of joking: "With this Herzl one must be careful. Perhaps he is right after all. When he comes into the room I have the feeling that Jesus Christ has entered."

In January 1898 the German Kaiser announced his intention to visit the Holy Land as a "pilgrim." The announcement enhanced the general interest in Palestine and in Zionism. Herzl had the feeling that if only the bank could be set up, an enormous step forward would be taken. On April 22 he convened his international Executive Committee to prepare for the second congress. Twenty-two members from Russia, Germany, and Austria gathered in Vienna. The Russians were critical of Herzl's policies. They wanted less diplomacy, more practical work in Palestine. The deliberations lasted three days. There was little support for Herzl's plan to convene another congress so soon. It was feared that after the euphoria of the first, the second congress might come as a letdown and dramatize differences of opinion. There was also fear that not enough people might attend. However, Herzl was obdurate. He argued effectively that a new constitution was needed, and an executive truly elected by the people rather than the current assembly of dignitaries. But above all it was important to stage another public demonstration and maintain the momentum of the movement; it might otherwise bog down.

He was convinced that the impact of the second congress would be greater than the first. His acute sense for pomp in politics told him how important it was to sustain the morale of "beggars and boys" through grand spectacle. Kellner reproached him for his showmanship: "This movement is all *noise!*"

"Yes, of course. But noise is everything!" Herzl replied irritably. "A sustained noise in itself is a remarkable fact. All of world history is nothing but clamor: clamor of arms, clamor of ideas on the march. One must make use of the noise and yet despise it."

The bank project too was heatedly discussed. Bigger financiers were still reluctant to join the syndicate. Herzl suggested that they begin selling one-pound shares immediately, on a popular basis, even before the establishment of a syndicate. The down payment would be only 10 percent. He swayed the participants with his fervor, and was pleased with the signs of deference he received. It was all the more depressing to rush off, between sessions, to his regular job. At the *Neue Freie Presse* he was a "hireling," serving other masters whose views were diametrically opposed to his own.

The next few weeks were taken up with preparations for the congress. He immediately began to practice what he had preached to Kellner. The clamor of the second congress must be as great and as impressive as that of the first. Once again he personally attended to every detail. He required that the major addresses be submitted in writing many weeks in advance. He urged Nordau to do his utmost that Asian Jews—Persians and Bokharans—be present at the congress. This was "very important" for the "picturesque" effect. The question of a flag was uppermost in his mind, for he had not been happy with Wolffsohn's spontaneous choice of the year before. Bodenheimer, the sober Cologne lawyer, was irritated by all this fuss over a piece of cloth tied to a wooden stick.

"Why can't we leave discussions on heraldics and such until after the establishment of the state?"

"No," Herzl retorted, "this is no trifle. When you want to lead people, you need flags and trumpets. Otherwise you cannot sound your *instructions* to the mass. I trust you don't consider me a fool!"

Characteristically, also, he asked his friend Oscar Marmorek, the architect, to design a proper congress building in Basel. "With nations," he insisted, "one must use a childish language—a house, a flag, a song are the symbols of communication." After the exodus, the building would remain one of the landmarks of Switzerland. Marmorek's preliminary sketch displeased him; it fell short of evoking what Herzl called a "neo-Jewish style."

He developed a sudden passion for architecture, "the art form that is most meaningful to me now," and handed Marmorek the following sketch as a suggestion for the facade:

"The main hall is the house. It opens onto the loggia
but is lighted from above like a parliament."

Meanwhile he worked on the financing of his bank. Wolffsohn's reports from London, Frankfurt, and Cologne were not good. By August initial subscriptions had brought in only 100,000 pounds, of which Herzl himself had subscribed 2,000. At Wolffsohn's urging, a small group of minor Jewish bankers agreed to meet Herzl on August 11 in Cologne, but a few days before the meeting they changed their minds. Herzl fumed at this "dirty trick."

"The rich fellows want to freeze us out. Our revenge will be terrible." To Wolffsohn he cabled, "Stiff upper lip." He decided to launch the bank at the congress itself. "It will be a popular bank, so much the better," he wrote to Wolffsohn on August 10.

With all these preoccupations, he somehow found time during these weeks to finish a new light comedy—*Unser Kätchen* (*Our Cathy*)—another farce on his perennial theme, the foibles of a modern bourgeois marriage. When he wasn't penning circulars to delegates of the forthcoming congress, he dispatched letters to actors and producers offering them his new play. He most probably wrote *Unser Kätchen* in the hope of making some money, for his

own resources were running dangerously low as a result of his
subsidies to *Die Welt*.

Before the congress he rejoined his family for a brief vacation
in the country. His marriage to Julie was neither better nor worse
than before. His attitude to women in general remained strained;
they were "the sex that sometimes mends our socks." In the thousands of pages of his diary Herzl often mentioned his children and
parents; there is not a single direct reference to his wife.

Julie still had very little understanding of the cause that was
driving him to the limits of his physical and mental capacities. She
was moody and ailing. He sometimes attempted to make up by
trying to be the gay, Bohemian husband Julie wanted him to be.
Maria della Gracia, a contemporary writer, recorded this impression of Herzl in his wife's company. "[Sitting] next to his beautiful
blond wife, it quickly became clear that she was annoyed at what
was his main purpose and aim in life . . . in her company he was
wholly and merely the spirited *feuilletonist*. Only then did I realize the whole tragedy of this life."

3

The second congress took place in Basel, August 28–31. A
cheering crowd greeted Herzl at the railroad station. He was "very
embarrassed" by the stir. Once again he engaged in a whirl of
emotions, excitement, receptions, and became the object of unbounded devotion. Serious, sober-minded men prostrated themselves before him. Herzl *was* Israel; his heart and Israel's were one
and indivisible. "It all vanishes from beneath me in a peculiar way,"
he noted in his diary, "as though I were ascending in a balloon. It
gives me no pleasure at all."

The general enthusiasm was as great as the year before. Three
hundred and sixty delegates came to the second congress, nearly
twice as many as to the first. In addition there were some five
hundred observers. The number of Zionist societies had increased
ninefold in the previous year. There were 273 organizations in Russia alone, another 250 in Austria-Hungary, 127 in Romania, 60 in
the United States, 26 in England, 25 in Germany, with the rest
scattered in several other countries—a world total of 913 clubs and
organizations. "The Zionist cause has made great progress in the
past year," the French consul at Basel informed the Quai d'Orsay.
No longer dismissing Zionism as the *divertissement* of *"les juifs de*

journalisme," the consul was impressed by what seemed a well-oiled machine of committees, press relations, and black-tie grand openings.

The participants this time were real delegates, elected by dues-paying members in almost four hundred "constituencies." There were many new personalities. The colorful Italian-Tunisian anarchist Marcou Baruch had crossed the Alps on foot to attend the congress. Some of the main figures in the future drama of Zionism and of Israel were present for the first time—Chaim Weizmann (still a chemistry student) and Dr. Stephen Wise, a young Reform Rabbi from the United States. From France came Bernard Lazare. This early sympathizer with the anarchist bomb-thrower Ravachol was now a Zionist of the socialist persuasion. "As a Jew it is less difficult to be humane," Lazare wrote. "Therefore one must remain Jewish." Lazare was idolized by the congress for his continuing fight to clear the innocent Dreyfus and to expose the conspiracy that had caused his conviction as a spy.

The first congress had been the surprising success of an improvisation; the second was better organized. It opened festively to the sounds of Wagner's *Tannhäuser*. Herzl's secretary, Heinrich Rosenberger, could not help wondering whether an audience of anti-Semites would have been "equally generous" in its applause for the Jewish composers Halévy and Meyerbeer, whose works were also played. The taste of that time and place was reflected also in the congress souvenir card, drawn in *art nouveau* style by E.M. Lilien, and picturing a Siegfried figure clad in medieval armor against an Oriental background.

The general enthusiasm was heightened by a happy incident that occurred a few hours before the festive concert. Just as the blue and white flag was formally unfurled, a procession of Swiss students, clad in picturesque armor and celebrating a local saint, passed under the windows of the congress building. Herzl, Nordau, and a few others watched the pretty pageant from a window. The students, as they passed the Zionist flag, shouted with all their might: "*Hoch die Juden!* [Long live the Jews!]" Everybody was terribly moved. It was a show of spontaneous sympathy "that, unhappily, one would find expressed in few civilized countries at the present time," wrote one observer. Nordau had tears in his eyes. "Such a thing has not been seen in the whole world for two thousand years," he said. "Deeply stirred," Nordau went to his room "to be alone."

Herzl referred to the incident in his opening speech. "Are these shouts already announcing the coming of better times? This we cannot tell. But we can resolve to be deserving of them." His speech, although devoid of all rhetorical pathos, was interrupted by long storms of applause. He could hardly finish a sentence. He referred to the Kaiser's visit to Palestine in the next month as proof of that country's importance for all mankind. But "if there is a single legitimate claim of sovereignty, all nations who believe in the Bible must recognize the claim of the Jews. They can do so without fear or envy, for the Jews are no political power and will never be a political power."

Herzl's formal address was again followed by Nordau's traditional jeremiad. "The situation has not improved anywhere and in some places has become worse." Not only had there been a new spurt of bloody pogroms in Galicia and Romania, but in the very home of liberty, in France, there had been an upsurge of violent anti-Semitism as a result of the Dreyfus controversy. In the anti-Semitic riots at Bordeaux, Marseilles, Clermont-Ferrand, Lyons, Rouen, Nantes, and Toulouse, there had been evidence of police complicity.

Herzl by now was almost bored with the theme, and although Nordau was a "colossal speaker," Herzl felt that he had had "little new to say." Long-winded self-pity was getting them nowhere. Impatiently Herzl besought the assembly to reach concrete results, and chief among those was his projected bank. There was some feeling among the conservative representatives that the bank project might be premature. Socialists, on the other hand, were suspicious of the very idea of a capitalistic bank; there was a proposal to establish a cooperative bank only. The program of the bank also caused a wrangle: a "Jewish Colonial Bank," intended to further agriculture and industry "in the Orient." Some of the purists, led by the volatile Ussishkin of Yekatrinoslav, were suspicious—and not without reason—of Herzl's commitment to Palestine; they feared the bank might enable Herzl to start colonization in some other country. After many hours of heated discussion, a compromise was reached and the resolution amended to read, " . . . in the Orient, especially in Palestine and Syria." There were other objections to the bank which even Herzl, in his own way, shared.

Late one night, after three sessions and no time for supper, Herzl wearily walked back to his hotel in the company of Marcou Baruch, the anarchist who had been "tamed by Zionism." The two men had more in common than it would seem. Anarchist and aristocrat, they shared an aesthetic disgust for money and a fascination with flamboyant intervention by individuals in the course of history. As they crossed the darkened street, Marcou Baruch said, "I am sorry you should put the bank ahead of the people of Israel. I should have preferred it otherwise—for history's sake." Herzl was ·very moved. Baruch had uttered the "first magnificent words of the entire congress."

The task of conducting the second congress proved more trying for Herzl than the first. The opposition was more vocal, and Herzl was often in a foul and irritated mood. Such critics of his leadership as there were, he hamstrung continuously. In his diary he vented his wrath at the "dirty little tricks of those Galician bastards." He was indignant also at the "narrow horizons" and stupidity of his closest Viennese stalwarts, Schnirer, Kokesch, and Marmorek. One cause for his indignation was their treatment of Nevlinski. Herzl was paying Nevlinski's expenses at Basel in the hope that he would report to the Sultan how strong the movement was. But Schnirer and Kokesch failed to understand why Herzl was allowing this destitute Polish aristocrat to run up an enormous hotel bill. And Marmorek made the terrible *faux pas* of publicly lauding Herzl for having accomplished so much although the movement had no money at all, while Nevlinski, who was supposed to believe the opposite, listened in the gallery. For a moment Herzl saw his entire house of cards collapse. He sent a note to Marmorek to shut up instantly, "otherwise I shall leave the congress."

There were also prolonged discussions on colonization work in Palestine. Rothschild's colonies came under heavy criticism. On this issue the movement was deeply and dangerously divided. To some of Herzl's opponents, colonizing Palestine was an end in itself. To Herzl it was only a means, and he had to steer very carefully to avoid an open split. But he repeated his injunctions against "the smuggling in of settlers" without prior agreement with the Turks.

It was the very first time in the history of Herzl's movement that the presence in Palestine of an Arab population was publicly noted. At the first congress, the delegate A.S. Yahuda, a young scholar specializing in Islamic studies, had made one or two attempts in private conversation to draw attention to the fact that there might be a problem here. But few had been interested.

Leo Motzkin gave the second congress an official report on current Palestinian conditions. Motzkin had just returned from Palestine, where he had been sent in April by Herzl's international Executive Committee. His report dealt mostly with general matters, but he did make a point of stressing the "established fact that the most fertile parts of our land are occupied by Arabs . . . 650,000 souls, but this figure is not verified." Motzkin also reported that in recent years "there have been innumerable clashes between Jews and incited Arabs"—he did not say why they were incited or by whom. Palestine, in his view, was a "colorful mixture of wilderness, tourism, and pilgrims . . . influenced by Europe in its forms but not in its essence, and dominated by neither element."

Another delegate noted that Palestine was 90 percent under-populated. Moreover, its sparse population was "Semitic, i.e., related to us by blood. We shall undoubtedly be able to get along with them." If the Boers had succeeded in establishing a state in the Transvaal, and even in defying England, the Jews need not expect too many difficulties in Palestine.

It is important to remember these early impressions (they sounded so convincing because they contained a large measure of truth) in order to understand the Zionists' early complacency about the Arabs. None of the men present at Basel ever expected that Israel would be established by a war, or sustained for decades only at the price of nearly permanent bloodshed. They considered themselves servants of one of the most humane, just, and worthwhile causes imaginable: the salvation of a pariah people, the renaissance of the most ancient national bond in existence. More susceptible than most people of their time to the power of ideas over the minds of men, they ignored the power that similar ideas might have over the minds of the Arabs. There are few things as egocentric as a national revival. The delegates were sure that the Arabs of Palestine would welcome their enterprise with open arms. Anyone who would have claimed the opposite, and there was no one, would have been dismissed as an utter madman.

For the time being, Herzl's view against small-scale infiltration of the country prevailed. He spent days and nights smoothing over the differences, by charm and persuasiveness, and sometimes high-handedly by enforced votes *en bloc*. On the third day, the machine he had created almost single-handedly was better organized and more solidly behind him than ever before. The final acclaim re-affirmed his supremacy in the movement.

An hour after the final session, a message from the Sultan arrived, acknowledging the homage the congress had paid the present ruler of Palestine. The message was couched in exceedingly gracious terms. Was something afoot in Constantinople? Herzl also received a summons to visit the Grand Duke of Baden immediately after the congress. Had Hechler finally achieved a breakthrough

with the German Kaiser? The Kaiser was about to go on his "pilgrimage" to the Holy Land. Herzl's mind reeled with a hundred
and one possibilities. Pleased with himself, he prepared for the next
step. The next few weeks would bring him tantalizingly close to his
coveted goal.

12

German Interlude I

THE NEXT STEP was an adventure in diplomacy and intrigue that sometimes reads like the libretto for a Gilbert and Sullivan opera. The action is fast, though convoluted, and the cast is spectacular. The hero, Herzl—idealist-adventurer, playing for high but not impossible stakes—arrives at a crossroad of world politics. He pursues his goal through a maze of seemingly impenetrable barriers.

Enter the German Kaiser in a Lohengrin-style helmet—excitable, a man of almost as many whims as uniforms (rumored to be hundreds), he changes both in each new scene. Herzl ignores the Psalmist's dictum and puts his trust in princes; the Kaiser, a megalomaniacal figure, toys with him in a mood of playful imperial arrogance, while his good queen smiles benevolently from afar. The cunning chamberlains plot at cross-purposes behind the Kaiser's back.

Enter the fabled Sultan in his silver brocades, surrounded by a thousand eunuchs, wives, and concubines in a court of Byzantine intrigue and barbaric splendor: silver trumpets, flying banners, camels in purple regalia.

In the background is a vast chorus of courtiers and attendants in resplendent uniforms and a mixed multitude of Prussians, Turks, Arabs, Armenians, and Jews who herald the swift changes of scene: the grim palaces of Potsdam; the Kaiser's hunting lodge on the swampy heath of East Prussia; Constantinople. The finale takes place in a bivouac of royal tents on a hillside overlooking the old city of Jerusalem.

The curtain first rises on a fairy-tale castle on the isle of Mainau, on Lake Constance. It is the summer residence of Herzl's patron, Friedrich, Grand Duke of Baden. On a misty morning in early autumn, Herzl and the Reverend Hechler arrived in Mainau directly from the congress in Basel. The Grand Duke received Herzl like an old friend; he had thrilling news. The German government, he said happily, was finally taking an active interest in Herzl's cause. Inquiries had been made, through the German ambassador in Constantinople, about the Turkish attitude to the Zionist movement. An answer had been received that the Sultan viewed Herzl's scheme "with favorable eyes."

The Grand Duke had also taken the matter up personally with his nephew, the German Kaiser. The Kaiser apparently saw great possibilities. The German ambassador in Vienna, Count Philip von Eulenburg, had been directed to make a close study of the matter and furnish the Kaiser with a report. The Grand Duke advised Herzl to contact Eulenburg immediately.

Speaking with great confidence, the Grand Duke unraveled to the astounded Herzl some of the secret imperial designs of his young, ambitious nephew, Kaiser Wilhelm. The Kaiser's much-heralded "pilgrimage" the following month to the Holy Land was in fact a political journey camouflaged as a religious act; his real purpose was to consolidate and extend German influence in the East. The Kaiser coveted a Turkish concession to build the strategically important railroad line to Baghdad; it would be a thorn in the flesh of the British Empire. Therefore the Kaiser was first going to Constantinople for talks with the Sultan. The Grand Duke's advice to the Kaiser had been that he take up Herzl's cause with the Sultan. "German influence in Constantinople is now unlimited," said the Grand Duke. "England has been crowded out completely, to say nothing of the other powers. . . . If our Kaiser drops one word to the Sultan, it will certainly be heeded."

Herzl was thrilled, but he was a little annoyed at Hechler. "He is good for the entrée," Herzl thought to himself, "but afterward one becomes a little ridiculous because of him." The clergyman interrupted the conversation with unctuous remarks on "the return of the Jews" according to the prophecy, which the Grand Duke welcomed with a benign smile.

"Such things are beyond my judgment," Herzl said, irritated. "I can only speak of what I see with my own eyes."

"Yes, yes," the pious Grand Duke now also agreed, "let us treat this as world history, not as a theological matter."

Herzl sensed the possibility of a quick breakthrough. Was this the explanation for the Sultan's remarkably cordial message to the congress? How much had the Germans already discussed in their exchanges with the Turks?

"We need a protectorate," he told the Grand Duke emphatically. "A German protectorate would suit us best." The Grand Duke liked the idea. An independent Jewish state would curb the drift of European Jews toward the revolutionary parties. At the same time a German protectorate in Palestine might open vast possibilities to German expansion in the East. Herzl pushed his case further by saying that Zionism itself was in a sense part and parcel of German *Kultur*: "German writers—though of Jewish descent—are leading the Zionist movement. The official language of the congresses has been German." With the return of the Jews, an important element of German culture would enter the Orient.

The Grand Duke liked this concept even more. He surmised that it was a complicated, possibly dangerous scheme, but not beyond the capabilities of Prince Bülow, the Kaiser's cunning Foreign Minister: "Bülow is the best man to deal with this matter," the Grand Duke said. He promised to approach the Kaiser once more and assured Herzl of his continuing support.

Herzl lost no time in contacting Eulenburg in Vienna. Eulenburg cabled Herzl to come to the German embassy the following morning. The Austrian Empress Elisabeth had just been assassinated by an anarchist and the German Kaiser was in Vienna for her funeral, staying at the embassy. As Herzl entered the German embassy he discovered that Hechler had preceded him. Hechler's prophetic charts were pinned to the walls of a little salon, and on a table his models of the ancient temple were on display for the benefit of the visiting Kaiser.

Eulenburg and Herzl briefly inspected Hechler's curiosities, then repaired to Eulenburg's study. The two men liked each other immediately, and for reasons that were revealing of both. Herzl's hero-ideal had always been the Prussian nobleman. "If there is one thing I should like to be, it is a member of the old Prussian nobility," he had confessed even after his conversion to Zionism. Eulenburg was a superb example of that landed aristocracy Herzl regarded as the embodiment of higher virtues. For his part, Eulenburg was equally impressed by Herzl. As with most of his class, anti-Semitism loomed large among his many prejudices. Yet Herzl's character, as he put it in a later memoir, "was without a trace of what we call the Jew-peddler."

The Count (later Prince) was a close friend of the Kaiser.

Until his downfall in 1909, the victim of a celebrated homosexual scandal, he was one of the most influential men behind the German throne. In 1898 he was at the peak of his power. Tall, with an immobile face and a pair of cold, expressionless steel-blue eyes, he is described in Herzl's diary as a man "locked tight, like an iron safe."

The conversation went well. Eulenburg had obviously received some word from Berlin. He promised at the very outset to persuade the Kaiser to see Herzl before leaving for the Holy Land. Then he voiced some misgivings. The soil of Palestine was too poor to support a bigger population; the Turks might fear a sudden influx of two million Jews. "The Sultan," Eulenburg said, giving Herzl a deep look, "is a downright paranoiac criminal." But as Herzl developed his case, repeating all the familiar arguments (his gift of persuasion often worked better with powerful Gentiles than with powerful Jews), the Count warmed to the idea considerably. Eulenburg was also a poet; the boldness of Herzl's plan, the sheer, almost insolent, simplicity appealed to his imagination. It would mean an end to anti-Semitism, the diversion of young Jews away from revolutionary parties, the improvement of the Turkish financial situation, and not the least important, an opportunity for Wilhelm II to play a flamboyant role in history by initiating the return of the Jews. The establishment of Western civilization in the Near East would safeguard that area for Europe. As Herzl spoke, Eulenburg's eyes deepened. The "iron safe," Herzl noted, "suddenly unlocked with nothing more than a softening of Eulenburg's hard eyes."

Herzl now shrewdly delivered his final coup. "Our movement exists," he said. "I expect that one or another of the great powers will espouse it. I once thought it would be England. It lay in the nature of things. I would like it much more to be Germany!"

With the mention of England, Eulenburg assumed a sudden note of urgency. He pressed Herzl to speak immediately with Prince Bülow, the German Foreign Minister, if possible the following day.

Herzl left the embassy feeling elated. Triumphantly, he wrote his wife: "Eulenburg is won, he is ready to do everything for us." Twenty-four hours later he returned to the embassy to meet the Foreign Minister. Prince Bülow received Herzl in his bedroom, where his traveling trunks still lay wide open. Herzl's vanity was flattered by this informality—within the hour he would bitterly regret it—and by the Prince's effusive charm. It was intoxicating to

be on such familiar terms with princes and great lords. The suave
and oily Bülow overwhelmed Herzl with captivating kindness. He
declared that he had read nearly everything Herzl had written, was
delighted to finally make his acquaintance, and so on.

> At this I grew weak [Herzl recorded]. Eulenburg, who re-
> ceived me coolly, I confronted with resolution; my words were
> ironlike and clear. In Bülow's presence I unfortunately became
> a vain writer. I strove harder to turn polished phrases than to
> talk seriously to the point. It was simply a fit of weakness, the
> result of his ingratiating behavior. Immediately after our talk I
> knew that I had been taken in.

He had little time to present his case properly, for in his dis-
armed state he allowed the conversation to remain a chat rather
than a tightly organized political exchange. The Prince was glad to
hear Herzl say that Jews were not by nature, or tradition, socialists.
He was all in favor of a Zionism that would divert the more restless
European Jews away from the Socialist party. Yes, too many Jews
were the lieutenants and generals of revolution. Yes, it would be
nice to see them occupied elsewhere, on more constructive business. But Bülow was not sure that the Kaiser should personally
initiate the return of the Jews to Palestine, at least not publicly.
Secret diplomacy was another matter. "We must move forward
carefully, otherwise the whole arrangement will be upset." Toward
the end of the conversation, Herzl repeated his request for a personal audience with the Kaiser, but Bülow was noncommittal. After
three-quarters of an hour he broke off the conversation abruptly,
saying he had to meet his imperial master at the railroad station.

Herzl did not know what to think. Had he been too talkative?
On the other hand, he surmised that German intentions were already so serious that the Prince had been deliberately guarded. He
waited by the telephone for the rest of the day, hoping against
hope that the Kaiser would decide to receive him on his short
stopover in Vienna. If he could only see the Kaiser, he was sure he
would sway him completely. The helpful Hechler posted himself in
the doorkeeper's lodge of the German embassy in order to spy on
the Kaiser's movements. After dinner he telephoned the bad news.
The Kaiser and Eulenburg had just left for the station, without
remembering Herzl. Or so Hechler thought.

2

A few days later Herzl left for Paris and London for a series of appointments in connection with the bank. Still very hopeful, he wrote to Richard Gottheil of New York,

Confidential!

20 September 98

... I have been called to a mighty statesman. In the past 1,800 years our cause has not stood so well as it does now. My lips have been sealed. Therefore—even in deepest confidence—I can tell you only that great things are afoot.

France was in a state of disarray. The Dreyfus affair was approaching its climax. "Everywhere one goes one hears only the screaming against Jews," Herzl wrote to his wife. "Everything in Paris is thereby made unbearable." Nostalgically, he stayed at the Hotel Castille, in the same room where he had written the first draft of *The Jewish State*. Sitting at his old desk, Herzl addressed another impassioned letter to Eulenburg, appealing to the "genius of the Kaiser through the kindness of your Excellency." The present moment, he assured Eulenburg, was especially opportune for a German *fait accompli* in Palestine. France, which he knew so well, was disorganized and weakened by the Dreyfus affair. She simply "must acquiesce to every *fait accompli* which does not irritate her almost to the point of insensibility."

He posted the letter through Wolffsohn in Cologne, to avoid French censorship. It was well timed, and he could not have found a better advocate than Eulenburg, for the Count was now steadily pressing Herzl's cause with the Kaiser. He first broached the subject at dinner in Vienna. The easily excitable Kaiser was interested, but there was not enough time to discuss it thoroughly. Then Eulenburg accompanied Wilhelm to Rominten, the Kaiser's hunting lodge in East Prussia. The wooden lodge, built in the so-called Norwegian style, overlooked the vast heath a few miles west of the Russian frontier. Eulenburg and the Kaiser marched out each morning to hunt pheasant and hare; in the evenings there were long drinking bouts by the fire and good man-to-man conversation.

Between rounds of pheasant hunting in the fog, Eulenburg and the Kaiser discussed the Jews. Eulenburg spoke highly of Herzl's character. As the Kaiser's close friend, he was able to push his case with persistence, charm, and unbounded flattery. Wilhelm's vanity made him the willing instrument of courtiers who were constantly assuring him he was the world's greatest sovereign.

There is little direct documentation of the events of the next few days, but the Kaiser's conversion to Zionism by Eulenburg can be construed fairly reliably from their letters and from the memoirs of the principal participants. There was little need to coax the Kaiser. Within a day or two he was "fire and flame" for Herzl's scheme. Wilhelm was not primarily concerned with the plight of the Jews, for he had very little sympathy for them, derisively calling them *Mauschels* (kikes). He was not an anti-Semite in the ordinary sense of the word. His mind was one of the more underdeveloped regions in the world of German culture, and he tended to regard the persecution of the Jews throughout history as largely deserved. Had they not killed Jesus Christ? Even nowadays, so many of them were harming good Christians by their usury—when they were not repaying his own tolerance of them by joining the socialist opposition. The chairman of the German Social Democratic party was Paul Singer, a Jew, and the Kaiser's special *bête noire*.

But as Herzl had rightly calculated, the drama of the return immediately touched the Kaiser's imagination. With his unique flair for the theatrical, he was quick to seize upon the possibilities of Herzl's scheme. It coincided well with his projected "pilgrimage" to the Holy Land, and fitted his overall scheme to outwit the British. In Damascus he would proclaim himself Defender of Islam; and in Jerusalem, Protector of the Jews.

He ordered Eulenburg to summon Herzl to an audience—not a private meeting, but a public audience in Jerusalem. Herzl must not come alone, but at the head of an official Zionist deputation. From Jerusalem, Wilhelm, the descendant of Crusader kings, clad in the shining armor he loved so well, would solemnly proclaim the beginning of the return. The idea of a German protectorate over a Jewish Palestine appealed to him greatly. For decades strategists had looked eagerly on the Mediterranean ports of Palestine as the "shortest route" to India. What if he were to seize Palestine, indirectly through the Jews, who, as Herzl had told Eulenburg and Bülow, were part and parcel of German *Kultur*? Who could oppose him? To Wilhelm, who believed that "there is no balance of power in Europe but me—me and my twenty-five army corps"—the risks appeared reasonable. France would not seriously assert her historic role at a time when she was enfeebled by the upheaval over Dreyfus. Russia would eagerly oust her surplus Jewish masses. In England the established church was in favor of restoring Jews to their historic homeland. The more Wilhelm heard of this man Herzl, the more he liked his plan. If, as an added bonus, Herzl's scheme would rid Germany of "many unsympathetic elements," and also cure Turkey's ailing financial situation—all through a *grand geste* by Germany—surely this was an enterprise seriously worth pursuing.

By the end of the week, the Kaiser's mind was firmly made up. As he rode out to the heath at 6:00 A.M. he was filled with his new role as restorer of Palestine to the Jews. Later, over a breakfast of caviar, boiled potatoes, and champagne, he spoke of his new task and his decision to make the most of it on his forthcoming tour of the Orient in the liveliest terms.* He did not doubt that the Sultan would heed his advice when he spoke to him. Those of his courtiers who thought otherwise—notably Bülow—dared not dampen his enthusiasm. On the contrary, Eulenburg clearly understood that Bülow was in full agreement. To the Grand Duke of Baden the Kaiser now wrote:

Rominten, 29 September 98

My most esteemed Uncle,

A momentary pause in the amorous concert of my deer permits me to dedicate you a few more lines. . . .

He thanked the Grand Duke for having brought this worthwhile cause to his attention. From the point of view of *Realpolitik* there was much virtue in Zionism, he wrote. It would be a "tremendous achievement for Germany if the Hebrew world looked up to us in gratitude." Moreover, Zionism would divert the

creative energies of the tribe of Shem to better purposes than to suck the blood of Christians, and so many Semites who at present incite the opposition and are obsessed with socialism, will proceed to the East, where they will likely find more worthwhile occupation that does not end them up in jail, as in the aforesaid case. . . .

Now I know well that nine-tenths of all Germans will turn away from me in utter disgust upon discovering that I sympa-

---

* In a letter that week to the Czar of Russia, the Kaiser protested the absolute innocence of his holy pilgrimage. There was no Christian piety left in Europe, he complained. "What is permitted to thousands of your wretched peasants [who go on pilgrimage each year] is permitted to me as well."

thize with the Zionists and place them under my protection. But
I do have to point out here that God knows even more than we
do that the Jews murdered the Savior, and He has duly pun-
ished them for it. But neither the anti-Semites, nor any others,
nor I myself, have been authorized by Him to deal with them
harshly in our own way *ad majorem Dei gloriam*. Here I think I
must also say, "Whoever of you hath not sinned, let him cast the
first stone." . . . I shall therefore intercede for them with the
Sultan, for the Scripture says, "Ally yourselves even with sloth-
ful evil Mammon, be ye as shrewd as snakes and without falsity
as doves."

Upon receipt of this letter the Grand Duke cabled Hechler: "I
regard the matter as accomplished. The protectorate will be declared. The intervention with ruler of desired country will take
place. . . . Tell all this to him who came with you to see me so that
he will place himself at the head of the deputation. Travel in peace
and return home in bliss. Friedrich Grand Duke."

Hechler received the cable at 1:00 A.M. He rushed to Herzl
early in the morning, having prayed all night to thank God for his
providence. To his dismay he discovered that Herzl was away in
Paris.

Eulenburg, meanwhile, wrote to Herzl directly:

I have only good news for you. . . . His Majesty the Kaiser, as I
had expected, has shown full and deep understanding for your
movement. I have been its eager advocate, for you had me
completely convinced. My friend Bülow thinks likewise. H.M.
has announced his readiness to press your interests with the
Sultan in the most thorough, and if possible, urgent manner.

Eulenburg informed Herzl that the Kaiser wished to receive
him in Jerusalem at the head of a Zionist delegation. "His Majesty
asked me to tell you that *Allerhöchstderselbe* [his Almighty Self] is
prepared to assume the protectorate." Further details would be
given Herzl in Berlin, where Eulenburg was expecting him within
the week.

Eulenburg's letter reached Herzl in Amsterdam. He had gone
to Holland for a day with Wolffsohn, to consult Jacobus Kann, a
young private banker and the only financier ready at this stage to
participate in the launching of the Jewish Colonial Trust. Herzl

read Eulenburg's letter with astonishment and joy. At first he "was dazed." His joy over the "colossal achievement" immediately gave way to anxiety. He had always craved a dramatic breakthrough, but now he suddenly feared the time was not yet ready for it. There was still no money to finance large-scale colonization; the bank had not even been launched. At this stage Herzl would have preferred a secret meeting with the Kaiser in Berlin to a public demonstration in Jerusalem. He was still employed by the *Neue Freie Presse*; if he now further extended his leave in order to go on a long journey to the Near East, he might lose his livelihood altogether. On the other hand, he could not ignore the Kaiser's wish. "I am caught in the coils. But I have no choice. I must risk my position as well."

Herzl withheld the contents of Eulenburg's letter from his friends. He took a long walk in the chilly autumn air alongside the Amsterdam canals. He wandered through the picturesque old Jewish quarter; it was Saturday and the shops were closed. Three Jewish youngsters, a boy and two little girls, were staggering, arms linked, along the Judenbreetstraat, pretending they were tipsy, stammering the Dutch national anthem. Later Herzl told Kann: "Ten years from now the children in all the Jewish quarters of the world must sing the Zionist anthem." The scene did much to improve his mood. His spirit was further soothed as he gazed at the Rembrandts in the Rijksmuseum; "The Night Watch" glowed with color and reminded Herzl of Corot. In the afternoon they returned to The Hague. Herzl still did not speak to Kann or Wolffsohn about Eulenburg's letter. At sunset he took a bicycle and rode out alone from The Hague to Scheveningen. He felt relaxed from the physical exertion and the beautiful view of the evening tide rolling in under a blood-red sky.

At the dinner table, after first swearing them to complete secrecy, Herzl finally revealed the contents of Eulenburg's letter to Wolffsohn and Kann. They were stunned. All agreed that this unexpected turn of events made it even more imperative to launch the bank as soon and as grandly as possible.

On the following morning, the three men crossed the channel to England. Wolffsohn did much to calm Herzl's anxieties. ("The man tends to lose the ground under his feet," he said of Herzl. "My job is to stand him up again.") Wolffsohn assured Herzl that, far from finishing him at the *Neue Freie Presse*, his meeting with the Kaiser in Jerusalem would only enhance his position on the newspaper. The two men spent the crossing pacing back and forth on the promenade deck, spinning plans and projects for the future Jewish state. Both men felt that it was almost a reality.

The confidence generated by Eulenburg's letter was further reinforced by the receipt of Hechler's message from the Grand Duke, which reached Herzl on his arrival in London. He cabled "profuse thanks to your Royal Highness for the great favor." The excitement of the past few days took its toll; on his first night in London he suffered a slight heart attack. Nevertheless, he delivered a rousing speech at a mass meeting in the East End. It was an incautious speech, and he would soon regret his rashness. The meeting was attended by seven thousand people; another seven thousand clamoring to enter were barely held in check by the police. Herzl had slept badly and had had little time to prepare his notes. Speaking extemporaneously, he dropped his customary reserve and went so far as to predict an imminent mass exodus: "I will not draw you a picture of the return, for it will soon begin. I can assure you of this, we are now not very distant from that date. I know well what I am saying. I have never spoken so positively. Today I tell you: the time is no longer distant when the Jewish people will set itself in motion."

The speech brought the audience of poor Eastern European refugees to their feet. "Do you believe the Jews will go if we get the land? Answer me! Answer me!" Herzl cried. "Yes!" roared the audience. "Yes!" News of Herzl's London speech traveled quickly through the Jewish world. In countless Jewish *shtetls* throughout Russia, people saw the day of the Messiah arriving, next week, next month. And everywhere Herzl's critics, within the movement and without, were eagerly sharpening their knives.

3

On Thursday, October 6, he traveled to Berlin to keep his appointment with Eulenburg. The Count was staying at Lieben-berg, his country estate in the Mark Brandenburg. His coachman met Herzl at the station. "Are you waiting for me?" Herzl asked. The coachman measured him haughtily. He had only been told to fetch "a tall gentleman with a long black beard." They rode for half an hour through the flatland; the coachman spoke of distances in terms of *dragoons*, and measured travel time in *uhlans*. An occasional bird flew off across the sunny fields. "I lack the shotgun and the skill for game," Herzl reflected. "These birds apparently have reproduced themselves since time immemorial for the noblemen who go out on fine autumn days to kill them."

At the end of a tree-lined driveway the manor house appeared behind hedges of roses. Two footmen were waiting at the entrance. The hall was lined with weapons and trophies, and through the tall French windows, the autumnal park shimmered in yellows and browns. Herzl wondered whether he was the first Jew ever invited to enter this citadel of Prussian nobility—not as a submissive, fawning assimilationist, but as a proud, "upright Jew." As usual, he had carefully planned his wardrobe and donned a gray frock coat to make clear that he was coming on business.

Eulenburg, in hunting costume, greeted Herzl cordially. The Countess and other members of the family were at the breakfast table. After introducing Herzl to the party, Eulenburg took him for a stroll through the park.

"The Kaiser is very warm to the project," Eulenburg began his report. He explained how important it was to keep the Kaiser enthusiastic; with so many matters bidding for his attention, he had a tendency to forget all but those that really excited him. "Fortunately for your cause, Bülow has also been won over. He is my best friend and a most outstanding statesman."

"Bülow did not seem too warm when I met him in Vienna," Herzl interjected. "I had the impression he was not very eager."

"He was merely reserved," Eulenburg explained. "At a first meeting, understandably, one is cautious. One does not let onself go immediately. The main thing is not what he said to you, but what he said to me when I urged him to agree. I have persuaded him."

Herzl spoke a few warm words of thanks. Eulenburg fixed him with his steely eyes. "Perhaps there will come a time when I shall ask favors of you."

Herzl was perplexed at this. What favors could he want? But he said, "Henceforth you will find me a devoted, grateful man."

Eulenburg drew a very rosy picture of the situation for Herzl. He related the events at the hunting lodge in Rominten. The Kaiser already was virtually "living the idea of the protectorate." Wilhelm was fully convinced that the Sultan would accept his advice, and he expected to receive Herzl at the head of a Zionist deputation in Jerusalem. He might also grant Herzl a private audience in Constantinople before going to the Holy Land. The Kaiser felt there was no sense hiding the matter. Since a German protectorate was involved, he would publicly espouse the Jewish cause. "It is best to come right out with it, demonstratively," Eulenburg said. "The world will just have to put up with it."

The two men walked at a leisurely pace through the magnificent grounds. A footman came after them with a telegram. The Count glanced at it and dropped it to the ground for the footman, who waited at a respectable distance to pick it up. Then they walked on through the park, to the nearby woods and back. Eulenburg was getting more confident every moment. He seemed to anticipate difficulties only from England and France. Russia did not worry him at all. "If worse comes to worse, our Kaiser will write a letter to the Czar and win him over to Zionism," he said. "Since Russia does not oppose the departure of the Jews, she will not put any obstacles in the way."

Herzl assured Eulenburg that there was little reason to expect any difficulties from France either. "France is in a severe crisis. Law and order are being championed by liars. France is too weak to act."

After about half an hour a gamekeeper with two dogs straining at the leash came into view. The Count had been showing signs of impatience. With the excuse that he had to hurry back to Berlin, Herzl refused his invitation to lunch. The Count promised to raise the matter again at the Kaiser's farewell dinner on the following day, at which the Grand Duke of Baden would also be present. "After the meal we shall all sit back comfortably and chat." Herzl said that in this case he would stay over for another day to thank the Grand Duke and to be on hand for further negotiations. They parted very amicably. Eulenburg ordered the coachman to take Herzl to the station by way of a scenic detour. In the gateway the two men waved their hats, then Liebenberg lay behind him.

Herzl drove back to the station, through lovely wooded flatlands, in an ecstatic mood. Ever since assuming his strange role, he had craved an alliance with a great power, particularly Germany. As he had told Baron Hirsch in 1895, "the German Kaiser will understand me. He has been trained to be a judge of great things." At the time, Hirsch had just blinked in amusement at this pipe dream. Now Herzl had achieved his aim. Back in Berlin Herzl rushed to his diary: "*Wunderbar, Wunderbar!* The intervention, the protectorate of Germany, is a *fait acquis.*" To Wolffsohn he wrote, "It is an unusual event which so many have never experienced. A dream suddenly comes true." Herzl knew well that many of his followers would shake their heads at the idea of a foreign, or

German, protectorate that fell short of full independence. But now that it had been offered, the only course was to accept it gratefully: "Surely none of us dreams of becoming king, since I do not." He marveled at Eulenberg's insistence on hiding nothing, on making everything public.

> This is the dashing, grand old style of Prussia. Aboveboard! That is how they have forced everything through. . . . Life under the protectorate of this powerful, great, moral, splendidly administered, firmly governed Germany, can only have the most salutary effects on the Jewish national character. . . .
>
> Through Zionism Jews will again be able to love this Germany to which, despite everything, our hearts have clung!

The next day he remained in his hotel room tensely awaiting further news. Excitedly he made hourly notations in his diary. In the afternoon a footman delivered Bülow's card. Herzl took this as a good sign. He put on his patent leather boots so as not to lose time in dressing when the summons came. Later a cable arrived from the Grand Duke, asking him to visit the imperial palace at Potsdam early the next morning.

In order to arrive on time—Potsdam was a train ride away—Herzl had to rise at 5:00 A.M. He almost missed the train when the hotel porter forgot to awaken him. Breathless, he reached the station at the last minute.

At the palace—Prussia's version of Versailles—he was conducted through a series of sumptuous apartments to the Grand Duke's study. Friedrich of Baden was more cordial than ever. Herzl thanked him for everything he had done. The Grand Duke waved his gratitude aside: "For me it is only the fulfillment of a duty."

He corroborated Eulenburg's report and told Herzl that the Kaiser had fully acquainted himself with his scheme. "He is full of enthusiasm. That word is not too strong! The Kaiser is completely and passionately taken by your idea." The Grand Duke returned again and again to the Kaiser's enthusiasm, as though to make Herzl feel more confident. The two men then compared notes on their respective difficulties in the past, the Grand Duke in pursuit of German unification, Herzl in the realization of Zionism. They agreed that heroes invariably reap ingratitude but that grand aims require great sacrifices. Finally the Grand Duke urged Herzl to see Bülow that same day in Potsdam, and advised him to wait at the nearby Hotel Einsiedler.

Herzl promptly checked into the hotel opposite the palace.

Through his window he admired the changing of the guard below and the stream of cadets in the square. They were the future officers of this "inexhaustible Germany which wants to place us under its protective wings." At midday Herzl was back in the palace to meet Bülow. His host was not alone. In the small rococo salon a frail old man, with a yellow sash across his blue court dress, was sitting next to Bülow. A dueling scar marked his left cheek. The lower part of his pale face was almost hidden by a drooping moustache, but under the low forehead the eyes were alert, and cold as ice. As he rose, the medals on his chest clanked together. This was the Imperial Chancellor, Prince Hohenlohe.

"Do you really think that the Jews will abandon their stock exchange and follow you to Palestine?" he asked menacingly. It was the first anti-Semitic remark that Herzl had heard in these exalted circles. Eulenburg and Bülow had pretended to be in love with all Jews.

"Your Highness," Herzl replied, "not Berlin West, but Berlin East, or North—I do not exactly know where the poor Jews live here—will go with us."

Bülow said, "In any event it would be the first eastbound Jewish migration. So far they have always moved westward."

"Not at all!" Herzl said elegantly. "It is westward as well. The Jews have already encircled the globe. East is West again." The Germans smiled, but not for long. They soon returned to their interrogation.

What exactly was the territory the Zionists wanted, Hohenlohe demanded. As far north as Beirut, or even beyond?

"We ask for what we need—the more immigrants, the more land. Of course we will purchase all land at market prices from the present owners."

"Who are they?" Hohenlohe asked.

"Oh, the whole mixed multitude of the Orient," Herzl said, "Arabs, Greeks."

"And *that* is where you want to establish a state?" Hohenlohe asked.

Herzl ignored the gibe. "We want autonomy and the right of self-protection."

"What does Turkey say to this?"

The question surprised Herzl. Was this a misunderstanding? Or a deliberate game? "The Grand Duke told me that *favorable* reports have been received from Ambassador Marschall in Constantinople."

Bülow, sitting in the corner with his lips pursed tightly, interjected: "I don't know anything about that. I have had no such
report from Marschall."

Herzl did not allow himself to be disconcerted. He said that he
had received his own reports that the atmosphere in Constantinople was favorable.

Hohenlohe continued to ply him with skeptical questions. How
many potential immigrants were there? More important, how much
money did they have? Herzl mentioned various Jewish foundations;
Baron Hirsch's foundation alone amounted to ten million pounds
sterling.

"That's a lot," Bülow said, again a little menacingly. Then,
pensively, he turned to Hohenlohe. "The money might perhaps do
the trick." After a short while the two Germans were suddenly in a
great hurry to go to a luncheon.

"See you in Constantinople, Herr Doktor!" Bülow exclaimed
jovially as he stood adjusting the gold shoulder cord on his court
dress.

Herzl barely had time to ask, "Where will the Kaiser receive
me? In Constantinople *and* in Jerusalem?"

"In any case, only once!" Bülow snapped, and was already in
the next room. Herzl heard him call out nervously for his valet:
"Neumann! Neumann!"

On this note the curious audience ended. Herzl left the palace
in an agitated state. Perhaps the Grand Duke was mistaken? Could
Eulenburg have misled him? Was he the butt of a court intrigue?
Perhaps Hohenlohe and Bülow disagreed with their imperial master but did not dare to contradict him directly? Was he being
tested? Perhaps it was all a diplomatic game? "If worse comes to
worse, our idea—even as the discarded mistress of the German
Kaiser—will be taken up by others. This adventure can only contribute to its advancement."

Herzl returned immediately to Vienna by night train. There
were only three days to prepare for the difficult journey to Jerusalem. He still had to assemble a deputation and arrange for another
prolonged absence from his job. The Kaiser had already begun his
"pilgrimage" and was due in Constantinople within the week.

The train shook badly and Herzl got little rest. The following
morning, in Vienna, he convened an emergency meeting of his
Executive Committee. Marmorek, the architect, could not join the
deputation; he was too busy at the moment on some building
project. Schnirer would go, but in addition to his traveling expenses

he also demanded compensation for lost wages. Having surrounded himself with mediocrity, Herzl now had to face the consequences. He cabled Nordau. But since he could not spell out the real purpose of the mission, his secrecy "irritated [Nordau] into refusing to join him." Mandelstamm of Kiev was unable to obtain a Russian passport on such short notice. Kann was busy elsewhere. Only the loyal Wolffsohn and the Cologne jurist Bodenheimer were ready and willing to depart immediately. Josef Seidener, a Vienna engineer, completed the party. He had the advantage of a previous acquaintance with Palestine.

At the *Neue Freie Presse* Herzl went through a painful scene with Benedikt and Bacher. The publishers were annoyed by this sudden development. Bacher foresaw embarrassing difficulties for the newspaper. Benedikt looked away, "wildly." Herzl noted that Bacher was causing him more anguish than Hohenlohe had! But he remained adamant.

On his day of departure he tore himself loose for a few hours to read his new light comedy, *Unser Kätchen*, to the actors of the Burgtheater. Herzl felt obliged to have the play produced, in case he was fired from the newspaper. He rattled through the banal text. His mind was in Jerusalem. From the theater he rushed home to pack his suitcases. There was a rumor that an attempt might be made on his life in Jerusalem. The parting from his family was tearful and uncommonly difficult. An hour before departure, six thousand gold francs arrived, the contribution of a Russian Zionist, to help defray the cost of the deputation's journey. Shortly before midnight, October 12, they boarded the train for Constantinople. Herzl's parents wept. "If I don't come back, only they will be disconsolate."

4

In Constantinople the deputation took over the entire second floor at the Hotel de Londres; the first floor was occupied by foreign royalty. The group was hounded by the usual contingent of fawning impostors and shady political agents offering their services. At first everything was utterly confused. No sooner had Herzl arrived and changed his clothes than he drove to Yildiz Kiosk to seek out his old Turkish contacts. But the viziers he sought were not present. Since the Kaiser's yacht was due in two days, Bodenheimer went to the German embassy to announce Herzl's arrival. Ambassador Marschall received him coldly.

"I do not know any Dr. Herzl," he said. Nor would he see Herzl, for he was leaving for the Dardanelles to meet the Kaiser's yacht.

During the next two days nothing happened. Herzl was too enervated even to note in his diary the magnificent sights of Constantinople that had so impressed him on his previous visit. He and his colleagues were shadowed by Turkish police agents whenever they went out, and their mail was opened by the post office. In the dining room the party conversed in code: "The old man" meant the Grand Duke; "Cohn" was the Sultan; "the nephew," the Kaiser; "printing office," Palestine. The meticulous Wolffsohn went so far as to say "The J.S." when mentioning Herzl's pamphlet *The Jewish State*.

From "the nephew," meanwhile, there was no word. On Tuesday morning, October 18, cannons announced his arrival in the city. His yacht, the *Hohenzollern*, sailed up the Golden Horn surrounded by warships. Herzl and his colleagues grew desperate. To reach Palestine in time they would have to leave Constantinople on the following morning. It hardly seemed conceivable that on the very first day of his state visit, the Kaiser woud find time to meet Herzl to discuss the Jews.

Undaunted, Herzl wrote to the Kaiser asking for a private audience immediately. Wolffsohn was charged with delivering the letter. He did not know one word of Turkish or of French, but managed to talk his way through tight security cordons, manned by grim Turkish and Prussian warriors. Security precautions were unprecedented, for the recent assassination of the Empress of Austria had roused suspicions of an anarchist plot against the Kaiser. The resourceful Wolffsohn nevertheless accomplished his mission. At the palace gate he drew himself up to his full height and announced in clipped military tones: "I must attend my Emperor immediately on a matter of highest importance." The Kaiser's entourage was almost as harassed as the Jewish deputation. As he delivered Herzl's letter to the Kaiser's court marshal, the latter said, "Please speak quietly; there are two fellows listening at every door."

At the hotel Herzl fretted nervously. After lunch a messenger arrived with a note. "Theodor Herzl to report to His Majesty at four-thirty. Yildiz." Everyone in the party was excited. Herzl gave

Seidener his hand to feel; it was quite steady. Schnirer, the physician, checked Herzl's pulse, which ran high. But Herzl refused his
offer of a sedative. He fussed over his clothes: "Careful toilette.
The color of my gloves was particularly becoming, a delicate gray."
Wolffsohn took along a clothes brush. Then they drove through the
festooned streets to Yildiz Kiosk. Their carriage joined a cavalcade
of imposing state coaches filled with gold-braided courtiers on their
way to one gala function or another for the visiting monarch. Herzl
mused to himself that "perhaps none of these state coaches was
carrying so much world history through the streets as my own
ordinary hackney cab."

Wolffsohn was detained in the forecourt. On the left, the Sultan's harem was enclosed behind a high stone wall. The park was
magnificent, though badly kept, and the masonry was crumbling
in the sun. Herzl entered the palace of the visiting Kaiser alone.
The Kaiser was still absent at some function, and none of the
German courtiers was present. Herzl was unceremoniously locked
off in a guardroom. After half an hour he grew anxious. Had there
been a mistake? Or had Bülow deliberately summoned Herzl to the
wrong palace to discredit him in the Kaiser's eyes?

Finally, at 5:30, he was called. As he climbed the wide staircase to the upper floor, he worried about the crease of his trousers.
His eye caught the slim figure of the German Empress behind one
of the stately columns. She had been standing there with Bülow,
observing Herzl. Bülow whispered something into her ear. Herzl
bowed. She smiled kindly and disappeared. Then, accompanied by
Bülow, Herzl walked briskly into the Kaiser's room.

The Kaiser, in dark hussar uniform and high boots, welcomed
Herzl at the door. His graciousness dazzled Herzl, who, not being
used to courts, did not realize that charm was part of a monarch's
trade and not necessarily a character trait. Herzl was quite be-
witched by the Kaiser's famous flashing blue eyes. He did not know
that this penetrating gaze was the product of long practice before a
mirror. ("They are truly imperial eyes. I have never seen such eyes.
They show a remarkable, bold, inquisitive soul.") The Kaiser, for
his part, was also impressed. He recorded his admiration of Herzl's
"shrewd, highly intelligent mind, expressive eyes, idealism, and
noble way of thought."

"Where shall I begin?" Herzl asked after the three had settled
into their armchairs—the Kaiser comfortably, with folded legs,
Herzl and Bülow stiff and upright.

"Wherever you like," the Kaiser said a little ironically. Herzl outlined his plan again. As he spoke, his heart pounded against his ribs. The sly Bülow watched his embarrassment with amusement, but the Kaiser nodded approvingly.

Herzl said, "I do not know—maybe I am crazy—but the whole thing seems perfectly natural to me."

The Kaiser's eyes flashed. "To me, too!" he said grandly. He made clear that he favored Herzl's scheme for imperial as well as for internal reasons. "Among your compatriots there are elements whom it would be quite beneficial to settle in Palestine. I am thinking of [the area of] Hesse, for example, where there are usurers at work among the rural population. If these people settled in the colonies with their possessions, they might become useful."

Herzl was annoyed by this identification of an entire people with a handful of dishonest men. He was so irritated that he suddenly regained his composure and gave the Kaiser a short lesson on anti-Semitism. Jews were neither better nor worse than other people, but anti-Semitism was stabbing the very best of them "right to the heart. We have been deeply hurt."

Bülow parried the blow by complaining that the Jews were ungrateful to the House of Hohenzollern. After all the kindness shown them by the Kaiser and his forefathers, they now had the audacity to join "the opposition parties. Yes, even the anti-monarchists!"

The Kaiser grumbled approvingly: "Singer!"*

Bülow said that the Kaiser was "hurt." It was like the cat complaining that the mice were unfair by allying themselves with the dogs.

Herzl repeated his familiar argument: "We will take the Jews away from the revolutionary parties." This in itself was good reason for Germany to support his scheme.

The Kaiser agreed that the Jews would join in the colonization of Palestine if they knew that he was keeping them under his protection. Thus they would not be leaving Germany, so to speak.

"And let us hope they will be grateful for it!" Bülow quickly added. It was clear that Bülow opposed Herzl's scheme though he did not dare contradict the imperial will openly. His objections were masked: "Well, yes . . . Yes, but . . . Yes, yes, if only . . ."

But the Kaiser visibly supported Herzl's argument with nods and encouraging glances. France was too weak at the moment to object . . . Russia and England were likely to be in favor . . . a role

---

* Chairman of the German Social Democratic party.

for Germany in the Near East . . . the shortest land route to India also would lead to the solution of the Jewish problem . . . the salvation of Turkish finances. He asked for a chartered land company along the lines of the East India Company. The *chartered company* was a household term in Europe ever since the Jameson raid in the Transvaal that had caused a rift between England and Germany.

The Kaiser grew more enthusiastic by the minute. He had some difficulty following Herzl's more complex proposals to cure the Turkish finances. But he found the scheme generally grand. It should be attempted. Yes, he would sponsor it.

"Well, yes—if only the Turks are willing," Bülow rejoined. "Perhaps you should approach the ministers. . . ." He rubbed his thumb against his finger as if counting out money. "After all, here they all take."

The Kaiser waved his hand. "But surely it will make an impression if the German Kaiser is involved, and shows an interest in it. . . . After all, I am the only one who sticks to the Sultan. He relies on me."

Toward the end of the long audience the Kaiser was so distinctly won over that even Bülow no longer resisted. It was all up to the Turks now; the Kaiser was sure the Sultan would heed his every wish. In this certainty the Kaiser wished to receive the Zionist deputation in Jerusalem. He asked Herzl to write out his formal address in advance and give it to Bülow. "I shall go over it carefully with him. . . . Now just tell me in one word what I should demand of the Sultan."

"A *chartered company* under German protection."

"Good!" said the Kaiser. "A *chartered company!*" He gave Herzl his hand, squeezed it hard, and went out of the room. Herzl and Bülow followed at a distance.

Bülow turned to Herzl: "That is a monarch of genius!" Walking down the stairs, the two men agreed on final arrangements. Herzl promised to deliver the text of his Jerusalem address before leaving Constantinople the next morning.

In the forecourt he joined the agitated Wolffsohn in the carriage. The colorful cluster of Turkish officers eyed them suspiciously. Herzl pressed Wolffsohn's hand warmly and said only one word: "Overwhelming!" At the Hotel de Londres his colleagues were clamoring for the news. He gave them only a summary report. He was exhausted from the great strain; his heart pained him and he had difficulty breathing. Then, while Wolffsohn packed his suitcases, he sat down to compose the difficult text of his address. He had promised Bülow and the Kaiser that he would deliver it before the morning. He worked for four hours. At 11:00 P.M., feeling he could do no more, he drank himself to sleep with a bottle of heavy Bavarian beer. At 4:00 A.M. he rose, lighted all twelve candles in his bedroom, and returned to his chore. But after half an hour of writing, his heart palpitations grew so intense that he had to lie down again. From 6:00 to 8:30 he wrote and rewrote a few more sentences, then sent Bülow what he had finished, promising to deliver the last part in Palestine: "I have spent a very difficult night, with all sorts of pains in my heart," Herzl wrote Bülow. "I am almost incapacitated for work." He had only a half-hour left to reach the Russian steamship *Imperator Nicholas II*, which would take them as far as Alexandria. It was pulling up anchor as he arrived.

The city was cast in glorious sunshine. The slim towers of the mosques receded into the distance, like lancets stuck in the ground. Herzl sensed a certain relief to be on board a Russian ship. In Constantinople he had half-expected an attempt on his life. He wondered how the Turks were reacting to his scheme now that, under the patronage of Wilhelm II, it was becoming so serious. He suspected more danger ahead in Palestine but kept his anxieties to himself. "I am obviously reaching the climax of my tragic undertaking," he noted in his diary. "If the expedition to Palestine is successful, the hardest part will have been accomplished." The remainder would be only detail. To his father he wrote of his "colossal success . . . I am convinced that at this hour every European government is intensely busy with our scheme."

The crossing was pleasant and uneventful. They dined on caviar, piroshki, and chicken Kiev. The lower deck teemed with poor Russian pilgrims and animals. To soothe his employers, Herzl wrote a little piece describing the sea voyage. The ship stopped at Piraeus on its way to Egypt. The company visited Athens and the Acropolis. Herzl was much more impressed a few days later by the Suez Canal—"the will of *one* man!" The new engineering works in the Egyptian desert touched his imagination more than all the glories of ancient Greece—facts were better than memories.

He was so sure of his success that from Alexandria he wrote the editor of *Die Welt* to hold the press for a sensational issue on the results of his mission to Palestine. In Alexandria the party purchased tropical suits and cork helmets and transferred to a smaller, slower vessel bound for Jaffa. It was unbearably hot in the cabin

that the five men had to share. On October 26, early in the morning
—Herzl had spent most of the night on deck—they began to peer
toward the horizon. At 7:00 A.M. the first pale, barren bit of land
was sighted at starboard. Wolffsohn wept. It was the land of their
forefathers. Herzl gazed at it "with mixed feelings."

13

German Interlude II

ERZL'S HEART SANK when he first laid eyes on Jaffa. The town was little more than a drab cluster of huts built of mud and porous sandstone. Its position on the sea was picturesque, but the squalor and the perennial stench of open sewers were repellent to most European travelers. A steep mound—the accumulated debris of innumerable civilizations—overlooked a shallow little bay. The population amounted to 32,000, of whom 3,000 were Jews. To the north (the future site of Tel Aviv) the city bordered on desolate swamps; in the south it touched on wandering sand dunes. Inland, toward the east, lay verdant orange and grapefruit groves.

Jaffa, the pilgrim's gateway to the Holy Land, was the main seaport of Ottoman-controlled Palestine. A single narrow-gauge railway led fifty miles up into the hills to Jerusalem, where in 1898 the Jews already constituted a majority. Jaffa had no proper harbor. Ships moored at some distance from the coast, and passengers and cargo were rowed ashore through rocks said to be those to which Andromeda had been chained by the dragon.

Herzl was feverish and had to limp ashore as the result of a bad fall on the ship's gangway. No Moses ever hoped to enter a promised land in as foul a mood. He almost expected to be sent back by the Turkish police. But on the eve of the Kaiser's arrival in the Holy Land, an advance party of German officials had virtually taken over the pier. While a Turkish policeman was snooping at his luggage, Herzl took one of the Germans aside. "We are here on the Kaiser's orders," he said. The German official swiftly ushered him and his four cork-helmeted companions through the Turkish controls.

Wolffsohn had cryptically alerted one of his Palestinian ac-

quaintances: "Arriving with four friends. Expect me Wednesday
morning Jaffa. *Aval hadavar jehe besod gadol.*"*

Despite all precautions, the news of Herzl's arrival preceded
him. A cluster of nervous and excited Jewish colonists spotted him
in the harbor. His name was a household word among the colonists,
and his face was familiar from photographs. No one knew the exact
purpose of his trip; there was plenty of conjecture, though (in the
Arab bazaar a rumor went round that the *Malik al Yahud*** had
arrived). Also present at the dock, discreetly keeping in the background, was Mendel Kramer, a Jewish agent of the Turkish secret
police, who had been alerted by cablegram from Constantinople.
Kramer had instructions to watch Herzl's movements, and in his
pocket he carried a signed order for Herzl's arrest which he was to
produce at the slightest provocation.

Herzl made sure there was none. He took pains to attract as
little attention as possible. He and his companions pretended to be
newspapermen covering the Kaiser's pilgrimage for the European
press. They avoided the more elegant, German-owned Hotel du
Parc and settled into a modest Jewish pension. Whenever people
gathered in the street to cheer, Herzl asked them to disperse quietly. He was very careful, as well, never to mount a white donkey
or a white horse. In Palestine this might have looked like the political demonstration of a messianic pretender.

The Kaiser was not due in Jaffa for another day. An hour after
disembarkation, Herzl and his companions set out to tour the
neighboring countryside. In 1898 some four thousand Jewish settlers were living in sixteen new colonies, of which thirteen were
subsidized by Edmond de Rothschild and administered by his
overseers. Seven colonies lay within a radius of twenty miles from
Jaffa. In the sweltering heat—after first successfully shaking off the
sleepy police spy—Herzl and his companions rode out to Mikve
Israel, an agricultural training school founded in 1870 by French
philanthropists to instruct Jewish youngsters in modern farming
methods. The school was, and still is, located on the main highway
to Jerusalem. Its big gate was festively decorated in honor of the
Kaiser, who was to ride by two days later. Herzl chatted with the
pupils and was shown around the grounds. Then the company
continued through a landscape ravaged by centuries of fever,
piracy, and neglect, to Rishon le Zion ("*The first to Zion* . . . that
bringeth good tidings to Jerusalem," Isaiah 41:27, italics my own),

---

* Hebrew: "But keep it a big secret."
** Arabic: "King of the Jews."

the first new colony established in 1882, where they spent the night in a farmer's home. The inexperienced settlers of Rishon had gone bankrupt within a year and had since become grateful recipients of Rothschild's charity. The population now amounted to about four hundred.

Thick dust lay on the roads and there was only a little greenery around the small stone houses. Herzl had never believed in these attempts at "infiltration" of the country by a handful of idealists living off a philanthropist's dole, without proper political guarantees. His visit to Rishon confirmed him in this prejudice. He was received with apprehension by Rothschild's administrator, who knew the settlers' sympathies for Herzl but also feared the Baron's ire and dared neither to be amiable nor hostile. In fact, fear of the Baron hovered over the village. "The poor colonists have swapped one fear for another," Herzl thought. He was shown through the elaborate wine cellars the Baron had built to produce a Bordeaux-type wine. But Herzl had never doubted that it was possible to build almost anything anywhere—with money. "With the millions that have been poured into the sand here, and been stolen and squandered, far different results could have been achieved!"

Meanwhile, news of Herzl's arrival spread through the little village. The younger colonists welcomed Herzl as a hero. He was touched by their worn faces. One man delivered a speech in which he tried to strike a careful balance between the settlers' obligations to Rothschild and their love for Herzl. Herzl answered briefly. The Baron's aim and purpose were different from his own, he said; nevertheless he advised the settlers to be grateful to their benefactor.

In the evening he had a frank talk with the colony's medical officer, Dr. Mazie. "Fever! All the colonies suffer from malaria!"

"When I get the charter," Herzl said, "I will bring in masses of laborers to drain and eliminate the swamps."

"I am afraid they'll all die," the doctor sadly rejoined.

"Nonsense," Herzl responded. "What about the Suez Canal?"

"The Suez Canal was built by African Negroes!" Mazie said.

But Herzl was not discouraged: "It will cost billions, but will also create billions of new wealth! As workers we might employ such Arabs as are immune to the fever."

On the following morning the group traveled farther south along the dusty track to visit three more hamlets. Everywhere they went, the entire population turned out to greet them. Children sang Hebrew songs and cried, "Long live Herzl, the President of the

Hebrew Republic!" Old men waited on Herzl with bread, salt, and wine, and he had to visit the home of nearly every colonist. In Rehovoth,* a little hamlet of 170 inhabitants who had managed somehow to remain independent of Rothschild's support, he was given the heartiest reception of all. A cavalcade of dashing Jewish cowboys astride Arabian horses swarmed about his carriage lustily crying *"Heddad!"* ("Hail!")

At the next hamlet, Ekron, the village elders were waiting at the roadside with scrolls of the Torah. Some knelt and kissed Herzl's footprints in the dust. He recoiled and withdrew to his carriage. Everywhere he spoke briefly in German. The majority of the settlers were from Eastern Europe, and some didn't understand him. But his presence was enough for many. They were a handful of idealistic men and women from various pogrom-stricken *shtetls* who had followed their hearts' dream to Zion and now eked out a meager living on remote farms; Herzl's very existence, his pamphlet, his congresses were proof that they were not alone, but pioneers of a mounting mass movement.

Throughout the long journey which also took them through at least a dozen Arab villages, and even in Jaffa itself, Herzl barely registered the presence of any Arabs, except once as a "mixed multitude of beggars, women, and children." There is no other reference to the native population in his diary, or in any of his subsequent written reports about the trip. The natives seemed to have vanished before his eyes as in their own *Arabian Nights*, or else they assumed no political importance at all in his mind. It is the happy faculty of idealists to overlook the visible—a price they pay for seeing the unseen.

2

The small party finally turned back to Jaffa at the place where the track leading into Ekron branched off the main route from Jaffa to Gaza, and on to Egypt in the south. The heat lay heavily in Herzl's limbs; his skin was caked with dust and sweat.

The Kaiser arrived in the afternoon. In Constantinople the Sultan had been the Kaiser's host in a new kiosk, built especially for the purpose, on the palace grounds. In Palestine Wilhelm was the

* Site of the future Weizmann Institute of Science.

guest of Thomas Cook Company, with twenty-six sleeping tents, six vast reception canopies, mobile kitchens, five hundred mules, and countless dragomans, cooks, waiters, valets, and water carriers. Jaffa was in complete turmoil; the combination of the Teutonic and the Eastern gave the busy scene an unreal, almost barbaric quality. Fierce Prussian warriors with straw-colored hair and knobby knees, and mounted Turkish Janissaries roamed the narrow streets. Courtiers in spectacular uniforms waded through the dust, and a cloud of pungent white smoke rose from a hundred sheep roasting on spits. The bazaars were jammed with souvenir hunters.

The indomitable Hechler had arrived in the Kaiser's tracks. In flowing robes and Arab headgear he drove through Jaffa's teeming streets triumphantly greeting the crowd with the cry: "He cometh! The Messiah cometh!" Try as he would, Herzl was unable to control Hechler's excitement. He asked Hechler to notify the imperial chamberlain of his arrival. He would await the Kaiser the next day along the highway outside of Mikve Israel.

Combating an attack of malarial fever, which he had contracted overnight, Herzl proceeded early next morning to Mikve Israel. He could scarcely manage even to stand on his feet in the intense heat. A chorus of pupils and a number of "somewhat baronial arrogant Rothschild administrators" were also awaiting the Kaiser at the gate. The Rothschild people were not altogether happy to see Herzl in their midst. Joseph Niego, the director of the training school, asked Herzl not to present him to the Kaiser; if the demonstration appeared to be a "Zionist demonstration," it might do the school harm.

Presently a regiment of mounted Janissaries galloped past at full tilt, and a detachment of Prussian dragoons with drawn swords heralded the approach of the imperial cavalcade. "The Turkish Crescent and the German Eagle mingled with the banners of Thomas Cook." The Kaiser rode a white stallion; his grayish khaki uniform was topped by a spiked gold helmet over a flowing white silk burnoose. He recognized Herzl from afar and drew rein abruptly. In the ensuing pileup, one of the courtiers fell off his horse.

"*Wie geht's?*" asked the Kaiser. The Empress, behind him, smiled at Herzl benevolently.

"Thank you, your Majesty, I am having a look at the country. How has the journey agreed with you so far?"

The Kaiser blinked. "Very hot. But the country has a future."

"At present it is still sick," Herzl answered.

"It needs water, very much water," the Kaiser observed from above.

"Canalization on a grand scale," Herzl suggested.

The Kaiser again said, "It is a land of the future."

The conversation lasted a few more minutes, while Niego and the Baron's men gaped timidly from a distance. Herzl considered the brief encounter a very good omen. The Empress cast Herzl another smile. They shook hands, and the Kaiser trotted off toward the Jerusalem hills.

In the scorching hot afternoon the Jewish deputation took the train for Jerusalem. Herzl's attack of fever grew worse, and his foot was swollen. He limped into the cramped, crowded compartment where the heat was even worse than outside. The train was delayed for an hour, and Herzl was accosted by Orthodox fanatics offended by his traveling into the Sabbath. Finally they departed. The train crossed the dismal coastal plain they visited the day before, and began its slow climb up the Judean hills. In 1898 the hills were still mostly barren rock and slopes that had eroded through centuries of neglect, with few traces of the ancient terrace cultivation. The fifty-mile journey took almost four hours, causing Herzl to grow weaker and more feverish. They arrived in full darkness, and although Herzl wanted to hire a carriage, his companions, because of the Sabbath, insisted they walk the half-hour distance from station to hotel.

Herzl tottered into town on a cane, his other hand braced around Wolffsohn's arm. He must have dreamed of a vastly different entry into the earthly Jerusalem. At the hotel he felt sicker than before. He swallowed a dose of quinine and vomited. Dr. Schnirer rubbed his skin with spirits of camphor and remained with him in his little room the rest of the night. His friends were frantic.

In the morning he felt slightly better. Still very feeble, he did not stir from the house but sat by the window staring out across the rooftops, ramparts, and domes at the surrounding mountains.

Hechler arrived for tea. "If, at the next vacancy of the Anglican diocese, I have anything to say, you must become Bishop of Jerusalem," Herzl proposed.

"No! No!" Hechler protested modestly. But Herzl said again, "Bishop of Jerusalem!"

He finished his address to the Kaiser and sent the full text off to the court marshal. In the afternoon he watched from his window as the Kaiser, clad in shining armor, triumphantly entered the

city. A section of the ancient battlements, twenty meters wide, had
been leveled to permit him to enter the old city without dismount-
ing: "I come as a knight of peace and labor, interested not in
riches, but in the healing of souls."

The beauty of Jerusalem in the diffuse moonlight impressed
Herzl greatly. But he was repelled by what he saw by daylight. His
diary reflects his distaste:

> When I remember thee in days to come, O Jerusalem, it will not
> be with pleasure.
>
> The musty deposits of two thousand years of inhumanity,
> intolerance, and filth lie in these foul-smelling alleyways. The
> one Man who has been here in all this time, the amiable
> dreamer of Nazareth, has only helped to increase the hatred.
>
> If ever we get Jerusalem . . . I would begin by cleaning
> it up.

While awaiting the Emperor's summons, the party took long
walks. The leaders of the local Jewish community were too afraid
of the Turks to risk being seen with Herzl, and studiously avoided
his company. When Herzl and his friends visited the Wailing Wall,
Wolffsohn and the others wept. To Herzl, try as he might, "a
deeper emotion refused to come," for at that last remaining bit of
stone of the ancient Jewish Temple, there were too many "hideous,
wretched, speculative" beggars. At dusk Herzl climbed the so-
called Tower of David. The city looked ghostly in the tempered
gloom; the distant mountains seemed to be melting away in the
evening mists. The imposing Herodian edifice built of enormous
blocks of stone now served as a Turkish jail. "It would be clever of
the Sultan to imprison me here," Herzl remarked to his friends, but
they did not consider it a joke. Mandel Kramer, the police agent,
was almost always within earshot. There were constant rumors of
an intended assault, and Wolffsohn at one point threw himself at
an innocent pedestrian in the bazaar whom he had momentarily
suspected of wanting to assassinate Herzl.

3

Three days passed and there was still no answer from the
Kaiser's encampment. The five men lingered about. No one knew
when, or if, the deputation would be received. The uncertainty was

unnerving. Herzl could only guess at the complications and intrigues being played over their heads and behind their backs. He was completely cut off from news sources and had seen no European newspaper in fourteen days. There was a rumor that France had declared war on England and that the Kaiser would abruptly return to Germany. Herzl had no idea how the Sultan had reacted to the Kaiser's entreaties. He was anxious to leave the country immediately after the audience, "before the Turks come to their senses and perhaps get me into trouble." The regular mail boat had just left Jaffa, and there would not be another for a week.

On Wednesday, their fifth day in Jerusalem, Herzl was finally called to the imperial encampment. He was received with some condescension by an arrogant young diplomat who waved Herzl's corrected speech at him and demanded that all passages crossed out (presumably by Bülow) be deleted: "I cannot allow you to say *this* to the Kaiser. . . . No, and *this* I just cannot allow you to say either." Herzl was requested to submit a revised text, together with the old one, so that the two could be compared. Herzl overlooked this impertinence and merely said, "Certainly." The audience was fixed for the next day.

In his excitement over the imminent meeting, Herzl at first overlooked the fact that key phrases in his text had been deleted by the Germans, particularly those that referred to a Jewish revival and to the possibility of a German protectorate. For Herzl's companions the final round of preparations for the audience proved arduous. Herzl controlled their diets to keep them in form, drilled them in court etiquette, and carefully checked their suits, shoes, cravats, shirts, gloves, boots, and silk hats. At the last minute he asked Bodenheimer to change his top hat, and Wolffsohn his cuffs. He would not allow any of them to take bromine, "for the sake of history."

In their heavy black evening clothes, the sweat running down their backs, the five men drove through the burning noonday sun and dust to the imperial tents. The Kaiser's encampment was perched—as in an old etching—under a forest of flags and silk banners on a rocky expanse overlooking the ramparts from the north, where so many conquerors of Jerusalem, from Nebuchadnezzar to the Crusaders, had paused before their final assault. Herzl's hopes still ran very high. If the Kaiser was only half as enthusiastic as he had been in Constantinople, his audience could change the course of history.

The Kaiser's aide-de-camp ushered them into a reception tent.

To get the full flavor of the ensuing scene we must picture the curious mixture of Oriental splendor and Teutonic might, reminiscent almost of the Crusades: the Kaiser's sumptuous brocade tent lined with magnificent Persian carpets and fitted in damascene mother-of-pearl furniture, and the five somber Jews in their black bourgeois clothes and starched shirt fronts. We must imagine the walled city close by, with its minarets and monasteries and synagogues, where the adherents of the various faiths had slaughtered each other since time immemorial in the name of the one true God. The calls of the muezzin mingled with the ringing of church bells, the wails of Jews sobbing at the Wall, and the tinny clatter, nearby, of the Prussian guards. In the distant hills were olive trees and the braying of donkeys and camels with their bright painted boxes and embroidered saddles. All this is bathed in brilliant, blinding light, under a translucent sky, and air purer than Herzl had ever dreamed of.

The Kaiser received them cordially. He held a riding whip in his good right arm; his left hand, malformed since childhood, was hidden in a glove. "*Ich bitte!*" he said in clipped military tones and reached out for his veiled Lohengrin helmet, which he put on. Bülow hovered in the background. The introductions were formal. As each name was pronounced, Wilhelm saluted. Herzl pulled out his corrected script and read it aloud, while Bülow, like a schoolmaster, ran his forefinger along another copy of the approved address. The gist of Herzl's speech was as follows (with the parts deleted at the Germans' request in parentheses):

A deputation of the sons of Israel approaches the German Kaiser with the deepest reverence—in the land which was our fathers' (but no longer belongs to us). We are bound to this sacred soil by no valid title of possession. Many generations have come and gone since this land was Jewish. If we speak of it now, it is only a dream of ancient days. But the dream still lives in the hearts of many hundreds and thousands; it was and still is a wondrous consolation in many an hour of pain for our (poor) people. (Whenever foes oppressed us with accusations and persecutions, whenever we were begrudged our little bit of right to live, whenever we were excluded from the society of our fellow citizens, whose fate we were also ready to share loyally—in our depressed hearts we remembered Zion.)

There is something eternal in this memory; its form, naturally, has undergone considerable changes, with people, with institutions, and with times. The Zionist movement today is an entirely modern one. It grows out of the conditions of present-day life and desires to utilize modern possibilities to solve the Jewish question. We believe that this can now finally be accomplished, because mankind has grown so rich in means of communication and technical achievements. Enterprises which only half a century ago appeared fantastic are now commonplace. Steam power and electricity have changed the face of the globe. Consequences, important for humanity, must be drawn from this as well.

(Above all we have aroused the national consciousness of our scattered brethren. At the congresses of Basel, the program of our movement was publicly formulated. It reads: "The establishment of a home for the Jewish people secured by public law.") This is the land of our fathers . . . it cries out for people to build it up. We happen to have among our brethren a distressing proletariat. These people cry out for a land to cultivate. We wish to derive a new welfare from these two conditions of distress—of the land and of the people—by a carefully planned combination of both . . . we are requesting your Imperial Majesty's exalted aid for this project.

We are thoroughly convinced that the implementation of the Zionist plan will contribute to the welfare of Turkey as well. Energies and material resources will enter the country; it is easy to foresee a magnificent reconstruction of desolate areas; from all this, more happiness and culture will arise for countless human beings. We plan to establish a Jewish Land Company for Syria and Palestine, to undertake the great enterprise (and for this company we request the protection of the German Kaiser).

No man's rights or religious feelings are threatened by our idea (which heralds a long-desired reconciliation). We understand and respect the piety of all faiths for the soil on which, after all, the faith of our fathers arose as well.

An Emperor of peace is making his great entry into the Eternal City. We Jews greet your Majesty in this high moment and wish with all our hearts that an age of peace and justice may dawn for all humanity. (For us also.)

When Herzl finished his speech he looked straight into the Kaiser's eyes. In the background Bülow made his presence known by fumbling with the papers. The Kaiser, who had been "fire and flame" for Herzl's scheme, now chose to remain noncommittal. He did not tell Herzl that in Constantinople the Sultan had simply refused to take his advice. Wilhelm had new hobbyhorses now with which to preoccupy himself. To Herzl he said, "I thank you for your communication. It interests me very much. The matter, in any case, still requires careful study and further discussions."

The Kaiser next lectured the deputation for a few minutes on the agricultural needs of Palestine, the importance of water and shade. He agreed that in Palestine "there is room for everybody. . . . Your movement, with which I am well acquainted, contains a sound idea."

Further than that he would not go. The entire company remained standing while the Kaiser complained about the heat. "The day we met at Mikve Israel was the hottest . . . thirty-one degrees [centigrade] in the shade, forty-one in the sun."

Bülow said sweetly, "As his Majesty the Kaiser was gracious enough to say, water is the main thing. Herr Herzl will know better than I what the Greek poet says: 'Ariston men udos' [Water is best]."

"We can bring the country water," Herzl said. "It will cost billions but will yield billions."

"Well, money you have got plenty!" the Kaiser said as he slapped his boot with his whip. "More money than any of us!"

Bülow hastened to endorse his master's judgment. "Yes, the money which gives us so much trouble, you've got plenty of it!"

A few minutes later the Kaiser closed the audience. The "charter," the "return," and the "protectorate" had never been mentioned. Herzl turned to leave; there was a bitter taste in his mouth. In Constantinople the Kaiser had been so much more forthcoming; clearly some difficulties had arisen since. Herzl had no idea what these were. Outside the tent, the Kaiser's aide-de-camp snidely asked, "*Already over*, the audience?"

Herzl did not respond. He turned to Schnirer and said only: "He said neither yes nor no." But in his heart he knew that the Kaiser had changed his mind.

There was more comic opera at the gates. The Turkish guards refused to allow them out of the imperial encampment. Fortunately Mendel Kramer, the police spy, who had been shadowing them since Jaffa, stood outside and made the guards open the gates for them.

On the way back Herzl hardly spoke. It had been a moment which, in the strain and anxiety of the recent weeks, he had antici-

pated with trepidation. Yet now it was here, it was like death. Suddenly he felt the heat and the flies and the dust pounding at his
body like a steaming rag. The light blinded him; his head ached. On
the roadside a tethered goat was munching away at the sparse
foliage, indifferent to all the Oriental commotion and the imperial
splendor that for a brief week in November was turning Jerusalem
into a Germanic outpost in the East.

4

In the afternoon, to escape the well-wishers pushing their way
into his living quarters, Herzl drove to Motza, in the mountains a
few miles west of Jerusalem. Motza was a colony newly founded in
the rocky wilderness by young Russian Jews. Samuel Broza, a thirty-
year-old settler from Mohilev, Russia, recited the hardships of settling and cultivating the remote and infertile spot. Herzl planted a
cedar sapling and wondered at Broza's courage and determination.

He could not for long ignore his own political preoccupations.
Fearing for his life, he felt he had to leave the country immediately. He still had no news from Europe, but suspected that his
approach to Wilhelm had irritated several European governments.
On the back of the original draft of his address to the Kaiser, which
Bülow had corrected, Herzl had seen the penciled words, "Tewfik
Pasha, Grand Hotel." Evidently the Turks now knew of his request
for a German protectorate in Palestine. How would they react? "If
the Turks had only a glimmer of political foresight," Herzl told
himself, "they would have to put a stop to my game now once and
for all." They might deport him ignominiously, or simply have him
attacked and killed by a few gendarmes conveniently disguised as
robbers.

He spent a sleepless night turning and twisting on his bed,
pondering the political consequences of his "pretender's journey" to
Palestine. Through the open window came the soothing breeze of
the night. He distrusted the Jewish well-wishers who in the past
few days had crowded into his parlor. With good intentions or bad,
they might betray him to the Turks—"whether to save imperiled
Jewry, to earn their thirty pieces of silver, or to obtain the good
graces of some pasha or Rothschild."

At 2:00 A.M. he rose to pack his suitcases. Shortly before dawn
the deputation left Jerusalem, almost stealthily, for the coast. The
police spy had not yet shown up for duty and Herzl asked the

innkeeper to keep his departure secret. In his haste he left part of his luggage behind.

A few hours later they arrived in Jaffa and went directly to the harbor. Three or four vessels were lying at anchor next to the German battleships. Herzl had himself rowed up to each of them, with the exception of a Turkish steamer, which he avoided. None was sailing that day for Alexandria. In his anxiety Herzl sent a note to Gordon Bennett, publisher of the New York *Herald*, whose private yacht was also in the harbor, asking for space for himself and only one of his four companions. In the afternoon he was dismayed to receive Bennett's negative response. The deputation was forced to spend another night in Jaffa. Kramer, the police spy, caught up with them in the evening and posted himself outside the hotel. Nothing happened, but Herzl would take no more chances. Early in the morning he and Wolffsohn rowed out to the *Dundee*, a small, miserable English freighter of only 350 tons' displacement, which was leaving for Alexandria that evening. Deciding to remain on board, Herzl sent Wolffsohn ashore to fetch the rest of the party and the luggage. Only now, on board this rocking little vessel, did he feel safe. His fellow travelers were reluctant to sail on the *Dundee*. Bodenheimer protested, but Herzl was determined not to return ashore. Only after he threatened that he might sail alone did they finally acquiesce. Finally, at sunset, the ship set sail. Sitting on an orange crate, Herzl watched the darkening coastline recede into the ashen mist. He had arrived in the promised land eleven days earlier with mixed feelings. He left it with a sense of great relief.

The passage on the *Dundee* was rough, and the entire deputation was seasick. In Alexandria Herzl and his associates raced through the French and English newspapers. There was not a word anywhere about their audience with the Kaiser. Herzl wired his father, who answered briefly, "Audience known." The uncertainty was tantalizing, but their two days in Egypt waiting for their boat were full of "joyful surprises" for Herzl. His colonizing zeal was fired by the irrigation works in the Nile delta and by the new residential quarters of Cairo. "Here one sees what industry and energy can achieve even in a hot country. Even though we do not have the Nile mud, the soil of Palestine offers a thousand possibilities which proper management can bring forth."

He had very little reason for optimism, yet was still bold enough to believe that the expedition had been a "fairly good success," or so he told his companions. Full of excited anticipation, the group boarded the Italian luxury liner *Regina Margherita* bound for Europe. Herzl's hopes were pinned on the Kaiser's promise to study the matter further. The full blow of disappointment awaited him at Naples. The German government had issued a colorless, meaningless court circular; it reduced the audience in Jerusalem to a routine social affair devoid of any political meaning. The statement first recounted the Kaiser's tour of the Mosque of Omar and his long visits with the Roman Catholic and Greek Catholic patriarchs of Jerusalem.

> Both received his Majesty at the entrance to their residences, surrounded by their entire clergy. Next the Kaiser received the French consul and afterwards a Jewish deputation, which presented him an album containing views of the Israelite colonies that have been established in Palestine. In reply to a speech by the leader of this deputation, Kaiser Wilhelm expressed his benevolent interest in all such endeavors that aim at the improvement of agriculture in Palestine for the welfare of the Turkish Empire and in full recognition of the Sultan's sovereignty.

Herzl suspected the hand of some irresponsible underling behind the official statement. The truth was that it had been written by Bülow himself with the approval of the Kaiser, but this became evident only much later. The deputation was thoroughly depressed. The expedition had been a waste of time, if this was its banal result. Even the faithful Wolffsohn faltered. Herzl hid his own depression and made strenuous efforts to cheer up his disappointed colleagues. Bodenheimer was especially taken aback. A practical man who believed only in what he saw with his own eyes, he was even beginning to wonder whether Herzl's report of his first audience with the Kaiser in Constantinople had not been slightly exaggerated. Herzl, sworn to secrecy by the Germans, had not shown Eulenburg's letters even to his close colleagues. He now had to reap the fruits of his zealous discretion. His credibility was damaged, and even his continued leadership was called into question.

He promised his associates that a suitable version of his encounters with the Germans would be published in due course. He also told them that despite this setback his tenacity alone justified his position as their leader: "I am neither smarter nor better than all of you. But I am undaunted. Therefore I deserve to be the leader. I never lost courage in darker moments than this and, in fact, always made even greater sacrifices."

He even dared to consider this setback "an excellent thing for the future development of our cause." Had the Kaiser kept his promise and assumed the protectorate in Jerusalem, it would have been only an immediate advantage. "But not in the long run. In the long run we would have had to pay the heaviest usurious interest. It would only have been more convenient!" Convenient, Herzl added maliciously, especially for the critical Bodenheimer, who could have returned to his native Germany "a made man, which, to be sure, is not now the case."

In his lifetime Herzl never learned all the reasons, grand and petty, serious and bizarre, that had caused the Kaiser's abrupt change of mind. It is now easier to reconstruct the behind-the-scenes events from the records preserved in the German and Austrian state archives. The Kaiser had indeed been "fire and flame" for Herzl's project; Wilhelm's own memoir of his conversation with Herzl in Constantinople fully bears out Herzl's version. In an unpublished memoir the Kaiser characteristically spoke of "the staging" of Herzl's project. He had in fact urged the Sultan to grant Herzl a charter for Palestine. The Sultan "promised me; even though he was not very sympathetic to this matter, he would readily instruct his ministers to consider the question and develop it further, for clearly a program sponsored by Me could not be detrimental to him and His people."

The Kaiser pursued the case further. He seems to have raised the matter again in Constantinople at least twice, but on each occasion the Sultan answered evasively and changed the subject. On one occasion the Kaiser bluntly said, "The Jews are a plague everywhere; we want to get rid of them." The shrewd Sultan—Bismarck had called him the cleverest diplomat in Europe—retorted, "I myself am very happy with my Jewish subjects."

The Kaiser had other things on his mind as well. The chief purpose of his pilgrimage to the Holy Land was to secure a concession for the construction of a strategic railroad to Baghdad. The idea of a German protectorate over a Jewish Palestine appealed to him briefly, but his main purpose remained the consolidation of a continental bloc against England. The Turks seemed to him better allies than the Jews, and the Turks did not want any more Jews in Palestine. Between Constantinople and Jerusalem—while Herzl believed himself on the threshold of success—the Kaiser began to hesitate. One enthusiasm quickly gave way to others. Haphazard moods and impressions, errors, momentary circumstances, which so often play a role in affairs of state, contributed to his change of mind. He set out to the East in the grandiloquent belief that he might sponsor the return of the Jews, yet the one thing he truly resented during his journey was the "predominance of the *Jewish* element in the city of Jerusalem; it already amounts to almost two-thirds of the population! Even the trade in Christian antiquities and sacred pictures is in their hands!" The Empress smiled at Herzl, but before leaving Constantinople for Jerusalem she reportedly said that the only thing she was sorry about was that she would have to see "so many filthy Jews."

The Kaiser's closest advisers—some working at cross-purposes —further confused matters. The Grand Duke of Baden was carried away by his enthusiasm. Hohenlohe, the Imperial Chancellor, considered Herzl a freak. He accused the Grand Duke of Baden of doing Germany and the Jews a disservice by showing interest in Herzl's cause. Marschall, the ambassador to Constantinople, was notorious in his opposition to some of the Kaiser's personal friends, notably Eulenburg, whose intrusion he resented. Far from reporting the friendly attitude of the Turks—as the Grand Duke had erroneously assumed he would—Marschall warned the Kaiser against rousing the Sultan's ire. Bülow was especially opposed to Herzl's scheme. In retrospect he was probably right, where Germany's interests in Europe and in Turkey were concerned. The Kaiser's trip had been something of a fiasco and was canceled in mid-course for fear of European complications. Bülow raised other objections as well. "These people have no money," he told a newspaperman a few months afterward. "The rich Jews don't want to participate, and with the lousy Jews of Poland you can't do a thing." On another occasion he announced that "beggars are unfit for establishing a state, even for colonization." Such riffraff might emigrate to Argentina, but a return to Palestine was sheer "romantic sentimentality."

The curtain fell. Many factors had gone into the making of this dénouement, the most serious crisis so far in Herzl's political career. Not the least of those factors had been Herzl's own infatuation with the person and would-be role of the Kaiser. Although he envisioned a better future, he was still subject to the prejudices of his own, raw bourgeois age. Herzl's own faith in the power of individuals to change the course of human history blinded him to the void that lay behind the Kaiser's spectacular facade. Yet it was this faith, after all, that had driven Herzl from the start, and he held to it, undaunted, for the rest of his life.

14

Days of Despondency

ON HIS FIRST DAY BACK at the *Neue Freie Presse*, Herzl noticed a change in the general attitude toward him. Instead of derisive laughter, he met occasional smiles of envy. The newspaper had refused to report Herzl's two audiences with the Kaiser. Benedikt made a "sweet-sour face." He asked what the Kaiser had said about Austria.

"Nothing," Herzl said bluntly.

Bacher was just studying the latest issue of *Die Welt*—which included Herzl's own carefully worded communiqué—and to his embarrassment had not had time to remove it from his desk before Herzl entered his office. He too quizzed Herzl, but received only vague answers. Herzl was pleased by Bacher's insistent curiosity. He said, "I shall enlighten you only after you publish the first Zionist article."

Otherwise there was very little satisfaction for Herzl. The next few months were frustrating in the extreme. Herzl's spirits reached an all-time low. His disappointment at the failure of the Palestine expedition was matched only by his resentment of what he considered the slovenliness of his colleagues in the movement. An anecdote was making the rounds in Vienna. The Kaiser had supposedly told Herzl: "Zionism is a splendid idea. The trouble is, it cannot be done with . . . Jews." Herzl recorded the anecdote in his diary with apparent approval; it reflected his own feelings. Desperately he tried to make the best of a bad situation. Steadily he pressed his followers everywhere to carry on. Let the bank at least be firmly established! The next diplomatic opening must not find them again without proper financial resources!

A few hours after his return to Vienna he sent off a stream of alarmist letters. The house was on fire: "let us not lose one day, one hour," he wrote Wolffsohn on November 18, "or else the loss might be tremendous." Five days later, he wrote to Wolffsohn again. "For heaven's sake, do not let things falter." And a week later he wrote, again to Wolffsohn, that he dared not make another approach to the German Kaiser—"for I might receive *too good* an answer"— while the money needed for the charter was not yet available.

He regaled other far-flung lieutenants with reassuring make-believe. "The results [of the Palestine expedition] surpassed all expectations," he wrote Nordau and half a dozen others in Europe and America. Even though he had admittedly been shortchanged by Bülow in the ensuing publicity, "the achievement is simply colossal."

He could hardly deceive himself, however. In one short, hot midday hour in Jerusalem the dream of a decisive, spectacular breakthrough—a dream he had nurtured for years—had popped like a soap bubble. He did not know why exactly, but he was fully aware of the fact. The slow progress of the bank added to his bitterness. "*Everything is bogged down,*" he confided to his diary on January 16. "*Something has to happen.* I have decided to re-quest an audience with the Czar through Berta von Suttner."

Baroness Berta von Suttner was the renowned Austrian pacifist and author of *Die Waffen Nieder* (*Put Down Your Arms*), for which she would receive the Nobel Peace Prize in 1905. She was very fond of Herzl personally and sympathetic to his cause. Suttner liked to address Herzl as "Dear Governor of Zion." Herzl had opened the columns of the *Neue Freie Presse* to her "war against war," but had excused himself for not personally joining her move-ment, for "I have just begun a 'crazy' war of my own, in which I fight like a fool."

Suttner was a lonely enthusiast like Herzl himself, and she admired his courage in pursuing a seemingly impossible ideal. As president of the World Peace Association, she was intrigued to discover the same banal arguments used against Zionism as against pacifism, often by the same people.

The Czar had just proposed an international conference on disarmament at The Hague. Suttner had many friends among the Russian aristocracy, and she warmly recommended Herzl to the Russian government. Count Muraviev, the Russian Foreign Minis-ter, responded evasively; an audience with the Czar at this time was out of the question, although Herzl's movement was regarded with sympathy. Nevertheless, a few weeks later, at Muraviev's own in-

stigation, the czarist government formally approached the Austrian
government on the subject of the activities of "a certain Dr. *Herzel.*"
His Zionist movement, according to the Russian note, was a cover
for socialist-revolutionary agitation.*

Herzl was unaware of this. But the Czar's refusal of an audience was enough to discourage him further. In his diary he noted,
"Days of despondency. The tempo of the movement is slowing
down. The slogans are wearing out. The ideas are becoming
declamatory, and the declamation is losing its edge."

Entries in his diary became rarer. In May 1899 he remarked,
"The well is running dry." His opponents, within the movement
and without, exploited the failure of his Palestine expedition in
order to criticize his strategy. In France Bernard Lazare resigned
from the international executive in protest against Herzl's secretive-
ness and his authoritarian regime. Herzl was variously accused of
being a Pied Piper, a fool, an irresponsible dreamer who had misunderstood the German Kaiser, even a liar who misrepresented the
true German policy; he had duped the poor masses with false hopes
of imminent redemption.

Herzl could not easily refute these charges. To do so he would
have to publish his Constantinople conversation with the Kaiser, or
reveal the specific assurances he had received in writing from Eulenburg and the Grand Duke. This he would not do, for the request
of the Germans, he had committed himself to complete secrecy. "I
cannot answer without getting into the most sordid scuffle."

He applied the same stricture to another attack, the most savage to date. It came from the scathing pen of Karl Kraus, a brilliant
young Viennese who would soon play a major role in modern German letters. Kraus had in fact contributed money to Herzl's cause,
and his name had appeared on a preliminary list of delegates to the
second Basel congress. In the fall of 1898 he changed his mind and
published a pamphlet entitled *A Crown for Zion.* The pamphlet
appeared shortly after Herzl returned from Palestine. It was an
instant success and the talk of Vienna. The title was a pun suggest-

* The Russian government demanded to know what the Austrians intended to do about this danger. A similar diplomatic note was sent to Germany.
The German government promptly initiated a thorough police investigation, and
the Russians were informed after a few weeks that their suspicions were un-
founded. The Austrian government, with characteristic *Gemütlichkeit,* ignored
the Russian query for almost a year. Only after repeated prodding by the
Russian embassy did Vienna send the Russians the noncommittal texts of a few
local police reports and a copy of *Die Welt.*

ing that Herzl sought both a crown (royal) and crowns (money).
Kraus was perhaps the greatest German satirist, with an uncanny
feel for language and nuance and all the inner turmoil of a Czech-
born Jew, living in Vienna, writing in German, successively converting to Catholicism and Protestantism. He was as much a product
of *fin de siècle* Vienna as was Herzl, and in many ways his exact
opposite. Filled with abysmal fears and an almost hateful disgust at
being alive, he played on the weaknesses of bourgeois society in a
ribald and grim style. Like so many gifted young Viennese intellectuals of Jewish extraction, he was tormented by the fact of his
origin to the point of neurosis. Some of his diatribes against Jewish
scribes and businessmen echoed those of Herzl's, but in his hateful
bitterness Kraus sounded like a precursor of Nazi propaganda. He
inveighed against the destruction of Austria by Jerusalem; he
regarded *Gemütlichkeit* and Jewishness as the driving forces of
Viennese decay. Sigmund Freud was another target. Kraus defined
psychoanalysis as that "mental disease which it pretends to cure."

Like Herzl, Kraus was a moralist obsessed with *Angst* of an
approaching apocalypse. But if Herzl believed in possible salvation
through technology, Kraus dated the destruction from the invention of modern machines. Both men, in a sense, were right and
wrong at the same time, and both drove themselves to frenzy.
Kraus believed that machines were becoming complicated, while
the minds of men, particularly in Vienna, became more primitive.
Like Herzl, Kraus had begun his literary career on the *Neue Freie
Presse*, but he soon left to become its most savage critic. The press,
he had decided, was poisoning the sources of language. Herzl's
particular métier, the *feuilleton*, he regarded as the incarnation of
the hypocrisy and decay of modern life. Herzl's Zionism was a mere
offshoot of the imbecility and inherent madness reflected in the
corruption of language in the modern press. He extended his
hatred of the press to Herzl's *Die Welt*. In Kraus's opinion, the men
of *Die Welt* were threatening no less than a religious war; they
were lending respectability to anti-Semitism. Kraus was appalled at
the notion of Jewish solidarity. In his pamphlet he ridiculed Herzl
as a "busybody *schmuck*," the self-proclaimed "historical advocate
of the Jewish people, with eyes strangely twisted toward the East,
agitating for the return of all other Jews to ancestral Palestine." He
mocked the "King of Zion" for planning to hold court in Jerusalem,
inspecting parades of phony neo-Jewish heroes, and distributing
badges of nobility among his foolish associates. In Kraus's view
there was no Jewish problem in the West. In the East there was

only poverty and ignorance, and a detestable tendency among Jews to cling to primitive tradition. It would be simpler, in his opinion, to civilize all Europe than to re-create a Jewish nation; mankind would be liberated even before the beginning of Herzl's exodus. Try as he might, Herzl would never lead the Jews back to Palestine. "It is hardly conceivable that this time the Jews will enter the promised land dry-shod. Another Red Sea—socialism—will block their way."

Kraus's attack on Herzl was not among the best examples of his wit. The posthumous editors of Kraus's work—to this day he remains very influential in German letters—wisely ignored it. But within the history of *fin de siècle* Vienna, it is a significant document. Its viciousness and unfairness must have driven Herzl to fits of anger and disgust. He revealed his feelings only in occasional asides to his diary. Outwardly he remained entirely unruffled.

2

He searched for ways out of the impasse. Despite the Jerusalem fiasco, he still hoped and planned for a link with Germany. Through Eulenburg and the Grand Duke of Baden he tried to reestablish contact with the Kaiser. The Kaiser refused to see him. Eulenburg and the Grand Duke remained sympathetic to Herzl's cause, but they could no longer help him. Both men informed Herzl that an important handicap was the Kaiser's "unpleasant impression" of the Jerusalem Jews. In March 1899 Herzl returned to Karlsruhe and had a long, very friendly interview with the Grand Duke. He asked the Grand Duke to assume the protectorate himself, in place of his nephew. This would have the advantage of being less conspicuous, without the smoke and fire of a formal commitment by the Emperor himself. The Grand Duke expressed his willingness but said he could do nothing without specific authorization from Berlin.

Even where the Grand Duke was able to act personally on Herzl's behalf, it turned out that Herzl had overrated his influence. The powerful *Deutsche Bank* ignored the Grand Duke's letter of recommendation and refused to act as receiving agent for down payments on shares of the Jewish Colonial Bank.

There was still no single reputable bank willing to act as receiving agent. All Jewish-owned banking firms seemed to be boycotting the Zionists. Everywhere he turned, Herzl was blocked.

Having failed with the Kaiser and the Czar, he turned his attention once more to the Sultan of Turkey. In order to keep his movement alive, he had to show something—somehow, somewhere—before the next congress convened in August.

In mid-March Herzl decided to dispatch Nevlinski, who had been bedridden the past few months, to Constantinople. A bad heart condition, which Nevlinski had had for fourteen years, suddenly became much worse, but he was ready, even eager, to go. There was something almost suicidal in this eagerness which Herzl did not perceive at the moment.

He was careful, however, to consult Nevlinski's doctor, who said it made no difference where Nevlinski was; he could have an attack at any moment, in bed or on the train. Since Nevlinski himself was so anxious to go, the doctor consented to the journey. Herzl discussed the matter quite frankly with Nevlinski's wife. She also tended to comply with her husband's wishes. Nevertheless, Herzl was very conscious of "a grave responsibility in allowing Nevlinski to go." He engaged a young Viennese doctor to accompany Nevlinski on the journey, and to be in constant attendance.

Nevlinski and his wife, accompanied by the physician, set out for Turkey on March 30. On April 1 he paid his first visit to Yildiz Kiosk and, as he immediately wrote Herzl, was summoned to call on the Sultan the following day. That evening he had a sudden stroke and died.

The news of Nevlinski's death reached Herzl early the following morning, just as he was awakening. Nevlinski's widow cabled for money, which had to be borrowed by Herzl's Actions Committee, since the Zionist coffers were empty. Herzl tormented himself over the extent of his responsibility in Nevlinski's death. He filled many pages of his diary, alternately reproaching himself for allowing Nevlinski to go and defending his action in having taken all reasonable precaution.

Herzl was extremely upset. He was not only afraid that he would be held responsible for the death of Nevlinski, a senseless victim of an "insane" movement, there was much more. A powerful fascination—almost even love—had bound Herzl to Nevlinski. In Herzl's political life, the Polish adventurer roused his sensibilities and imagination more deeply than any other person, except perhaps the Kaiser. A Cagliostro figure, Nevlinski resided on the borderline between life and letters that was Herzl's natural abode. Now his corpse lay across Herzl's path. Although Herzl never fully trusted him, a curious camaraderie had prevailed between the two. Long ago they had sworn to each other eternal friendship.

With him the saga of the Zionist movement loses one of its most remarkable figures. He was a *grand seigneur déchu* [a fallen aristocrat], likable despite certain questionable qualities, and of a truly charming manner. . . .

He cost me a good deal of money and also drew a subsidy from the committee. To this day I do not know whether he did anything—or even if he was in a position to do anything for us with the Sultan. He never furnished any proof; he only introduced me to various Turkish dignitaries. Perhaps he merely used me, as an editor of the *Neue Freie Presse*, to advance his own interests. He took this secret with him to the grave.

Still, even as regards my shekel-payers, my conscience is clear. Although he could not help us, he certainly might have done us frightful harm. He sometimes hinted as much, and I hastened to make him a friend before he could become an extortionist.

There was a macabre scene at the railway station when Herzl went to meet the widow and the coffin. The atmosphere was almost gay; even Nevlinski's children laughed a great deal. An odd assortment of people—relatives, diplomats, friends of the family, "agents," Austrian politicians, newspapermen, the Turkish chargé d'affaires—were regaled by Nevlinski's lawyer with stories of stag supper parties with *dames nues* and similar orgies in Constantinople. Mme. de Nevlinski tottered down the steps and fell sobbing around Herzl's neck. Later, at home, she was "composed, clearheaded, and covetous." She expected Herzl to take care of her and her children. Herzl reassured her that she would receive her husband's subsidy if she continued to publish the newsletter. Later, a more permanent arrangement could be worked out.

A postmortem examination showed that even had he remained in Vienna, Nevlinski could hardly have survived for more than a few weeks. For the first time it dawned on Herzl that the doomed man might have gone on the journey wryly calculating that his death would place the Zionists under perpetual obligation to his survivors. "He sold us his corpse, as it were. Surely nothing as strange as this occurs in novels."

The suspicion evoked more tenderness in his heart for the dead

man's soul. What a splendid exit for a man who, in his lifetime, had
gone on "artistic *tournées*" in diplomacy! Herzl admired Nevlinski's
courage; his manner of dying proved his tender love for his children. "He looms head and shoulders above all this riffraff," Herzl
wrote. "To get mixed up with this rotten bunch was the tragic
blunder of his life."

A few days later Nevlinski's mystery was unraveled further.
His newsletter, *Correspondance de l'Est*, through which he had
pretended to wield power in diplomatic circles, turned out to be a
swindle. When Herzl checked the account books he discovered that
the newsletter had only a dozen subscribers, of whom Herzl was
one. Still Herzl somehow felt in Nevlinski's debt. "His greatest
service was to teach me not to have any respect for pashas."

3

At this time there occurred an event that, in retrospect, is of
particular interest. Its impact on Herzl at the time is not clear, but
in view of subsequent events, the chronicler of his life cannot omit
it. Early in March a distinguished Palestinian Arab was aroused
enough by Herzl's movement to protest its feasibility from the
point of view of the indigenous Arab population of Palestine. Yus-
sef Ziah el-Khaldi, a former mayor of Jerusalem, was living in
Constantinople as a deputy representing Jerusalem in the Ottoman
parliament. On March 1, 1899, he wrote a long letter to a Jewish
acquaintance, Zadok Kahn, the Chief Rabbi of Paris, whom el-
Khaldi associated with Herzl's movement. Kahn decided that Herzl
should answer el-Khaldi directly and passed the letter along to
him.

El-Khaldi was the scion of an old aristocratic Arab family,
prominent in Jerusalem for many centuries. He was a man of mature judgment, liberal and tolerant. In his letter to Rabbi Kahn he
readily acknowledged the "beauty and justice" of the Zionist idea.

> Who could deny the rights of the Jews to Palestine? *Mon Dieu*,
> historically it is certainly your country. And what a marvelous
> spectacle if the Jews were reconstituted once more as an inde-
> pendent nation, happy and respected . . . as in days gone by.
> But unfortunately the destiny of nations is governed not only by
> abstract concepts, however pure and noble they might be. One
> must consider reality and respect established facts, the force,

yes, the *brutal* force, of circumstance. The reality is that Palestine is now an integral part of the Ottoman Empire and what is more serious, it is inhabited by others than Israelites.

El-Khaldi went on to say that Turks and Arabs were now the guardians of the Holy Places and would never relinquish them to the Jews. He warned Kahn that Palestine could not be bought; the realization of Zionism in Palestine required "more formidable means than money, [it would mean] cannons and cuirasses." Who would give such power to Herzl—the Russians, Wilhelm, France?

It is therefore pure folly on the part of Dr. Herzl, whom I greatly esteem as a man, as a writer of talent, and as a truly patriotic Jew, to imagine that even with the consent of the Sultan he shall one day obtain Palestine.

Zionism, in its present *geographical* sense, must therefore cease. Let them find a country elsewhere for the unfortunate Jewish nation. [There is] nothing more just and equitable. *Mon Dieu*, the earth is big enough, there are still uninhabited parts. ... But in God's name, let Palestine be left alone.

We have seen earlier that Herzl had tended so far to ignore the presence of a sizable Arab population in Palestine. He had told Hohenlohe they were a "mixed multitude," and on his recent expedition to Palestine he had scarcely given them a thought. On one occasion, his traveling companion Seidener had drawn his attention to some Arab villagers who in past years had resisted the Jewish colonists with violence. This had merely strengthened Herzl in his opposition to small-scale infiltration without a political charter. He believed that with a charter all local difficulties could be removed. Zionism would triumph as a bloodless crusade, so to speak; the natives would gratefully welcome the wealth it would bring them.

Herzl answered el-Khaldi to this effect on March 19. The exchange can be seen as the first of many futile contacts between leaders of the two camps that were destined to be locked in war for most of the ensuing century.

Herzl assured el-Khaldi that his fears were groundless; there was no question whatsoever of using force. "As you yourself said, there is no military power behind the Jews. As a people they have long lost the taste for war, they are a thoroughly pacific element, and fully content if left in peace. Therefore there is absolutely no

reason to fear their immigration." Nor did the Holy Places present
a problem. They would not be touched; the Holy Places must not
be the exclusive possession of any religion.

> You see another difficulty in the existence of a non-Jewish popu-
> lation in Palestine. But who wishes to remove them from there?
> Their well-being and individual wealth will increase through
> the importation of ours. Do you believe that an Arab who owns
> land in Palestine, or a house worth three or four thousand
> francs, will be sorry to see their value rise five- and tenfold? But
> this would most certainly happen with the coming of the Jews.
> And this is what one must bring the natives to comprehend . . .
> if one looks at the matter from this viewpoint, and it is the right
> viewpoint, one inevitably becomes a friend of Zionism. . . . You
> tell M. Zadok Kahn that the Jews would do well to turn else-
> where. This may well happen on the day we conclude that
> Turkey refuses to see the tremendous advantages offered her by
> our movement. [In that case] we will search for—and believe
> me, we shall find—what we need in another place.

For Herzl the Zionist idea was also "a colonial idea"; he said as
much in a speech in London a few weeks later. His letter to el-
Khaldi must be seen in the context of the time. The turn of the
century was the heydey of the Age of Colonialism and Herzl fully
shared in its pious hopes and pious delusions. By returning to Palestine, the Jews were assuming a burden not merely for their own
welfare, but in Herzl's words, "for the wretched and poor" of all
mankind.

4

Criticism of his German adventure came to a climax at the
third Zionist congress at Basel in August. Herzl defended himself
inadequately. In his opening speech he asked the delegates not to
debate the Jerusalem audience for "propriety's sake." The past year
had not been a bad one for the movement, he said; "it has been a
good year . . . the fact alone that that genius, the Kaiser, has turned
his attention to our national idea should suffice to give us some
confidence. Insignificant movements are never noticed from such
heights . . . the German Kaiser assured us of his benevolent
interest."

Herzl's vagueness did not enhance credibility or silence his detractors. But he kept the promise of secrecy he had given the Germans, for he still hoped to deal with them. The critics were not numerous, but for the first time their language was robust, sharp, and sometimes violent. The organized opposition proved the vitality of the parliamentary mood Herzl himself had instilled, and which at the first congress he had regarded as his major achievement. He did not think so now. Herzl was alternately "bored" and "angered" by the attacks, as he sat most of the time stone-faced and stiff in his chair.

He was taunted for his rash prediction, one year before, that the exodus would soon begin. His caustic reply that in the future he might suppress all good news was not calculated to restore the calm he desired. His authoritarian manner and failure to consult the international executive also came under attack. The mounting pressure forced him to present a more detailed statement on the finances of the movement, rather than informing the congress of the total receipts against expenditures as he had planned.* Herzl was also severely criticized for having assigned founder shares of the bank to certain members of the executive. The bank's 100 founder shares bore no dividends, but controlled as many votes as the remaining 1,999,900 shares, which, after all, anybody might buy. This was done to protect the bank against a possible take-over by opponents of the movement. Herzl's critics understood the need for founder shares, but protested Herzl's assigning them without consulting the congress. Herzl was angered by the insinuations and suspicions; he threatened a showdown by offering his resignation, whereupon the opposition faltered and he finally prevailed.

The incident showed that despite a widening mood of opposition, Herzl had not lost his hold on the movement. In fact, his control had grown stronger in the past year. The number of Zionist societies had risen from 913 to some 1,300; in Russia alone, membership had increased by nearly one-third, and elsewhere there was a 25 percent increase. Although Herzl had again arrived empty-handed before a congress that expected a concrete achievement, he remained irreplaceable. Even his critics, in the final hours, joined in the tumultuous applause that greeted his reelection, and the third congress closed on a note of ecstasy reminiscent of the first and second. Amid thunderous hurrahs, roared in a dozen languages, Herzl was acclaimed: "Next year in Jerusalem!" Herzl stood mo-

* The official budget had risen in the past year from 63,000 to 158,000 francs. The lists of political expenditures omitted names in order to protect Herzl's various "agents" and recipients of bribes in Turkey.

tionless on the dais; the delegates cheered and cheered, but his face remained pale and frozen. The delegates had never seen a man who looked so wistfully at the day.

5

The political outlook seemed to him so cheerless that he contemplated seeking another homeland, one sooner attainable than Palestine. The Ottoman Empire might take another decade to disintegrate or to reach Herzl's point of view, but masses of poor Jews were in need of immediate help. For the time being he had to keep these thoughts to himself, for the mood of most Zionist activists was sentimental and the movement would have broken apart if he had as much as hinted that he was willing to forgo Zion for another territory. Herzl was haunted by the upsurge of anti-Semitic riots in France, Romania, and in nearby Bohemia (two hours by train from Vienna), where a Jewish cobbler named Leopold Hülsner had just been accused of the ritual murder of a Gentile girl and the Austrian prosecutor had been forced by public opinion to put him on trial.*

Early in November Herzl resolved that if by the next congress no progress had been made with the Turks, he would urge, and if necessary, force the congress to accept another country—"any country." He thought of the island of Cyprus. It was close enough to Palestine to appear as a "first step," and was furthermore under the enlightened rule of England, where Zionism was espoused by such leading Conservatives as Lord Salisbury as well as by the established church. Herzl knew how difficult it would be to convince his followers. For instance, at the third congress, Davis Trietsch had aroused a furor by daring to address an informal gathering of delegates on the subject of Cyprus as a "side entrance" to Zion. The Russian delegates had run from the room crying "Shame!" Herzl believed that he might get around the purists by first securing a British commitment and then presenting the congress with a *fait accompli.*

---

* The case won additional notoriety through the courageous defense of Hülsner by Thomas Masaryk, the future President of Czechoslovakia. The jury, intimidated by anti-Semitic rioters, found Hülsner guilty. It was beyond the Emperor's power to set Hülsner free although there was little doubt that Hülsner was innocent. Instead his death sentence was commuted to life imprisonment in 1901, amid the outraged protests of anti-Semites in the parliament and the press. A few years later Hülsner was quietly released.

If he were only free from his daily work, Herzl reflected bitterly, he could travel to England, Karlsruhe, and Constantinople, playing Turkey against England and Germany, or Palestine against Cyprus. "But I am the little clerk of Messrs. Bacher and Benedikt. I must show up at the office every day, even though I don't do much there." Bacher and Benedikt refused to grant him another leave of absence, and he dared not defy them again for fear of endangering his family's livelihood.

The larger part of his inherited capital was spent. Less than half of Julie's dowry remained. *Die Welt* alone had swallowed some fifty thousand gulden, and the bulk of his travel expenses still came out of his own pocket. The thought that he might leave his children penniless tormented him. Accustomed to riches, Julie could not cut down on the household expenses. They continued to grow because the family now occupied an elegant, large villa at Carl Ludwig Strasse 50,* in the so-called Cottage section of Vienna. The children were educated at home by a succession of German governesses and French and Austrian private tutors. The growing expenditures shackled him even more to his position on the *Neue Freie Presse*. He poured forth his bitterness upon his return from the recent congress: "After having been a free man and a great lord at Basel, I must enter the room of Big Boss Bacher like a meek little boy."

In the past his disciples had often asked him to devote himself to the movement on a full-time basis. But the idea of receiving a salary from the Zionists was anathema to this proud, self-reliant man.

To recover his losses—and in the hope of regaining a measure of economic freedom—he briefly returned to his theater work. This included some frivolous assignments that made him loathe himself. He even dug up an old farce he had written in 1885 as a law clerk in Salzburg, and rewrote it for the popular Viennese comedian Girardi. In the latter half of 1899 he was at work on at least three new plays and on two novels. His literary work helped him at least to fight his depression. On the train, traveling to the third congress, he noted in his diary: "Even more than my still unfinished congress speech, and the princes and my slave drivers at the *Neue Freie Presse*, what preoccupies me these days is the plan of my new play *Die sündige Mutter* (*The Sinful Mother*), which delights me in my thoughts." The new plays differed little from his old bedroom

* Today the embassy of the People's Republic of China.

comedies; they were duly produced, but rather than bringing in riches or much fame, they tended to compound his difficulties.* Many Zionists considered these superficial farces as beneath the dignity of the recognized leader of a Jewish renaissance, and anti-Zionists regarded them as proof of Herzl's shallowness and mediocrity.

Herzl was convinced that the bad critical reception of his plays was caused by his Zionist activity. "Zionism is costing me money and should not yield me any," he mused on November 8. "On the other hand [through Zionism] I have done myself great harm as a 'German author.'" On January 13, 1900, after his latest play, I Love You, had been assailed by the reviewers, he wrote Hermann Bahr, one of the few who had come to his defense: "I am being persecuted so hatefully in the theater for my political 'fallacy' that when I am treated kindly for a change, as I am treated by you, I feel I am dreaming." Despite the reviews, some of his comedies played to full houses and went on extended tours in the provinces. But Herzl eventually tired of the effort. Before the year was out he wrote Nordau: "I daresay I shall never again write for the theater. There one is helplessly exposed to gangsters—I am thoroughly hated."

Meanwhile he did not neglect his cause. Just as he had tenaciously marched from one producer to another as a struggling playwright, so he pursued every possibility that offered itself in the diplomatic field. He made further attempts to reach the Czar, all of which failed because the Russians continued to regard Zionism as part of the dangerous social revolutionary movement. The Russian police inhibited the sale of bank shares, and for a time the subscriptions, higher in Russia than in all other countries combined, had to continue clandestinely.

Nevlinski's death only briefly severed Herzl's line of communication with Constantinople. Within weeks he was in touch with several high-ranking Turks. Among them were his old acquaintance Nuri Bey, the avaricious Secretary-General of the Turkish Foreign Ministry, and Tahsin Bey and Izzet Bey, the Sultan's first and second secretaries.

He had to spend more money on bribes than before. There was nothing unusual about this in Turkey, where bribery was the rule and most European governments resorted to it to facilitate

---

* A friendly critic, Rudolf Lothar, wrote in Die Wage (1900): "For many years now he has tried to establish himself on the stage. He never succeeds. His plays are interesting; his dialogue and talent are praised, but they lack the dramatic power which alone guarantees success."

their dealings with the *Sublime Porte*. Even the Sultan regarded
bribery as less than odious, since he did not pay his ministers
regular salaries. Izzet Bey, the Sultan's most trusted adviser, had
amassed a fortune in Swiss bank vaults as a result of engineering
the Turkish-German alliance.

In his dealings with corrupt Turkish statesmen and a medley
of shady Levantine agents, Herzl was hardly at his best. Nuri Bey
visited him in June; he made things easier for Herzl by being
perfectly straightforward, even cynical.

"There are people who want to make money," he said. "I will
organize a syndicate for you that will do the job at Yildiz. To put it
simply, this man must get so much, and that one must get so
much." He gave Herzl a list of eleven names, which included the
Grand Vizier, two ministers, and an assortment of imperial chamberlains and favorites. In Nuri's words, it was all a question of
paying money to the right people.

Nuri Bey made other outlandish propositions. Would the Zionists be interested in acquiring real estate in Constantinople on a
mortgage basis? Within a few years they could own all of Constantinople. He offered to sell Herzl the entire "public opinion" of
Turkey for a mere three or four hundred thousand francs.

Herzl quickly reiterated that he was interested only in a chartered company for the settlement of Palestine, under the Sultan's
sovereignty. As a first step he must talk with the Sultan; he offered
to pay Nuri twenty thousand francs on the day he was received by
the Sultan to present the Zionist plan to him. This of course would
be only an advance; the actual granting of the charter would bring
Nuri considerably more.

In Nuri's opinion twenty thousand francs was not enough.
"Any banker would give me twice that in return for an audience
with the Sultan," he said.

"Don't let it worry you," Herzl replied drily. "You shall have
your forty thousand."

The Turkish statesman suggested they communicate further
through a middleman, one Eduard Crespi, who was his special
agent for all matters too delicate for Nuri Bey to acknowledge
officially. It meant paying Crespi another "ten, fifteen, or twenty
thousand francs" to work up a favorable attitude at court. "I am
speaking to you as a friend, and I tell you, you must sow before you
can reap."

Herzl responded quite firmly: "I shall give you ten thousand francs in advance and thirty thousand on the day of the audience. How you spend the money is your business. I shan't ask you what you do with it."

"Agreed," Nuri said. "I will have to add to it from my own pocket, but the gamble is worth it. I think I can make a couple of million on you. For that I'll risk a little." He boasted some more of what he could do, and Herzl pretended to believe him. "I am now going up to Semmering," Nuri said. "Have the ten thousand francs ready. But it must be paid to me in cash, without witnesses or receipts."

"I will send you the money through my advocate," said Herzl, who had no intention of paying Nuri without a receipt. Since there was little money in the Zionist till, the ten thousand francs was raised through a private loan against future shekel revenue. The Turkish statesman gave a written receipt after all: "Received the sum of ten thousand francs which was due me—Nuri."

Herzl eagerly awaited the results. On August 31 he wrote to de Haas that "big things are in the works." A few days later, in anticipation of his audience with the Sultan, he asked Bodenheimer to prepare the draft of a Turkish charter based on the charter Cecil Rhodes had written for Africa. Herzl was ready to risk the journey although he did not put it beyond Nuri Bey to have him beaten up or killed by some hired assassin once he set foot on Turkish soil.

There was no word from Nuri. Having cashed in his sizable advance, the Turkish statesman took his time. "His Excellency Eduard Crespi," Nuri's agent, titillated Herzl with vain promises; he alerted Herzl to be ready to leave for Constantinople immediately, and then he let weeks pass without any definite summons. Weeks became months, and early in 1900 Herzl began to suspect that the whole thing was a fraud.

The impasse continued into the new year. Surprisingly, Herzl's position on the *Neue Freie Presse* improved. After Herzl made a futile attempt to break out of his subservient position by offering to buy Bacher's share in the newspaper, the publishers consented to a very considerable increase in Herzl's salary.

In February 1900 he struck up a rather intimate relationship with Ernest von Koerber, the new Austro-Hungarian Prime Minister. It began when Koerber, as a personal favor to an editor of the powerful *Neue Freie Presse*, intervened with the Austrian treasury to lift its ban on the sale of shares in the Jewish Colonial Bank. The reasons for banning the bank in Austria-Hungary were largely technical, but the blow to Herzl's cause was not inconsiderable. On a bleak February morning he poured his heart out to the Prime Minister, who promised Herzl that in this case the authorities would "look the other way."

"I admire the tenacity with which you have been pursuing this work for years," Koerber said.

"It is really the most beautiful task a man could set himself in life," Herzl answered, "although I know that people laugh at me."

"Yes, I know that too," Koerber smiled.

"But I pay little attention," Herzl added.

From then on Koerber often asked Herzl to his office to discuss Austrian politics or to deplore the *Presse*'s unfriendly attitude to his regime. Koerber's endless tales of woe, intoned in the folksy Viennese dialect, his weary acceptance of the general turmoil in Austrian affairs and the incompetence of government were a good index of the rapid decline of the Austro-Hungarian Empire. There was little this friendship could do for Herzl's cause, and Herzl asked nothing of Koerber, except an occasional word in his behalf with the Sultan.

6

From Constantinople there were still only vague promises. To Nordau, who wondered at his listlessness, Herzl wrote on March 6: "No, I wasn't sick. But I am greatly troubled for our cause. *We need success like a bite of bread.*"

His troubles mounted. The Rabbi of Gur, powerful head of a Hassidic sect with a fanatic mass following throughout Eastern Europe, attacked Herzl and his followers as a band of "criminals in a conspiracy of evil," for they were presuming to force the hand of the Lord. The difficulties over the Jewish Colonial Bank still seemed almost insurmountable. Nordau and Wolffsohn had just made one more unsuccessful contact with Edmond de Rothschild. The Baron's opposition to Herzl had softened somewhat since their disastrous meeting four years earlier. But Rothschild was still unwilling to step in, although he was ready to promise "on his honor" that once their bank was set up he would sell them his Palestinian colonies at a "bargain price." Nordau, furious at this gibe, threatened the Baron with "all-out war" unless he agreed to collaborate immediately with the Zionists.

"Herr Doktor," said Rothschild, rising to leave, "the House of Rothschild, thank God, does not yet have to fear Zionism for its existence."

More than 100,000 individual subscribers had signed up, mostly small shareholders in Eastern Europe, but according to the bank's own regulations, it could not begin to function before the accumulation of a paid-up capital of 250,000 pounds. That minimum had not yet been reached. Sharp disputes developed over the management of the bank, and in his impatience, Herzl accused the directors of slovenliness and ineptitude. Eager to see results, Herzl overstepped his authority as chairman of the board by issuing orders without consulting the other governors of the bank. They protested Herzl's high-handed measures; even the faithful Wolffsohn rebelled and boycotted a board meeting Herzl had convened in London for April 25.

Herzl went to England on April 21, traveling by way of Karlsruhe, where the Grand Duke of Baden again reassured him of his personal support but regretted that Germany was unable to act until its sea power was on a par with the British navy. England was at war with the Boers, and Herzl heard talk of little else. He spent a happy weekend in the country with Alfred Austin, the poet laureate, to whom he had been recommended by Nordau. They talked mostly of the war, which the conservative Austin supported with all the supreme confidence of a self-confessed jingo. A frail old man of small stature—his wife towered over him—with a fierce moustache, Austin talked endlessly of England's might and grandeur. An armchair strategist, the poet's idea of heaven was "to sit in a garden and receive a flow of telegrams announcing alternately a British victory by sea and a British victory by land." Austin readily volunteered to recommend Herzl to Lord Salisbury, the Prime Minister, but Salisbury proved too busy with the war to see Herzl immediately. Herzl spent perhaps the most pleasurable hours of the past few years in Austin's company. He forgot his cause long enough to admire the English gentry; he had become even more enamored of it than of the Prussian aristocracy: "How well I understand them, the assimilated Jews of England! If I lived in England I might also be a *jingo!*"

The main purpose of his English visit, however, was the bank. Its skeleton staff responded wearily to his orders to speed up the procedures. But as a result of his unconstitutional zeal, board member Jacobus Kann of The Hague sent in his resignation, and even Wolffsohn threatened to quit. Wolffsohn felt that Herzl's high-handedness might frighten away all but the most servile and unimaginative on the bank staff. In Wolffsohn's opinion Herzl had little experience in business and none at all in banking, and could endanger the whole project through his meddling.

To Herzl, Wolffsohn's criticism was a terrific blow. He accused the loyal Wolffsohn of looking for an excuse to withdraw from Zionism altogether. "If you have arrived at this stage, you don't have to search for excuses," he wrote Wolffsohn on May 5. "Just say frankly: 'I have had enough.' "

For once Herzl's most steadfast and obedient lieutenant firmly stood his own ground. A furious correspondence ensued. Herzl gradually calmed down and grudgingly gave in to Wolffsohn's patient admonitions that he show more confidence in his colleagues. On June 18 Wolffsohn visited Herzl in Vienna and the quarrel flared up again. The following morning, as he sat at his desk at the offices of *Die Welt*, overwrought by anguish and excitement, Herzl had a sudden attack of dizziness, which was diagnosed by the doctor as "brain anemia." While he was talking to an assistant, he blacked out for a few moments. He went directly home. The doctor ordered complete rest for two or three days, but the next morning Herzl was up again to resume negotiations with Wolffsohn. Whether it was because of his recent illness, or because by now he had had enough of banking, Herzl agreed to stay out of the daily management of the bank and to allow Wolffsohn and Kann a free hand.

Other concerns soon diverted his attention. A fourth congress was scheduled for August. Would he have to face it empty-handed once more? It had been decided to hold the congress in London. "I am taking my show to London, for I have reason to fear that I shall no longer find an audience in Basel," Herzl noted sarcastically. On Whitmonday, 1900, he gloomily recorded the fifth anniversary of his visit to Baron Hirsch. Five years and still nothing concrete achieved: "This is how a lost battle looks."

He was seized by further premonitions of approaching death. The incessant exertions, his despair, and the failing state of his health were physically telling on the forty-year-old. His black beard was streaked with premature white, and under the pale forehead, lined as though by scars, his eyes seemed to have sunk deep into their sockets. His swinging step was gone; he had a slight stoop now. His home life gave him little solace, except for his children, whom, however, he could enjoy only briefly each evening. In May 1900 he revised his will, appointing his parents as his sole heirs, and his children after them. Julie was completely left out; she was to receive the share prescribed by Austrian law for widows only if she was otherwise without any means of sustenance.

From Nuri Bey there were still only evasive promises. Nuri and his agent, Crespi, had extracted nearly fifteen thousand francs in advance payments. Herzl dared not interrupt the flow, for fear of the damage Nuri might do him in revenge. But realizing that he was being defrauded, he made haste to approach the Sultan through a different route.

7

Herzl's gallery of colorful middlemen, which included Nuri, Nevlinski, and Hechler, now gained a new figure, even more colorful but, for a change, considerably more effective. He was Arminius Vámbéry (1832–1913), a world-renowned explorer, anthropologist, linguist, adventurer, personal friend of the Sultan, Turkish agent, and former English spy. Like Herzl, he was a Hungarian-born Jew. He had since professed four other religions, two of them as an ordained priest; with such intimate knowledge of several faiths, it was hardly surprising that by the time Herzl met him he had become an atheist. He had begun his astonishing career in 1856 as a singer in a Constantinople café. Within a year he had advanced to the position of French tutor to the ladies of the Sultan's harem and intimate adviser to the Grand Vizier. He first befriended the present Sultan when he was a sixteen-year-old prince. In 1861, on behalf of the Hungarian Academy of Science, he traversed Central Asia, the ancient homeland of the Hungarians, disguised as a dervish; after sundry adventures in Persia, Bokhara, Turkestan, and Samarkand, he returned to Europe to become consultant in turn to Sultan Abdul-Hamid, Queen Victoria, Disraeli, Lord Palmerston, and finally King Edward. A superb storyteller, his reputation among European royalty was that of a male Scheherazade, and his voluminous *Travels in Central Asia* was considered a classic of its kind. He spoke twelve languages fluently, and although he was no longer sure whether he was more Turk than Englishman, he definitely considered himself a German writer. Now nearly seventy, he was professor of Oriental languages at the University of Budapest.

Herzl went to see Vámbéry on June 17, after Nordau arranged the introduction. Vámbéry was at Mühlbach, a resort town in the Tirolean Alps, nursing one of the ailments he had contracted in the

East. When Herzl met him the explorer was dressed in a mixture of European and Turkish clothes and sat smoking a nargileh. He received Herzl most graciously, and the two men achieved instant rapport. They spoke of their youth in Budapest and exchanged notes on their subsequent adventures. Vámbéry took Herzl into his confidence and confessed that his professorship at Budapest was merely window dressing. "I am no *wanz-melamed*"* he said, and swearing Herzl to secrecy, he admitted that he was still a secret agent for both England and Turkey. He spoke alternately English and German, with a heavy sprinkling of Hungarian and Yiddish expressions. His table was full of books and "secret documents," which Herzl could only admire but not read, since they were written in Turkish. He told Herzl he had just begun to write his memoirs.

Herzl asked for his help. Vámbéry accepted his cause not so much because he believed in Zionism but for the sake of Herzl, whom he recognized somehow as a kindred spirit.

"I want no money," he declaimed. "I am a rich man. I cannot eat gold beefsteak. I've made a quarter of a million and I cannot spend half the interest I receive. If I help you, it is for your cause."

Herzl told Vámbéry he believed that he might be able to convert the Sultan to Zionism through a personal audience. Vámbéry knew the Sultan better and doubted this very much; the Sultan was a *"mamser ben-nide"*** and a madman. Whatever the outcome, Herzl protested, an audience would be useful in itself, as a first step, especially if it came *before* the next congress. There was always time to discuss details later; all he wanted now was an audience before the congress in order to maintain the momentum of the cause. He became very emotional.

"Vámbéry *bacsi*,"† he pleaded, "please write and ask the Sultan to receive me. Tell him I can render him a service in the world press, and that the mere fact of my appearance will raise his credit with others. I should like it best if you would come along as interpreter," he added.

Vámbéry shook his head; at his age he was afraid of the difficulties in traveling to Turkey in the summer. He asked Herzl for time to think it over. As Herzl took leave they kissed and embraced like old friends. From Vienna the next morning Herzl wrote Vámbéry: "I understand what you would like to achieve with your

* "Imbecile-scholar" (Yiddish).
** "Foully conceived bastard" (Hebrew-Yiddish).
† "Uncle" (Hungarian).

autobiography. Build yourself a royal sepulchre. Crown your pyramid with the chapter, 'How I helped prepare the return of my people, the Jews.' Your whole remarkable life will appear as though it had been planned for just that."

Vámbéry replied, "You are an incorrigible *giaour* [infidel] who rushes uphill and down without heed for Turkish ditches." The Turks could not be rushed, he added. Still, Vámbéry had written to the Sultan, but he was not certain that the letter would actually reach his hands. "Telegrams and letters are futile at a place where the spoken word is quickly forgotten and where one deals with one of the world's arch liars, the very personification of distrust!"

Vámbéry asked Herzl to be patient. His efforts were to bear fruit, but not as quickly as Herzl hoped.

8

Before proceeding to London for the fourth congress, Herzl joined his wife and children at Aussee for a brief rest. On July 11 he had another sudden seizure of brain anemia and blacked out. A bit ironically, he wrote Kellner: "Thus the Jewish people is losing— or has already lost—one of the finest energies it had at its disposal." He and Julie got on no better than usual, so the vacation at Aussee gave him little rest. "The two weeks I spent here at first soothed, but then pained my nerves," he wrote his lawyer (Julie's cousin), "for everything remains as before."

Herzl arrived in London a week ahead of the date set for the opening of the congress. During the channel crossing he felt unwell, and at Dover he dragged himself ashore with some difficulty. In London he was stricken by severe chills and high fever, and his whole body shook violently. At first it appeared that he might not be able to attend the congress. He asked that his illness be concealed from his family and demanded to be treated only by a Vienna-trained doctor who was also a Zionist.

Jacob de Haas rushed out into the night and managed to find a physician who filled the requirements. Two nurses hovered over Herzl night and day. In the delirium caused by the high fever, "the most colorful hallucinations" (he remembered later) danced before his hot and tired eyes. On August 13 he recovered sufficiently to deliver his inaugural address, but his knees were still shaking from weakness.

It was the largest congress ever, and the best organized as well. Four hundred delegates, almost half from small towns in the Russian Pale of Settlement, "floundered in the maze of a city whose vastness in turn amazed and humbled them," de Haas recorded. The international and the English press were present in force. Herzl was pleased by this, for the main purpose of the fourth congress was to stage a demonstration and solicit England's support for the movement. "England, great England, England the free, England commanding all the seas—she will understand us and our purpose," Herzl said, to applause, in his opening speech. Otherwise his remarks offered no new thoughts; he was beginning, inevitably, to repeat himself. But not Nordau, whose annual summation of woe, suffering, and persecution drew more attention than usual. This had been the worst year since the beginning of the movement; anti-Semitism was spreading on the continent like a forest fire, from the ritual murder trial and riots of Polna to the ruthless expulsion of Jews from Romania. "But this is only the beginning," Nordau warned, not knowing how right he was. "It will get worse, much worse."

The opposition demanded more concrete remedies and chastised the deliberate vagueness of Herzl's political report. But the fervor of the critics had been spent in the year before; the fourth congress was the calmest thus far. The ovations were as big as always: Herzl was smothered under royal honors, he was handed children to kiss, and he was introduced to the ladies. More important, Herzl lunched with Eric Barrington, Lord Salisbury's private secretary, and talked himself hoarse in an effort to win Barrington's interest. As the next two years would show, he was not unsuccessful.

He rejoined his family at Aussee to recover from the lingering aftereffects of his illness. But some symptoms continued to bother him for the rest of the year, and it is not clear from the record when or whether he ever fully recovered. He continued to feel faint and generally weary, and he looked ten or fifteen years older than his age. But he was no sooner back in Vienna than he prepared to travel to Budapest on September 16, for another session with Vámbéry.

The city of his youth cast a melancholy spell. Herzl walked the familiar streets of Pest to Vámbéry's home. He was treated to more of the explorer's reminiscences of Asia, but nothing else. Vámbéry swore that the Sultan would definitely receive Herzl by the following May. Herzl had heard too many promises to take this one seriously. However, he was a weary man and had no alternative but to assure Vámbéry of his gratitude.

In this mood he resumed his regular work on the newspaper. During the next few months he produced a series of sad, incisive journalistic vignettes on Viennese life and manners, marked by an almost baroque infatuation with the "aesthetics" of death and decay. The man whose great goal was to initiate a national rebirth wrote about funerals, cemeteries, and men struck by fatal disease. When not running his movement, he was required to write witty comments on some fashion show or the skill of Japanese trapeze artists. He was leader and clown at the same time. He could also be suave and gallant.

"What would be the use of a Jewish state?" a charming young lady asked him at a party.

"The glamour of your company in Jerusalem," said Herzl, "would increase our enjoyment of life considerably."

On October 15 Nuri Bey suddenly contacted him to announce that the Turkish government had "a pressing need for seven or eight hundred thousand Turkish pounds." If Herzl could arrange an immediate loan at 6 percent, or 6.5 percent per annum, he would receive his audience with the Sultan as a reward. The Turkish Consul General visited Herzl to confirm the offer. Herzl immediately obtained a binding letter of intent from Jacobus Kann's Dutch banking firm. A protracted correspondence ensued during which Nuri Bey attempted both to increase the amount of the loan and to lower the interest.

Undoubtedly Herzl's offer was used by the Turks as a lever to extract better terms from other possible creditors and as a source of personal income for rapacious diplomats. Nuri's agent, Crespi, came to Vienna to negotiate. He had to be paid one thousand francs for his trouble, but willingly signed a receipt. Crespi did not know how difficult it had been for Herzl's aides to raise even this relatively small sum. In his diary Herzl described the empty Zionist coffers as one of "the curiosities of this episode," since he and Crespi spoke so grandly of the millions and millions the Zionists might be able to offer the Sultan. Crespi, who was accompanied by the Turkish Consul General, was a lean, black-bearded Levantine, slightly brash and rather loud in his dress; his face was emaciated and sallow. But he was forthcoming, and he didn't make a bad impression on Herzl. Crespi knew of Vámbéry's intervention with the Sultan, which he said had done Herzl an enormous amount of good. Crespi assured Herzl he was ready henceforth to be his faithful servant, provided he was paid a monthly salary.

But nothing came of these negotiations, for while Crespi was still in Vienna, the Turkish government concluded the loan with the *Deutsche Bank*. Although the bank had offered terms less beneficial than Herzl's, it had apparently been more lavish in its distribution of *baksheesh*. Crespi pretended to be shocked by this development; he promised Herzl he would cable the Grand Vizier. The Consul General whispered in Herzl's ear that he would make sure Crespi really sent the cable. And here the matter rested.

Herzl promptly traveled to Budapest to consult Vámbéry on these developments. At their first meeting in Mühlbach Vámbéry had proudly announced that if he helped Herzl it would not be for money. It now transpired that he expected a commission of five thousand pounds. "Only fools and knaves work for nothing," Vámbéry said. Herzl answered that he had always meant to pay him adequately, and added, "I am actually looking for an opportunity to give you pleasure."

Vámbéry again wrote to Constantinople. The only response was an announcement that Turkey opposed the re-creation of the Kingdom of Judea; henceforth Jews would no longer be permitted to enter Palestine. Herzl took this as a good sign. He wrote Vámbéry on December 28. "The whore wants to raise her price, so she says she cannot be had. Am I right?"

Vámbéry thoroughly agreed with him. He had been to Constantinople meanwhile to meet his friend the Sultan. From Constantinople he wrote Herzl that the Sultan had expressed himself on the question of Jewish immigration to Palestine quite differently from the official announcement. "He does not give a hoot. All he wants is gold and power."

However, despite Vámbéry's urging, the Sultan was not yet ready to meet Herzl. Four months passed in an agony of suspense and false hopes. On May 2, 1901, Herzl's forty-first birthday, he noted in his diary,

> The wind blows through the stubble,
> I must my pace redouble . . .
>   It is almost six years since I started this movement which has made me old, tired, and poor.

The six years seemed like sixty. Early in May Vámbéry made another trip to Constantinople to press Herzl's case. For two long weeks Herzl waited impatiently. Finally, as Vámbéry had correctly predicted, the Sultan yielded.

9

Herzl went to meet Vámbéry at the Budapest railroad station to receive the good news in person. The Orient Express from Constantinople was late. Flustered, Herzl paced the platform puffing one cigar after another. It was long past midnight when the old man finally stepped off his train emitting a volley of complaints, oaths, and recriminations. No porters were at hand, so Herzl carried his luggage to the waiting carriage. They drove through the darkened streets to Vámbéry's house. Vámbéry heaped abuse upon the lunatic Sultan, who had detained him for almost two weeks and had made him come back six times before granting his request.

"The fellow is completely crazy and a robber. But he will receive you! Not as a Zionist but as *Chief of the Jews!* And as an influential journalist. You must not speak to him about Zionism. That is phantasmagoria. Jerusalem is as sacred for them as Mecca. And yet they don't mind seeing a good side to Zionism as well—as a weapon against the Christians.

"I want Zionism to continue to exist," Vámbéry added. "That's why I got you this audience. Otherwise you couldn't have faced your congress. I want you to gain time, and keep Zionism alive somehow."

At Vámbéry's door the two men kissed and embraced several times. Vámbéry's achievement fell short of complete success, but Herzl was more than satisfied. "If [the Sultan] should want to sell me Palestine right now, I would be extremely embarrassed. After all, I must first raise the money."

Plotting a dozen new schemes to raise the money somewhere, somehow, and to whet the Sultan's appetite, he drove to his hotel through the darkened streets of Pest, past his parents' old home on the Tabakgasse and the haunts of his youth. It had never appeared so distant. He slept only two hours, and at 5:00 A.M. he was up and planning the next step. He cabled Wolffsohn to join him immediately for the journey east, and headed back to Vienna to pack his bags. He consulted his colleagues on the Executive Committee, a stream of letters went out to his far-flung lieutenants, and an elaborate code was devised for secret communication. To spare himself the nervous strain of another clash with his employers, he informed them of his departure by letter. He strongly suspected, however, that this escapade would cause his prompt dismissal.

He was feeling too tired and faint to think much about the audience, for which he had waited so long, but like a man possessed, in "a complete daze," almost in a "stupor," he flung himself into this new adventure. Within forty-eight hours he boarded the train for Constantinople; his companions, Wolffsohn and Marmorek, carried the requisite *baksheesh* money—forty thousand francs. In the thirty months that had passed since Herzl's abortive meetings with the Kaiser he had grown wiser and more cynical in his attitude toward mighty princes. The Sultan, as Vámbéry had said, was a lunatic, a robber, and a murderer of children, but in his bloodstained hands he held the keys to the Holy Land. To wrest them from him would not be easy.

15

Turkish Imbroglio I

HE STOPPED OVER BRIEFLY in Budapest to see Vámbéry, and the old man gave him final instructions and a sealed letter for the Sultan.

"You will not get the charter now," said Vámbéry. "That will take a few years and can cost up to three million gulden."

"Done!" cried Herzl. "You will get three hundred thousand as well as the everlasting gratitude of *Kol Israel*."*

Yet Vámbéry was much cooler than he had been three days before. It seemed to Herzl that he already regretted the service he had done him. Vámbéry wanted money right away. When Herzl told him that he would have to pay Nuri Bey and his cronies the thirty thousand francs that he had promised a year ago for the interview with the Sultan, Vámbéry exploded in wild rage. He shouted and cursed; he had done everything, and now others were reaping the fruits. Herzl explained that he was aware that Nuri had cheated him but that he simply had to honor his words. "You are a thorough gentleman," Vámbéry admitted, and calmed down somewhat. But he wanted the 30,000 for himself, perhaps as an advance toward the 300,000 gulden. Herzl could promise him only a share, for even this sum had been raised with the greatest difficulty by the Executive Committee. Their parting was rather strained.

Two days later Herzl was in Constantinople, in the same rooms at the Hotel d'Angleterre & Royal he had occupied with Nevlinski five years earlier. A changed man, he looked impassively out the windows. The beauty of the Golden Horn and the rose-tinted towers and rooftops no longer moved him. "For me the

---

* "All Israel" (Hebrew).

world is no longer Representation, but Will," he noted, echoing Schopenhauer. "It is strange how one's entire *Weltanschauung* involuntarily and unconsciously assumes another character when one gets caught by a chain of circumstances as I have been."

His arrival set off a string of rumors. The London *Times* reported from Constantinople that Herzl had come on behalf of Rothschild and Bismarck's banker, Bleichröder, to offer the Sultan a loan. The Austrian embassy informed Vienna that he had come to open a bank in Constantinople. Herzl had hardly unpacked his luggage when "the Levantine scissors grinder Crespi" arrived, greedily reminding Herzl of his debt to the members of Nuri's "syndicate." Herzl received Crespi in a friendly manner, and asked him to return the next day with a list of all those officials and courtiers who would share in the bribe.

Herzl announced his presence to the palace and settled down to await his summons. The party went sightseeing to Hagia Sofia and the bazaars. Day and night Herzl pondered the words he would say "in the moment of my desire." In his hipbath, in front of a mirror, he rehearsed the conversation as it might possibly unfold:

> *Will his Majesty permit me to speak plainly, frankly, seriously?*
> *I have not come to render small services but great ones. . . .*
> *Newspaper articles can be bought for fifty to five hundred*
> *gold pieces. As for me, I cannot be bought—I give myself. . . .*
> *Androcles and the Lion—your Majesty is the lion, perhaps*
> *I am Androcles who pulls the thorn from your Majesty's foot. . . .*

The summons arrived on the fourth day. After the colorful *salamlik* ceremony, Herzl was led from one kiosk to another. On the square in front of the palace, the processesion of pashas and eunuchs and heavily veiled harem ladies swept by to the sound of martial music and calls of the muezzin. The last minutes before the audience were a mixed *entr'acte* of comic opera and serious endeavor. Ibrahim Bey, the Sultan's chief of ceremonies, informed Herzl that his Majesty had conferred upon him the Order of the Medjidiye Second Class.

"Thank you most kindly, but I do not want any decoration," Herzl said firmly. He added, somewhat distorting the facts, "I was given the Medjidiye Order Third Class five years ago by mistake. At that time I accepted it only out of courtesy. The least I could accept *now* is the First Class."

Ibrahim Bey became flustered and withdrew to inform the

Sultan of his refusal. Herzl was passed from one servant to the next. Presently Ibrahim Bey returned, beaming and laughing. He informed Herzl that the Sultan had indeed bestowed upon him the First Class Grand Cordon—Turkey's highest decoration—as requested. Finally he was conducted to the audience chamber.

The Sultan gave him a bony, shaking hand and then sat down with his sword between his knees. He was a small man of Mediterranean complexion, with a prominent aquiline nose, thick and fleshy lips, full beard, dyed red with henna, and his fez pulled down low over his forehead. In a weak and trembling voice he assured Herzl that he read the *Neue Freie Presse* every day. Herzl thanked him for the high decoration. The Sultan inquired about the health of the Austrian Emperor and was delighted to hear that Franz Josef was fine. Then Herzl pulled his notes out of his glove, where he had deliberately placed them, for if he had reached into his breast pocket Abdul-Hamid might think he was taking out a gun. In fact, under similar circumstances, the Sultan was known to have shot and killed people, including recently a small child.

Herzl found ample opportunity to tell the Sultan everything he had rehearsed so well, because the conversation lasted more than two hours. He heeded Vámbéry's advice and did not utter the words "Palestine" or "Zionism," but even without using these key words he managed to lead the conversation where he wanted it. He offered the Sultan his services, "naturally not minor services—there are plenty of other people for that—but major ones." The Sultan took two cigarettes out of his case and offered one to Herzl.

"When Professor Vámbéry told me that your Majesty wished to receive me, I was reminded of the good old story of Androcles and the Lion. Your Majesty is the lion. I am Androcles and perhaps there is a thorn I might remove. May I continue to speak plainly, frankly, seriously?" The Sultan begged him to. The thorn, Herzl said, was the Ottoman Empire's humiliating indebtedness to the foreign creditors who had declared Turkey bankrupt and had seized her public revenues. If that thorn could be removed, "Turkey would regain its vitality, in which I have great faith."

"Yes," answered the interpreter, Ibrahim Bey, for the Sultan. "Ever since the beginning of his glorious reign his Majesty has sought in vain to remove this thorn. This thorn was acquired under his Imperial Majesty's exalted predecessors. Alas, it seems impossible to remove it. If Monsieur Herzl could help, it would be ever so nice."

"Well then," Herzl said, "I believe I can. But the first and fundamental condition is absolute secrecy."

The Sultan raised his eyes to heaven, placed his hand on his breast, and murmured in French, "*Secret! Secret!*"

Herzl now developed his plan. He and his Jewish friends were devoted to his Majesty because he was so good to the Jews. They were ready to buy up the Ottoman public debt on all stock exchanges of Europe. The Sultan was to reciprocate by adopting a measure particularly friendly to the Jews and by proclaiming it publicly.

Herzl did not specify the measure; the Sultan sensed a bargain and stepped into the breach. He had a Jewish court jeweler, he said, to whom he might say "something favorable about the Jews," and allow him to release it to the newspapers. Ibrahim Bey listened approvingly to his master's voice and translated with a beaming face. "His Imperial Majesty also has a rabbi for his Jews. He could say something nice to him as well."

"No, that would not serve the purpose," Herzl replied. Unfortunately such a kindness would not have the necessary resonance in the world outside of Turkey. When the proper moment arrived he would suggest to the Sultan the form of a truly imposing proclamation. Meanwhile, what Turkey could most use was the industrial energy of the Jews. In short, the Jews should flock to Turkey from the lands of persecution, develop Turkey's resources, and remain here, unlike all the other Europeans, who enriched themselves quickly only to rush off again with their spoils.

The Sultan nodded contentedly. Ibrahim Bey repeated his words with exuberant joy. Yes, that might be a very good thing. Vast treasures as yet unexploited existed in the country. "Only today his Majesty received a telegram from Baghdad that oil fields have been discovered there, richer than those of the Caucasus."

Here was a field on which they might collaborate, the Sultan said. He asked Herzl to recommend a capable financier who could develop new sources of revenue. This expert would report directly to the Sultan, and to Herzl, and would be in charge of development. Herzl was flattered by this offer and promised to inform the Sultan of a sufficiently reliable and competent expert as soon as he could find one. The Sultan had another wish: he needed 1.5 million pounds urgently to cover the previous year's deficit. Could Herzl help? He outlined a third current scheme—the consolidation of the state debt by borrowing new money to pay off the old loan. In the

Sultan's opinion, this transaction might produce a net profit of 1.5 million pounds.

"What? So little?" Herzl cried. The Sultan also regretted that it would not be more. Herzl told the Sultan he was not at all sure that the plan was such a good idea. More effective measures were needed to free Turkey of her shackles. He asked for a full, detailed accounting of the state finances and of the proposed consolidation plan in order that he might give a final judgment. The Sultan promised the details would reach him by the following day.

Herzl now marshaled all his powers of persuasion to draw the Sultan a vivid picture of the future, all the wondrous things that could be accomplished through electrification on a large scale. In Constantinople alone vast improvements were called for—new residential quarters, new avenues, and the construction of new bridges high enough to permit the biggest ships to pass into the Golden Horn. The Sultan mentioned that his palace already had an electric generator and that he was pleased with the light. "It is better than the other kind." Yet he requested Herzl to forget these magnificent projects for the moment and occupy himself first with removal of the thorn—the public debt.

By now Herzl had spun all the threads he had wanted to. He had not mentioned Palestine, but felt fairly certain that he had begun a permanent relationship with the Sultan that could lead toward the granting of a charter. In conclusion he asked again for utmost secrecy about their intentions and understanding. The Sultan repeated, "*Secret, secret.*"

Ibrahim Bey conducted Herzl back through the maze of kiosks and passages and gravel paths to his office, and there handed him the red case with the Grand Cordon. In the anteroom, and again at the gate, a scuffle for *baksheesh* broke loose. Herzl calmed it with a shower of gold coins. Guards, servants, and doormen met him with outstretched hands, while high-ranking courtiers, expecting more lavish remuneration later, smiled at the lurid scene from the sidelines.

Herzl was no sooner back at the hotel than Crespi, Nuri Bey's agent, showed up. He demanded the reward for what Vámbéry had done. Herzl decided to deal directly with his employer, and drove immediately to the Foreign Ministry. Nuri Bey pretended that he had played a large role in the current negotiations; Herzl did not challenge him but rather thanked him most effusively for his kindness. His "group" would be fully paid. To himself he reflected that one of the arts of being a *grand seigneur* was to allow oneself to be robbed gracefully. Herzl asked whether his inter-preter, Ibrahim Bey, was on Nuri's list.

"Alas, he is not!" replied the Secretary-General of the Foreign Ministry. He advised Herzl to send Ibrahim a fine carriage and a span of horses, preferably through Crespi. Herzl asked how much Nuri intended to give Tahsin Bey and Izzet Bey, the Sultan's first and second secretaries. "Between seven and eight thousand francs," said Nuri. Herzl did not believe a word he said and was certain that Nuri was pocketing the entire amount of thirty thousand francs. But he only nodded, and then insisted that a list of the supposed recipients be drawn up. Although Tahsin Bey's name appeared on Nuri's list, Herzl was afraid to take a chance. Tahsin was Vámbéry's friend and the Sultan's first secretary. Herzl sent him ten thousand francs in cash and a silver powder box for his wife. "A bagatelle," he wrote Tahsin, and "the first proofs of my gratitude . . . for the great service you have just rendered me."

Paying off Nuri proved to be more difficult. Wolffsohn, charged with presenting the thick pad of bank notes, demanded a receipt from Nuri on his own visiting card. Nuri was rising to his feet in a show of offended innocence when Herzl intervened and said the Bey could sign any way he liked. Still offended, Nuri refused to touch the money. "Give that to Crespi," he said disdain-fully. "That gentleman," he told Herzl, pointing at Wolffsohn, "won't do much business around here. . . . On *you* I rely as a . . ." and he gave Herzl's wrist the Freemason's grip.

"You know me," Herzl replied and amused himself by return-ing the sign.

The negotiations at the palace continued for three days. "We are probably on the eve of receiving the charter," Herzl wrote Mandelstamm, "but it will cost us terrible battles. May God give me the strength to persevere. We need money in piles. Gather as much as you can."

There were day-long sessions with Ibrahim Bey and Izzet, during which Turkish delicacies and cups of coffee were consumed in great amounts. In the strange surroundings of Yildiz Palace—partly stage set and partly thieves' den—Herzl cut a rare figure. At the Sultan's order he was presented with the details of the proposed consolidation plan. He proclaimed it "harmful" to Turkey because of a severely usurious rate of interest. His own proposal, which he submitted to the Sultan in writing, was that shares of the Turkish debt be quietly and gradually bought back at the various European stock exchanges, to prevent a sudden rise in price. The 1.5 million

pounds needed to cover the last year's deficit must be found elsewhere. Ibrahim Bey went back and forth conveying Herzl's offers
to the Sultan and bringing back to Herzl the Sultan's reaction.
Meanwhile more sweet black coffee was served in small, diamond-
studded cups.

Herzl's judgment of the proposed consolidation plan aroused
Izzet's rage. He waved Herzl's memorandum furiously in his face.
Izzet, like Nuri, had his own little syndicate, and Herzl possibly
had just thwarted one of its designs.

Herzl now stepped fully into his new role as a Levantine ne-
gotiator. He tried to distract Izzet with meaningful winks. He did
not know in whose syndicate Ibrahim was a partner and dared
not speak in his presence. Instead he dropped veiled hints to
Izzet—"With us you will do well"—and with his eyes tried to make
him understand. Izzet regained his composure. Ibrahim went off to
report to the Sultan and returned with a new offer: Herzl and his
Jewish friends should take over the exploitation (and financing) of
all Turkish mines, oil fields, and other state monopolies. There was
only one small hitch: a matter of some four million pounds which
the Sultan needed immediately to pay for some warships he had
ordered. Would Herzl please find that sum for him right away?

Herzl replied that he could, but it would depend on the Sultan's attitude toward Jewish investors, experts, and colonists who
came to settle in Turkey. The Sultan sent word that Jews would be
welcome as colonists if they became Turkish subjects, served in the
army, and so forth. At the same time, "colonization cannot take
place in masses. But, for example, five families here, five families
there—scattered without connection."

So you may plunder and slay them all the more easily, Herzl
thought to himself. Outwardly he was receptive. He would not
mind such dispersion, he said, but weren't there good technical and
economic reasons against it? Would it not be more efficient to set
up a great land company under Ottoman law? This company might
be assigned some uncultivated territory on which to settle Jews.
"Surely there is enough land in Palestine that could be used for
such a purpose." The land company would produce a sizable income for Turkey, in concession fees and in taxes. Herzl could submit definite proposals within the month.

In this harmless form Herzl first propounded the idea of the
charter to the Sultan's men. He contented himself with having at
least roused their interest. There would be time to elaborate on
details later; at this stage Herzl had reason enough to believe that if

Izzet and his cronies had any misgivings, they could be promptly swept away by gold.

Izzet disappeared to inform the Sultan of Herzl's plan. He returned with a farewell greeting. His Majesty was interested and expected a definite proposal from Herzl within four weeks. Herzl was very encouraged at his departure. "We have actually entered upon negotiations for the charter. All it takes now to carry out everything is *luck, skill, and money*."

2

Of his three prerequisites, Herzl immediately set out to find the last—money. The Sultan had given him four weeks' time. To Mandelstamm Herzl wrote on May 28: "The success with Cohn* surpassed my boldest expectations. If our friends now do their duty and assemble the *means*, then the final achievement is much closer than we ever dreamed. Every man aboard! Or else we shall bog down on the very threshold of success. I embrace you. . . ."

On the following morning, only five days after his return to Vienna from Constantinople, Herzl left for Paris and London to see how much money he himself could raise in the West. On his way to Paris he stopped briefly in the Tirol and at Karlsruhe to visit Vámbéry and the Grand Duke of Baden.

Vámbéry congratulated him on what he considered a tremendous success. He now believed that Herzl might actually obtain his charter "this very year." He offered to go himself to Constantinople in the autumn and induce the Sultan to sign the charter there and then, without even telling his viziers. If he could manage that, Herzl assured him, his reward would be 300,000 guldens in cash and a name in world history. Vámbéry seemed receptive to both.

The Grand Duke, whom Herzl visited the next day, was similarly impressed. He regarded the Sultan's readiness to negotiate with Herzl, following his rebuff of the mighty Kaiser in 1898, as an enormous success.

The rich Jews of Paris, however, reacted differently. Herzl talked himself hoarse in vain efforts to engage the financial support of several millionaires. He needed 1.5 million pounds, in addition to funds already subscribed to the Zionist bank. Rothschild remained unapproachable, as did the Jewish Colonialization Associa-

---

* Code name for the Sultan.

tion, a foundation endowed with some ten million pounds sterling by the late Baron Hirsch. Rothschild made things worse by dissociating himself publicly from Herzl's enterprise in the *Financial Times*. Others were ready to offer money if and when Herzl actually had the charter, but he needed money in order to obtain the charter. The problem was how to break this vicious circle.

Nordau irritated Herzl with his constant nagging criticism. He agreed that Herzl's audience with the Sultan had been an important event, but felt that he had tremendously blundered by playing *va banque*—all or nothing. "People will later say that you forced yourself on the Sultan under false pretenses."

Herzl did not take this kindly. He rebuked Nordau; above all he now needed his friends' forbearance, not their constant criticism: "A man on a tightrope should not be made dizzy!"

"You are right," Nordau countered pleasantly. "All we can do for you now is to run along with a mattress to break your fall."

In his diary Herzl complained that all this criticism, which offered no constructive alternatives, was insidious enough to give a man a stroke. On June 5, while driving through the Bois de Boulogne, he suffered another seizure. He staggered from his carriage to lie down on two chairs hidden in the bushes, and blacked out for a few moments. After a while he drove home, though he was barely conscious. Next morning he felt better, "but my nerves are gone."

Still hoping to achieve more in London, he wrote the Sultan on June 6 from Paris: "Matters stand well . . . I hope to succeed within a very short time. The lion shall be relieved of his thorn."

Although he was received grandly in London, the money he needed to open serious negotiations with the Turks was not forthcoming there either. He addressed a large and distinguished audience of Jewish bankers, businessmen, and public servants. His main theme was a frank appeal for 1.5 million pounds, to allow "a very definite step forward." But he was handicapped by the air of secrecy he felt he had to maintain on behalf of the Sultan at this stage of the scheme. Everywhere he went he was asked: "What is the Sultan prepared to do?" He parried the question in the old Jewish fashion, by posing another one himself: "What are *you* ready to do?"

He was in great demand socially, mostly among non-Jews, and was feted by a succession of society hostesses. In London society Herzl and his cause became fashionable, at least for a fortnight. He met the Bishop of Ripon, Dr. Boyd-Carpenter, who assured him of his own complete support and that of Bishop Bramley Moore of the

Irvingite Apostolic Church, who was Hechler's friend and an ardent Zionist.

The rich Jews, however, remained aloof. Before a charter was actually granted, they were not prepared to risk a penny. Among his English lieutenants Herzl now counted not only his first convert, the young, ebullient Jacob de Haas, but also older, more experienced men. Among them were the barrister Sir Francis Montefiore, the businessman Joseph Cowen, and Leopold Greenberg, a future editor of the *Jewish Chronicle*. But their combined efforts produced few results. Aided by Lady Battersea (née Rothschild), they made vain efforts to induce Lord Nathaniel Rothschild to receive Herzl. But at this point Herzl was still as odious to Lord Rothschild as to his French cousin Edmond.

"In fifty years their graves will be spat upon," Herzl wrote Mandelstamm. "I almost *concluded* with the Sultan but could not raise the filthy money."

At the same time he was swamped by innumerable demands for charity. One typical request came from a poor Jew in Plonsk (Russian Poland) who asked Herzl to help in the education of an unusually talented sixteen-year-old son. The man's name was Abraham Grien, and the boy afterward immigrated to Palestine and changed his name to David Ben-Gurion.

Seeing that he was getting nowhere at all with rich Jews, Herzl turned to rich Gentiles. He thought first of Sir Cecil Rhodes. The great English imperialist and head of South African mining companies was powerful enough, financially, to buy up the Turkish public debt. Herzl hoped that Zionism would appeal to Rhodes's colonizing zeal, as well as to his business instincts. "Rhodes and his friends can make two million pounds and more if they help us," Herzl wrote to Cowen. "You know, Joe, that I am no illusionist or prattler. I know what I am saying."

But Rhodes—although he had once declared he was sorry he could not colonize the stars ("I would annex the planets if I could")—sent back word, through Cowen, that he was not interested. In Rhodes's view, Palestine and Syria should be assigned to Germany. England could not rule the whole world; it needed a buffer between itself and Russia. "But if Herzl wants a tip from me," Rhodes added, echoing Shakespeare's Iago, "tell him to put money in his purse."

This Herzl knew only too well. Shortly before leaving England he sent another long letter to the Sultan. Carefully worded, its main purpose was to keep the line of communication open. He and his friends, Herzl wrote, were still doing their utmost to procure money for Turkey. They would be able to do infinitely more after the establishment of an Ottoman-Jewish development company. The Sultan did not respond, but his ministers continued to approach Herzl through their "agents" with various shady offers which Herzl rejected. In his desperation Herzl turned to Vámbéry. The explorer consoled him with the thought that things were always very slow and convoluted in Turkey. The Turks could not be rushed, but his day would come.

The Sultan, meanwhile, was becoming bolder with his European creditors. That fall he suspended payment on bills due to a French company. France resorted to gunboat diplomacy; French troops landed at Miytilene to enforce payment, and the Sultan gave in. Herzl was convinced that his own scheme, though not at all selfless, but advantageous to both Jews and Turks, might have shielded the Sultan from his gunboat creditors. He wrote the Sultan again but received no reply. He was not sure that his letters had penetrated the court clique to reach the Sultan. In the hope of circumventing the court clique and the interpreters, he began to study Turkish; next time he would be able to address the Sultan directly. Vámbéry was his only direct link with the Sultan, and certainly the safest. He urged Vámbéry to act, repeating his promise that in return for the charter, Vámbéry would receive a commission of 300,000 guldens.

Herzl's latest appeal to Vámbéry evoked a strange response. Vámbéry informed Herzl that he was ready to stage a *coup d'état* in Constantinople; he would overthrow Izzet Bey and take his place, or even overthrow the Sultan himself by calling in the Young Turks. Herzl reacted to this hyperbole in good humor: "I have read your youthfully audacious letter with great joy. You are really a divinely favored man. May God keep you!"

He urged Vámbéry to deal with the Sultan after all and to induce him to allow the establishment of an Ottoman-Jewish company in Asia Minor, Palestine, and Syria. The company would guarantee an answer to Turkey's financial problems within five years.

A few days later, on the occasion of the Sultan's birthday, Herzl cabled congratulations and a reminder that it was still possible to extract the thorn from the Sultan's foot. This message, for a change, was gratefully acknowledged. Herzl consoled himself that at least the thread was not broken.

For some months this was all he heard. He did not delude himself about the prospects of his dream. The ensuing depression combined with the bad state of his health to produce more thoughts of death. On November 8 he wrote Wolffsohn: "I am repeatedly seized by a premonition that my days are numbered. . . . For me this thought connotes nothing awful. I am prepared to face it every moment."

These premonitions contained a faint suggestion of relief, and the satisfaction of a life well spent. A few weeks later, on an almost wistful note, he wrote, "Zionism was the Sabbath of my life."

3

In this mood he faced his annual congress, the fifth, on December 26, 1901, in Basel. The parliamentary procedures Herzl had introduced during past congresses were now routine. The years had not cooled the enthusiasm generated by the national assembly of a people dispersed on five continents. New faces replaced the old; the psychological and dramatic effect of the first assemblies continued.

The movement had made further strides in 1901. Its steady growth contrasted with the deadlock on the diplomatic front. With its main office in London, the Jewish Colonial Bank was finally operational; it prepared to open branches in Russia and Palestine. It was still a small operation based not on the wealth of Jewish high finance, but on the accumulated pennies of the poor. Yet the bank was capable at least of issuing the relatively modest letters of credit Herzl needed in the first stage of possible negotiations with Turkey.

These negotiations were on everybody's mind. In his opening speech Herzl briefly referred to his audience with the Sultan. He disclosed no details. "I gained the conviction that in the reigning Caliph the Jewish people have a friend and protector." The negotiations, he said, would continue.

As at previous congresses, the opposition gathered its forces. Disdainful of "diplomacy" and anxious to "establish facts" in Palestine, many dismissed Herzl's endeavors as useless bourgeois games. Some were shocked to discover that relatively large sums had been spent on *baksheesh*. The opposition was strengthened by the presence of a vocal contingent of radical Jewish Russian students attending nearby Swiss universities. But the opposition was again easily outvoted, and Herzl's position as the virtually unchallenged leader was reconfirmed.

In closed sessions Herzl explained that he certainly did not rely on the Sultan's promises alone—he was not so naïve as that—but on the Sultan's vital needs. The Turkish public debt was preventing the Sultan from ruling his own house. Herzl estimated its market price at twenty-five million pounds; certainly the Jewish people could raise this sum in return for a charter for Palestine. The Sultan, he argued, *must* grant the charter in order to resolve this most pressing problem.

"Jewish culture" was another important item on the congress agenda. The opposition urged that the new nationalism be deepened through the reaffirmation of a specific Jewish *Kultur*, instead of proceeding mainly from negative postulates (the existence of anti-Semitism) as Herzl had done. Among the chief spokesmen for this course were Chaim Weizmann, the future President of Israel, and Martin Buber, the philosopher. Weizmann proposed the establishment of a Jewish university, possibly in Jerusalem. Herzl was much more congenial now than in former years to this point of view. Since assuming his new role, he had learned a great deal about himself, his own people, and their culture—which he had once believed was nonexistent, in a modern, secular sense.

Another leading spokesman for *Kultur* was the gifted young artist E.M. Lilien, whom Martin Buber hailed as the most serious interpreter of the Jewish cultural renaissance. Lilien, a disciple of Aubrey Beardsley and the new school of *art nouveau*, was a superb draftsman and illustrator. His delicate pen drawings, celebrating the return, and his fine portraits of Herzl and Nordau circulated throughout the Zionist world. Zionism was a back-to-the-earth movement; but its most celebrated artistic image was created by a member of the Escapist school, which stressed the decorative, the voluptuous, and the luxurious.

16

Turkish Imbroglio II

I N THE NEW YEAR, events quickly came to a head. On February 4, 1902, Herzl received a telegram from Ibrahim Bey urgently requesting him to come to Constantinople. He was needed to furnish "certain explanations of your scheme." Herzl was puzzled by this sudden summons which came at an inconvenient time. "We have no money as yet . . . just now I would not know what to do with the charter." Yet after learning from reliable sources that Ibrahim was acting on instructions from the Sultan, Herzl realized he had no alternative.

On a bleak winter day he left for Constantinople, accompanied by Joe Cowen, whom he had called in from London because, as an Englishman, Cowen would enjoy better diplomatic protection. The journey was long and arduous. The main line to Constantinople was damaged by floods at Philippopolis. The two men were forced to travel through Romania and from there by steamer across the rough Black Sea to Constantinople, where they arrived on a Friday, two days late. Herzl drove straight to the palace from the boat. The ceremony of the *salamlik* had just ended; the Sultan was too tired to receive Herzl immediately. Instead he was welcomed effusively by Ibrahim Bey and asked to return on the next day, for his Majesty had certain "imperial decrees and perhaps some propositions to make to you."

Herzl bowed silently. Ibrahim further said that Herzl would be the Sultan's guest during his entire stay. Herzl again bowed silently; this was a new and unaccustomed honor. A few pleasantries were exchanged, but when Herzl announced that he had brought some fresh fruit from Vienna for the Sultan, an embarrassed silence followed. The Sultan was so fearful of poison that he never touched any food that had not been grown on the premises. The courtiers agreed, however, to consume the fruit themselves and on this note they parted amiably. For the first time in days Herzl enjoyed a good night's sleep.

At eleven the next day the negotiations began in earnest; there was none of the polite pretense of the previous year. Herzl dealt openly as head of the Zionist movement, offering a Turkish-Jewish alliance in return for a charter. The Turks would be freed of their foreign creditors and the Jews permitted to colonize Palestine. This was the moment Herzl had anticipated for years, and he threw himself into it with gusto. For the first time the Turks wanted something of him. He spoke openly and candidly, and so did they. Turkey was represented by Ibrahim and Izzet Bey, who went back and forth submitting Herzl's proposals and conveying the Sultan's responses.

There were some bizarre moments. At the end of the first day of negotiations, Herzl was taken aside by Ibrahim Bey and told that Izzet Bey's "confidence man," a certain Monsieur Caporal, would call on him to discuss his master's "personal interests." On another occasion he was requested, in the Sultan's name, to ask Benedikt how much money it would require to secretly turn the *Neue Freie Presse* into an unofficial Turkish organ.

The atmosphere was promising. Ibrahim Bey seemed carried away by the possibilities of what he called a "defensive and offensive alliance" between Turks and Jews; he raved about the marvelous improvements that would ensue throughout the empire. Then Izzet, speaking for the Sultan, made a counterproposal.

"I shall give it to you straight," he said. "The Sultan, in his lofty wisdom, is prepared to open his empire to Jewish refugees from all countries. On two conditions: they must accept Ottoman citizenship. And they may settle anywhere in the empire with this single exception—*at first*—they must not settle in Palestine." In return for this concession, Izzet went on, the Sultan asked Herzl to form a syndicate for the consolidation of the public debt on terms better than those currently offered by other financiers. Furthermore, Herzl must undertake to develop the entire present and future mining resources of the empire, under an imperial concession.

"What mines?" Herzl asked.

"All the mines . . . gold and silver, coal and oil!" Izzet cried. He hid his face in his hands, and bending down over his knees, emitted a roguish laugh! "It is because we know that you want *something* *else!* That is why we entrust the mines to you. *You* won't exploit us!"*

Herzl asked for time to consider these unexpected offers. Next morning he handed over his reply, a memorandum addressed to the Sultan. He accepted the economic proposal in principle, but he rejected Izzet's demand that colonization be restricted. Much time was spent in translating his response, which was done by Ibrahim, writing in the Turkish fashion, on his knee, as Herzl bit his fingernails. At long last Izzet returned with the Sultan's reply. The Sultan still refused to open Palestine to Jewish colonization, but he offered Herzl Mesopotamia, Syria, and Anatolia for large-scale settlement. In fact, anywhere at all, but not Palestine. It was a regular charter, but not for Palestine! Herzl refused immediately.

In addition to all the other proposals agreed to, he offered to establish an Ottoman-Jewish bank, which would modernize the entire Turkish credit system; but there must be no geographic restrictions on settlement. The Sultan replied that, even if he wanted to, he could not agree to this. Izzet grinned, "You see, it is an error to believe that an absolute monarch may do as he pleases." The talks had reached a deadlock. Izzet appealed to Herzl "as a friend"; he implored him to enter the country as a financier first, to make friends, open a bank, and take the mining business into his hands. "Later on you can do what you want."

A good way for Herzl to begin, Izzet suggested, was to present impressive letters of credit and prove his financial backing. In order to keep the discussions alive, Herzl immediately responded to this proposal. Here was an opportunity to flash money before greedy Turkish eyes without involving the Zionists in actual outlays.

A final memorandum was drafted. Herzl was slightly taken aback when a messenger from the Sultan arrived with two hundred pounds in gold coin as reimbursement for his traveling expenses. He could not refuse the money. He considered leaving the little cloth sack with their Excellencies, who would not be reluctant to accept it on some pretext, but decided rather to keep it for the poor Zionist treasury.

"Gentlemen and dear Excellencies," said Herzl, "even though officially we have not yet reached agreement, let me express a hope that we shall meet again. I shall follow your advice and seek a

---

* It is odd to ponder what might have happened if Herzl had accepted this offer. Herzl would have replaced Goubeluian, and after World War I the Zionists might have had a share in Iraqi and Arabian oil.

solution that is good for your country as well as for my Jews, and which might at the same time satisfy mankind."

"May God hear you," said Izzet unctuously. "We are your partisans! *Inshallah!*" Herzl left the palace, scattering the requisite shower of gold coins on doorkeepers and guards. He headed directly to the harbor, where Cowen was waiting with their suitcases alongside the Black Sea steamer leaving for Romania. Five minutes later the ship sailed.

Herzl's comings and goings in the palace for four full days had caused considerable nervousness among other financiers in the wings. Had the whole purpose of the exercise been to tantalize them? There were also diplomatic inquiries. A German diplomat approached Ibrahim Bey soon after Herzl's departure. What had Herzl requested? Ibrahim replied laconically: "*Des choses impossibles.*"

Herzl thought just the opposite. As he saw it, the Sultan was asking too much and still offering too little. But if Turkey's situation worsened, a compromise might be reached. The erosion in the Turkish position since Herzl's last visit to Constantinople had been considerable; there were good reasons to expect more. Yet Herzl realized that, for the time being, he would obtain no Turkish charter for Palestine, except through the circuitous route of a heavy involvement in Turkish finances. Tossing about on the miserable little Romanian steamer, he plotted his next step. The sea was rough and cast in a thick fog. The Sultan's two hundred pounds weighed heavily on his mind: "If we collided with another boat and went under—then at some future date the receipt for the two hundred pounds would be found in Yildiz—perhaps when the Russians or Bulgarians occupy the city? Then I would appear as a hireling of the bloodstained Sultan, a sort of Nevlinski. . . ."

Cowen, who carried the heavy money bags on his person, was tortured by similar fears. He told Herzl the next day that he had determined, at the first sign of shipwreck, to throw the money overboard lest it drag him under.

The next few months were spent in futile attempts to initiate a preliminary financial program with the Turks. Although Izzet, speaking "as a friend," had proposed the program himself, he now chose to ignore Herzl's practical steps. When Herzl presented the requested three letters of credit—one million francs for the mines, one million for the proposed bank, and another for the Ottoman-Jewish company—a surrealistic exchange of letters ensued. It seemed that either the Sultan had not received Herzl's letter informing him of the deposits or else he had chosen not to inform his ministers about it. The Turkish ambassador in Vienna was asked by Constantinople who Dr. Herzl was and what all this money was for. As the confusion began to clear, the Turkish ambassador in Vienna called on Herzl in embarrassment to apologize. "Between ourselves," he said, "I must confess that order in our country leaves much to be desired." Two weeks later word came from Constantinople that the whole affair had been a "misunderstanding." At the same time there were press reports that the Sultan had approved the so-called Rouvier project for the consolidation of the debt.

Rouvier was a former French cabinet minister; he enjoyed a considerable advantage over Herzl in that he was supported by one of the great powers. In Herzl's eyes this latest development was a veritable disaster. In 1898 the German Kaiser had failed him; now, after another promising beginning, it was the Sultan. At the moment there was nowhere he could turn.

2

He withdrew briefly to the one place he could call his own, the world of fantasy. In March and April Herzl finished a utopian novel he had been writing intermittently in the few quiet moments he had had during the past three years. Entitled *Altneuland* (*Old-Newland*),* it involved an imaginative projection of his plan up to the year 1923, which, he thought, would be long after its full realization in practice.

The main purpose of *Altneuland* was to prove that the utopia need be no elusive pipe dream; it was within reach. Inscribed on the title page was the motto, "If you will it, it is no fairy tale." In Herzl's words, it was also "a story I am telling by the campfire to keep my poor people in good cheer on their journey. Endurance is *everything.*"

Imagination, he might have added, was perhaps even more. Among the many social utopias that were conjured up in the nineteenth century, *Altneuland* is probably the only one written by an active politician. Full of autobiographical suggestions, the novel's main protagonists are thinly disguised portraits of Herzl's closest aides, Wolffsohn, Cowen, Greenberg, Hechler, Marmorek, and

* In the Hebrew translation: *Tel Aviv*. The city, founded in 1912, was named after the book.

Mandelstamm. The plot is simple and at times so thin it is almost trite; no nineteenth-century political utopia so closely resembles a contemporary Viennese melodrama. Yet there is in *Altneuland* a stirring tragic beauty; it was a last attempt by Herzl to live, at least through literature, what was being denied him in real life.

Even as a political utopia, *Altneuland* is in the mainstream of *fin de siècle* Viennese art. Its pursuit of arcadian bliss within a mystic community and its haunted preoccupation with dreams recall Gustav Mahler's music and Hugo von Hofmannsthal's poetry. "Dream and deed are not as different from one another as many believe," Herzl wrote in his postscript to the novel. "All deeds of men are dreams at first, *and in the end become dreams again.*"

The plot can be summed up briefly. Mr. Kingscourt, an immensely rich, eccentric, Anglicized Prussian nobleman (Herzl's hero-ideal), and Dr. Friedrich Loewenberg, a melancholy, suicidal young Jewish intellectual (a combination of Herzl himself and his dead friend Heinrich Kana), tire of the corrupt life in *fin de siècle* Europe. They withdraw together to an island in the Pacific, where they live in total isolation from the world, "hunting, eating, drinking, sleeping, and playing chess." After twenty years, they return, on Mr. Kingscourt's yacht, to inspect a changed world. Their first stop is Palestine, which they had viewed twenty years before in its desolation. The two recluses hardly believe their eyes. Zionism has become a reality; not only have the Jews returned and has anti-Semitism in Europe ended, but Palestine is now a model society that has successfully solved the cultural and political problems of all mankind.

Altneuland marked a dramatic departure in Herzl's political thinking. The sharp contrast with Herzl's earlier tract *The Jewish State* is immediately evident. *Altneuland* reflected a new development in Herzl's theory of power and sovereignty, a development that set him apart from, and above, most nineteenth-century nationalists. In *Altneuland* Herzl no longer contemplated a nation-state, but a new society well outside the accepted framework of European nationalism.

"We are not a state like the Europeans of your time," David Litwak (Wolffsohn), the main protagonist in the novel, tells Kingscourt. "We are a *Gemeinschaft* [commonwealth]," based on new cooperative forms of voluntary association. The trappings of sovereignty and power that had once beguiled Herzl were forgotten. Instead he devised an original kind of polity, based on syndicalist ideals and derived in part from French anarchist thinking. There was little or no state coercion and almost none of the forms of sovereignty associated with the European nation-state. The society functioned primarily on good will, generated by far-reaching social reforms. All land was publicly owned; industries, newspapers, banks, and department stores were cooperatively owned by workers and consumers. The new polity was a triumph of modern technology; it avoided the blights of industrialization by not repeating the mistakes of Europe. Its cities were airy and well planned, featuring a fabulous mass transit system, powered by odorless, noiseless electricity, including a monorail. A huge tunnel connecting the Mediterranean and the Dead Sea was harnessed to generate electrical power. Vast irrigation works made the desert flourish. There was a seven-hour work day, and women had the vote.

The protagonists of *Altneuland* hoped that the new social system would be applied everywhere, to cure the evils of industrial capitalism without resorting to socialist authoritarianism. In the words of one character, the scientist Steineck (Marmorek), the experience of *Altneuland* might even point a way toward ameliorating the tragedy of the American Negroes: "Only a Jew can fully measure all its depths of pain." For this reason, Steineck, as a scientist, worked to combat African diseases. "After having experienced the return of the Jews I would like to help prepare the return of the Negroes. . . . All people must have a home. Then they would be more benevolent toward one another."

Culturally, the new polity of *Altneuland* was not Jewish, but cosmopolitan. It was an open, secular, pluralist society of Jews, Christians, Moslems, and Buddhists speaking a wide variety of languages. There was no official tongue, although German seemed to predominate (in the rural areas Yiddish was spoken). Hebrew was used by Jews only for prayer and at funerals. The citizenry attended German opera and French theater, and engaged in English outdoor sports. The new polity was not self-centered. In the words of one character, it was built not in Palestine but in "England and America, in France and in Germany"; it grew out of the experience and the best "books and dreams" of all mankind. *Altneuland*'s guiding principle was a high form of tolerance. The official motto was "Man, thou art my brother." Hence, the return of the Jews did not generate any tension with the native Arab population, although the new community extended beyond Beirut and Damascus. The Arabs were enthusiastic members of the *New Society* which had no interest in whether men worshiped the eternal in "synagogue, church, mosque, in the art museum or the philharmonic concert." And when Mr. Kingscourt challenged a local Arab leader with the words "You are very curious, you Mohammedans. Don't you consider these Jews as intruders?" the Arab retorted, "Christian, you speak very strangely. Would you consider him a robber who takes nothing from you, but gives you something? The Jews have made us rich. Why should we scorn them? They live with us as brothers. Why should we not love them?"

3

Altneuland aroused wide interest and was translated into many languages. At the same time it was savagely attacked by Herzl's opponents in the movement for its alleged rootless cosmopolitanism and lack of specific Jewish content. Asher Ginzberg, best known under his Hebrew pen name, Ahad Haam, and one of the most influential Jewish thinkers in Eastern Europe, wrote that *Altneuland* was written to curry favor with non-Jews; its spirit, he said, was so cosmopolitan it might also serve as the blueprint of a Negro republic in Africa. Martin Buber complained that *Altneuland* had "no single quality expressive of the folk characteristics of the Hebraist" revival.

Of the two critics, Ahad Haam was more formidable. As editor of the Hebrew monthly *Hashiloah*, published in Odessa, Ahad Haam had raised an entire generation of modern Hebrew poets, novelists, and essayists. In 1897 he had gone to the first Zionist congress, but "like a mourner among bridegrooms." He had avoided all subsequent congresses, for he distrusted Herzl's rationalist scheme of political and material amelioration without first instigating a "moral regeneration" through the revival of a true national culture. Israel will be saved by "prophets," not by "diplomats," he claimed. His argumentative spirit found a predestined target in Herzl. In the past five years Ahad Haam had conducted a relentless war against Herzl's politics. His assault on *Altneuland* surpassed all the other attacks he had launched on Herzl so far.

Herzl was incensed at Ahad Haam's attack ("He seems to be running for Pope!") and asked Nordau to respond. Nordau's public reply surpassed that of Ahad Haam in its viciousness. The West European arrogance with which he dismissed his Eastern European opponent harmed Herzl. Nordau argued, somewhat lamely, that if none of the protagonists in *Altneuland* spoke Hebrew, it was simply because Herzl had written the book in German, and his heroes spoke German just as Shakespeare's Julius Caesar spoke only English.

Herzl regarded *Altneuland* as his "best book." It helped him preserve a touching vision of himself and gave pathetic expression to his tragic failure as a writer. We glimpse this in a revealing diary entry on June 4, 1902, during a brief stopover in Paris, where Herzl had just been hailed by his disciples as a great historical figure. A prematurely aged, ailing man, Herzl laments that he is renowned for the wrong reason. As a politician he is world famous, even though in politics "I have accomplished next to nothing intellectually, I have merely displayed average skills. . . ." On the other hand, "as a writer, particularly as a playwright, I am considered nothing, less than nothing. People merely call me a good journalist. And yet I *feel*, I *know* that I am a writer of great merit who simply did not give his full measure because he became disgusted or discouraged."

4

His fame as a politician brought him to London three days later to testify before a Royal Inquiry Commission investigating the immigration of "poor aliens"—a euphemism for Russian and Romanian Jews—who had been flocking to England in recent years to escape the misery and persecution of Eastern Europe. For some time laws had been proposed to block their entry into England. The agitation stemmed primarily from a desire to curtail the influx of cheap labor. Yet the restrictions, if imposed, would have meant the first breach in England's traditional open door policy for the persecuted of the continent.

Baron Nathaniel, the first Lord Rothschild, was the only Jewish member of the commission. He had vigorously opposed summoning Herzl as a witness, claiming that he was a windbag, but he had been overruled. Now, after years of refusing to receive Herzl, he was suddenly anxious to meet him before he testified, in the hope of coaching him a little.

Herzl looked forward eagerly to the meeting, for he sensed, rightly, that after so much misunderstanding in the past, the moment might be psychologically ripe to achieve a reconciliation. He also anticipated the opportunity to propagate his view that while restrictions on immigration would be odious, the only true remedy in the long run was the establishment, somewhere, of a semi-autonomous Jewish territory.

His keen preparations were aborted by a sudden disaster. On the eve of his meeting with Lord Rothschild he returned from the theater late at night to find a cablegram from his wife. "Papa very ill. Come at once Vienna." Herzl sensed instinctively that this was his father's end; in a near trance he packed his bags and canceled all his arrangements. There was no boat or train before early next morning, so, breathing heavily, he lay on his bed in the dark. At 6:00 A.M., just as he was leaving the hotel for Victoria Station, the concierge handed him another cable from the family doctor, confirming his worst fears. "Father passed away after sudden stroke, painlessly." On shaking legs Herzl dragged himself onto the train and spent the next thirty-two hours in a numb daze, lulled and aggravated by the monotonous motion of the speeding train. He felt like a man who had had his arm shot off. He could not forgive himself for not having been at his father's side: "My dear, my good, my golden one . . . how greatly I remain in his debt, although I haven't been a bad son. (I owe him everything.) He stood by my side like a tree. Now that tree is gone."

Wolffsohn, alerted by the family, boarded Herzl's train in Cologne, wanting to keep him company until Vienna. "You can't help me now," Herzl said. The two men sat silently in Herzl's compartment for a few minutes. They embraced; Wolffsohn's face touched Herzl's wet cheek, then he left. Herzl wanted to be alone, to nurse his wound "like a runover dog."

The funeral took place the next day, and Herzl, overcome with grief, mourned his father's death for two weeks. Sitting idly at his desk, he gazed for hours at his father's photograph. Jakob Herzl was laid to rest in a temporary grave; Herzl did not buy a family vault, thinking that his father's remains would soon be transported to Palestine.

Now only his mother was left to him. But he did marshal enough strength to oppose her wish to come and live with him and his family. Herzl knew both his wife and his mother. "On the second day there will be quarrels and discontent, if not on the first. After fifteen years we ought to know better! It is impossible!"

Early in July he returned to England to keep his appointment with Lord Rothschild and to address the Royal Inquiry Commission. Rothschild received him in his office at New Court. He was a sturdy-looking man of sixty-two, of medium height, with a bald head and large warm eyes, and very hard of hearing. A man of fabulous wealth, even richer than his Paris cousin, whom he disliked, he was the first Jewish peer to enter the House of Lords without first converting to the Church of England. His father had helped Disraeli acquire the Suez Canal for England; he was a director of the Bank of England and played an important role in public life.

Rothschild began by telling Herzl that he was an Englishman and planned to remain one. Zionism was wrong; the great powers would never permit the Zionists to have Palestine. He very much "wished" that Herzl would tell the commission certain things and not tell the commission certain other things. Herzl tried to break in, but the old man was so hard of hearing he did not notice. Herzl lost his patience and began to shout so loudly that Rothschild, astounded, held his tongue. Nothing like this had happened in years.

Herzl cried: "I shall tell the commission what *I* think is proper! That has always been my custom and I shall stick to it this time too. And it is not true that the powers are against our going to Palestine. I have made Germany and Russia favorably disposed toward our cause. England, I think, would have no objections. And I am *persona grata* with the Sultan."

"Certainly," said Lord Rothschild, "the Sultan treats you nicely because you are Dr. Herzl of the *Neue Freie Presse*."

"That is not true!" Herzl shouted. "The *Neue Freie Presse* does not enter into this at all! Its publishers are mortal enemies of my Jewish plan. They have not printed the word 'Zionism' in their newspaper to this day. I never spoke to the Sultan about the *Neue Freie Presse*."

The conversation continued for a while in this tone, leading the two men nowhere at all. Herzl said that "charity has become a machine for suppressing cries of distress." Rothschild gasped. Then they went to an adjoining room for lunch, where they were joined by Rothschild's younger brothers, Alfred and Leopold. Leopold quarreled with Herzl, but then invited him to his next garden party; Alfred was supercilious. Colonization was a fine thing, he said, but God Almighty, why in Palestine? "Palestine sounds too Jewish!"

After lunch the atmosphere improved somewhat. The old man was beginning to like his visitor.

"Would you like to hear my scheme now?" Herzl asked.

"Yes," replied Rothschild. Herzl moved his chair close to his better ear and cried, "I want to ask the British government for a colonization charter!"

"Don't say 'charter.' The word has a bad sound right now."

"Call it whatever you like. I want to found a Jewish colony in a British possession."

"Take Uganda," Rothschild lightly suggested.

"No, I can only use this. . . ." He did not want the others to overhear him and so wrote on a slip of paper: "Sinai Peninsula, Egyptian Palestine, Cyprus." He added, aloud, "Are you for this?"

Rothschild thought it over for a while. Then, smiling, he said, "Very much so!"

Herzl sensed a victory for which he had been waiting seven years. He added on the piece of paper: "Prevent the Sultan from getting money!"—alluding to the Rouvier scheme to consolidate the Turkish public debt. Rothschild said that although he had prevented anti-Semitic Romania from obtaining money, he could not prevent the consolidation of the Turkish debt; the great powers wanted it in return for railroad concessions.

"The Sultan offered me Mesopotamia," Herzl said.

"And you refused?"

"Yes, I did," Herzl said grandly and rose to leave. "*Nous sommes gens de revue* [We are all showmen]," he said to himself; this was the moment to conclude their first meeting. They agreed to meet again in a few days to discuss the matter further. Herzl left New Court in an elated mood; he had not completely converted Rothschild, but the ice was certainly broken. Later in the afternoon his mood further improved when, unexpectedly, the Turkish ambassador to London informed him that the Sultan had cabled, urgently requesting Herzl to come immediately to Constantinople. The Rouvier scheme had not gone through after all. Herzl now played hard to get. He replied that he was tied up with the commission, and could only leave in a week. In any case, he would like more details by wire.

His appearance, later in the week, before the Royal Inquiry Commission, drew an unusually large crowd. Rothschild greeted Herzl as an old friend and introduced him to the other commissioners. In his prepared statement Herzl announced that the flight of Eastern European Jews to the West was the inevitable result of persecution; yet their course could be *diverted*, to a legally recognized national Jewish home, where Jews would no longer be regarded as aliens. He was subjected to a thorough cross-examination.

Major Evans-Gordon, a Conservative member of Parliament, who favored restrictions, tried to draw Herzl out to support his cause, but Herzl did not yield. He was opposed to legal restrictions of any kind. At the same time, he urged, the problem must be assaulted at its roots by recognizing the Jews as a people like all others, with a right to call one corner of the globe their own. The Jews needed a country, not charity. Rothschild questioned him closely on the compatibility of being a Zionist and a loyal English patriot. Herzl's use of the English language was halting, but his seriousness impressed the commission. The publicity following his appearance enhanced the sympathetic mood toward the Zionist aspirations in England.

Two days later he returned to New Court for another frank talk with Rothschild. The reconciliation was complete. After pledging Rothschild to secrecy, he showed him Eulenburg's letter of 1898 from Rominten, reporting the Kaiser's short-lived promise of a German protectorate, as well as the Grand Duke's letter announcing the same in even more definite language. He had not shown these letters to anyone, not even his closest associates. To Rothschild they came as a surprise, for like so many people, he had regarded Herzl as a windbag who was deluding the masses with pipe dreams.

"I am doing this, my lord, to show you how unfairly I have been judged. And also so that you may tell the British government, 'It is all right to deal with this man. He does not compromise his friends.'"

The old man was impressed and was ready to help. He still had serious reservations in principle about the very notion of a "Jewish" state, which he regarded as a retrogressive step. But he sensed something personal in Herzl, something appealingly audacious in his scheme, which moved him.

Herzl explained the plan of a Jewish company for the settlement of Sinai, Egyptian Palestine, and Cyprus. "Call together the leading figures in the City, from the Jewish company, and you will be doing England a patriotic service. But no philanthropy; it must be *business*."

"Put that in writing," Rothschild said, warming to the subject. He favored only a small experiment, 25,000 settlers at the most. In his opinion, there was no money for more.

"I must do it on a large scale or not at all," Herzl said.

They argued the point for a while, and no agreement was reached. The important thing was that Rothschild was ready to help. He promised Herzl that he would speak to the Colonial Secre-

tary, Joseph Chamberlain, two days hence. That talk would bear
fruit sooner than Herzl imagined

5

Herzl remained in England for another week. The Turkish
ambassador returned almost daily with cabled requests from Constantinople that Herzl come without delay. The Sultan was demanding his immediate appearance. The Rouvier group had made
a definite offer to consolidate the national debt at a cost to the
Turkish taxpayer of 32 million pounds. Could Herzl offer more
advantageous terms? If so, the Sultan would "give the Israelites
proofs of sympathy and protection."

Herzl suspected that the Turks might use him only to obtain
more favorable terms from Rouvier. Nevertheless he promised to
give a definite reply within a short time. Once more, as so often in
the past, he walked the tightrope between genius and adventurism,
for the Jewish Colonial Bank by itself was too small to raise 32
million pounds; its capital amounted to less than 10 percent of that
sum.

Messages from the Sultan, conveyed through the ambassador,
became more urgent and insistent every day. On July 15 an "ultimatum" arrived requesting Herzl to submit his proposal within
one day. Herzl replied that he could not properly carry out so
difficult an operation in fewer days than Rouvier had had months.
But he did indicate that his own offer might save the Turks two
million pounds at the outset and considerably more at a later stage.
He urged the Sultan to reject the French proposal because it was
advantageous only to the financiers and the imperialist powers
backing them.

On July 18 he returned to Austria, where he was bombarded
by more telegrams urging him to come to Constantinople. On July
23, accompanied by Wolffsohn, Herzl finally left for Turkey. They
arrived two days later. From the station Herzl drove straight to
Yildiz Palace. The heat, the dirt, the noise, and the uncertainty
grated on his nerves. It was his fifth visit to Turkey, a "wonderland," where, as he put it, "diplomacy was the art of dealing with
robbers."

The *baksheesh*-snatchers at the palace gates greeted him with
familiar grins, anticipating the gold showers that would mark his
exit. Inside the palace the reception was more cordial than ever

before. Beaming with satisfaction, Ibrahim Bey, the Sultan's master of ceremonies, welcomed Herzl effusively. Tahsin Bey, the Sultan's first secretary, informed Herzl that he was the Sultan's guest and that a carriage with footmen would be placed at his disposal. So impatient was the Sultan to receive Herzl's offer that Tahsin demanded an immediate written memorandum. Herzl, exhausted by the long journey, pleaded to be allowed an extra day. Tahsin made a doubtful face. Presently, the Sultan sent word that he would wait until the morning. To escape the stifling heat, Herzl retired to a hotel on Therapia, an island in the Sea of Marmara. Wearily he sat down and worked on his memorandum until 11:30 P.M. Ibrahim Bey was waiting in the palace to translate it into Turkish that very night.

The memorandum was in the form of a personal letter to the Sultan. Herzl offered to carry out the consolidation of the Turkish debt at 31.4 million, 1.6 million less than the French financiers had demanded. In return, Herzl demanded "a charter or concession for the Jewish colonization of Mesopotamia, as Y.I.M. deigned to offer me last February, plus the territory of Haifa and its environs in Palestine." The colonists naturally would pay the Turkish government an annual tribute in addition to all regular taxes and levies.

On the following morning, a Friday, Herzl arrived at the palace at noon. The foreign ambassadors, gathered in the forecourt for the *salamlik* ceremony, viewed him suspiciously. After waiting for two dreary, hot, demoralizing hours in Ibrahim's office, he was excused until 6:00 P.M. because the Sultan needed that much time to study his memorandum. But an hour later he was urgently recalled to the palace by cablegram, only to discover that his memorandum, which he had been urged to complete the night before, had not even been translated. At Yildiz Palace the reasons for haste, as for procrastination, always remained inscrutable. Karatheodory Pasha, an elder statesman who had represented Turkey at the Berlin conference of 1878, was now charged by the Sultan with urgently translating Herzl's four-page memorandum. Groaning and sweating, Karatheodory labored at his task until after midnight, interrupting himself occasionally to entertain Herzl with anecdotes of Bismarck and Disraeli. At 12:30 A.M. Tahsin Bey took the translation to the Sultan and Herzl was given an appointment for the next morning.

But when Herzl showed up punctually at ten, there was none of the urgency of the previous night. Herzl hung around for hours. After an elaborate lunch in Ibrahim Bey's office, Tahsin Bey brought a message from the Sultan, who wished Herzl to consult with Said Pasha, the Grand Vizier, about his memorandum. The Grand Vizier could see Herzl only on the following day, for he was suffering from a cold and an abscessed tooth.

On Sunday afternoon Ibrahim Bey, and another chamberlain, followed by three bodyguards, ceremoniously conducted Herzl to the Grand Vizier's office at the palace of the *Sublime Porte*, on the other side of town. The beggers and *baksheesh*-snatchers huddled in their rags as the procession of carriages charged through the gilded gates. At the Sublime Porte there was more waiting while Tahsin and Ibrahim disappeared into the Grand Vizier's office. Finally the door opened and Said Pasha, a small, pudgy, sick old man in a dressing gown, asked Herzl to come in.

Herzl repeated his proposals. The Grand Vizier asked Herzl if the Jewish colonists would accept Ottoman citizenship and serve in the army. As so many times in the past, Herzl declared that they most certainly would. The potential colonists were poor, persecuted Jews from Russia and Romania, he said; they were neither dangerous nor troublesome but a sober, industrious, loyal element bound to the Moslems by racial kinship and affinity.

The Grand Vizier congratulated Herzl on his campaign to aid the persecuted Jews; it was very humanitarian and commendable. But then, with a long side-glance at Tahsin and Ibrahim, he asked Herzl to give the names of the financiers who formed his syndicate. (This sidelong glance, Herzl told himself, and the shrewdness it reflected, are what make him the Grand Vizier!) Aloud he said he could not divulge the names at this particular moment; since the deal with Rouvier was said to be almost concluded, such a disclosure would not be ethical.

The Grand Vizier conceded the justice of this claim and did not press further. But with all his amiability, Said Pasha remained reserved. Amid more compliments and salaams, Herzl was dismissed. With the courtiers and the bodyguards he drove back through the teeming, dusty streets to the Sultan's palace.

At Yildiz a surprise awaited Herzl. The Sultan sent word that Herzl should not only write out a report of his conversation with the Grand Vizier, but also arrange for its translation by a confidant of his own. Apparently the Sultan wanted to check the accuracy of his own ministers' reports. For one long afternoon Herzl raced about Constantinople in search of a reliable translator; it was not an easy task in a city where he knew few people and trusted even fewer. He finally found a young Jewish student, whom he interviewed in a little cotton goods shop owned by the boy's uncle. It took the young man almost twenty-four hours to complete his task. Herzl told himself this might well be the first time one of his letters would actually reach the Sultan unadulterated by court intrigue or careless translation. But the main result was that the Turks gained more time to exploit Herzl's visit in their continuing talks with the Rouvier group.

On the following day Herzl was conducted a second time to the Grand Vizier, with as much pomp and ceremony as before. The interview began promisingly. Said Pasha said that the Sultan had been very satisfied by his two memoranda and was prepared "in principle" to go ahead with Herzl's propositions. Herzl's heart pounded as he bowed deeply. But then the conversation became hazy and inconsequential as innumerable cups of black coffee were passed around and the room was enveloped in cigarette smoke.

The procrastination continued for two more days. The boredom of endlessly waiting in Ibrahim's or Tahsin's office between interviews was excruciating, like a cramp slowly spreading from the nape of one's neck. Herzl's stomach rebelled against the greasy, lukewarm palace food which had to be swallowed with unending exclamations of happiness and satisfaction. By now Herzl was convinced that the Sultan had forced him to come to Constantinople only to squeeze better terms out of Rouvier.

Another man might have despaired. Herzl consoled himself that it was all for the best: most assuredly at their next financial crisis the Turks would be eager to settle with him. And that crisis was bound to come as soon as the meager profits from the Rouvier operation were squandered or stolen by the corrupt state machine.

At the week's end the Turks concluded their deal with Rouvier. On Herzl's last day in Constantinople, the Sultan, through Tahsin Bey, asked him to accept a sizable subsidy for the *Neue Freie Presse*. Herzl refused immediately, but he accepted, "for my poor," a red silk money bag the Sultan had sent him as reimbursement for his cash expenses.

17

The Sinai Wilderness

AS THE TRAIN SPED through the Bulgarian countryside, Herzl wryly plotted his next steps. He would henceforth approach his goal by an indirect route. His ultimate aim remained the opening of Palestine to large-scale Jewish immigration under adequate legal guarantees. But if Palestine could not be obtained at the moment, he was determined to find a substitute territory, perhaps nearby, to absorb the persecuted masses.

Recent directives against the Jews of Romania reinforced Herzl's sense of urgency. The vast majority of native-born Romanian Jews were excluded from Romanian citizenship. Now an arbitrary new law sought to exclude them from pursuing any useful livelihood; reduced to beggary, they would have to emigrate. While Herzl had been in Constantinople, protest meetings against the new law had been held in many European countries, as well as in America. The United States had lodged an official protest against the discriminatory measures; the Romanian government chose to ignore it.

In his search for a temporary "substitute" to Palestine, Herzl pinned his hopes on the benevolence of the English. As he had told the fourth congress in London, "England, great England, England the free, England commanding all the seas—she will understand us and our purpose!" England controlled two territories adjacent to Palestine—Cyprus and the Sinai Peninsula. The latter was known as Egyptian Palestine. If the British government agreed to grant Herzl a "charter" for the colonization of Sinai or Cyprus, he could wave it before the reluctant rulers of Turkey. Such a charter, Herzl felt, would benefit both British and Jewish interests:

It must be made clear to the British government that we are ready and able to serve as pioneers of the British interests. . . . Here is an opportunity for England to stop the spread of French influence in Syria and Palestine. *We* are that opportunity. We could serve them as a cover. England should support us, and we shall remain within the British sphere of influence.

On his return to Vienna Herzl immediately instructed Leopold Greenberg in London to seek a meeting with the British Colonial Secretary, Joseph Chamberlain. And he tried once again to cultivate the sympathies of the still vacillating Lord Rothschild. In an August 12 letter he pleaded with Rothschild:

Ah, if you only had some inkling of the boundless misery and distress of our poor *honest* people—I am not talking of *schnorrers* [beggars] and rabble—you would listen to me more fully. There is no counting the heartbreaking letters from workers, business people, men of academic training, that I receive. I must answer all with a sigh: "I cannot help you."

Rothschild sidestepped his urgent pleas. "I should view with horror the establishment of a Jewish colony pure and simple," he wrote Herzl on August 18. "Such a colony would be *imperium imperio*; it would be a ghetto with the prejudices of the ghetto; a small petty Jewish state, Orthodox and illiberal, excluding the Gentiles and the Christians."

In his pique at this accusation, Herzl sent Rothschild, on August 24, a copy of *Altneuland*, his blueprint of a liberal, open, tolerant commonwealth:

I cannot agree that the Jewish commonwealth I intend to set up simply must be narrow-minded, Orthodox, and illiberal. . . . Were the founders of other states, which are now great, any mightier, cleverer, better educated, richer, than we Jews of today? Poor shepherds and huntsmen have established humble communities that later became great states. Greeks, Romanians, Serbs, Bulgarians have established themselves in our own day—why should we be incapable of doing so? Our race is more capable than most other peoples of the earth. This, in fact, is the reason for the great hatred. We have not had self-confidence until now. On the day when we begin to believe in ourselves, our moral misery will end.

Meanwhile, in London, Leopold Greenberg pleaded Herzl's cause at the Foreign and Colonial offices, and on September 22 cabled that Joseph Chamberlain was ready to grant Herzl an interview. Herzl was elated, but was unable to depart at once because his employers on the *Neue Freie Presse* demanded his help in combating a newly established rival daily. A month later, on October 19, Herzl finally "bolted from the office like a schoolboy," without informing his employers. Again he feared that he might lose his livelihood. He was still troubled by his heart condition. In the train he rehearsed his forthcoming audience. "Mr. Chamberlain," he would say, "you are accustomed to seeing great historical questions suddenly rise before you. . . . In collaboration with the Jews, England might powerfully enhance its position throughout the eastern Mediterranean."

Two days after his arrival Herzl had his first meeting with Chamberlain at the Colonial Office. Chamberlain listened, poker-faced, to his detailed exposition. The great colonialist, who had begun political life as a radical, had come around in recent years to "think imperially." Chamberlain was not another Reverend Hechler. His interests were political and financial. He shared none of the romantic philo-Semitism of the English Protestant clergy. He is said to have told Baron Sonino, the half-Jewish Italian statesman, in 1899: "There is, in fact, only one race I despise—the Jews, sir. They are physical cowards." But as he listened to Herzl, his cold, calm face gradually melted into a sympathetic smile. Herzl appealed not to his sentiment, but to his political imagination, and occasionally to his sense of humor.

"I am negotiating with the Sultan," Herzl said. "But you know what Turkish negotiations are. If you want to buy a carpet, you must first drink half a dozen cups of coffee and smoke a hundred cigarettes. Then come the family stories and from time to time a few more words about the carpet. Now *I* have the time to negotiate, but my people do not. They are starving in the Pale. I must bring them immediate help." He asked Chamberlain outright to give him Cyprus and the Sinai Peninsula for Jewish colonization.

Chamberlain replied that, as Colonial Secretary, he could speak only in terms of Cyprus. British-controlled Sinai was not a colony and therefore came under the jurisdiction of the Foreign Office. He doubted that Jewish colonization was possible in Cyprus; its Greek and Moslem populations would undoubtedly oppose it and provoke as big a storm as the Australians had recently raised against Indian immigration. He was, however, prepared to help.

He liked the idea of Zionism, Chamberlain said. He assured Herzl that "personally" he had nothing against Jews; on the contrary, if by chance he had a drop of Jewish blood in his veins, he would have been proud of it. Herzl wrote later, "But *voilà*—he didn't have a drop!"

Chamberlain thought Sinai was a better proposition. A Jewish colony at El Arish in the unpopulated Sinai wilderness was much more politically acceptable than a colony on Cyprus. He did not exactly know where Sinai was, so Herzl pointed it out to him on a map. To Herzl he seemed like the manager of a big junk shop who knows he has a certain article in his store but must rummage about to find it.

As they were poring over the map, Chamberlain noticed Sinai's proximity to Egypt. "Oh, wouldn't we have the same difficulty with the natives in Egypt [as in Cyprus]?"

"No," Herzl replied jokingly, "we shall not go to Egypt: *we have already been there.*"

Chamberlain laughed. For the first time he seemed to fully understand Herzl's scheme to gain a foothold in the immediate vicinity of Turkish-controlled Palestine.

"El Arish and Sinai are vacant land. You could give us that," Herzl said. "In return England would reap increased power and the gratitude of ten million Jews. Would you agree to a Jewish colony in the Sinai Peninsula?"

Chamberlain brightened. "Yes," he said, "if Lord Cromer favors it." Lord Cromer, nominally "British Agent and Consul General" in Cairo, was the undisputed ruler of Egypt; he was responsible to the Foreign Office.

Chamberlain promptly arranged for Herzl to meet Lord Landsdowne, the Foreign Secretary, and promised to warmly recommend Herzl's scheme. But, he warned, "be sure to assure Landsdowne that your proposed colony is not a jumping-off place aimed at the Sultan's possessions."

He smiled mischievously as he said this. Herzl replied, "There can be no question of that. I intend to go to Palestine only with the Sultan's consent."

Chamberlain continued to smile, as if to say, "Let the Sultan believe *that!*" Aloud he repeated, "Reassure Lord Landsdowne that you are not planning a Jameson Raid* from El Arish into Palestine."

---

* Sir Leander Jameson, British colonialist, in 1895 attempted to force the issue of Transvaal (the last remaining obstacle to a South African federation

"I shall certainly set his mind at rest," Herzl said, also laughing.

On the afternoon of October 23, Herzl had his first talk with Lord Landsdowne at the Foreign Office. The ground seemed to have been well prepared by Chamberlain. Landsdowne gave Herzl a very sympathetic hearing. Herzl proposed the establishment of a Jewish Eastern Company, with an initial capital of five million pounds. The company would be granted a concession to develop roads, harbors, railways, industries, and mines in the Sinai Peninsula, and to parcel out land for masses of poor Jewish immigrants. Eventually this "Egyptian province of Judea," as Herzl called it, would be granted some sort of semi-autonomy, under the British crown. England would gain a rich and loyal colony; ten million grateful Jews would proclaim British grandeur and influence; the poor persecuted Jews of Eastern Europe would gain a safe haven.

Lord Landsdowne refused to commit himself before consulting with Cromer in Cairo. But to Herzl he seemed most agreeable to the scheme. Everything now depended on Lord Cromer's advice. Leopold Greenberg, as Herzl's agent, would proceed to Cairo immediately. That evening Herzl triumphantly noted in his diary that it had been "a great day in the history of the Jewish people."

2

He returned to Vienna in poorer health but hopeful of an imminent breakthrough. Greenberg's first message from Cairo reached him on November 7. "Everything all right," Greenberg cabled. He was on his way to Vienna to report to Herzl directly.

"Could it be that we are on the eve of obtaining a British charter and the establishment of a Jewish state?" Herzl wondered. "My total exhaustion makes it seem credible." He made elaborate plans to establish huge fisheries, canning factories, harbors, artificial lakes, railroads, and dikes for the collection of rainwater, all on the barren coast of Sinai. In his mind's eye he saw Sinai as one of the main industrial centers for the whole of Asia.

Herzl's optimism was not wholeheartedly shared by his colleagues in the movement who were just then gathered in Vienna

---

under the British flag) by invading, with a force of about five hundred men, Transvaal without the British government's consent. The raid failed. Jameson was later tried in England under the Foreign Enlistment Act. From 1904 to 1908 he was Prime Minister of the Cape.

for the annual conference of the Zionist Actions Committee. The Sinai wilderness belonged to Egypt, which was theoretically still a vassal of the Ottoman Empire even though it was in fact ruled by Britain; was it wise to become a *fourth* party to this complicated arrangement? Leon Kellner was one of the few with the courage to tell Herzl "very quietly, trying not to excite him," that he considered the whole project impossible. As far as Kellner knew, Sinai was a waterless stretch of lunar desolation unfit for human habitation. Herzl expressed his conviction that there was enough water in the Nile to make that desert flower. And even if Sinai was a desert, he liked the powerful symbolic gesture of pitching the Zionist tent in Sinai as a prelude to settlement in Palestine. He accused Kellner of distracting him with unimaginative pedantry at a time when he sorely needed all his strength. Kellner stuck to his argument and the two men parted, both greatly upset.

Herzl's spirits were restored when Leopold Greenberg, passing through Vienna on his way from Cairo to London, reported "complete success." He had talked to Lord Cromer and the Egyptian Prime Minister Boutros Ghali Pasha. Both, he said, had been won over to the cause.

Meanwhile, Cromer discussed Herzl's scheme with Chamberlain, who was visiting Cairo on his way to East Africa. Cromer's first reaction was positive. He "saw no political objections to the establishment of a [Jewish] colony" in the Sinai Peninsula. The one political condition he raised did not seem unreasonable. There was a long-standing conflict between Britain and Turkey over the exact delineation of the border between (Turkish) Palestine and (British-Egyptian) Sinai. Therefore, Cromer insisted, there could be no settlement in the contested areas north and east of El Arish. There was, however, enough vacant land elsewhere in the vast wilderness. As for the economic feasibility of settling it, Cromer pleaded ignorance and suggested an inquiry commission be sent to the area. Although he had been the virtual ruler of Egypt for almost two decades, he confessed that he himself had never visited Sinai.

Three weeks later, on December 18, the British government made its first move. In a letter to Herzl, Sir Thomas H. Sanderson, Permanent Undersecretary of Foreign Affairs, suggested that the Zionists dispatch a commission to explore actual conditions on the peninsula. Pending a favorable report, Sanderson agreed to the establishment of a Jewish colony in Sinai. The settlers would have to renounce their original nationality, be wholly subject to Egyptian (i.e., British) rule, and pay Cairo an annual subsidy for the maintenance of order within the colony and without. They might, however, be exempted from taxation on whatever land they might bring under cultivation. As long as the British occupation of Egypt lasted, they would be assured of just and impartial treatment.

Herzl was in a state of near euphoria. Sanderson's letter was "a historic document." It recognized Herzl as a partner in serious international negotiations and held the promise of an important beginning. "We are about to emerge from the realm of dreams and set our feet on solid ground," he wrote to Otto Warburg, the noted German botanist who had recently been converted to the Zionist cause. In his diary he envisaged a flourishing "Egyptian province of Judea," with its own elected governor and protected by a Jewish defense force commanded by Anglo-Egyptian officers.

The next step was the speedy dispatch of experts to explore actual conditions in the area. Herzl had little doubt that they would find Sinai suitable for settlement. In the first week of January he traveled to Paris and London to conclude all practical arrangements for the inquiry. He had barely arrived in London when Rothschild—more sympathetic to his cause than ever before—came to see him in his hotel. "Two years ago," Herzl commented, "he would not even meet me at Lady Battersea's." He showed Rothschild his correspondence with the British government and begged him to find three million pounds for the Jewish Eastern Company; he hoped to raise the remaining two million pounds by popular subscription. He offered Rothschild the financial leadership of the entire project.

"No, no, you will be at the head, Dr. Herzl," protested Rothschild. "I only want to be your co-worker. I will be pleased if I can be of help to you."

Later in the day, Herzl and Greenberg went to Downing Street to see Sir Thomas Sanderson. The three men agreed on the itinerary of the proposed expedition and its membership. The leader would be Leopold Kessler, a mining engineer with considerable experience in South Africa. Other members selected were Jennings Bramley, a surveyor formerly employed in the Sudan, whom Lord Cromer had recommended as the greatest living expert on Sinai, and George H. Stephens, an expert on irrigation, also recommended by the British. Herzl's Viennese colleague, Oscar Marmorek, the architect, would explore the problems of urban development; Emile Laurent, a Belgian scientist and expert on the Congo, would report on agrarian aspects. The remaining members were Dr. Hillel Joffe, a Jaffa physician; and the romantic Colonel

Albert Goldsmid, whose short-lived enthusiasm for Herzl's cause had been rekindled by the Sinai project. He would serve as quartermaster and liaison officer with the British government.

Two weeks later the expedition arrived in Egypt and was briefed by Lord Cromer and members of his administration. On February 11, 1903, mounted on camels and attended by an exotic array of servants, cooks, water carriers, and runners supplied, along with their tents, by Cook's Travel Office, the experts crossed the Suez Canal at Kantara and headed northeast toward El Arish. Leopold Greenberg returned to Cairo to negotiate details of the concession with the Egyptian government. Herzl wrote Rothschild on February 10: "I hope that the expedition will return safe and sound in just a few weeks and soon afterward I shall be in possession of the charter."

But Lord Cromer and the Egyptian government were not to be rushed. On February 16 Greenberg cabled Herzl that the Sultan's representative in Egypt was doing all he could to obstruct their scheme. Herzl, in his answer, suggested that Greenberg offer him a bribe. On the following day Greenberg cabled that it appeared absolutely impossible to obtain a charter, but that he had suggested an alternative to Cromer which was now under consideration. Herzl was dumbfounded. "Do not understand what you mean by alternative," he cabled back. "Please give full explanation." Greenberg's evasiveness alarmed and amazed Herzl. Still without an explanation of what had happened, Greenberg answered that he was returning to London and asked Herzl to meet him in Paris. Herzl was vexed and replied, "I will not come Paris. I am anxiously awaiting report as soon as possible."

On February 26, as he was leaving Cairo, Greenberg informed Herzl that Cromer's last words to him had been "Above all, tell Dr. Herzl he will wreck everything and accomplish nothing if he tries to hurry things in this country." Egyptian Prime Minister Boutros Ghali had, however, given Greenberg a "document" that Greenberg considered "very satisfactory." Although it was not the desired charter, it stipulated the establishment of a Jewish "municipality" in El Arish.

Meanwhile the Sinai expedition was slowly making its way across the desert. Its preliminary findings were encouraging and suggested that large-scale settlement in Sinai was possible. On March 16 Greenberg finally arrived in Vienna. Herzl was thoroughly dissatisfied with his report. He felt the paper that Greenberg had received from Boutros Ghali was meaningless and noncommittal; it made no mention of Herzl or of the Zionist movement. Greenberg would have liked to return to Cairo, but Herzl had lost faith in him. He decided to go to Cairo himself. The Italian steamer *Semiramis* was sailing for Egypt from Trieste on the following evening. Herzl took a train for Trieste that same night.

3

He arrived in Cairo on March 23 and took rooms at Shepheard's Hotel. Still hopeful, he rationalized the setback as a result of Greenberg's ineptitude. He wrote Mandelstamm in Kiev: "I am out to win the Archimedean point. There is hope, although as yet no certainty, that I shall be successful." The expedition was still in Sinai, charting the lagoons and interviewing Bedouin fishermen, so Herzl sent a camel rider out to summon its leaders to Cairo.

On March 25 he had his first meeting with Lord Cromer. The interview was not a success. "Lord Cromer is the most unpleasant Englishman I ever faced," Herzl commented in his diary. The great colonial administrator announced that he was willing to support the scheme, but would not share Herzl's enthusiasm. When Herzl developed his program to construct ports and railroads, Cromer cut him short: "We will talk about this later." He disliked the Zionist leader's effusiveness and left no doubt in Herzl's mind that he would have preferred to transact business with Englishmen rather than with emotional foreigners. "When is Mr. Greenberg coming back?" he asked pointedly. Herzl winced at this hint, which he attributed to a case of tropical madness and vice-regal hauteur. "My lord," he replied, "I do not see him coming back."

Cromer repeated that he would like to see the Sinai project succeed but insisted that nothing be hurried, that everything be done in a businesslike way. The settlers could not expect more than municipal autonomy. Britain's delicate position as one alien people controlling a second (the Turks), by whom they were disliked, in the government of a third (the Egyptians), precluded the granting of a formal charter to still a fourth (the Jews).

"Should I visit the Turkish representative?" Herzl asked.

"No, he has no say here," Cromer said. "I don't recognize him. Do not contact him at all." But he urged Herzl to see Egyptian Prime Minister Boutros Ghali. For the rest, Cromer wanted to

A Jewish colonist in Palestine at the time of Herzl's visit.

Herzl at the gates of Mikve Israel expecting the Kaiser's cavalcade.

Above: Kaiser Wilhelm's triumphal entry to Jerusalem: "He will understand me. He is trained to understand great things."

Left: Herzl greeting the Kaiser at Mikve Israel: "The land needs a lot of water." (Wolffsohn's hand trembled as he took the shot. The picture was later reconstructed through the combination of two shots.)

The expedition explores the proposed site for a Jewish colony in Sinai, a stepping-stone to Palestine: "A miniature England in reverse. Let us establish the colonies first and the motherland later."

Herzl in Egypt negotiating for the lease of Sinai with the British.

Anti-Semitic cartoon, the Knights of Zionism:
"Well, dear coreligionist—will you follow us
to Zion?" The coreligionist: "Nu, what could
one nebbish do in Zion? But I'll buy from
you."

Viennese cartoon,
"The Biggest Jew Alive."

Herzl and his mother surrounded by delegates to the sixth congress.

Herzl in 1903.

Facing page: Herzl's funeral in 1904: "They streamed through the streets of Vienna on their way to the Promised Land."

The tomb on Mount Herzl. In the background the new government quarter and University of Jerusalem, in the distance the mountains of Moab, where Moses had viewed the Promised Land he could not enter.

await the return of the experts and the government's reaction to their report.

Herzl drove directly to the Prime Minister's office. Servants idled in the corridors, and through the open doors, the Premier's British aides could be seen sipping their eleven o'clock tea. Boutros Ghali Pasha received Herzl immediately. "Where are you going to get water from?" he demanded.

Herzl explained that the water would be pumped to Sinai from the Nile, but only surplus water that otherwise flows into the sea. "We will build reservoirs for it." The two men drank Turkish coffee, and the Prime Minister of Egypt seemed to agree with all that Herzl proposed. Herzl took his leave. "An Egyptian Ministry," he commented in his diary, "in which the Egyptians cannot give any orders."

The expedition was not due back until three days later. Herzl was in a terrible mood, his health was poor, and he attributed the failure of his interview with Cromer to his own general exhaustion: "I was not in full possession of my faculties." He attended a lecture by Sir William Willcocks, a celebrated irrigation expert, who spoke on the canalization of Chaldea, the area in Mesopotamia that the Sultan had offered him the year before. Bored by the lecture, he was fascinated by the audience. A mass of eager, intelligent-looking young Egyptians packed the hall. Herzl was struck by what he had so blatantly overlooked on his visit to Palestine in 1899—the potential force of the native population. "They are the coming masters," he noted in his diary. "It is surprising that the English do not see this. They think they are going to deal with *fellahin* forever. One wishes one could come back in fifty years to see how it has turned out."

At the same time he was completely shattered by the misery of the *fellahin* he saw on a visit to the Pyramids. "I resolve to think of the *fellahin* too, once I am in power," he commented in his diary. A few days later the expedition returned to Cairo. Kessler and Goldsmid bounded into Herzl's room at 11:00 P.M., suntanned and in high spirits. Goldsmid read Herzl the preliminary report until 12:30 A.M. In most of its findings the report was encouraging enough. There were great prospects in the fields of mining, fishery, and shipping. But the key sentences read, "Under existing conditions the country is quite unsuitable for European settlers. If, however, sufficient water resources are made available . . . it could support a considerable population."

This was the crux of the matter—*water*. In the next few days Herzl and the experts conferred several times with Lord Cromer. Herzl proposed that they syphon Nile water to Sinai via a pipe under the Suez Canal. George Stephens, the expedition's British irrigation expert, insisted that there was sufficient water in the Nile to satisfy the needs of both Egypt and the proposed Sinai colony. Cromer, suffering a bad cold, reacted sourly to Stephens' entreaties and demanded time to study the water problem more closely. He also wondered whether Herzl and the Zionists had sufficient funds to realize so ambitious a program as the development of Sinai and the subsequent purchase of Palestine.

"Do not think that I am entirely powerless," Herzl snapped at Cromer at one point. "If I call upon twenty thousand young Jews to join me in seizing Palestine by force of arms, I tell you they shall respond!" Yet, he assured him, he preferred to proceed by peaceful means. Cromer relented a little; he asked Herzl to begin negotiating legal details with the Egyptian government. At Cromer's suggestion Herzl hired a local attorney, a Belgian by the name of Carton de Wiart. He instructed de Wiart to draft a lease of Sinai for ninety-nine years in return for an annual tribute. "We will give up the word 'charter,' but not the thing itself." He reminded de Wiart of Talleyrand's dictum that a good constitution "must be short and—*obscure*." But the outcome still depended on a solution of the water question, which would not be decided before the return to Egypt, in May, of Sir William Garstyn, Cromer's chief expert on public works.

Herzl left Egypt on April 4; Goldsmid remained behind as his representative. Herzl paused only a few days in Vienna before rushing on to London to see Chamberlain. Lord Cromer had upset him. His final words to Herzl had been that "many modifications" would have to be made in the draft concession before it could be accepted. Herzl pinned all his hopes on Chamberlain. "He is more detached [than Cromer] and therefore has a higher view—*and* he does not know the value of the big tract of land I am demanding."

Cromer had anticipated Herzl's intervention in London and had already cabled a warning to the Foreign Office. "He is a wild enthusiast. Be careful not to pledge yourself to anything in dealing with him."

Chamberlain received Herzl amicably, like an old friend. He had been to Egypt, East Africa, and back, and seemed to Herzl a great deal older and more world-weary. "Since we last met I have seen quite a bit of the world," he said, a little tiredly. The report of the Sinai expedition lay before him on his desk.

"It is not very favorable," he remarked.

"Well, it is a very poor country," Herzl said, "but we will make something out of it."

Chamberlain waved his hand and gave the conversation an unexpected turn. "I think I have seen *another* land for you on my recent travels. *Uganda!*" he said. "It is hot on the coast, but farther inland the climate is excellent, even for Europeans. You could plant sugar and cotton there. So I thought to myself, 'That is a land for Dr. Herzl. But of course he is sentimental and wants to go to Palestine or thereabouts.'"

"Yes I do," replied Herzl. "We must have the base in or near Palestine. Later on we might also settle in Uganda, for we have masses ready to emigrate. But we must build on a national base— that is why we must have the political glamour of El Arish."

Chamberlain did not press the issue. But he regretted that Herzl seemed so committed to the politics of sentimentalism. Chamberlain was also dubious of the Zionists' chances in the Near East. He feared that there might soon be a showdown there among France, Germany, and Russia. "What would then be the fate of your Jewish colony in Palestine, supposing you have succeeded in establishing it?"

"Our chances would then be even better," Herzl replied. "For we shall be used as a small buffer state. We shall [keep Palestine] not from good will, but from the jealousy of the powers."

There the matter rested. Within a few months Chamberlain's unexpected offer of Uganda would cause the most shattering, most tragic turn in Herzl's entire career. At the moment, neither he nor Chamberlain was aware of that.

Herzl had a few more futile meetings in London and Paris with Rothschild and other Jewish millionaires, who showed interest in his Sinai project but announced they could not raise more than one million pounds. In a bad state of health, embittered at his failure, Herzl returned to Vienna on April 30. At home he was subjected to a nerve-shattering scene by his wife. Julie had been under psychiatric treatment in recent months; in addition to other maladies that remain obscure, she suffered from recurrent attacks of hysteria. Julie sobbed and screamed at Herzl that Zionism had cost her a husband, and their children a father, as the frightened children huddled with their German governess in the nursery. Why

was he constantly away? Where was he going next? Herzl calmly
but vainly pleaded with his wife.

A few days later, more shattering news arrived from Goldsmid
in Cairo. Sir William Garstyn, upon his return to Egypt, had vetoed
the Sinai project because, in his view, there was not enough water
in the Nile. On May 7 Goldsmid cabled: "Lord Cromer recom-
mends abandonment." Cromer had concluded that even if there
were enough water in the Nile the cost of "syphoning it to Sinai
under the Suez Canal would be prohibitive." Moreover, construction of the syphons would interrupt traffic in the Suez Canal and
disturb British trade with the Far East.

The Sinai project was dead. "I considered [it] so completely
certain that I no longer sought to buy a family vault in the Döbling
cemetery, where my father is provisionally laid to rest," Herzl
wrote in his diary on May 15. "I now consider the affair so hopeless
that I have already been to the district court and I am acquiring
vault number 28." Jakob Herzl was exhumed, to be buried in the
new vault. Herzl's aides urged him to absent himself from the
ceremony in view of his heart condition, but he ignored their advice. Gazing tremblingly into the vault, he murmured, "Soon, soon,
I too will lie down there."

18

Split over Uganda

ON APRIL 19 an outrage occurred in the small Bessarabian town of Kishinev, which, in less than 48 hours, left 45 local Jews lying dead, and nearly 600 wounded; 1,500 shops and homes were pillaged or destroyed. The church bells were ringing on Easter Sunday, when a wild mob, undoubtedly acting on a given signal, rushed through the narrow streets killing Jews and setting fire to their homes and stores. In the past few decades Kishinev's Christian population of some 60,000 had lived peacefully alongside 50,000 Jewish artisans and small shopkeepers. The only newspaper in the town was a sensational anti-Semitic journal, the *Bessarabitz*, subsidized by the czarist Ministry of the Interior from a special slush fund. In recent months the *Bessarabitz* had waged a vicious campaign against the Jews of Kishinev, accusing them of the ritual murder of Christian babies and of sponsoring, at the same time, both socialist revolution and the capitalist exploitation of Christians.

The police made no attempt to interfere in the widespread killing, looting, and arson. For almost twenty-four hours, while the army was ordered by the provincial governor to remain in its barracks, the mob ran amok. Nails were driven into victims' skulls, eyes gouged out, and babies thrown from the higher stories of buildings to the pavement. Men were castrated, women were raped. The local bishop drove in his carriage through the crowd, blessing it as he passed. Only on the evening of the second day did the police appear on the scene to disperse the mob. By then the devastation had been accomplished. It was generally believed that Konstantin Pobedonostsev, the Czar's close adviser and head of the Holy Synod, had inspired the outrage in order to divert popular sentiments from the social revolutionists.

Pobedonostsev's own solution of the Jewish problem was known to be three-pronged: a third would convert, a third would emigrate, and a third would die. It was widely reported that Wenzel von Plehve, the czarist Minister of the Interior, had instructed the provincial governor of Kishinev not to be overzealous in his protection of the Jews. At Kishinev the government was testing a new technique to drown the revolutionary fervor in Jewish blood. News of the pogrom was suppressed in the Russian newspapers, which merely stated that there had been a sudden outbreak provoked by the Jews.

To modern eyes the Kishinev outrage may seem "small" in comparison to the disasters of World War II and its aftermath. In the quieter days of 1903 the sudden slaughter produced so traumatic a shock that everywhere in the East, Jews began to reassess their entire outlook on life. Many began to search for radical solutions—in revolution or in its twin phenomenon, Zionism. Tolstoi denounced the Kishinev outrage as a direct result of government propaganda. Chaim Nachman Bialik, the greatest living Hebrew poet, wrote in a fit of poetic rage that the Devil himself had not yet invented a fitting revenge for the blood of a small Kishinev child.

2

News of the Kishinev pogrom reached Herzl in London, before his final interview with Chamberlain. The disaster confirmed the dire predictions he had repeated *ad nauseam* over the past eight years. He felt sure that Kishinev was not the end; worse was to come. He was still hoping to convince Chamberlain that Cromer was overcautious, and that the Sinai project was feasible. Sinai could serve as a first way station toward national reconstruction for hundreds of thousands of rescued Russian Jews.

In the first week of May it became clear that the Sinai project was doomed. Brooding over this new failure, Herzl feverishly searched for yet another solution. His next scheme was twofold.

First, he decided to reconsider Chamberlain's offer of Uganda. Time was running out in Russia. Undoubtedly Palestine was a better choice than Uganda, but one had to begin *somewhere*. On May 20 Chamberlain met Leopold Greenberg in London and repeated his offer. The British government was ready to lease the Zionists a vast area, not actually in Uganda, but in what is now Kenya, in the valley rift between the Mau escarpment in the west and the Kikuyu in the south. Here Chamberlain was prepared to grant the Zionists a form of "self-government" in an area big enough to absorb one million settlers.

Herzl cabled Greenberg that Chamberlain's proposal must be given "serious consideration." In June the London law firm of George, Roberts & Co. was engaged to draft a charter in time for the forthcoming Zionist congress. The senior law partner in charge of these preparations was Lloyd George, the future Prime Minister.* The colony was to be called New Palestine; its stated purpose was to foster the welfare of the Jewish people and to further the national Jewish idea.

But Uganda was only one pebble in the political mosaic Herzl began to construct in the aftermath of Kishinev. His scheme was more complex, more fantastic, and called for what Herzl defined as a "miniature England in reverse": the creation of a far-flung colonial empire to precede the actual establishment of a homeland. As he prepared to secure a British charter for Uganda, he struggled at the same time to obtain similar concessions in the Congo from the Belgian government, from Portugal in Mozambique, and from the Italian government in Tripoli. He proposed to create half a dozen Jewish colonies in Africa and elsewhere, to be used as national bases and training stations for the eventual repossession of Palestine by the Jews. For Jews, everything always was upside down anyway. With all other peoples, colonies were founded by the motherland; in this case the colonies would come first and later establish a motherland. At the same time Herzl renewed his contacts with the Turkish Sultan, whose offer of Mesopotamia he had rejected in the past. "Events are pressing," he wrote the Sultan's secretary, Izzet Bey, on June 4. "You have certainly heard of the Kishinev atrocities. Our poor Jews are miserable, and something must be found for them." If Palestine and Mesopotamia were not obtainable, "we shall be obliged to find another territory. There is no lack of opportunity." In a separate envelope he enclosed the following lines to Izzet:

> My dear friend:
> Permit me to call you that and to speak as a friend. How much do you want for yourself if the scheme works? Write me the amount and the way in which I should make it available to

* Under Lloyd George's premiership, the Balfour Declaration was issued in 1917, which stipulated "the establishment in Palestine of a national home for the Jewish people."

you on an unsigned piece of paper, and put it in a sealed envelope on which you put only my name.*

The first warning of trouble among Herzl's closest associates came from Max Nordau. Better than Herzl, he sensed the passionate attachment of Eastern European Jews to Palestine, and Palestine alone, which no substitute Zion could replace. Herzl replied on July 13:

> Have you suddenly lost all faith in me? Do you consider me wholly thoughtless in such serious matters? When we failed at El Arish I simply had to return [to the Uganda offer]. An English colonialist will declare Uganda much better than El Arish; a Zionist will say it is much worse. This then is the purpose of leadership, to point the way, which even by an apparent detour, leads our people to the goal. *Moses had to do the same.* If there is to be a storm, we shall have to quell it.
>
> When I asked Jewry for money for the Sultan—by which we could have made [Palestine] easily—I did not get any. *Eh bien, quoi?* We will just have to try another way, and this is it. We shall colonize [Uganda] on a national basis, with a flag, *s'il vous plaît*, and self-government.
>
> We make the formulas; we are not their prisoners. Where we will first break ground is only a question of opportunity, if only we are clear in our minds what kind of house we are building on the foundation.
>
> The settlement between Kilimanjaro and Kenya could be our first *political* colony. You already guess what I mean: a miniature England *in reverse*.

Next, as the second part of his new plan, Herzl decided to approach Russia directly. For most Jews of his time, the czarist regime was the very incarnation of evil. But in order to save his people and alleviate their suffering, Herzl was ready to deal with the Devil himself. Since Russia was so obviously and so brutally anxious to rid itself of its Jewish population, which it considered "alien" and revolutionary, Herzl believed that he might induce the Russian government to at least tolerate the Zionist movement (which was still illegal in Russia). As a world power, Russia might

---

* At this time a great Arab landowner in Palestine offered Herzl a huge tract of land in the Esdraelon valley. Herzl was reluctant to buy it without adequate international guarantees. Moreover, the area—although only sparsely settled—was not empty. Herzl said, "We cannot disinherit these poor *fellahin*."

even exert diplomatic pressure on the Turkish government to permit a form of Jewish autonomy in Palestine.

His first written appeal to Plehve and Pobedonostsev remained unanswered. At Herzl's request Berta von Suttner wrote to the Czar, pleading with him most urgently to receive Herzl as a man of peace. "I shall do it, although it is an audacity," Suttner commented in her diary, "and it will not work, but I will try just the same." Within a week she was informed by Count Lamsdorff, the Russian Foreign Minister, that an audience with the Czar was out of the question. Early in July Herzl remembered that he knew an influential Polish noblewoman living in St. Petersburg, the writer Paulina von Korvin-Piatrovska, who was said to be on friendly terms with Plehve. He asked Korvin-Piatrovska for help. A few days later she replied with good news. Not only was Plehve "delighted to meet as interesting a personality as Dr. Herzl," but he was even more interested in Herzl's proposal to organize Jewish emigration from Russia "without right of reentry."

Herzl's Russian disciples reacted to his decision to meet the butcher of Kishinev with mixed feelings. One leading Russian Zionist considered it his "sacred duty" to travel from St. Petersburg to Vienna to warn Herzl against taking this trip. He brought with him "material proof" that Plehve was directly responsible for the Kishinev pogrom. Plehve might exploit his meeting with Herzl to whitewash his tarnished reputation in the eyes of an aroused public in the West. Herzl would not listen; his journey to Russia would proceed as planned.

3

He left on August 5, having first submitted to the humiliating procedures mandatory at the time for men of the Jewish religion seeking entrance into czarist Russia.* Before leaving Vienna he paid a solemn visit to his father's grave. He had a dread of Russia, and on the train he was plagued by terrible headaches. At the border he was exposed to a rigorous search. His journey had been kept secret from most of his colleagues, but excited well-wishers greeted him at the railway station. "They are so badly off," Herzl remarked, "poor devils, I seem to them like a liberator!" Dr. Nissan Katzenelson, the leading Russian Zionist and a private banker in

---

* Even as foreign nationals, Jews were forced to apply for special permission from the Department of Foreign Religious Cults in St. Petersburg.

Libau, was his sole traveling companion. He plied Herzl with all sorts of advice, for he was worried that Herzl might compromise whatever little ground the Russian Jews still held. As the train passed through the dreary Lithuanian countryside, the two men relaxed over a pocket chessboard, replaying the Andersen-Kieseritzky "immortal game." Katzenelson implored Herzl to deal carefully with Plehve.

"Don't worry," Herzl said, "I shall strive to play a good game."

Katzenelson said: "Play the immortal game!"

"Yes, I shall sacrifice neither the castles nor the queen."

The dreaded Plehve received Herzl on August 8. A tall, slightly obese man of about sixty, he greeted Herzl with a sallow smile and offered him a cigar, which Herzl refused. They spoke French. "I have granted you this interview which you requested, *Monsieur le Docteur*, in order to come to an understanding with you." Herzl immediately sensed that Plehve was most anxious to prevent a discussion of Kishinev at the forthcoming Zionist congress.

"The Jewish question is not vital for us, but still it is a fairly important matter," Plehve said. "We are trying to bring it to an end in the best possible way." He explained that the Russian state must insist on the *homogeneity* of its population. In Plehve's view the Jews were an alien element within the state; it was therefore justified in suppressing them. He was ready to concede that education might facilitate the assimilation of this alien element into the culture of Holy Russia; on the other hand, he could allow only a limited number of Jews to receive higher education, "for otherwise there would soon be no positions left for Christians." To make things worse, most Jews were poor and tended to join the revolutionary parties. There were 7 million Jews within the general population of 136 million, but alas, he pointed out, 50 percent of all revolutionaries were Jews.

This in essence was how Plehve viewed the Jewish problem in Russia. For this reason he proclaimed himself an ardent supporter of Zionism. "You are preaching to a convert," Plehve told Herzl. However, he added, in recent months he had noticed a change in Russian Zionism. "There is less talk now of Palestinian Zionism than there is about culture, organization, and Jewish nationalism [within Russia]. This does not suit us."

Plehve seemed to be remarkably well briefed on Herzl's internecine squabbles with the Russian proponents of Jewish cultural separatism. "Your Excellency," Herzl assured him, "all the Russian leaders are on my side, even if they oppose my position now and then. . . . Their opposition to me is a phenomenon which Christopher Columbus also knew. When after many weeks no land was yet in sight, his sailors began to grumble. What you see among us right now is a revolt of the sailors against their captain." He raised his voice: "Help me to reach land sooner, and the revolt will end. The defection of Jews to the socialists will end as well."

"What sort of help?" asked Plehve.

Herzl made three specific requests. First, the Russian government should pressure the Turkish Sultan to grant the Zionists a charter for colonization everywhere in Palestine except in the Holy Places. Second, the Russian government should support Jewish emigration to Palestine by means of subsidies derived from taxes paid by its Jewish subjects. Third, the government should allow the organization of Zionist societies operating within the framework of the Basel program.

Plehve immediately agreed to all three demands. He asked Herzl to draft a memorandum, after which they would meet again. "I am very happy—don't think these are just words—to have made your personal acquaintance," Plehve said.

After Herzl left, Plehve told an acquaintance that before meeting Herzl, "I did not know there were Jews who did not crawl"—a strange remark, considering the large number of Jewish revolutionaries Plehve was contending with almost daily. Herzl's impression of Plehve was sharper; Plehve struck him as a "strong, sinuous, unrelenting beast, whose every move was a guarded offense." The two men believed they could use one another.

Herzl next visited Count Serge Witte, the czarist Minister of Finance. Only Witte could end the current Russian ban on the sale of Jewish Colonial Trust shares. He was a plump, knock-kneed man, with none of Plehve's ingratiating suavity. Before Herzl could broach his subject, Witte launched into a little discourse on the Jews.

"One has to admit that the Jews provide enough reasons for hostility. There is a characteristic arrogance about them," he announced. "Most Jews, however, are poor, and because they are poor, they are filthy and make a repulsive impression. They also engage in all sorts of ugly pursuits, like pimping and usury. So you see, it is hard for friends of the Jews to come to their defense."

His next remark came as something of a surprise. "And yet, I am a friend of the Jews," said Witte. If so, thought Herzl, "we certainly don't need enemies."

It was difficult to defend the Jews, Witte added, for it would

immediately be said that one had been bought. He also complained
bitterly that so many Jews participated in the revolutionary movements.

"To what circumstance do you attribute this?" Herzl asked.

"I believe it is the fault of our government," Witte admitted.
"The Jews are too oppressed. I used to say to the late Czar Alexander III, 'Majesty, if it is possible to drown the six or seven million
Jews in the Black Sea, I would be absolutely in favor of that. But if
it is not possible, one must let them live.' This is still my point of
view."

Herzl now expounded his own solution, an orderly, well-
organized exodus of Jews to a territory of their own. Witte picked
at one point and another, and finally asked, "What, then, do you
want from the Russian government?"

"Certain encouragements," Herzl answered.

"But the Jews are given encouragements to emigrate. Kicks in
the behind, for example."

Herzl drew himself up and said icily, "This is not the kind of
encouragement I wish to speak about. This kind is already known."
He repeated the three requests he had presented to Plehve, and
asked Witte, by way of supporting the movement, to remove the
ban on the purchase of Jewish Colonial Bank shares. Witte promised
his help. Herzl left this disagreeable man with the satisfaction that
at least he had obtained what he wanted.

His second meeting with Plehve on August 13 was even more
favorable than the first. Plehve announced that he had submitted
Herzl's three requests to the Czar for his approval and they had
been granted. At the same time the Czar had complained of the
attacks upon himself in the foreign press. He was extremely hurt by
the accusations that his government had been implicated in the
Kishinev pogrom. The Czar wished Herzl to know that he was
equally well disposed toward all his subjects.

"I cannot deny that the situation of Jews in the Russian empire
is not particularly happy," Plehve admitted. "If I were a Jew I
would probably also be an enemy of the government. This is how
things are; we can only continue to act the way we have acted until
now. Therefore we would very much like to see the creation of an
independent Jewish state capable of absorbing several million
Jews. Of course we would not like to lose *all* our Jews. We should
like to keep the very intelligent ones—the type of which you, Dr.
Herzl, are the best example. But we should like to rid ourselves of
the weak-minded and those with little property."

Herzl begged Plehve to alleviate, in the meanwhile, the lot of those Jews who remained in Russia. Why not extend their restricted rights of domicile? Plehve was willing to consider this. He presented Herzl with a letter that the Czar had approved and which he authorized Herzl to publicize at will. In the letter the Russian government formally pledged its support of the Zionist cause on the condition that the Zionists encourage Jews to move from Russia to a Jewish state in Palestine. There could be no organizing them, however, on a national basis within the empire. The letter held out a promise of emigration facilities, financial help, and Russian intervention on behalf of the Zionist cause in Constantinople.

Before leaving, Herzl pressed Plehve once more for just such an intervention. He told Plehve that everything depended on the efficacy of such a move. In his view, Russia was now in a favorable position to enforce Turkish compliance. The best thing, Herzl suggested, would be for the Czar to intervene personally with the Sultan.

Plehve listened with a "thoughtful look." He seemed to be agreeing with Herzl. He promised to take up the matter with the Czar, and to press it most energetically. As for getting Herzl an audience with the Czar, he said: "We shall see—after the congress."

Herzl clearly understood that Plehve expected him to curb international criticism of the czarist government. He was fully prepared to do so in order to further his cause. He was satisfied with the political results of his trip. This was an instance, he felt, when evil could be made to serve good. Not only had he succeeded in lifting the czarist ban against Zionist organization and fund raising, but after the Kaiser's abortive attempt of 1898, Plehve's promise to intervene in Constantinople was the first of its kind by one of the big powers. It could well provide the lever necessary to obtain the charter from the Sultan. Herzl and Plehve parted amicably.

That evening Herzl addressed a small group of Zionist activists in a local banquet hall. There was some concern about Herzl's apparent cooperation with Plehve; the communal leaders distrusted Plehve's promises. Herzl asked his audience to concentrate on Zionist agitation rather than on a national Jewish culture within Russia itself, and to thereby avoid Russian suspicions. He warned also against Jewish involvement in socialist activities. This, he intimated, was putting the cart before the horse.

"In Palestine, in our own land, an extreme Socialist party will be perfectly in order," he said. "Once we are in our land such a

party would vitalize our political life—and then I shall determine
my own attitude toward it. You do me an injustice if you say that I
am opposed to progressive social ideas. But now, in our present
condition, it is too soon to deal with such matters. They are ex-
traneous. Zionism demands complete, not partial involvement."

His remarks did not go unchallenged. At least one person retorted that even as Zionists they could not turn a blind eye toward
the pressing and political problems of the day. This was especially
true after Kishinev.

4

Meanwhile, the news of Herzl's arrival had spread to countless
towns and hamlets throughout Russia and Ukraine. The mystery
that surrounded the visit released a string of absurd rumors. Telegrams arrived in St. Petersburg from ten different cities inquiring
whether it was true that Herzl had been assassinated. It was not
clear whether he was presumed shot by the government or by the
socialists. Herzl's last day in Petersburg was spoiled by hysterical
admonitions from local leaders not to stop anywhere on his way
back to Austria, and to leave the country by the shortest possible
route.

He dismissed all the warnings impatiently. He desired to see
Eastern European Jewish life at its worst, those places where both
the suffering and the messianic fervor were a cause, and the supreme justification, of his life's work. On August 16 he arrived in
Vilna. His brief stay there was one of the most moving, and most
shattering, experiences of his life. Vilna was in the heart of the
Jewish Pale of Settlement, where millions of Jews had been herded
together in tightly restricted areas, somewhat like the Bantus in
modern South Africa. A renowned center of Talmudic learning—
Napoleon passing through Vilna had called it "the Jerusalem of
Lithuania"—Vilna was a prime example of the traditional and the
new, of Orthodox lore and revolutionary strivings, of the gloom and
the violence generated over the past two decades among the Jewish
masses of Eastern Europe. Vilna was a center of revolutionary
activity, a stronghold of the clandestine *Bund* of Jewish Workers,
which was aligned with Lenin's Social Democratic party. Vilna was
also a citadel of left-wing Zionist activity. The Zionists and the
Bund had in fact grown intertwined within the history of Russian
radicalism. If many of the Zionists were left-wing socialists, the

Bund affirmed Jewish nationhood, but within Russia proper. (Plekhanov called the Bundists "Zionists afraid of a sea voyage.") Herzl visited Vilna just when the reaction to the pogroms in Kishinev and elsewhere was at a fever pitch. Only a few months earlier a young Jew, Hirsch Leckert, had given vent to his fury and despair by killing the czarist governor of Vilna.

A tumultuous reception awaited Herzl at the Vilna railroad station. The police drove back the crowd with sticks and clubs, but it surged forth desperately with cries of "Herzl, Herzl!" and "Long live the King!" A dark mass, seething with excitement, crowded the narrow streets. Herzl drove into town surrounded by grim police and a detachment of plainclothesmen. To prevent further demonstrations, the police requested Herzl to withdraw to a hotel. They forbade any public meeting, including one that had been scheduled in a synagogue. A luncheon in Herzl's honor was canceled. Nevertheless he visited the office of the community center. It was a "small and stuffy, dingy chamber—symbolic of the ghetto itself." The aged Rabbi, with shivering hands, offered Herzl "our community's dearest, holiest possession," an ancient scroll of the Torah. As the Rabbi pronounced a blessing and hailed Herzl as the "greatest son of the Jewish people," the assembled notables broke out in sobs. Herzl, forcing back his tears, thanked the assembly for the great honor, which he declared was undeserved—his work was not yet accomplished. He was convinced, however, that the Jewish state would finally be realized. The suffering was too enormous, he added; it was growing daily. The Jewish people could not wait much longer.

Although his telephone was tapped, and he was constantly shadowed by police agents, Herzl managed to steal off in the evening to attend a private dinner given by a local Zionist activist in Werki, a small village an hour's drive from Vilna. The dinner was interrupted by a crowd of Jewish youngsters who had walked all the way from Vilna to hail the leader. One young worker, in a blue workman's shirt, whom Herzl took for one of the revolutionary Bundists, surprised him by drinking a toast to the time when King Herzl would reign. "This absurdity," Herzl noted in his diary, "produced a remarkable impression in the dark Russian night."

After dinner Herzl drove back to Vilna. At 1:00 A.M., almost furtively, he left the hotel for the railroad station. The town was wide awake. Despite a heavy downpour, crowds lined the streets, and hailed him from the balconies as he drove by. Near the station the crowd was thicker and a wild scene ensued. Mounted cossacks threw themselves against the running, screaming, sobbing crowd, brutally lashing out with whips and rifle butts, trampling stragglers under the hooves of their horses. Shouts of "Hail Herzl!" mingled with the cries of the beaten and trampled. Herzl was shattered. "Why are they beating these people?" he cried. "What barbarism!" To the small group of communal leaders assembled on the platform he cried, "Gentlemen, do not despair! A better day will come! We are working for it!"

He boarded the night train for Berlin with a very heavy heart. He was so agitated that he could not sleep all night. His mind dwelled on the horror, the squalor, the sadness and despair of the past twenty hours.

He had other matters to consider as well. During his short stay in Vilna he had received a message from Leopold Greenberg in London reporting a momentous breakthrough in the negotiations with the British government. Two days earlier, on August 14, the British, anxious to promote "the amelioration of the Jewish race," had formally proposed the establishment of a Jewish colony in East Africa. In the words of Sir Clement Hill, chief of the Protectorate Department of the Foreign Office:

> If a [suitable] site can be found, Lord Landsdowne will be prepared to entertain favorably proposals for the establishment of a Jewish colony or settlement on conditions which will enable the members to observe their national customs. For this purpose he will be prepared to discuss (if a suitable site has been found, and subject to the views of the advisers to the Secretary of State in East Africa) the details of a scheme comprising as its main features the grant of a considerable area of land, the appointment of a Jewish official as the chief of the local administration, and permission to the colony to have a free hand in regard to municipal legislation as to the management of religious and purely domestic matters [with] His Majesty's Government exercising general control.

In the early hours of the morning, the train crossed the Russian-German frontier. Herzl had made up his mind. The next Zionist congress was only six days away, on August 23. Uganda was not Zion, this he knew well, but his Russian journey had shown him once more that there was no time to lose. It was a time for rescue, not for ideology, however dear.

5

He paused for only one day in the mountain resort of Alt-Aussee, where his family was again spending the summer. His heart condition was affecting him, and he sporadically gasped for breath. Next morning, accompanied by his worried mother, he continued to Basel. In the train he happened to meet his old ally Count (now Prince) Eulenburg, the German ambassador to Vienna. Impressed by Herzl's accomplishments in Russia, Eulenburg said he would inform the Kaiser immediately. Eulenburg bowed deeply over Mrs. Herzl's hand and told her how much he admired her son.

In Basel the delegates were beginning to assemble. The Russian pogroms had swelled the Zionist ranks. Since its last convocation, the movement had again grown considerably. There were 592 delegates (one had walked 42 days from a small town in Bulgaria) and a large number of observers, including the usual Russian and Turkish spies. Only a handful of Herzl's aides had been informed of his recent achievements in Russia and England. Most delegates expected the usual debate on "culture" and "practical work" in the Palestinian colonies.

The delegates were shocked by the change in Herzl's physical appearance. Fatigue and illness showed in his lined face and stooped figure. "He looked old and worn. There were brown and gray streaks in his erstwhile jet-black beard." The opposition to his leadership had grown since the last congress. Herzl, as blind to the weakness of his friends as to the strength of his critics, convened the Actions Committee in advance of the congress. After pledging them to secrecy, he reported on his negotiations with the Russian government and presented Plehve's letter. Most of the Russian members were shocked that Herzl had shaken hands with the butcher of Kishinev. They seriously doubted the sincerity of Plehve's pledges and begged Herzl to withhold publication of the letter, which, as Russian subjects, they dared not criticize in public. Herzl would not hear of it. He next reported on the latest British offer of Uganda and read them Sir Clement Hill's letter. There was even greater shock, not only among the Russian members. The delegate from Kishinev remarked bitterly that "under present circumstances the Russian Jews would even go to hell." Alex Marmorek, Herzl's close Viennese aide, called the East African scheme a "death blow for Zionism." Could it be that the age-old history of Israel would end in an African jungle?

It was not what Herzl had expected. He was shaken by the

hostility and by the vicious attacks hurled against him personally. He was so tired, so busy, and so disgusted that he hardly registered his impressions in his diary, except once, on August 22.

The old hullabaloo.

My heart is palpitating from fatigue.

If I were doing it for thanks I would be a great fool.

Yesterday I gave my report to the Greater A.C. I presented England and Russia. Not for a single moment did it occur to any of them that for these greatest of all accomplishments to date I deserve a word of thanks, or even a smile.

Instead Messrs. . . . criticized me.

On the following morning, however, Herzl's public opening speech to the congress was received with tumultuous applause. Speaking slowly, in a firm, well-modulated voice, he reviewed the most recent disasters. "Many of us believed that things could not become worse, but things have become worse. Like a floodtide, misery has swept Jewry. . . . Kishinev is every place where Jews are physically or morally afflicted, dishonored, impoverished because they are Jews. Let us save those that can still be saved."

He recounted the failure of his negotiations with the Turks, and with the British government over Sinai. But now, he stated, the British had offered him a substitute territory for autonomous Jewish colonization: Uganda. "The new territory does not possess the historical, poetic, religious, and Zionist value that even Sinai would have, but I do not doubt that the congress will welcome the new offer with warmest gratitude."

The British government, he added, was fully aware of the movement's ultimate aims in Palestine. Uganda was not and would never be Zion. It would serve merely as a "provisional site for colonization on a national, self-governing basis." He therefore urged the congress to accept the British offer "without renouncing any of the great principles on which our movement is based."

A storm of applause followed this last remark. But the applause barely concealed the abyss between Herzl and his opponents. The movement itself was threatened. While the speech making continued, the various factions went into consultation. The most tumultuous was the Russian caucus. One of the sharpest attacks on Herzl came from a young Russian student, Chaim Weizmann: "If the British people and government are what I think they are," said the young man, who, thirteen years later would obtain the Balfour Declaration from the British government, "they will make us a better offer." Some of the Russian opponents of Uganda declared a hunger strike; others furiously tore from the wall a map of East Africa that roughly delineated the area offered by the British. The Russian caucus resolved to thank the British government for its offer but to reject it as incompatible with the official Zionist program.

In the plenary session, meanwhile, Nordau rallied to Herzl's support. He was by no means convinced of the wisdom of Herzl's East African project, much less his imperious tactics. But in loyalty to his old friend he relentlessly defended him. Far from repudiating the idea of Zion, Nordau said, Uganda was in fact a much needed way station. Uganda could be a "shelter in the night" for the suffering and persecuted, a field base where Jews would learn the art of political independence which they could afterward apply in Palestine. Nordau's eloquence swayed many a fence-sitter. At the same time his imagery incited even greater opposition. "Night shelter" was the German title of Gorki's play *The Lower Depths*, which portrayed a ghastly scene of drunkards, gamblers, and thieves, and which was just being presented on the German stage.

Most of the delegates who spoke in favor of East Africa came from Western Europe or, like Cyrus Sulzberger, from New York. Israel Zangwill favored Uganda because he feared the religious and atavistic revival that a Jewish state in Palestine might provoke, precluding all modernity. "You are a photographer of the ghetto, not its psychologist," Weizmann complained to him. Members of the ultra-Orthodox religious bloc, *Hamizrachi*, were prominent among Eastern European supporters of Herzl's scheme. The ultra-Orthodox had always distinguished between the Zion of faith (as a messianic idea beyond time or space) and the earthly Zion as a political goal, which could be established just as easily outside of Palestine. Herzl did not participate in the debates. With all his array of fantastic projects, he was an eminently rational man. He loved not Zion, but the Jews. He was more concerned with their suffering than with the desolation of the ancient homeland. The most fervent nationalists in the debate, ironically, were socialists from Russia.

In the face of so much opposition and the very real threat of a split, a mild resolution was actually put to a vote; it merely called for the dispatch of an expedition of experts to the proposed East African region. The roll call was by name. Two hundred and ninety-five delegates voted for the resolution, 178 voted against, and 99 abstained. Among the Westerners voting against were Martin Buber and the painter Lilien. Although technically a victory for Herzl, the vote heralded his defeat. A storm broke loose. Threatening secession, the Russian members of the Actions Committee left their seats on the dais. Followed by their supporters, they marched out of the hall. Once outside, according to Israel Cohen, an eyewitness, "they gave vent to indignation and grief, without restraint. Many fell on one another's necks and wept. One man fainted, and all presented the most doleful and mournful looks, as though Zion had been abandoned forever." Leon Trotsky, observing the stormy scene from the press gallery, predicted the imminent collapse of the Zionist movement.

Late at night—two hours after the plenary session had ended —the secessionists were still meeting in caucus. In the words of another eyewitness, Jacob de Haas, men sat "on the floor, mourning in Orthodox fashion for a dead Zion." Others wept. Word of the demonstration reached Herzl at his hotel. He swallowed his pride and rushed back to the congress building. "The nays had locked themselves in. Shouting his name, he hammered at the door." Inside the room a vote was taken on whether he should be admitted. One man screamed "Traitor." Herzl, pale, bent, with the tragic air of a man who walks alone, mounted the rostrum. He pleaded with the dissenters; his voice secured an instant of silence. "There was in his attitude," said de Haas, "something so strong, so earnest, so much sympathy for their pleading and so much unexplained assurance that he would win Zion itself, that at two A.M. the caucus yielded without terms or conditions, and decided to return to its seats at the morning session."

In his closing speech, the last he was ever to deliver to any congress, Herzl returned to the British offer of East Africa. He described it as a temporary expedient. Then, slowly raising his right hand, he cried, in Hebrew, "If I forget thee, oh Jerusalem, may my right hand lose its cunning."

Later in the day, completely worn out, as he sat with his friends in his hotel room sipping a glass of mineral water, he said, "If the expedition to Uganda makes a favorable report, I shall present it to the movement and resign. I shall now tell you the speech I shall deliver at the seventh congress—that is, if I live to see it. By then I shall either have obtained Palestine or realized the complete futility of all further efforts. In the latter case my speech will be as follows:

It was not possible.

The ultimate goal has not been reached. But a temporary result is at hand: Here is a land in which we could settle our suffering masses on a national basis and with the right of self-government. I do not think that we can deny the unfortunate this relief for the sake of a beautiful dream or a legitimistic banner. . . . Palestine is the only land where our people can find rest. But hundreds of thousands need immediate help.

There is only one way to resolve this conflict. I must resign from the leadership . . . my best wishes for those who work for the fulfillment of the beautiful dream.

I have not made Zionism poorer, but Jewry richer.

Adieu!

19

The Price

THE SIXTH CONGRESS, in which the movement had almost split apart, was barely over when opposition to Herzl's Uganda scheme arose in another quarter. The London *Times* printed a number of hostile letters from British settlers in the East African protectorate, protesting the influx of undesirable Jews. The settlers did not want to see the "best portions of the Protectorate" handed over to foreigners. Lord Delamere cabled the *Times* from Nairobi, "Feeling here very strong against introduction alien Jews." Editorially the *Times* voiced the same objections as Herzl's Zionist critics. The *Spectator*, too, asked, "What are the Jews to do in Uganda that they should be bribed to go there?" Palestine, according to the *Spectator*, was a much better place for Jews to learn the art of self-government.

There was at that time only a handful of British settlers in East Africa. Only a few weeks earlier they had welcomed Joseph Chamberlain in Nairobi as the architect of a vast British program of expansion; they were stunned by this sudden invitation to the Jews. The settlers' hostility to the Jews was matched only by their massive opposition to the influx of Indians imported as laborers for the Kenya railway. Their newspaper, the *East African Standard*, lashed out at what it called "Jewganda" and protested the introduction into East Africa of "Jewish hawkers who from the manifold pockets of their rags will offer for sale anything from a comb to a bar of soap, for neither of which they have any use."

Herzl was undaunted by these protests. Sensing that he had only a few months to live, he pursued his task with dogged determination. With barely a moment's respite, he left Basel for Mainau Castle to consult with his old ally, the Grand Duke of Baden. The two men strolled for two hours in the park; the Grand Duke was moved to tears when Herzl said, "We would gladly renounce the good land in Africa for the poor land in Palestine. It might vindicate us avaricious Jews if we gave up the rich country for the poor one."

But the Grand Duke gently passed over Herzl's suggestion that the Kaiser should again lead the Zionist campaign, now that England and Russia were supporting it.

Next day Herzl returned to his family in Alt-Aussee. But he still got no opportunity to rest. Julie became seriously ill when a sudden attack of appendicitis was aggravated by pneumonia. She was unconscious part of the time. At one point the doctors gave up hope. Herzl wrote Wolffsohn about these "fearful days of horror." He did not mention that after his return from Basel he himself had had another heart attack and had also suffered from leg cramps and insomnia. While tending his sick wife, he pursued his elusive quest by correspondence. An endless stream of letters went out. There was something desperate, almost fanatical, in his zeal and energy, as in his early days in the movement, immediately after his ecstatic awakening in Paris.

He wrote Plehve a detailed report on the deliberations of the congress. The congress had proved most dramatically that a massive and "permanent emigration" of Russian Jews "can only be directed to Palestine." He asked Plehve once more to urge the Czar to put pressure on Constantinople. A Russian intervention, he wrote, would "probably have a decisive effect, all the more so because we are willing to offer financial advantages to the Ottoman treasury" and because England and Germany would support it.

At the same time, ignoring what had happened in Basel, he wrote to Leopold Greenberg in London: "We must forge the iron while it is hot. Make an intensive (but secret) effort to speedily obtain the charter for East Africa." He made still another attempt to enlist the support of the German Kaiser: "I have always placed great hopes in German assistance. There is in our movement an element of German culture which should not be underestimated and which has not escaped the German Kaiser's genius." Simultaneously, and for the first time since his conversion to Zionism, he tried to enlist the active assistance of officials of his own native country, Austria-Hungary. Seeking "the support of the government of my fatherland," he wrote his old acquaintance Koerber, the Austrian Prime Minister: "A settlement of Jewish masses in Palestine could only stimulate and increase the monarchy's trade relations" with the Near East. The evasive replies he received did not discourage Herzl but merely caused him to renew his efforts in other directions. He sent Colonel Goldsmid to Balmoral to talk to the King of England, and Felice Ravenna, the Italian Jewish lawyer, to the Pope. At the same time he sought experts to join the proposed fact-finding commission to East Africa.

By October Herzl was back in Vienna at his regular job on the newspaper; he could not relinquish his only means of support. Wolffsohn proposed that he accept an annuity from the movement and devote himself to Zionism on a full-time basis. For Herzl, this was simply unthinkable: "And my self-esteem? Do you think I could bear such a shameful situation? May the God of Israel save me from ever becoming dependent [financially] on the Zionist movement!"

The continuing frenetic pace and resultant fatigue were affecting his health. Heedless of all advice, he plodded on. George Sil Vara, the writer, met him in the street and warned, "Don't work so hard. You will ruin yourself."

"I want to work until I am ruined," Herzl answered.

Meanwhile, more trouble was on its way from the Russian Zionists. The opponents of Herzl's East African project had not been reassured by his conciliatory remarks in Basel, or by his dramatic announcement that his right hand would lose its cunning should he ever forget Jerusalem. The leader of the anti-Ugandists among the Russian faction was M.M. Ussishkin. A man of massive build with an enormous chest, his tone was as fierce as his appearance. In a weak moment Herzl had once asked him if he really believed that they would obtain Palestine. "Yes," Ussishkin retorted angrily, "and if you do not believe, then there is no place for you at the head of this movement." Ussishkin had been away in Palestine during the last congress. He was shocked to discover that many of the depressed settlers in Rothschild's colonies (including the father of modern Hebrew, Ben-Yehuda) were actively in favor of the Uganda project. Upon his return from Palestine in October, Ussishkin called eight other leading anti-Ugandists to a conference in Kharkov. The conference voted (seven against two) to present Herzl with an ultimatum. Either he commit himself in writing to change his autocratic manner and completely renounce the East African project, or they would split the movement. Membership fees would no longer be transferred to the Vienna headquarters but would be retained in Russia. Thus a worldwide personal campaign against Herzl would begin. The decision was taken in secret, and a deputation was appointed to deliver the ultimatum to Herzl.

Rumors of the decision reached Herzl before the arrival of the deputation later in the year. He contemplated resigning and drafted an open "Letter to the Jewish People":

> The road parts, and the split cuts straight through the leader's breast. When I started on my course I was only in support of a Jewish state. I have become a lover of Zion. For me there is no other solution than Palestine. But I cannot overlook the fact that in the Jewish problem there is also an element of bitterest misery [that I believe can be resolved through an interim device and that] I am not entitled to reject. . . . If it should come to a split, my heart will remain with the Zionists and my mind with the [Ugandists]. Such a conflict I can only resolve with my resignation.

But he put the letter aside. (It was found after his death among his papers.) Although he was in turmoil over Ussishkin's "open rebellion," he ordered Greenberg to reduce his activities on behalf of East Africa, and he increased his own pleas to Plehve for a pro-Palestinian intervention by the Russian government in Constantinople. Bilinsky, the Austrian Finance Minister, to whom he reported his exchanges with Plehve, noted in his diary, "Long live Theodor the First by the grace of Russia."

Early in December Plehve finally acted. He wrote to Herzl on October 6 that the Russian Foreign Minister, Count Lamsdorff, would instruct the ambassador in Constantinople to inform the Turkish government of "the friendly reception which the imperial government has given the Zionist project to resettle their coreligionists in Palestine. [The Ottoman government would be told] that by favorably receiving the Zionist request, it will attest to the bonds of friendship between the two empires." Plehve asked Herzl to contact the Russian representative in Constantinople directly.

This Herzl promptly did. Zinoviev, the Russian chargé d'affaires in Constantinople, procrastinated. Although he had received his instructions, he did not hide the fact that he despised Plehve. "No, I have not yet done anything in this matter," he told Herzl's agent in Constantinople. "It will not be easy. Tell Dr. Herzl that; it will not be easy."

To calm the mounting storm within the movement, Herzl was now ready to admit that, in view of the British settlers' opposition, the East African project was "impractical." He did so on December 12, in a public letter to Sir Francis Montefiore. Only five days later,

Max Nordau was attending a Hanukkah ball in Paris when a demented Russian Jewish student, Chaim Luban, suddenly drew a
gun and fired two shots at him, crying, "Death to Nordau, the East
African!" Both bullets missed their target, but the attempt indicated the turmoil and the violent passions generated by the controversy. It was ironic that Nordau was the intended victim, for he
had actually opposed the East Africa scheme and had rallied to
Herzl's defense solely out of personal loyalty. "I now await a similar
act of gratitude," Herzl wrote Wolffsohn. And to Nordau: "If they
shoot at you, undoubtedly there is a bullet ready for me too. It is
hard to prove the connection, but I am convinced that Luban's gun
was loaded in Russia. Already in the ultimatum announced by the
men of Kharkov, I recognized the shotgun's barrel."

A few days later two representatives of the Kharkov deputation arrived in Vienna to present their ultimatum. Herzl would
meet them as individuals, but not as a delegation. He also refused
to accept any "ultimatum." Their mission produced no results, instead the two men (Ussishkin was not among them) were brow-
beaten by accusations of disloyalty and treason. Under the impact,
undoubtedly, of the attempt on Nordau's life, they did not press
their case. By the sheer force of his imperious personality, Herzl
scored a remarkable victory. Far from being pleased by his success,
he went about his business almost mechanically, a beaten old man,
feeling stale, flat, and unprofitable.

2

That fall Herzl had been considering Italy and the Holy See as
new intermediaries. He was sure of Germany, Russia, and England,
but he needed more. On January 21 Herzl arrived in Rome. Wan,
stooped, breathing with difficulty, and suffering from insomnia, he
prepared to win the King of Italy and the Pope to his cause. His
first meeting was with Cardinal Merry del Val, the papal Secretary
of State. He told the thirty-eight-year-old prelate that he had come
to seek "the good will of the Holy See."

"I do not quite see why we should take an initiative in this
matter," the Cardinal replied. "As long as the Jews deny the divinity of Christ we cannot declare ourselves in their favor. Not that we
wish them ill. On the contrary. But how could we agree to the
repossession by the Jews of the Holy Land without abandoning our
highest principles?"

"We only ask for the profane earth," Herzl declared. "The Holy Places shall be extraterritorialized."

"Oh, but enclaves of that sort will not do."

Herzl told the Cardinal how in the past few years he had gone from one great power to another and secured their consent. He presented Plehve's last letter. "But I would like also to obtain the spiritual approval of the Roman Church."

The Cardinal read and reread Plehve's letter attentively. He then promised consideration of Herzl's request. He would ask the Pope to grant Herzl an audience. That night Herzl had a curious dream, which a Freudian analyst might have found revealing: he was alone with the German Kaiser in a rowboat on the sea.

On the following morning Herzl had an audience with the King of Italy. Victor Emanuel III assured him that nowhere in Italy was there discrimination against Jews. Italy was the only country on the continent where all posts in the army, in the cabinet, and in the diplomatic service were open to Jews. At the same time the King, who had been to Palestine himself, displayed great interest and much sympathy for Herzl's cause. "The country is very Jewish," he said. "It will, it must, fall into your hands. It is only a question of time. Once you have half a million Jews there—"

"They are not allowed to enter, Sire."

"Bah!" said the King. "Anything can be done with *baksheesh*." He told Herzl that he was pleased that the Zionists had given up East Africa. "I admire this love of Jerusalem." But on practical matters—Herzl's request for Italian intervention in Constantinople —the King excused himself. He was a constitutional monarch; this was a matter for his Foreign Minister.

Two days later Herzl met with Pius X. Herzl did not kneel, nor did he kiss the Pope's extended hand. The Pope seemed annoyed. When Herzl apologized for his halting Italian, the Pope said, "No, no, you speak very well." He addressed him as "*Signor Commendatore*," because Herzl, for the first time, was wearing his Ottoman decoration as Commander of the Medjikiye Order.

Herzl repeated his request for the good will of the Roman Church.

"We cannot approve of the Zionist movement," said the Pope. "We cannot prevent the Hebrews from going to Jerusalem, but we could never sanction it. The Hebrews have not recognized our Lord, therefore we cannot recognize the Hebrew people."

Herzl, trying nevertheless to remain conciliatory, recited his old plan for the extraterritorialization of the Holy Places. The Pope was not impressed.

"*Gerusalemme* must not fall into the hands of the Jews," for they had denied Christ and still refused to recognize His divinity.

"But Holy Father," Herzl said, "the Jews are in terrible straits. I do not know if your Holiness is familiar with the full extent of their sad situation. We need a land for the persecuted."

"Does it have to be *Gerusalemme*?"

"We do not ask for Jerusalem but for Palestine, only the profane earth."

"We cannot be in favor of that."

"Holy Father, do you really know the present situation of the Jews?" Herzl pleaded. The Pope would hear nothing of it.

"We pray for the Jews," he said. "May their minds be enlightened . . . and so if you come to Palestine and settle your people there, we shall keep churches and priests ready to baptize all of them."

There the matter rested.[*] After about twenty-five minutes Herzl took his leave. He spent the next hour walking through the Vatican Museum. In the Raphael rooms he saw the picture of an emperor kneeling to be crowned by a seated Pope. "That is how Rome would wish it," he thought.

3

The pace now slackened, though there was still considerable activity. Herzl now very much resembled the protagonist in Schnitzler's novel *Der Weg ins Freie*, who said of himself: "I start a great deal but I never finish anything." In London Leopold Greenberg continued his negotiations with the Foreign Office. Herzl had no sooner returned to Vienna than he received a message from Greenberg stating that the Foreign Office was now ready, even anxious, to grant the Zionists a charter for East Africa. But in view of the British settlers' opposition, the area now offered was more

---

[*] According to Heinrich York-Steiner, one of Herzl's aides, the Pope—or at least his aides—apparently regretted his brusque manner. A few weeks later Cardinal Merry del Val told York-Steiner: "If the Jews believe they might greatly ease their lot by being admitted to the land of their ancestors, then we would regard that as a humanitarian question. We shall never forget that without Judaism we would have been nothing." (Christopher Sykes, *Two Studies in Virtue*, London, 1954, p. 199.)

remote and less promising than that originally discussed. Herzl made preparations to send an expedition into the field. He had promised the congress that the costs of the expedition would not come from Zionist funds; they were eventually contributed by an English Christian woman sympathetic to the cause.

Herzl's physical condition continued to deteriorate. Berta von Suttner noted in her diary on February 2, 1904: "With Herzl, who seems sulky and haggard." A few weeks later Stefan Zweig ran into him in the park. He was shocked by his slow walk and pale face. The old jaunty step was gone.

"It was my mistake that I began too late," Herzl said. "Victor Adler was leader of the Social Democrats at thirty, in his best fighting years, to say nothing of other greats in history. If you knew how I suffer at the thought of the lost years and that I did not approach my task sooner! If my health were as good as my will, all would be well. But one cannot buy back lost years!"

There was a slightly outlandish quality in some of the schemes that now reached his desk. A Swedish adventurer married to a Turkish princess visited him on February 23 with a proposal that he purchase two cruisers, sail up the Bosporus, shell the Sultan's palace, depose him, and set up a new government that would grant the charter for Palestine. The price of two cruisers was a mere 400,000 pounds; the remainder of the scheme would cost another 100,000 pounds. The entire operation would cost no more than half a million pounds, and the Swede was ready to head it. Born with the name Nordling, the Swede converted to Islam and was now known as Ali Nouri Bey. "After mature deliberation—I cannot discuss the matter with anyone—I have decided to reject Ali Nouri's proposal," Herzl noted in his diary two weeks later. If the plan should fail, he argued, there would be a horrible massacre of Jews in Turkey.

On April 11 Zionist leaders from ten European countries and the United States assembled in Vienna to attend an extraordinary session of the Actions Committee. Herzl had convened the meeting in an attempt to pacify the malcontents and prevent a possibly disastrous split. It was as if Herzl, already dying, was making a last-minute effort to save the movement he had almost single-handedly brought into being. The Kharkov rebels were present. None imagined that this was their last exchange with Herzl. Ussishkin attacked Herzl vociferously and threatened to part company with all those who continued to support East Africa. The violent discussions lasted three days and ended, finally, in reconciliation. Herzl above all wanted to end, or postpone, the bitter controversy. He was uncommonly conciliatory and ignored the violent attacks on his person. Yet he did not give ground, insisting that the only real political success thus far had been the British offer of East Africa. All other attempts in Constantinople had failed. East Africa was no substitute for Zion, but it could not be rejected out of hand. He himself would not go to East Africa, although he had been accused of wanting to become viceroy. "I will not characterize the British offer with the controversial term 'shelter for the night,'" he said. "I say only: 'Here is a piece of bread!' I, who perhaps have cake to eat, have no right to reject this piece of bread which is offered to the poor. I am obliged at least to put the question to the people." Accused of being an autocrat, he replied,

> Here in this city of Vienna, I one day tore myself loose from the entire circle of my life, from all my acquaintances and all my friends and, as a lonely man, stood up for what I considered right. I do not feel the need for a majority. I need only to be in harmony with my own conviction. Then I am content, even if no dog accepts a piece of bread from me.

4

Two weeks later he had a last conversation with Count Agenor von Goluchowski, the Polish-born Austrian Foreign Minister, who advised him that the Austro-Hungarian monarchy might endorse Zionism, if England took the initiative. Herzl made plans to travel to England, but his heart trouble grew worse. A panel of physicians, alarmed by a sudden deterioration of his heart muscle (myocarditis), ordered him to Franzenbad for a cure. Two days later, on May 2, he celebrated his forty-fourth birthday. With some difficulty he set out on the long train journey. He carefully concealed his condition from his mother. To his wife, who knew everything and with whom he had achieved a kind of rapprochement since her last illness, he wrote on May 3: "I know well that I will not find a better one than you, dear brave mother of my precious children. I wish, *Schatz*, that we were both in better health. I like you so. . . . " And to David Wolffsohn, on May 6: "I take the heart cure. My mother does not know. She thinks I am only resting here. *Don't do anything foolish when I am dead.*"

He was completely fatigued and had trouble breathing. Dr. Katzenelson, with whom he had traveled to Russia, visited him on May 9. "Let us not fool ourselves," Herzl said. "With me it is after the third curtain." On May 13 he felt completely "broken down." He wrote Plehve to continue negotiations with his friend Katzenelson. The doctors were still hopeful. Their diagnosis read: "Heart muscles completely degenerated. But as yet no heart expansion. Chances for recuperation not unfavorable." To his mother, who had again complained of Julie's insolence, he wrote on May 20: "I am tired of these fights and excitements over nothing. As the mother of our marvelous children, and as a sick person, Julie deserves the most tender consideration."

The diary breaks off on May 16. It was probably the new tension between his mother and his wife that caused the sick man to interrupt his cure and return to Vienna. He spent two weeks in bed. His condition did not improve. On June 3 he accepted his doctors' advice and entered a sanatorium in Edlach, on the Semmering. Julie accompanied him on what was to be his final trip. The clean cool air descending from the Alps briefly invigorated him. The mountains, as often in spring, were transfigured by the haze rising from forests and lakes. Julie sat by him compassionately, nursing him tenderly through the nights. After fifteen years of acrimonious marriage, they seemed to have achieved the rapport that had eluded them for so long. Herzl began to work again and planned a trip to Hamburg to visit a famous heart specialist. He dreamed of the seashore. "To lie in the hot sand—to gaze silently— to recover, to recover!" Hermann Bahr, the enlightened anti-Semite of his student days, came to visit and walked with Herzl on the terrace. The doctors complained that Herzl was overtaxing his strength. As he took leave of another visitor, his cousin, Raoul Auernheimer, Herzl became for a moment the dramatist of earlier days. Looking deep into Auernheimer's eyes, and stepping back on the terrace into the falling darkness, Herzl gestured grandly at the evening, and said, "*Le soir—mon soir—bon soir!*" He still had the gift of endowing every moment of his life with melodrama. No man was ever more Viennese and less Viennese at the same time.

The improvement in his health was brief and deceptive. On June 29, according to his doctors' report, "he had a wild scene with his wife, who succumbed to an attack of hysteria. I was called twice to his bed; he did not sleep all night." On July 1 he contracted a bronchial catarrh, which developed into pneumonia.

Feverish, semi-conscious, and unable to breathe properly, his body shook violently; he coughed up blood. Wolffsohn came, and left weeping after conferring with the doctors.

On July 2 he became more lucid. The Reverend Hechler came and sat by his bedside. Speaking softly, he promised Herzl that they would soon go to Palestine and "see Jerusalem again from the Mount of Olives."

Herzl replied, "Greet Palestine for me. I gave my heart's blood for my people."

Impatiently he asked for his mother and children. In his sleep he muttered incoherently and seemed to be lecturing the congress about East Africa. His hands seemed to have shrunk and were nervously moving over the sheets. His eyes opened and he turned to his secretary. "Hear, Reich, *this* piece of land"—his fingers pointed to a spot on the bed—"the National Fund must buy it!" Once more he asked for his mother and the children. Julie had another nervous relapse. When his mother finally entered the room, he raised himself in his bed. "How are you, dear mother?" he asked smilingly. "It is good, dear mother, that you are already here. How well you look. I do not feel so well, but soon I shall be better." Then his strength left him and he fell back on the bed.

An hour later he again lifted himself "imperiously," and, pointing to the students who stood guard in the garden outside his room, told his doctor: "They are marvelous, good people, my compatriots! You shall see, they shall enter the promised land one day!"

The children were brought in to see him. After a few moments he turned his head and said, "Well, my dear ones, you saw me and I saw you. Now go home." The ashen-faced, hushed relatives and companions waited in the adjoining room. Herzl fell silent. Then his lips moved again. In the twilight of consciousness he was at one moment in Palestine and in the next addressing the congress in Basel.

It had all happened so quickly and been so inconclusive: the moments, the minutes, the madness, the melodrama, the daring, the solid achievements, the dreams and disappointments of a short life—the taste of dust and sun on his dry tongue at the gates outside Jaffa, waiting for the Kaiser, the sound of cossack whips lashing the dark, crying crowd at Vilna, the view of Sinai from across the Suez Canal at Port Said, a lunar desolation of sand and rock. Yet beyond it, the prospects of a New Land—a Good Society —and the reconstruction of a downtrodden people. Perhaps he also remembered the advice he had given long ago, as a young dandy, to aspiring playwrights: "Last (pacifying) thought. After us—others flop."

The end came suddenly. The doctor heard a deep groan. He turned and saw Herzl's head fall back. The injection came too late. Herzl died at 5:00 P.M. on July 3, of cardiac sclerosis.

5

To friends and foe alike, Herzl's death came as a terrible shock. Thousands rushed to Vienna from almost every European country to attend the funeral. The coffin was transferred to Vienna and lay in Herzl's study. The tall windows overlooking the stately chestnut trees were draped in black. From the next room his mother's wail pierced the muffled silence: "Theodor, my son, my son." It was typical of Viennese morbidity that rumors soon circulated that Herzl had committed suicide.

The *Neue Freie Presse* printed a long front-page obituary that lauded his role as a littérateur and foreign correspondent, but dismissed his Zionist activities in two final sentences. Berta von Suttner noted in her diary: "Stupid world which permits such men to die prematurely." The anti-Semitic weekly *Kikeriki* wrote:

> He would have liked the Jews to leave,
> A thought which makes us grin.
> But his biggest fault was this,
> That he did not begin.

The liberal and the Jewish press celebrated his memory as one of the great men of the century. The Socialist *Arbeiterzeitung* wrote, "It is amazing how many people now pretend to have been his friend, and proclaim their disconsolateness on paper." Israel Zangwill wrote, "He had a dream and he has paid the price. To save a people, leaders must be lost, by friend and foe alike be crucified."

Georges Clemenceau, when told that Herzl had fought for the recognition of Israel, snapped, "Nothing of the sort! It was his own people he fought." To Clemenceau, Herzl was a Jacob battling the angel as in the Delacroix painting in St. Sulpice.

Tens of thousands of condolence messages streamed in from all parts of the world. Ahad Haam, one of his great Russian critics, wrote, "He died at the right time. His career and activities during the past seven years had the character of a romantic tale. If some great writer had written it, he too would have had his hero die after the sixth congress."

Chaim Weizmann, the future president and Herzl's true heir, who was at the time still an unknown, struggling scientist, wrote his bride Vera on July 6: "I feel that a heavy burden has fallen on my shoulders."

In the small town of Plonsk, in Russian Poland, the eighteen-year-old David Ben-Gurion was overcome with grief for days. "What a loss," he wrote a friend. "Nevertheless, today more than ever, I believe we shall succeed. I know the day will come—it is not far—when we return to the wonderful land, the land of truth and poetry, of roses and prophetic visions."

The funeral was one of the biggest and strangest Vienna had seen in many years. Every train brought additional mourners. Western, Eastern, Russian, German, and Turkish Jews hurried anxiously to the house. The shock of the news could be seen in their faces. Many Viennese were startled. In the words of Stefan Zweig, only now did people realize that "it was not just a writer or a mediocre poet who had passed away, but one of those creators of ideas who disclose themselves triumphantly in a single country, to a single people, at vast intervals." More than six thousand followed the hearse. The funeral went on for hours. Hermann Bahr said that only at the funeral did he begin to understand who Herzl really had been. "I realized I was moving in an alien world. The dark mass of people silently whispered sounds I could not comprehend; it rolled through the streets of Vienna on its way to the promised land. This is Herzl's deed. He gave his people the feeling that they had a homeland once again."

Chaos broke out at the cemetery. A sobbing, wailing crowd pressed into the narrow enclave. Stefan Zweig noticed an "elemental and ecstatic mourning such as I had never seen before." It made him too realize for the first time how much passion and hope this lonesome man had borne into the world through the power of a single thought.

At the open grave his thirteen-year-old son read the *kaddish*. In his final testament, Herzl had asked to be buried next to his father in a metal coffin "until the day when the Jewish people transfer my remains to Palestine." He desired a poor man's burial, "no flowers, no speeches." Nevertheless David Wolffsohn delivered a short eulogy. He swore that Herzl's name would "remain sacred and unforgotten for as long as a single Jew lives on this earth. In this heavily laden hour we recall the oath you took at the sixth congress and we repeat it: If I forget thee, O Jerusalem, may my right hand lose its cunning."

Yet even as he was laid to rest in Döbling cemetery, in view of the vineyards and forests on the rolling slopes of the Wienerwald, hundreds of young men were packing their little bags in the distant townlets of Poland, Russia, and Romania. The departure of these early Zionists was sporadic and disorganized, but Herzl had started them moving. They embarked at Odessa or Trieste, to settle as pioneers in Ottoman-controlled Palestine. Ben-Gurion was among the men and women who in the next four decades would lay the foundations of the modern state of Israel. Everything remained to be done. But Herzl had cast the mold.

Epilogue

The View
from Mount Herzl

O N THE WESTERN OUTSKIRTS of Jerusalem a wide, busy, tree-lined thoroughfare—Herzl Boulevard—crosses a new green suburb and leads south through the hills to the picturesque little village of Ein Kerem, birthplace of St. John the Baptist. Along the way to Ein Kerem, the traveler reaches a wooded slope enclosed within a low stone wall. A broad flight of steps leads through a massive gate covered with creeping vines and flowers.

Here, on a hill west of Jerusalem, the highest point in the modern city, Theodor Herzl has found his final resting place. The magnificent site is known as Mount Herzl. In 1949, forty-five years after his death, his remains were flown to Israel from Vienna. The new state had come into being only fifteen months before and had just emerged victorious, though without permanent peace, from its first war with five neighboring Arab states.

The grave is reached through a fine park of magnificent pines, cedars, and cypress trees. The solemn simplicity of the site—a square block of black marble inscribed "Herzl"—is enhanced by the rugged mountain landscape that surrounds it. The view is barer than the European eye desires, but it is softened in the long summer months by the shimmer of the great heat, and in winter by the fog that rises from valleys briefly bathed in green. A graveled square nearby is used for state ceremonies.

A few yards to the left is the grave of David Wolffsohn, who succeeded Herzl as president of the Zionist organization. The Zionists wanted the more formidable, more famous Max Nordau to assume Herzl's mantle, but Nordau refused: "I do not have Herzl's faith. . . . Herzl managed to build a facade without a house and believed that it would not occur to anyone to look behind it. He could do so because he had such immense faith in himself. I am a different man."

Close to Wolffsohn's grave, Herzl's parents and his sister Pauline rest under three bright, simple marble slabs surrounded by petunias and laurel. Jeannette survived her son by seven years. Herzl's wife and three children were not buried in Jerusalem. Julie died in 1907 at the age of thirty-nine, a lonely, embittered, ill woman. She had never made her peace with Herzl's chosen vocation, and she felt that the Zionists had robbed her of a husband in her lifetime, and after his death robbed her of her children. She was cremated in Gotha. The urn containing her ashes disappeared; according to one version, her son Hans inadvertently left it behind in a railroad compartment. Herzl's three children, for whom he had such great hopes, all ended disastrously. His eldest daughter, Pauline, suffered from a serious mental disorder and was hospitalized for long periods; a drug addict, she died in 1930 in Bordeaux of an overdose of heroin. Hans Herzl, whom his guardian, Wolffsohn, had sent to a public school in England, was treated by Sigmund Freud, who considered him to be suffering from an extreme Oedipus complex. On the twentieth anniversary of Herzl's death, Hans converted to Christianity, and then became in quick succession Baptist, Catholic, Quaker, Unitarian, and finally Lutheran. Shortly after Pauline's death he committed suicide in Bordeaux.

The third child, Trude, spent most of her life in mental clinics. She married a Mr. Neumann, by whom, in 1918, she had a son, Stephan Theodor. Shortly after his birth Trude was committed to the mental hospital of Steinhof, near Vienna. In 1942 the Nazis dispatched her, with the other Jewish patients, from Steinhof to the concentration camp of Theresienstadt. There Trude died of hunger and ill treatment on March 15, 1943. The fate of her son, Herzl's only surviving descendant, was equally tragic. Stephan Theodor attended public school in England and served as a British officer in World War II. In 1946 he visited Israel (then still Palestine) and was publicly hailed as a descendant of the great visionary. He was given a tour both of the Herzl Archive in Jerusalem, then already a formidable research institution, and also of his grandfather's study which had been transported to Jerusalem from Vienna in 1937. Stephan Theodor was greatly moved and promised to return. However, only a few months later he committed suicide by jumping off a bridge in Washington, D.C., where he had accepted a post in the British embassy.

2

Before he died it seemed to Herzl that his life was ending in failure. Even though his own effort was cut short, like a pruned tree it provoked new life. Flying Dutchman, Don Quixote, Eternal Jew —he had set in motion forces that continued long after his death. His prediction after the first congress on September 3, 1897, that in Basel he had founded the Jewish state and that within fifty years everyone would realize it, was fulfilled with astonishing punctuality on May 15, 1948. On that date the state of Israel was established. Today Herzl is venerated in Israel as the father of modern Jewish nationhood. He was only forty-four when he died, and had he enjoyed normal health, he might have lived at least thirty years longer. If he had lived another fourteen years, he would have witnessed the granting of the Balfour Declaration by Britain—the formal charter for Palestine which had eluded him in his lifetime. In the 1930s, as a man in his seventies, he might have witnessed the steady growth of the Jewish National Home which made inevitable the final breakthrough to independence in 1948.

The final years of Herzl's life were spent in a unique attempt to create a state out of a deep sense of pessimism. By temperament an aristocrat, he became a populist rouser of masses. By conviction a conservative, he initiated the great Jewish heresy of the nineteenth century. Contemptuous of democracy, he constructed a Jewish parliament. A profoundly pessimistic man, he helped to mold Eastern European Israeli pioneers into a movement of incurable optimists, fired by a messianic dream of a new world, another Eden purged of suffering and sin. In a short story written in 1898, one of Herzl's characters remarked that, for a pessimist, only the future is not disappointing, because it is unattainable.

The brightest dreams of freedom are born in prison. In real life, as Herzl well knew and often wrote, *"rien n'arrive jamais, ni comme on le craint, ni comme on l'espère"* (nothing ever turns out as badly as we fear, or as well as we hope). Herzl lived in constant fear of imminent disaster, but not in his most terrible nightmares could he have even remotely contemplated the possibility of the Nazi holocaust which wiped out six million European Jews. He assessed anti-Semitism more accurately and realistically than most of his contemporaries; yet he deluded himself when he thought he "understood" anti-Semitism, for he grossly overrated its rational component at the expense of the psychotic. Herzl's Jewish State did not put an end to anti-Semitism as he had hoped, but instead even promoted it in such places as the Arab world that had seemed historically immune. The supreme goal of his life was to restore a measure of security to the persecuted. Seventy years after his death a sense of security still eludes the Jewish State.

Herzl was a man of peace. In his time there was little, if any, indication of Palestinian-Arab nationalism. The supreme irony of Herzl's Zionism was its role as midwife of Palestinian-Arab nationalism. This nationalism gathered strength with every year that passed and with every Zionist success. Ultimately a kind of Arab Zionism came into being, a mirror image of Herzlism, driven by the myth of a lost homeland and the bitterness of dispersion. There was no symmetry between Arab and Jewish grievances. The Jews were always ready for a compromise; the Arabs have not yet contemplated the possibility of accommodation. The Palestinian dispersion was largely self-inflicted; unlike the Jews, they could live full Arab lives in any of a dozen other Arab countries.

The violent passions generated among Arabs were nevertheless powerful enough to deny the nascent Jewish State its most cherished goal, security and peace. This was not how Herzl had envisioned it. He was sure that Jews and Arabs could live together peacefully and amicably for the benefit of both. He never contemplated the possibility that the new Jewish State would be assaulted by ferocious enemies from its first day, or that it would be forced by its foes and a complacent world to fight for its very survival and to live for decades as an armed camp. Nor did he consider it possible that Israel would become a pawn in the struggle between superpowers. Herzl regarded his enterprise as a great act of historical reconciliation between Gentile and Jew; and so, perhaps, it might have been had it been realized a few decades earlier. For what appeared perfectly natural in 1899, or 1903, was considered by the Arabs some forty years later as an outrage against nature itself. Herzl did not even envisage military conscription: "After a hundred years we ought to introduce universal military service; but who knows how far civilization will have progressed by then."

He once said that he who *wills* something great—not he who achieves it—is a great man, "for in achievement luck plays a part." Much of what has been achieved by Herzl and his successors—and

the price paid for it—is actually visible from the vantage point of
Mount Herzl. As one stands at Herzl's grave on a clear day, a vast
and varied panorama unfolds in all directions. In the south the ever-
expanding green of newly cultivated land pushes into the desert a
hundred miles away. In the west the Mediterranean Sea lines the
horizon under a blanket of low white clouds broken by the thrust of
Tel Aviv's new skyscrapers. And on either side lie the fertile
coastal plains that three generations of pioneers, fired by Herzl's
vision, have turned from desolate, malaria-infested swampland into
a veritable garden. On a clear day from Mount Herzl one can
glance at almost all of it. Between the craggy foothills and the
silvery sea one sees new towns, villages, industrial centers, recrea-
tion areas, and superhighways, where only a few decades ago there
was little more than a mournful expanse, ravaged by centuries of
warfare, fever, piracy, and neglect. In 1974 there were three million
Jews in Israel. More than half of them were native born, who had
never tasted what it meant to be a Jew in the diaspora, dependent
on the ever-shifting moods of tolerance.

Today, this past is a lengthening shadow that diffuses as the
years go by; but it continues to cast a spell that few Israelis, including the young and native born, can ignore. As one turns right at
Herzl's grave, the massive walls of Yad Vashem come into full
view. The memorial center of Yad Vashem occupies the western
slope of Mount Herzl; it honors the memory of the six million
slaughtered Jews of Europe whom Herzl had tried so desperately
to save. The memorial center is dedicated to the impossible task of
tracing and registering the name of every single man, woman, and
child for whom the realization of Herzl's dream had come too
late.

Nor had the suffering and the bloodshed ended when Herzl's
Jewish State was established in 1948. The north slope of Mount
Herzl bears mournful witness to the price still being paid. It is
covered almost in its entirety by a huge military cemetery, a reminder of the four wars Israel had to fight since 1948, and of the
many bloody skirmishes in between. Each war proved more costly
than the last, and the end is not yet in sight.

Turning eastward again from Herzl's grave, one has a magnificent vista of Jerusalem, old and new. The pink hilltops and olive-
green valleys, the golden towers and domes, and the ramparts and
new residential areas gleam in a steady blazing mountain light of
crystalline clarity. Directly in front is the new campus of Hebrew
University. To the left lies the great rectangle of the Knesset, Is-

rael's parliament, where a portrait of Herzl looks down a bit wryly at the deliberations from the wall behind the Speaker's chair. Beyond the Knesset building, the low-flung glass and stone pavilions of the new Israel Museum nestle gracefully into the rocky landscape, as if they had been part of it since time immemorial. Farther east, over the rooftops and towers and trees, the pink-yellow mountains of Moab, luminous and bare, beckon in the distance. From Moab, Moses had seen the promised land, but like Herzl could not enter—a land of milk and honey, a time of roses and peace, peace above all earthly dignities.

Acknowledgments

N o BIOGRAPHY is ever definitive. One can never gain definite
knowledge about oneself, let alone about another person.
But this biography could never have been researched or written
were it not for the wealth of material diligently gathered by the staff
of the Central Zionist Archive in Jerusalem over the past four decades. I am indebted to its staff and in particular to its director, Dr.
Michael Heyman; Mr. M. Winkler, head of the Herzl Section; Mrs.
Adina Haron; Mr. E. Cohen; and Mr. M. Scharf. They spared no
energy and gave generously of their time to make available the vast
material collected in the past forty years. Closed sections of the
Archive were made available for the first time since Herzl's death by
special decision of the late chairman of the Jewish Agency, Mr.
Aryeh Pincus, who overturned an earlier ruling that they should not
be opened before 1987. I am also indebted to the Austrian State
Archives, the German Foreign Office Archive, and the Public Record
Office in London, all of which made available material on Herzl and
other related documents.

Throughout the writing of this book I have enjoyed the generous aid and advice of the retired director of the Zionist Archive,
Dr. Alex Bein. Dr. Bein, author of an earlier Herzl biography
(1934), has since been the enthusiastic mentor of all subsequent
students of the theme. No attempt has been made in the past four
decades to arrive at a fresh appraisal of Herzl's career from the
vantage point of twenty-six years of Israeli statehood and on the
basis of Israeli, German, British, and French archives since opened
to the public. The present work is based also on the unpublished
memoirs of some of Herzl's most important Jewish and non-Jewish
contemporaries, which have since become available.

Other students of Herzl's life have overemphasized his "ideological" development at the expense of his emotional development,
and have tended to ignore or belittle the impact on his character of

the Viennese milieu. The present work is predicated on the assumption that this milieu is vital to an understanding of the man.

My friends Gertrude and Erich Lessing have rendered invaluable assistance in tracing Herzl's environment and have been the kindest of hosts on my frequent visits to Vienna; I owe them a great debt of gratitude. Dr. Hilde Spiel of Vienna graciously shared her profound knowledge of *fin de siècle* Austrian culture. The learned researches of Professor Carl E. Schorske of Princeton University, a pioneer in Austrian studies, have been a rich source of inspiration, for which I am extremely grateful. My good friend Karl E. Meyer read the manuscript and offered invaluable advice. The responsibility for the result is, of course, completely my own. I must express gratitude to my Austrian publisher Fritz Molden, who facilitated my researches at the Austrian State Archives; his generosity and Viennese hospitality approached the proverbial. Finally, I am greatly indebted to my American editor, Thomas Wallace, who has labored over this book as on my two others; and to David Baker, whose meticulous attention to detail proved invaluable in preparing the manuscript for the printer.

The bibliography is not limited to the sources cited in the text. Primary sources are referred to in the notes by their abbreviations. Jacob de Haas's two-volume study of Herzl's life (1927) sometimes approaches the value of a primary source, for de Haas was Herzl's close collaborator. Equally valuable are many of the entries in the six volumes of the *Herzl Yearbook* published by the Herzl Institute of New York. The letters to and from Herzl are identified in the text (or in the notes) by their dates, and except where otherwise stated can be found in their proper chronological order in the Central Zionist Archive. All other archive material is identified by file numbers. Herzl's political diary has been translated by the author from the original German manuscript in Herzl's hand, and not from the published version (1922) which was censored and incomplete. For another English translation of the complete text, see Primary Sources.

Bibliography

Primary Sources

CZA-H   Central Zionist Archive, Jerusalem (Herzl Section).
RTB   Herzl's *Reisetagebuch* (*Travel Diary*).
JTB   Herzl's *Jugendtagebuch* (*Diary of His Youth*).
D   Herzl's Political Diary (1895–1904).
HHSA   Haus Hof u. Staatsarchiv (Austrian State Archives), Vienna.
HHSA-IB   Haus Hof u. Staatsarchiv, Intelligence Section.
AVA   Allgemeines Verwaltungsarchiv (Administrative Archive), Vienna.
FO   Foreign Office Papers, in the Public Record Office, London.
FO (Germany)   German Foreign Office Archive, Bonn.
NFP   *Neue Freie Presse* (1891–1904).

Stenographic Protocols of the Zionist Congresses I–VI (in German). Vienna, 1897–1903. CZA-H

T. Nussenblatt (ed.), *Zeitgenossen über Herzl* (*Contemporaries on H.*). Brunn, 1927.

M. W. Weisgal (ed.), *Theodor Herzl, A Memorial* by various (contemporary) writers. New York, 1929.

Hermann Ellern: *Herzl, Hechler, the Grand Duke of Baden, and the German Emperor.* A collection of documents in facsimile found in the Grand Duke's archive, Tel Aviv, 1961.

Works by Herzl

ZIONISM

Der Judenstaat, Versuch einer modernen Lösung der Judenfrage. Vienna, 1896. English translation by S. D'Avigdor. London, 1896.

Altneuland. Leipzig, 1902. English translation by de Haas, *The Maccabean.* New York, 1902–1903.

Zionistische Schriften. Edited by L. Kellner. Berlin, 1920.

413

Tagebücher. 3 vols. Berlin, 1922. English (uncensored) translation by Harry Zohn; edited by R. Patai. New York, 1960.

JOURNALISM AND TRAVEL

Neues von der Venus. Leipzig, 1887.
Das Buch der Narrheit. Leipzig, 1888.
Palais Bourbon. Sketches of French parliamentary life. Leipzig, 1897.
Feuilletons. 2 vols. Edited by R. Auernheimer. Vienna, 1911.
Philosphische Erzählungen. Berlin, 1919.

LIGHT COMEDIES AND DRAMA (*Printed or Produced*)

Kompagniearbeit. Comedy in 4 acts, 1880.
Causa Hirschkorn. Comedy in 1 act. 1882.
Tabarin. Play in 1 act. 1884.
Muttersöhnchen. Comedy in 4 acts. 1885.
Seine Hoheit. Comedy in 3 acts. 1885.
Der Fluchtling. Comedy in 1 act. 1887.
Wilddiebe. Comedy in 4 acts. 1888.
Was wird man sagen? Comedy in 4 acts. 1889.
Die Dame in schwarz. Comedy in 4 acts. 1890.
Prinzen aus Genieland. Comedy in 4 acts. 1892.
Die Glosse. Verse play in 1 act. 1894.
Das neue Ghetto. Drama in 4 acts. 1897.
Unser Käthchen. Comedy in 4 acts. 1898.
Gretel. Drama in 4 acts. 1899.
I Love You. Comedy in 1 act. 1900.
Solon in Lydien. Drama in 4 acts. 1904.

Secondary Sources

Ahad Haam. *Collected Works* (in Hebrew). Tel Aviv, 1931.
Akademische Lesehalle, Vienna. *Jahresbericht 1879–1880* (Herzl and Schnitzler).
Arendt, Hannah. *Origins of Totalitarianism.* New York, 1958.
Auernheimer, Raoul. *Wien, Bild u. Schicksal.* Vienna, 1938.
———. *Das Wirtshaus zur verlorenen Zeit.* Vienna, 1948.
Avinery, Shlomo (ed.). *Karl Marx on Colonialism.* New York, 1969.
Bahr, Hermann. *Der Antisemitismus.* Berlin, 1894.
———. *Selbstbildnis.* Vienna, 1923.
Bein, Alex. "German Documents," *Shivat Zion*, Jerusalem, 1950.
———. *Theodor Herzl.* Vienna, 1934. (English translation by M. Samuel. New York, 1941.)
Ben-Gurion, David. *Igrot* (letters), vol. 1. Tel Aviv, 1972.

Bialik, C. N. *Collected Works* (in Hebrew). Tel Aviv, 1959.

Bloch, Joseph S. *Reminiscence.* New York, 1921.

Blumenthal, Pinkhas. *Ejn Su Agada (It Is No Fairy Tale).* Tel Aviv, 1964.

Brainin, Reuben. *Chajej Herzl (Herzl's Life)*, vol. 1. New York, 1919.

Braunthal, Julius. *Auf der Suche nach dem Millenium.* Vienna, 1966.

Buber, Martin. *Die jüdische Bewegung.* Berlin, 1916.

Bülow, B. von. *Denkwürdigkeiten.* 2 vols. Berlin, 1930.

Citron, S. L. *Herzl, chajaw ufaala.* Vilna, 1921.

Cohen, Israel. *Herzl.* New York, 1960.

Cohn, Norman. *Warrant for Genocide.* London, 1970.

de Haas, Jacob. *Theodor Herzl, A Biographical Study.* 2 vols. Chicago, 1927.

De Lagarde, Paul. *Juden und Indogermanen, Eine Studie aus dem Leben.* Göttingen, 1887.

Delhorbe, Cécile. *L'Affaire Dreyfus et les Ecrivains.* Paris, 1932.

Dessauer, Fritz. *Grosstadtjuden.* Vienna, 1910.

Die Welt (official Zionist weekly). Vienna, 1897–1904. CZA.

Dubnov, Simon. *History of the Jewish People*, vol. 10.

Dühring, Eugen. *Die Judenfrage als Racen Sitten u. Culturfrage.* 1881.

Fisher, H. A. L. *History of Europe.* London, 1942.

Fraenkel, Josef. *Theodor Herzl, des Schöpfers erstes Wollen.* Vienna, 1934.

——— (ed.). *The Jews of Austria.* London, 1967.

Friedemann, Adolf. *Das Leben Theodor Herzls.* Berlin, 1919.

Friedman, Isaiah. "The Austro-Hungarian Government and Zionism." Doctoral thesis, Hebrew University, Jerusalem, 1962.

Fuchs, Albert. *Geistige Strömungen in Österreich, 1867–1918.* Vienna, 1949.

Goldhammer, Leo. *Die Juden Wiens.* Vienna, 1927.

Gordon, J. L. *Collected Works.* Tel Aviv, 1928.

Graetz, Heinrich. *History of the Jewish People.* London, 1908.

Grunewald, Max. *Vienna.* Philadelphia, 1926.

Grunwald, K. *Tuerkenhirsch.* Jerusalem, 1962.

HYB. *Herzl Jahrbuch* I. Edited by T. Nussenblatt. Vienna, 1937.

HYB. *Herzl Yearbook* II–VI. Edited by R. Patai. New York, 1960–1972.

Haslip, Joan. *The Sultan.* New York, 1972.

Heer, Friedrich. *Land im Strom der Zeit.* Vienna, 1958.

Hertzberg, Arthur. *The Zionist Idea, An Anthology.* New York, 1920.

Heyman, Michael. *The Uganda Controversy.* 68 original documents. Jerusalem, 1970.

Hitler, Adolf. *Mein Kampf.* Berlin, 1938.

Hofmann, Martha. *Theodor Herzl, Werden u. Weg.* Frankfurt, 1966.

Jenks, William. *Hitler's Vienna.*

Jones, Ernest. *The Life and Work of Sigmund Freud.* 3 vols. New York, 1953.

Jubilee of the 1st Zionist Congress. Jerusalem, 1947.

Kautsky, Karl, *Aus der Frühzeit des Marxismus.* Prague, 1935.

Kellner, Leon. *Theodor Herzls Lehrjahre.* Vienna, 1920.

Klausner, J. *Opposizia le Herzl.* Jerusalem, 1960.

Kohn, Hans. *Schnitzler, Kraus, Weininger.* Tübingen, 1963.

Kraus, Karl. *Eine Krone für Zion.* Vienna, 1898.

————. *Untergang der Welt durch Schwarze Magie.* Munich, 1960.

Landau, S. R. *Sturm und Drang im Zionismus.* Vienna, 1937.

Langer, William L. *The Diplomacy of Imperialism, 1890–1902.* New York, 1935.

Laqueur, Walter. *The History of Zionism.* New York, 1972.

Lazare, Bernard. *Job's Dungheap.* New York, 1948.

Leblond, Denis. *Zola.* Berlin, 1932.

Lessing, Theodor. *Der jüdische Selbsthass.* Berlin, 1930.

Millin, S. G. *Rhodes.* London, 1939.

Morris, James. *Pax Brittanica, The Climax of Empire.* London, 1968.

Mumford, Lewis. "Herzl's Utopia," *Menorah Journal,* August 1923.

Musil, Robert. *The Man Without Qualities.* Translated by E. Kaiser. London, 1968.

Namier, Lewis. *Vanished Supremacies.* London, 1958.

Nordau, Anna and Max. *Max Nordau, A Biography.* New York, 1943.

Nordau, Max. *Die conventionallen Lügen der Menschheit.* Leipzig, 1909.

————. *Degeneration.* London, 1895.

————. *Paradoxe.* Leipzig, 1886.

Nussenblatt, T. *Ein Volk unterwegs zum Frieden. Herzl und B. von Suttner.* Vienna, 1933.

Ost u. West (magazine). Vienna, 1904.

Patai, Josef. *Herzl.* Tel Aviv, 1936.

Pinson, K. S. *Modern Germany.* New York, 1954.

Rosenberger, E. *Herzl as I Remember Him.* New York, 1960.

Roth, Joseph. *Radetzkymarsch.* Cologne, 1961.

Rudorff, Raymond. *Belle Epoque, Paris in the Nineties.* London, 1972.

Sacher, Harry. *Zionist Portraits.* London, 1946.

Salten, Felix. *Geister der Zeit (Erlebnisse).* Berlin, 1924.

Schnitzler, Arthur. *Der Weg ins Freie.* Vienna, 1908.

————. *Youth in Vienna.* New York, 1970.

Schnitzler, Olga. *Spiegelbild der Freundschaft.* Vienna, 1970.

Shoub, David. *Sichronoth lebejth David* (memoirs). Jerusalem, 1937.

Sokolov, Nachum. *History of Zionism.* London, 1919.

Sperber, Manes. *Alfred Adler.* Vienna, 1970.

Spiel, Hilde. *Wien, Spektrum einer Stadt.* Munich, 1971.

Steed, Wickham. *The Hapsburg Empire.* London, 1914.

————. *Through Thirty Years.* New York, 1925.

Stern, Fritz. *The Politics of Cultural Despair.* Berkeley, Calif., 1961.

Taylor, A. J. P. *The Hapsburg Monarchy.* London, 1967.

Teweles, Heinrich. *Theater u. Publikum.* Prague, 1927.

Tietze, Hans. *Die Juden Wiens.* Vienna, 1933.

Toussenel, B. *Les Juifs, Rois de l'epoque.* Paris, 1845.

Trebitsch, Siegfried. *Chronicles of a Life.* London, 1954.

Tuchman, Barbara. *The Proud Tower.* London, 1966.

Vámbéry, Arminius. "Personal Recollections of Abdul Hamid and His Court," *Nineteenth Century,* June 1909.

———. *The Story of My Struggles.* 2 vols. London, 1912.

Wandruszka, Adam. *Die Neue Freie Presse, Geschichte einer Zeitung.* Vienna, 1958.

Wardi, A. *Malki be Zion (Herzl in Palestine).* Jerusalem, 1922.

Weigel, Hans. *Karl Kraus.* Vienna, 1972.

Weisbrod, L. *African Zion, the Attempt to Establish a Jewish Colony in East Africa.* Philadelphia, 1968.

Weizmann, Chaim. *Letters and Papers,* vol. 3. Oxford, 1972.

———. *Trial and Error.* London, 1949.

Wilhelm II, Kaiser. *Briefe an den Zaren.* Berlin, 1923.

Wilson, C. *The East African Protectorate.* London, 1905.

Witschenik, A. *Umgang mit Österreichern.* Nuremberg, 1959.

Yisraeli, David. "The Problem of Palestine in German Politics." Doctoral thesis, Hebrew University, Jerusalem, 1972.

Zangwill, Israel. *Articles, Speeches, Letters.* Edited by M. Simon. London, 1921.

Zweig, Stefan. *The World of Yesterday.* London, 1940.

Notes

The quote on p. xiii is from Hardy, *Late Lyrics and Earlier, Collected Poems* (London, 1952), p. 569.

Chapter 1

"*Afraid of going insane,*" D, 16 June 95. "*Crazy,*" "*crippled inspiration,*" D, 11 June 95. "*World history begun,*" D, 16 June 95. "*Bismarck*" and "*Napoleon,*" H. to Hirsch, 3 June 95. "*Savonarola,*" H. to Teweles, 6 June 95. "*Limits of consciousness,*" D, Pentecost 95. "*To his beloved,*" D, 5 June 95. "*See a doctor,*" Brainin, p. 11. *Wagnerian music,* Autobiographical Sketch in Herzl, *Schriften,* p. 15. "*Volcanic eruption,*" Olga Schnitzler, p. 94. "*Promised land,*" D, 16 June 95. *Schnitzler,* quoted from *Paracelsus. Hofmannsthal* quoted from Introduction to Schnitzler's *Anatole. Herzl's medical examination papers,* French Prefecture, CZA–H NI A. *Freud:* HYB 1:266. *Sultan and Ibrahim Bey,* de Haas, 1:369. *Rosenzweig,* HYB 1:1. *Nordau,* in *Ost u. West,* Aug. 04. *Buber,* in *Jüdische Bewegung.* "*The Bible spared,*" Kellner, p. 6. *Kaiser's deformity,* D, 9 Apr. 96.

Chapter 2

Birth certificate, CZA-HI A 1. *Denounced in synagogue,* Herzl, *Schriften,* p. 23. *J. L. Gordon,* p. 28. "*Greatest Hungarian,*" Taylor, p. 26. *Rabbi Kohn,* HYB 7:285. *Herzl's royal blood,* Blumenthal, p. 13. *Genealogy,* CZA-HN I K 2. "*Novel of my life,*" D, Pentecost 95. *Tale of two brothers,* Brainin; repeated as fact, among others, by Kellner, Friedemann, Patai, Cohen; Bein, more circumspect, states that "so far there has been no basis for considering this story as anything but a legend," Bein, *Herzl,* p. 29. "*Prussian nobleman,* D, 5 July 95. *Dream of Messiah,* Brainin, p. 18. *Freud's mother,* Jones, 1:4. "*Unwilling pupil,*" Kellner, p. 8. *Reading and writing,* A. Iricz, H.'s tutor, *Die Welt,* 20 May 10. "*Moral weakness,*" Kellner, p. 9. "*Cornelia, mother of,*" Olga Schnitzler, p. 81. "*Never a happier pair,*" Kellner, p. 8. *Freud's father,* Jones, 1:19. *Marry a princess,* RTB, 18 July 83. "*Thrashing*" *and Lesseps,* Autobiographical Sketch in

Herzl, *Schriften. Old Jewish teacher*, Patai, p. 7. *Chevra Kadisha*, Patai, pp. 8–9; CZA-H NX 71. *"Confirmation,"* CZA-HI IV A 2–3. *"Moses and Jesus,"* CZA-H IV A 32. *Fellow student's testimony*, CZA-H NX 71. *Herzl's cousin*, unpublished ms. in CZA-H NX 87. *Wir, protocols*, CZA-H IV A 2. *Freud's father*, Jones, 1:192. *Luther poem*, CZA-H IV B. *"As the Messiah,"* D, 10 Mar. 96. *"Looked like my grandfather,"* D, 17 June 96. *Alkalai*, in Hertzberg, *Zionist Idea*, pp. 103–107. *"Easy grasp"* and *"memory,"* CZA-H NX 71. *Holderlin*, qu. in Patai, p. 10. *"Simple-minded confidant,"* ms. in CZA-H II A 11. *"Only love,"* JTB, 10 Jan. 86. *"I hid my love,"* CZA-H II A 11. *Jensen's heroes' "compelling beauty,"* CZA-H IV A. *"German writer,"* CZA-H III B 2. *English dictionary*, CZA-H IV B. *Letter to newspaper editor*, CZA-H III C 4a. *"Heart went out for Vienna,"* CZA-H II A 11. *Jeannette "did not cry,"* ibid. *Letter to aunt*, HYB, 1:69.

Chapter 3

City of "pains and travails," H. to Schnitzler, 29 July 92. *Writing "not really a career,"* Patai, p. 11. *Budapest "shrunk and narrowed,"* CZA-H II A 11. *"Since I left Hungary,"* H. to Kana, March 82. *"Out of time and place,"* Taylor, p. 3. *"Born in Vienna,"* Auernheimer, *Wirtshaus*, p. 11. *"Nowhere easier,"* Zweig, p. 29. *"Every . . . lady a Marie Antoinette,"* Auernheimer, *Wirtshaus*, p. 11. *"They looked like gods,"* Roth, p. 193. *Schiller on the Viennese*, qu. in Witschenik, p. 4. *"Thou art no more,"* qu. in Auernheimer, *Wien*, p. 75. *"Subconsciously every citizen,"* Zweig, p. 30. *"Cosmopolitans in our buttonholes,"* qu. in Spiel, p. 34. *Graetz*, vol. 11, Intro. *"Severe attack of diabetes,"* Steed, *Hapsburg Empire*, p. 29. *"Mutual dislike,"* Musil, 1:68. *"Only good horses,"* Feuilletons, 1:192. *"From this single enthusiasm,"* CZA-H IV A. *"A fleeting carnality,"* Steed, *Hapsburg Empire*, p. 30. *"I have much cause to complain,"* H. to Kana, 4 Sep. 79. *"I can only be happy,"* ibid., 23 Mar. 82. *Fritz Mauthner*, qu. in Weigel, p. 18. *Wagner as idol*, Bahr, *Selbstbildnis*, p. 139. *Girardi*, qu. in Spiel, p. 50. *"The French disease,"* Kraus, *Untergang*, p. 188. *"On February 1,"* CZA-H IV A 190. *"At the sound of music,"* CZA IV A 189. *"Impotence! Impotence,"* JTB, Feb. 82. *"It is in writing,"* ibid., 2 May 82. *"No success,"* ibid., 27 Nov. 83. *"Come Book,"* ibid., 11 Oct. 85. *Zweig on Victorian sex*, in *World*, p. 62. *Schnitzler and his father*, in *Youth*, p. 71. *"It is strange how dreams,"* RTB, 26 July 83. *"A girl as sweet,"* H. to Kana, 5 Mar. 82. *"Blond, clever-eyed little girl,"* RTB, July 83. *"Pure untouchable love,"* CZA-H IV A 17. *"Have I already told you,"* H. to Ludassy, 22 Nov. 83. *Dieppe beach scene*, Herzl, *Buch der Narrheit*, p. 192. *"Snake-girls,"* CZA-H IV B 71. *Venereal infection*, H. to Kana, 8 June 80; Kana to H., 20 June 80, 25 July 80. *Army rejection*, CZA-H I C 2. *Kana-Herzl correspondence*, 15 Mar. 82; 20 June 82; 3 Aug. 83; ? May 85.

Chapter 4

Deutsche Lesehalle, CZA-H IV B. Kralik on young Adler, Geschichte u. Gestalten, qu. in W.J. McGrath, Journal of Contemporary History 2, No. 3 (1967): 183. "One must be blond," CZA-H IV A 182b. Schnitzler, qu. fr. Youth, p. 129; Olga Schnitzler, p. 80. Herzl's Mensur, Fraenkel, Herzl, p. 120. Drinking song, CZA-H IV B 74. "Patronizing mockery . . . ," Bahr, in Weisgal. Book reviews, JTB, CZA-H II A. Rohling's Der Talmudjude, qu. in Bloch, p. 29. Pinsker and Jellinek, qu. in Sokolov, 1:188. Taafe, Taylor, p. 169. "Emancipation from yoke of Judaism," Wagner, "Das Judentum in der Musik," Neue Zeitschrift für Musik, 3 Sep. 50. Bahr's speech, in Bahr, Selbstbildnis, p. 119. Albia correspondence, CZA-H III, Mar.–Apr. 83. Paul v. Portheim and Albia, qu. in Fraenkel, Herzl, pp. 117–131. Schnitzler, letter in CZA, 5 Aug. 92. Herzl and Friedjung, D, Pentecost 95. Herzl and Bahr, Fraenkel, Herzl, p. 127.

Chapter 5

"Just a writer of sorts," D, Pentecost 95. Freud's father, in Freud, The Interpretation of Dreams, stand. ed. (ed. J. S. Strachey), p. 196 ff. "Spiritually almost more," Schnitzler, Youth, p. 6. "As a Jew you had the choice," ibid. "Never fear, your Excellency," Bloch, p. 171. "Anti-Semitism did not really succeed," Schnitzler, Youth, p. 7. De Lagarde, in Juden u. Indogermanen, p. 339. Zweig on Jews in Viennese culture, in World, pp. 27–28. Schnitzler, in Der Weg ins Freie, p. 299. Kautsky on Austrian anti-Semitism, in Frühzeit, p. 122. "Yesterday grande soirée," H. to parents, 25 Nov. 85. "Many Viennese Jews here," ibid., 28 Aug. 85. Weininger, in Lessing, p. 42. Prince Schwarzenberg, Bloch, p. 329. "Wherever he went," Schnitzler, Der Weg ins Freie, p. 45. Heine, in Zeitgedichte. Mahler, qu. in Leo Baeck Institute Yearbook, London, 5:266. Dessauer, in Grossstadtjuden, pp. 162, 306. "Nothing on earth," CZA-H IV A 182b. "It seems you have still not found," H. to Kana, 4 July 83. "My precious child," qu. in Kellner, p. 10. "If ever I get married," JTB, 25 July 83. "Shall I describe," H. to parents, 26 July 83. "Sexual love," CZA-H IV A 182 B 311. "I have a mistress," JTB, New Year's eve 84. "I read, dream," JTB, 31 Dec. 84. "Too haughty, cool," Ludassy to H., 20 Aug. 84. "Affairs of honor," protocols in CZA-H IV B; letter to challenger, 26 Feb. 1902. "I beg of you again," H. to parents, 28 June 85. "Parentagogy," in Buch der Narrheit, p. 23. "I eat very well," H. to parents, 23 June 85. "I would like to receive," ibid., 27 June 85. Herzl in Salzburg, Autobiographical Sketch in Herzl, Schriften. Heidelberg, H. to parents, 18 Aug. 85. "Jokai, like Turgenev," ms. in CZA-H IV B 100. "Will get to the Burgtheater," H. to parents, 6 Dec. 85. "Miserable life," JTB, 11 Oct. 85, 31 Dec. 85. "Infatuation with Magda, JTB, 10 Jan. 86, 13 Jan. 86. "J'y étais," ticket in CZA-H II A. Encounter with Julie, JTB,

28 Feb. 86 to 29 May 86. *"Á l'attente de Julietta,"* JTB 1886, CZA-H II
A2. *"Seeing makes me unhappy,"* CZA-H IV A 182b. *"You undoubtedly
have talent,"* Hartmann to H., 7 Feb. 87. *"Mother is right,"* Kellner, p. 71.
"This wild unnerving," H. to parents, 12 Mar. 97. *Rome ghetto,* in Herzl,
Buch der Narrheit, p. 243. *"I have found my good Julie,"* JTB, 7 Sep. 87.
"The applause," H. to parents, 21 Mar. 88. *"I am so happy,"* Kana to H.,
19 Apr. 88. *Herzl tired of Vienna,* fragment in CZA-H IVa 6/206. *"Name
in marble,"* Zweig, *World,* pp. 85, 89. *"When one is . . . alone,"* H. to par-
ents, 3 Aug. 88. *Mainz incident,* D, Pentecost 95. *"Once more,"* H. to
Kana, 1 Aug. 89. *What Will People Say?,* in Herzl, *Was wird man sagen?*
pp. 10, 11, 25. *State of Julie's nerves,* CZA-H N III 305. *Bein,* qu. fr.
Herzl, p. 113. *To Teweles,* H. to Teweles, 17 Feb. 90. *"My poor good
Theodor,"* Kana to H., 13 Sep. 90. *"It's the same,"* H. to parents,
15 Feb. 91. *"The performance of one's duty,"* H. to parents, 9 July 91.
Güdemann refuses divorce, unpublished memoirs in CZA. *Divorce, contemplated,* H. to parents, 2 May 90, 28 May 90. *"You know well,"* H. to
parents, 27 Sep. 91. *"Thirst for power . . . ,"* in Herzl, *Feuilletons,*
1:111–151. *Novel on Kana,* D, Pentecost 95. *Wittmann on Herzl,* qu. in
Kellner, p. 102. *"Night of appointment . . . ,"* note in CZA-H IV A 133.

Chapter 6

Freud and Nordau, Jones, 1:188. *"Paris correspondent,"* H. to parents, 10 Oct. 91. *Bahr,* in *Selbstbildnis,* p. 120. *"My beloved good
parents,"* H. to parents, 23 Dec. 91. *"Children are . . ."* and *"The only
thing,"* in Herzl, *Feuilletons,* 2:210–212. *"Life has an attraction,"* H. to
parents, 5 Feb. 92. *"For what you are,"* H. to parents, 17 Jan. 92. *"Your
position is so strong,"* H. to mother, 19 Mar. 92. *French police spy,* French
Ministry of Interior, photostat in CZA-H N I 5: "Herzl paraît disposer de
ressources importantes . . . habite avec ses parents, qui fort avares,
dit-on, lui reprochent d'être trop prodigue." *"I am not giving,"* H.
to parents, ? Mar. 92. *"A democracy which produces,"* H. in NFP, 29
Apr. 92. *Deadlines and Sunday cables,* Bacher to Herzl, CZA-H VIII 35.
"Gladly permit him," ibid. *Shy of famous persons,* D, Pentecost 95. *"This
treatment,"* Bacher to H., ibid. *"A play . . . to amuse the Gods,"* H. in
NFP, 11 Feb. 92. *"The republicans are raising,"* ibid., No. 9767. *"Dreamer
or mean knave,"* ibid., 24 Apr. 92. *"Unrecognized through the crowd,* D,
Pentecost 95. *"What a perplexity,"* H. in NFP, 29 Feb. 92. *Roundup on
French anti-Semites,* NFP, 3 Sep. 92. *"By rabbis and monks,"* ibid. *"To
excuse it,"* D, Pentecost 95. *"Rendezvous"* and *"salon,"* NFP, 3 Sep. 92.
Freycinet, NFP, 26 June 92. *Maupassant,* in Herzl, *Feuilletons,* 1:254.
"Stared at each other" Schnitzler, *Youth,* p. 129. *Herzl-Schnitzler correspondence,* 29 Jul. 92, 5 Aug. 92, 16 Nov. 92, 2 Jan. 93, 13 May 93. *"By
the way, I like your style,"* Hofmannsthal to H., 24 Nov. 92. *Duel with
anti-Semitic leaders, contemplated,* D, 12 June 95. *"Let us stick to anti-*

Semitism," qu. in HYB 3:77-90. *Herzl-Leitenberger correspondence,* drafts in CZA-H III. *Mass conversion plan,* D, Pentecost 95. *Benedikt "combined the pathos of,"* Fuchs, p. 22. *Déroulède and Renan,* qu. in Fisher, p. 1006. *"David Copperfield,"* Palais Bourbon, p. 247. *"Gone are the days,"* qu. in Kellner, p. 141. *Lafargue in Lille,* in Herzl, *Palais Bourbon,* pp. 25–27. *Malaria in Toulon,* H. to Teweles, 19 May 95. *Aftereffects of malaria,* de Haas, 1:39. *"In a few years,"* H. to Teweles, 19 May 95. *"Completely forgotten,"* H. to Burckhard, 4 May 95. *"When a theater director,"* aphorisms, in Herzl, *Buch der Narrheit. "Fired only by his intellect,"* Zweig, *World,* p. 46. *"How strange it all is,"* qu. in Kohn, p. 11. *Boat ride in Aussee,* Olga Schnitzler, p. 92. *Conversation with Speidel,* D, Pentecost 95. *"Saujud" incident, ibid. World survey on Jews, ibid. Herzl against Jewish nationalism,* review of Dumas' *Femme de Claude,* NFP, 6 Oct. 94. *Discussion with Beer,* H. to Schnitzler, 9 Jan. 95; H. to Teweles, 19 May 95. *"A piece of Jewish politics,"* H. to Teweles, 19 May 95. *The New Ghetto,* various drafts in CZA. *"Write himself free,"* D, Pentecost 95. *Paris synagogue, ibid. "Hide and bury,"* H. to Schnitzler, 8 Nov. 94. *"It is arrogance," ibid. Anatole France,* qu. in Delhorbe. *Lazare on French Jews,* in *Job's Dungheap,* p. 97. *"The fact that the arrest,"* H. in NFP, 1 Nov. 94. *"Where? In France,"* Herzl, *Schriften,* 2:123–124. *"Evil-smelling fog,"* Herzl in *Die Welt,* 9 May 99. *Herzl's psychological theory on Dreyfus' innocence,* Herzl, *Schriften,* 2:122. H. *at Dreyfus trial,* NFP, 22 Dec. 94. *Degradation ceremony,* NFP, 5 Jan. 95. *Dreyfus as symbol,* Herzl in *Die Welt,* 15 Sep. 99. *Censored dispatch,* Bein, *Herzl,* p. 218. *Léon Daudet,* qu. in Rudorff, p. 279. *Austrian Diet,* NFP, 6 Feb. 95. *Pobedonostsev,* Dubnov, 10:123. *Secret Police,* photostat of report in CZA-H NI 5; in Archives of Paris Prefecture, translations of intercepted letters to and from H. *Alphonse Daudet,* D, Pentecost 95. *New novel, ibid. Zola's Zionist novel,* Leblond, pp. 302–303. *"They will pray . . . ,"* D, 17 June 95. *Letter to Hirsch,* draft in Diary, Pentecost 95.

Chapter 7

Hirsch, Grunwald, pp. 65, 72–73, 90, 113. *Evasive answer,* Hirsch to H., 20 May 95. *"As soon as I find the time . . . ,"* H. to Hirsch, 24 May 95. *Interview with Hirsch,* D, 2 June 95; Herzl's preparatory notes in CZA-H IV C4. *"For some time past,"* D, Pentecost 95. *"Insane,"* D, 16 June 95. *"I think that for me . . . ,"* D, 11 June 95. *"Because of your impatience,"* H. to Hirsch, 3 June 95. *Opera,* D, 5 June 95. *Savonarola,* H. to Teweles, 6 June 95. *"The harmlessly joking,"* Teweles, p. 124. *The new exodus "compares . . . ,"* D, 7 June 95. *Order of procedure,* D, 6 June 95. *"First dig the canals,"* D, 7 June 95. *Ship of coffins,* D, 11 June 95. *"A lot of toasts,"* D, 11 June 95. *Coronation ceremony,* D, 15 June 95. *Telegram to Hans,* D, 11 June 95. *Gambetta's statue,* D, 7 June 95. *"Today*

I say," D, 8 June 95. *German Kaiser, ibid. "I should still be capable,"* note inserted in D ms., 16 June 95; CZA-H II C 1. *"Smacked of megalomania,"* D, 11 June 95. *"Tragicomedy,"* inserted note no. 95 to D. *"How one learns,"* CZA-H IV A 197. *"I must above all,"* D, 16 June 95. *"My God,"* D, 12 June 95. *Speech to the Rothschilds,* D, 13–17 June 95. *Güdemann-Herzl correspondence,* H.'s letters in D; Güdemann, CZA-H VII. *Schiff's visit,* Brainin, pp. 109–114; D, 17–19 June 95; Autobiographical Sketch in Herzl, *Schriften,* p. 9. *Tuileries and Schiff's "cure,"* D, 18 June 95. *Bismarck,* D, 19 June 95, 22 June 95. *Paoli poem and notes,* CZA-H N III. *"I no longer think,"* H. to Schnitzler, 22 June 95. *"Logically entered new stage,"* D, 23 June 95. *Democracy,* D, 21 June 95. *Albert Rothschild,* D, 28 June 95. *Bismarck's rebuttal,* CZA-H NX A 5. *"Such fellows,"* D, 28 June 95. *"Splendid, great romance,"* H. to Julie, 19 June 95. *"A lucky thing,"* D, 16 July 95. *Taverne Royal,* D, 20 June 95. *Nordau,* D, 6 July 95. *"School of Journalism,"* in Herzl, *Palais Bourbon,* p. 248. *Schiff,* D, 15 July 95. *Güdemann-Herzl correspondence,* 17, 21, 23, 25 July 95. *Salzstangel and Capital City,* D, 23 July 95. *Munich conference,* D, 13 Aug. 95. *Güdemann to his wife,* G.'s unpublished memoirs, qu. in Landau, p. 254.

Chapter 8

Auernheimer, in *Wirtshaus,* p. 37. *Freud in 1895,* qu. in E. Simons, "Freud the Jew," *Leo Baeck Institute Year Book* (London, 1957), p. 276. *Bahr,* in *Antisemitismus,* pp. 1–4. *Election day,* D, 20 Sep. 95. *Freud on Lueger's suspension,* qu. in Jones, 1:311. *Herzl and Badeni,* D, 3 Nov. 95. *Nordau,* in *Degeneration,* p. 5. *"Every man of action,"* 27 Jan. 82 in CZA-H N III. *"Dammed up, if not arrested,"* Jakob Herzl to H., 26 Oct. 95. *"Julie liked society,"* de Haas, 1:85. *"At night it burns,"* Maria della Gracia in Weisgal, p. 69. *Negotiations with publishers,* D, 20 Oct. 95. *Parnell of the Jews, ibid. "Electric light,"* D, 6 Nov. 95. *Güdemann,* D, 3 Nov. 95. *Kahn,* D, 16–18 Nov. 95. *Nordau, ibid.;* HYB 7:31. *Zangwill,* D, 21 Nov. 95; Weisgal, p. 43. *Montagu,* D, 24 Nov. 95; de Haas, 2:295–304. *Goldsmid,* D, 25–26 Nov. 95. *"Good lungs,"* D, 28 Nov. 95. *"Force of Nature" and utopias, Der Judenstaat,* p. 4; H. to Gudemann, 21 Aug. 95. *Christmas tree incident,* D, 24 Dec. 96. *"We are a people . . . ,"* in Herzl, *Judenstaat,* p. 13. *"I do not agree,"* Cranbach to H., 20 Dec. 95. *Bacher and Benedikt,* D, 2–4 Feb. 96. *Pamphlets and father,* D, 14–15 Feb. 96. *Zweig,* Nussenblatt, *Zeitgenossen,* p. 257; Zweig, pp. 86–87; private Zweig memoir in CZA-H NX 49. *Derision,* D, 1 Feb. 96, 23 Mar. 96; Kellner, p. 124. *"My warmest supporter,"* D, 4 Mar. 96. *Ludassy's attack, etc.,* D, 1 Mar. 96; Bein, *Herzl,* p. 281. *Bismarck,* de Haas, 1:135. *Schnitzler,* Olga Schnitzler, pp. 95–96. *Beer-Hofmann,* letter to H., 13 Mar. 96.

"*Surely the Jewish people,*" Braunthal, p. 37. *Holman Hunt,* qu. in *Öster-reichische Wochenschrift,* Vol. 14, 1896. *Pinsker's tract,* D, 10 Feb. 96. *Sokolow's reaction, Hazephira,* Vol. 142, 1896. *Ben-Gurion's reaction,* Israel radio interview, 1 July 1966 ("Beit Avi" series). *Mazzini,* in *Duties of Man and Other Essays* (London, 1915), p. 53. "*The credibility of strangers,*" H. to Teweles, 28 Feb. 90. *Weizmann's reaction,* in *Trial and Error,* pp. 61–62. *Heart ailment,* D, 17 Mar. 96. "*I already have my reward,*" H. to Henrichsen, 8 Apr. 96. *Daily Chronicle,* 16 Apr. 96. *Simonyi's visit,* D, 30 Mar. 96. *Wolffsohn,* Bein, *Herzl,* pp. 290–291. *Ussishkin,* in Nussenblatt, *Zeitgenossen,* p. 240.

Chapter 9

Hechler-Herzl encounters, interview with Hechler in CZA-H NX A 18; Bein, *Herzl,* p. 294; Rosenberger, p. 57; D, 14–16 Mar. 96, 14–16 Apr. 96. "*If Hirsch will withdraw,*" H. to Nordau, 21 Apr. 96. *Reaction to Hirsch's death,* D, 21–22 Apr. 96. *Hechler's talks with Kaiser, etc.,* D, 23 Apr. 96; Ellern documents. *H. interview with Grand Duke,* D, 23–25 Apr. 96. "*I do not think I am in error,*" H. to Nordau, 6 May 95. *Nevlinski,* HHSA-1B, 455/1886, 3 231/1888, 974/1889; HYB 2:152; D, 7 May 96, 9 June 96; de Haas, 1:105. *Journey to Turkey,* D, 15 June 96, 17 June 96; Brainin, p. 169. *Herzl and Nevlinski's negotiations and talks,* D, 17–29 June 96. *Cyprus lease by Britain,* Morris, p. 68. *Salisbury,* Langer, pp. 196–202, 209–210. *Marx and Engels,* Avinery, pp. 10, 472. *Herzl on Sultan,* D, 19 June 96. *Lufti Aga's dreams,* D, 27 June 96. "*The Sultan said that . . . ,*" D, 29 June 96. "*The great of this earth,*" ibid. *Sofia,* D, 30 June 96. *Nevlinski's reward,* D, 1 July 96. *Montagu,* D, 5 July 96, 11 July 96; de Haas 1:120. *Montefiore and Mocatta,* ibid. *East End meeting,* D, 13 July 96; de Haas, 1:121. "*Looking as kings wish,*" S. Münz, in *Contemporary Review,* July 1924. "*I saw and heard my legend,*" D, 15 July 96. "*You have been utterly defeated,*" de Haas, 1:118. "*Didn't these people ask,*" D, 18 July 96. *Clemenceau on Rothschild,* qu. in Arendt, p. 103. "*These are my colonies,*" HYB 7:31. "*Purchase Rothschild's,*" D, 17 July 96. *Herzl-Rothschild interview,* D, 19–20 July 96. "*There is only one answer,*" H. to de Haas, 20 July 96, 27 July 96. *Meeting with King of Bulgaria,* D, 22 July 96. *Moses and Amalekites,* de Haas, 1:141. "*Organize!,*" de Haas, 1:129. *Seldom sped forward,* de Haas, 1:111. *Herzl and Bacher,* D, 3 Aug. 96. *Bacher, Nevlinski,* D, 5 Oct. 96. *A madman,* D, 24 Sep. 96. "*If it was one of your overzealous,*" D, 22 July 96. "*A person . . . out of conviction,*" D, 1 Dec. 96. *Suspicion of bribery,* D, 10–11 Oct. 96. *Rival paper and Badeni's offer,* D, 22 Oct. 96. "*I seem to be your only,*" D, 11 Dec. 96. *Last wills,* orig. in CZA-H II D.

Chapter 10

"Certainly," D, 6 Jan. 97. "Everybody is waiting," de Haas, 1:142; H. to
de Haas, 8 Feb. 97. "Let us guard ourselves," H. to de Haas, 12 May 97.
"From Constantinople," H. to Cohen, 1 Sep. 97. "In Palestine," D, 20 Feb.
97. "My dear friend," CZA-H NX HL. "If I had relented," D, 5 Feb. 97.
"Well then . . . ," D, 10 Mar. 97. Provisional agenda, Bloch's Öster-
reichische Wochenschrift, 9 Apr. 97. Weizmann travels, qu. in Jubilee of
the 1st Zionist Congress, p. 9. German Rabbinical Council, Herzl, Schriften, pp. 211–212. New York resolution, de Haas, 1:154. Herzl's response, Herzl, Schriften, pp. 211, 216. Güdemann's attack, D, 17 Apr. 97.
Bambus' perfidy, D, 24 Apr. 97; H. to B., 24 Apr. 97. "I am proud of
you," H. to E. Rosenberger, 18 Oct. 99. Schnitzler's affront, Olga Schnitzler, p. 80. One-man rule, Patai, p. 147; D, 12 May 97. "Un très beau
poème," Daudet to H., 24 Mar. 97. "A veritable scene," D, 25 Apr. 97.
Fights with publishers, D, 3–5 June 97. "I knew what I was doing," N. to
de Haas, 5 June 1901; de Haas, 1:178. "No need to worry," de Haas,
1:194–195 (note). 1st congress, D, 20 Aug. 97 ff.; Stenographic Protocols,
1897. "But we do have a flag," Wolffsohn in CZA-H NX 19. Nordau in
synagogue, Anna Nordau, p. 101. "Hosanna of king," de Haas, I, 160 ff.
"Dancing among eggs," D, 24 Aug. 97. Leib Jaffe, Zangwill, qu. in Jubilee
of the 1st Zionist Congress, pp. 54, 80. Bialik, "The Zionist Delegates,"
in Collected Works. Austrian legation report, HHSA, Pal. A xxvii, box 43,
No. 64B. French legation report, photocopy in CZA CM 210. Kaiser's
marginal note, German Foreign Office Archive (Turkey 195K; 175903-
10). Basel Congress and anti-Semitic myths, qu. in Cohn, pp. 75–76.
Mark Twain on congress, in "Concerning the Jews," Collected Works
(New York, 1901), 22:272. Students' farewell, Allgemeine Schweizerische
Zeitung, 1 Sep. 97. "The man who had brought," D, 27 Oct. 97. "How
ashamed," H. in Die Welt, Sep. 97. "I don't want to hear," D, 4 Sep. 97.
"Were I to sum up . . . ," D, 3 Sep. 97.

Chapter 11

Jews' seizure of Holy Places, press report qu. in D, 4–9 Sep. 97. Taliani
qu. Jews, Nussenblatt, Zeitgenossen, p. 139. Interview with Taliani, D,
8 Feb. 99. Nevlinski "tells me . . . ," D, 23 Sep. 97. Herzl and Tewfik,
D, 4–5 Feb. 97. Lucanus, ibid. Bank idea launched, Die Welt, No. 25,
1897. Kokesch, D, 12 May 98. "We are like soldiers," de Haas, 1:214.
"Scoundrels and malefactors," H. to Nordau, 25 Apr. 98. "Sooner or
later . . . ," D, 23 Sep. 97. "Revenge," D, 2 June 97. Mauschel, Die Welt,
No. 27, 1897. Wolffsohn's imitation, private memo, 17 Apr. 99 in
CZA-H NX 48. "You take advice with difficulty," HYB 2:178. "The
Menorah," Die Welt, No. 31, 1897: 1. Poznanski, D, 11 Dec. 97. Censor's
ruling, Vienna police archives, qu. in Fraenkel, Herzl, p. 112. "Nobody

felt insulted," Teweles, p. 129. *"I am very weary,"* H. to Nordau, 15 Feb. 98. *"I am tired,"* D, 12 Mar. 98. *"Night after night,"* de Haas, 1:214. *"With this Herzl . . . ,"* D, 18 Mar. 98. *Noise,* D, 12 May 98. *"Picturesque,"* H. to Nordau, 19 May 98. *Flag,* H. to Bodenheimer, 11 June 98. *"With nations . . . ,"* D, 10 July 98. *"The art form . . . ,"* ibid. *"Dirty trick,"* D, 3 Aug. 97. *"The sex which sometimes,"* Herzl, Feuilletons, 2:16. *"Next to his beautiful blond wife,"* M. della Gracia, in Nussenblatt, *Zeitgenossen,* p. 85. *"Very embarrassed . . . ,"* D, 25, 29 Aug. 98. *French consul,* 27 Aug. 98, photocopy in CZA CM 210. *"As a Jew it is less difficult,"* Lazare, p. 98. *Tannhäuser,* Rosenberger, p. 158. *Nordau's tears,* in *Nordau, A Biography,* p. 141. *Herzl and Nordau's speeches,* protocols of 2nd congress (Vienna, 1898). *Baruch,* D, 29 Aug. 98. *"Dirty little tricks,"* D, 2 Sep. 98. *Mitzkin's report,* protocols of 2nd congress, p. 103.

Chapter 12

With Grand Duke, D, 3 Sep. 98. *"If there is one thing,"* D, 5 July 95. *Eulenburg's memoir,* unpub. ms., German Foreign Office Archive. *Conversation with Eulenburg,* D, 16 Sep. 98, 21 Sep. 98. *"Eulenburg is won,"* H. to his wife, 16 Sep. 98. *Bülow,* D, 18 Sep. 98. *"I have been called to a mighty,"* H. to Gottheil, 20 Sep. 98. *"Genius of the Kaiser,"* H. to Eulenburg, 24 Sep. 98. *Wilhelm "fire and flame,"* Bülow, 1:254. *"There is no balance of power,"* Pinson, p. 278. *"Many unsympathetic elements,"* Bülow, 1:254. *"What is permitted,"* Wilhelm II, Briefe, 18 Aug. 98. *"Tremendous achievement for Germany,"* Kaiser to Grand Duke, text in Ellern. *"I regard the matter,"* original in CZA-H. *"I have but good news,"* qu. in Bein, "Erinnerungen. Dokumente ü. Herzl's Begegnung mit Wilhelm," *Zeitschrift für die Geschichte der Juden. "Was dazed . . . ,"* D, 2 Oct. 98. *Wolffsohn on Herzl,* qu. in Blumenthal, p. 182. *Speech in London, Jewish Chronicle,* 7 Oct. 98; *Die Welt,* No. 41, 1898. *Visit to Liebenberg,* D, 7 Oct. 98. *"Wunderbar," ibid. "It is an unusual event,"* H. to Wolffsohn, 7 Oct. 98. *"Surely none of us,"* D, 8 Oct. 98. *"This is the dashing,"* D, 7–8 Oct. 98. *Hohenlohe interview,* D, 7–10 Oct. 98. *Invited Nordau,* de Haas, 1:245. *Assassination rumor,* Wardi, p. 13; Bodenheimer in Nussenblatt, *Zeitgenossen,* p. 38. *Parents,* D, 14 Oct. 98. *Marschall,* D, 15 Oct. 98. *Wolffsohn's adventure,* CZA-H NX 48. *Kaiser interview and preparations,* D, 19 Sep. 98. *"Imperial eyes," ibid. "Shrewd, highly intelligent,"* Kaiser's memoirs, Hauptarchiv (form. Geheim Staats archiv), Berlin-Dahlem, p. 8, photocopy in CZA-H EV 9. *"Overwhelming,"* CZA-H NX 48. *"I have spent,"* H. to Bülow, 19 Oct. 98. *"I am obviously reaching,"* D, 19 Oct. 98. *"Colossal success,"* H. to his father, 20 Oct. 98. *"Will of one man,"* Herzl, Feuilletons, 2:179. *"Mixed feelings,"* D, 27 Oct. 98.

Chapter 13

On Kaiser's orders, D, 27 Oct. 98. *"Arriving with four friends,"* Shoub, p. 23. *Malik al Yahud*, Wardi, p. 78. *Kramer, ibid.*, p. 18. *"The poor colonists,"* D, 27 Oct. 98. *Dr. Mazie, ibid.*; Wardi, p. 179. *Mixed multitude*, D, 29 Oct. 98. *Cook's preparation*, Haslip, p. 241. *"The Messiah . . . ,"* Wardi, p. 35. *"The Turkish Crescent . . . ,"* Haslip, p. 241. *Mikve Israel*, D, 29 Oct. 98; eyewitnesses in Wardi, pp. 131–144. *"Bishop of Jerusalem,"* D, 31 Oct. 98. *"Knight of peace,"* Haslip, p. 241. *"When I remember thee,"* D, 31 Oct. 98. *Wailing Wall, Tower of David*, Wardi, p. 28. *"Before the Turks come,"* D, 1 Nov. 98. *Audience with Kaiser*, D, 2 Nov. 98; ms. of Wolffsohn memoir in CZA. *Address text with deletions*, copy in CZA by courtesy of Dr. Alex Bein. *"If the Turks had only a glimmer,"* D, 5 Nov. 98. *Egypt*, D, 8 Nov. 98. *German announcement*, Bülow's instruction to Berlin, in Bein, *Shivat Zion*, 1950–1951, p. 376. *Leadership*, D, 15 Nov. 98. *Kaiser's record*, Wilhelm's unpublished memoirs, copy in CZA-H EV 9. *Too many Jews in Jerusalem*, Calice, Austrian ambassador in Constantinople to Foreign Ministry, HHSA, Turkei Berichte 1898, X–XII. *Empress's resentment*, D, 15 Dec. 98. *Hohenlohe*, Bilinsky papers, copy in CZA-H NX A 5, p. 22. *Bülow*, interview with B., *Breslauer Jüd. Volksblatt*, 14 Oct. 1904, in CZA-H NX A6; also D, 29 Mar. 99.

Chapter 14

At N.F.P., D, 18 Nov. 98. *Kaiser anecdote*, D, 17 Apr. 99. *"Let us not lose,"* H. to Wolffsohn, 18 Nov. 98. *Too good an answer*, H. to Wolffsohn, 29 Nov. 98. *Colossal results*, H. to Nordau, 29 Nov. 98; to Kellner, 21 Nov. 98; to Gottheil, 25 Dec. 98; to Stephen Wise, 26 Dec. 98. *Suttner and Herzl*, Nussenblatt, *Ein Volk unterwegs*, p. 101. *Russian fears of Zionism*, 3 May 99, HHSA (Russland); 25 Apr. 99, qu. in Bein, *Shivat Zion*, pp. 384 ff. *Days of despondency*, D, 11 Feb. 99. *"The well is running dry,"* D, 23 May 99. *"I cannot answer,"* D, 6 Dec. 98. *"Mental disease,"* qu. in Sperber, p. 211. *"Busybody schmuck,"* Kraus, *Krone*, p. 8. *"Unpleasant impression,"* Grand Duke to H., 5 Dec. 98. *"With him the saga,"* D, 2 Apr. 99, 7 Apr. 99. *"Sold us his corpse,"* D, 8 Apr. 99. *El-Khaldi-Herzl exchange*, CZA-H III D 13 (in French). *Seidener on Arabs*, qu. in Nussenblatt, *Zeitgenossen*, p. 184. *"Colonial idea . . . ,"* speech in London, 26 June 99, *Zionistische Schriften*, pp. 102–103. *Third congress*, protocol, 1899; D, 17 Aug. 99, 21 Aug. 99. *Take "any country,"* D, 8 Nov. 99. *Trietsch*, de Haas, 1:303. *"But I am the little clerk,"* D, 8 Nov. 99. *Spent dowry*, Herzl's second testament, in CZA-H. *"After having been a free man,"* D, 24 Aug. 99. *"Even more than unfinished speech,"* D, 6 Aug. 99. *"I daresay I'll never,"* H. to Nordau, 14 Sep. 1900. *Nuri*, D, 17 June 99, 29 Aug. 99; Nuri's receipt in CZA-H. *Koerber*, D, 16 Feb. 1900. *Hassidic leaders' protest,* H. to Rabbi of Gur, 2 Apr. 1900. *Nordau's interview with Rothschild,* unpublished ms. by Adolf Friedemann (17 Apr. 99) in CZA-H NX 48. *Austin's jingoism,* Tuchman, p. 41. *"How well I understand them,"* D, 22 Apr. 1900. *"I am taking my show to London,"* D, 11 June 1900. *Revised will,* dated 23 May 1900, text in CZA-H. *Herzl and Vámbéry,* D, 17 June 1900; H. to Vámbéry, 26 June 1900, 3 July 1900. *"Thus the Jewish people is losing,"* qu. in HYB 2:179 (in French). *"The two weeks I spent here,"* H. to M. Reichenfeld, 31 July 1900. *Sickness,* fever charts in CZA-H 1 I 1; de Haas, 1:321; D, 10 Aug. 1900. *Fourth congress,* de Haas, 1:321; protocols, Vienna, 900; D, 10–29 Aug. 1900. *"What would be the use of a Jewish state,"* de Haas in Nussenblatt, *Zeitgenossen,* p. 89. *"A pressing need,"* D, 15 Oct. 1900. *"The curiosities of this episode" and Crespi,* D, 16 Nov. 1900, 3 Dec. 1900. *Vámbéry's 5,000 pounds,* H. to Vámbéry, 23 Dec. 1900. *"He does not give a hoot,"* Vámbéry to H., 29 Dec. 1900; D, 31 Dec. 1900. *"The fellow is completely crazy,"* D, 8 June 1901.

Chapter 15

With Vámbéry, D, 10 May 1901; Kellner, p. 13. *"For me the world,"* D, 13 May 1901. *"Times" report,* de Haas, 1:370. *Austrian embassy report on Herzl,* HHSA, 1B 1901, 1636; AVA Z 4483. *Crespi,* D, 13 May 1901. *"Moment of desire" and rehearsal,* D, 15 May 1901, 17 May 1901. *Decoration and audience with Sultan,* D, 19 May 1901. *Nuri,* D, 19 May 1901, 20 May 1901. *Tahsin's bribe,* H. to Tahsin, 19 May 1901. *Negotiations with Turks,* D, 21 May 1901. *Nordau,* D, 1 May 1901, 8 May 1901. *London speech,* de Haas, 2:8–11; Herzl, *Schriften,* 2:207. *Ben-Gurion's father,* A. Grien to H., ? Nov. 1901. *"In fifty years,"* H. to Mandelstamm, 18 Aug. 1901. *"Rhodes and his friends can make,"* H. to Cowen, 4 July 1901. *"I would annex planets,"* Millin, p. 138. *Rhodes's advice,* Cowen to H., 25 Jan. 1901. *Vámbéry,* H. to V., 11 Aug. 1901, 21 Aug. 1901; D, 22 Aug. 1901. *Sabbath of my life,* D, 24 Jan. 1902. *Fifth congress,* protocols, Vienna, 1902; de Haas, 2:29–35.

Chapter 16

Certain explanations, D, 5 Feb. 1902. *"We have no money . . . ," ibid.* *"Imperial decrees,"* 15–18 Feb. 1902. *"Des choses impossibles,"* Marschall to Bülow, 19 Mar. 1902; German documents qu. in Bein, *Shivat Zion.* *"Between ourselves,"* D, 26 Mar. 1902. *Preliminary notes for Altneuland,* CZA-H IV A 177. *"A story I am telling,"* H. to Grand Duke of Baden, 5 Oct. 1902. *"Dream and deed,"* Herzl, *Altneuland,* p. 343. *"We are not a state," ibid.,* pp. 90, 328. *"American Negroes," ibid.,* p. 193. *"Synagogue, church," ibid.,* p. 297. *"You are very curious . . . ," ibid.,* p. 140. *Attacks* on *Altneuland*, Ahad Haam: *Al Parashat Derachim*, vol. 3. *"Running for Pope,"* H. to Nordau, 16 Mar. 1903. *Nordau's response, Die Welt*, No. 11, 1903. *"Best book,"* Friedemann, p. 59. *"Papa very ill,"* Julie to H., 9 June 1902. *Doctor's cable,* D, 10 June 1902. *"My dear, my good . . . ,"* D, 10 June 1902. *"You can't help,"* D, 11 June 1902. *"Runover dog,"* D, 11 June 1902. *"On the second day,"* H. to mother, ? July 1902. *With Rothschild,* D, 5 July 1902. *"A charter or,"* H. to Sultan, 23 July 1902. *Negotiations in Constantinople,* D, 25 July–4 Aug. 1902.

Chapter 17

"It must be made clear to the British," H. to Cowen, 13 Nov. 1901. *"Bolted like schoolboy,"* D, 20 Oct. 02. *"You are accustomed,"* 20 Oct. 1902. *"Think imperially,"* Tuchman, p. 65. *Chamberlain's anti-Semitism,* Steed, *Thirty Years,* 1:163. *Conversations with Chamberlain and Landsdowne,* D, 23, 24 Oct. 1902. *Herzl's Sinai industries,* CZA-H VI C 41. *Kellner's objections to Sinai,* HYB 2:180. *Greenberg's report,* D, 13 Nov. 1902. *"No political objections,"* Cromer to Landsdowne, FO 78/5481. *Sanderson's letter,* FO 78/5490. *"Historic document,"* D, 22 Dec. 1902. *"We are about to emerge,"* Friedemann, p. 68. *"Egyptian province of Judea,"* D, 22 Dec. 1902. *Meetings with Rothschild and Sanderson,* D, 15, 17 Jan. 1903. *Herzl-Greenberg exchanges,* D, 16–23 Feb. 1903; Greenberg to H., 26 Feb. 1903. *"Archimedian point,"* H. to Mandelstamm, 20 Mar. 1903. *Cairo visit,* D, 24 Mar.–4 Apr. 1903; eyewitness account, CZA-H VI 27. *Expedition's report,* CZA-H, 26 Mar. 1903. *"Do not think I am powerless,"* Friedemann, in Nussenblatt, *Zeitgenossen,* p. 74. *"He is more detached,"* D, 7 Apr. 1903. *Herzl's plans to go to London,* Cromer to Sanderson, FO 78/5479. *Chamberlain interview,* D, 24 Apr. 1903. *Domestic trouble,* CZA-H N III 305. *Cost of "syphoning water under canal,"* Cromer to Landsdowne, 14 May 1903, FO 78/5479. *Family vault,* D, 16 May 1903. *"Soon, soon,"* qu. by H.'s secretary in Nussenblatt, *Zeitgenossen,* p. 159.

Chapter 18

"Miniature England," H. to Nordau, 13 July 1903. *Footnote on "poor fellahin,"* Friedemann, p. 20. *"I shall do it,"* Suttner diary, qu. in Nussenblatt, *Ein Volk unterwegs,* p. 141. *"Sacred duty,"* Belkovsky, *Hazioni Haklali* (Tel Aviv), 3:16. *Visa difficulties,* CZA-H VI D2. *"They are so badly off,"* D, 7 Aug. 1903. *"Immortal game,"* D, 10 Aug. 1903. *First Plehve interview,* D, 10 Aug. 1903. *"Jews who did not crawl,"* qu. in Zangwill, p. 133. *"Strong, sinuous,"* H. to de Haas, in de Haas, 2:145. *Witte and second Plehve interview,* D, 11–14 Aug. 1903. *St. Petersburg speech,* contemporary report qu. in Heyman, pp. 95–96. *Vilna visit,*

Goldberg in Nussenblatt, *Zeitgenossen*, p. 80; secret contemp. reports B'nai Brit Mitteilungen, Austria XXVIII; Boris Goldberg qu. in de Haas, 2:151–156; Boris Goldberg, *Die Welt*, 20 May 10; D, 17 Aug. 1903. *"Small and stuffy dingy chamber,"* qu. in Cohen, p. 318. *Sir Clement Hill's letter*, CZA-H VII. *"He looked old and worn,"* de Haas, 2:150. *Actions Committee*, minutes in Heyman, pp. 101–102. *Sixth congress*, protocols, Vienna, 1903; Nussenblatt, *Zeitgenossen*; D, 22 Aug. 1903, 31 Aug. 1903; Heyman, p. 89; Sacher, p. 22; *Die Welt*, 13 July 14; de Haas, 2:159–183; Weizmann, *Trial and Error*. Trotsky, J. Nedava, *Trotsky and the Jews* (New York, 1973), p. 196. *Eyewitnesses to turmoil*, Cohen, p. 531; de Haas, 2:177; Jabotinsky, "Herzl bei den Neinsagern," *Die Welt*, 3 July 14. *"If expedition makes a favorable report,"* H. to Nordau, 23 Dec. 1903. *"Speech" to seventh congress*, D, 31 Aug. 1903.

Chapter 19

Protests in East Africa, Weisbrod, p. 68; de Haas, 2:189–198; Y. Friedler, *Jerusalem Post*, 17 Dec. 71. *"We would gladly renounce,"* D, 1 Sep. 1903. *"Fearful days of horror,"* H. to Wolffsohn, 18 Sep. 1903, 30 Sep. 1903. *Heart attack after Basel*, H. to York-Steiner, 8 Sep. 1903, qu. in Friedemann, p. 83. *Letter to Plehve*, 5 Sep. 1903. *Letter to Greenberg*, 5 Sep. 1903. *German assistance*, H. to Eulenburg, 11 Sep. 1903. *Austrian assistance*, H. to Koerber, 13 Sep. 1903. *"And my self-esteem,"* H. to Wolffsohn, 9 Jan. 1904, 14 Jan. 1904. *"Don't work so much,"* Sil Vara, in Nussenblatt, *Zeitgenossen*, p. 242. *Ussishkin*, qu. in Sacher, p. 54. *Kharkov conference*, Klausner, p. 237. *Open Letter to Jewish People*, draft in CZA. *Ussishkin's "open rebellion,"* D, 4 Jan. 1903. *Bilinsky*, qu. in HYB 1:215. *"The friendly reception,"* Plehve to H., 6 Dec. 1903. *Zinoviev's response*, Wellisch to H., 30 Dec. 1903. *"I now await,"* H. to Wolffsohn, 23 Dec. 1903. *"If they shoot at you,"* H. to Nordau, 23 Dec. 1903. *Sure of Germany, Russia, England*, de Haas, 2:216. *Visit to Rome*, D, 23–26 Jan. 1904. *Suttner*, qu. in Nussenblatt, *Ein Volk unterwegs*, p. 142. *"It was my mistake,"* Zweig, pp. 90–91. *Ali Nouri Bey*, D, 23 Mar. 1903, 10 Apr. 1903. *Actions Committee meeting*, minutes, 11–13 Apr. 1904; CZA Z 193; speech qu. in Friedemann, p. 27. *"Broken down,"* D, 13 June 1903. *Doctor's diagnosis*, Dr. Asch to Wolffsohn, 26 June 1904, 27 June 1904. *"To lie in the hot sand,"* S. Werner qu. in de Haas, 2:241. *"Le soir,"* Auernheimer, *Wirtshaus*, p. 42. *"Wild scene with wife,"* Dr. Max Asch, CZA-H N VIII. *Hechler*, Friedemann, p. 90. *Julie's breakdown*, CZA-H N VIII A 2. *Reich and mother*, Nussenblatt, *Zeitgenossen*, pp. 160, 189; de Haas, 2:248. *"Last pacifying thought,"* in Herzl, *Buch der Narrheit*, p. 74. *"Theodor, my son, my son,"* Rosenberger, p. 241. *NFP Obituary*, 4 July 1904. *"Stupid world,"* Suttner qu. in Nussenblatt, *Ein Volk unterwegs*, p. 142. *Kikeriki*, issue of 10 July 1904. *Zangwill*, de Haas, 2:334. *Clemenceau*,

Pierre van Paassen, in Weisgal, p. 129. *Ahad Haam*, in HYB 2:151. *Weizmann*, in *Letters and Papers*, 3:270. *Ben-Gurion, Igrot* (letters), 1:20. *Zweig on funeral*, in *World*, p. 91. *Bahr*, in Nussenblatt, *Zeitgenossen*, p. 21. *Wolffsohn*, de Haas, 2:252.

Epilogue

Nordau's refusal, Weizmann, *Letters and Papers*, 3:264. *Children's fate*, Dr. Arthur Stern: "The Genetic Tragedy of Herzl's Family," *Israel Psychiatric Journal*, Jerusalem, 1965. "*Nothing ever turns out as badly*," CZA IV A 189. "*After a hundred years*," D, 7 June 95.

Index